John Calvin's American Legacy

John Calvin's American Legacy

Edited by

THOMAS J. DAVIS

OXFORD
UNIVERSITY PRESS

2010

OXFORD
UNIVERSITY PRESS

Oxford University Press, Inc., publishes works that further
Oxford University's objective of excellence
in research, scholarship, and education.

Oxford   New York
Auckland   Cape Town   Dar es Salaam   Hong Kong   Karachi
Kuala Lumpur   Madrid   Melbourne   Mexico City   Nairobi
New Delhi   Shanghai   Taipei   Toronto

With offices in
Argentina   Austria   Brazil   Chile   Czech Republic   France   Greece
Guatemala   Hungary   Italy   Japan   Poland   Portugal   Singapore
South Korea   Switzerland   Thailand   Turkey   Ukraine   Vietnam

Published by Oxford University Press, Inc.
198 Madison Avenue, New York, New York 10016

www.oup.com

Oxford is a registered trademark of Oxford University Press

Library of Congress Cataloging-in-Publication Data

John Calvin's American legacy / edited by Thomas J. Davis.
p. cm.
ISBN 978-0-19-539097-1; ISBN 978-0-19-539098-8 (pbk.)
1. Calvinism—United States—History. 2. United States—Civilization.
I. Davis, Thomas J. (Thomas Jeffery), 1958-
BX9422.5.J64 2010
284′.273—dc22   2009020972

9 8 7 6 5 4 3 2 1

Printed in the United States of America
on acid-free paper

In the words of William Walsham How,
"For all the saints, who from their labors rest"

Acknowledgments

There is considerable overlap between this book and a set of panels
held in Geneva on May 24–27, 2009, as part of the John Calvin and
His Legacy, 1509–2009 international conference organized by the
Association Calvin 2009, the Institut d'histoire de la Réformation,
the Faculté autonome de théologie protestante of the Université de
Genève, and the Société du Musée historique de la Réformation et
Bibliothèque Calvinienne and co-sponsored by twelve other scholarly
organizations worldwide. The occasion for this conference was the
500th anniversary of John Calvin's birth. Many (though not all) of the
contributors to this volume gave presentations of abbreviated
versions of their chapters at this conference (and some scholars
contributed to the conference but not to the book; there is not a perfect
overlap between the two). I was asked by one of the collaborating
organizations, the American Society of Church History (ASCH), to
propose panels on its behalf to the organizing committee. I accepted
the responsibility and then immediately thought that this would
make for a good opportunity to pull together a book that would
examine John Calvin and Calvinism's role in American culture. So, in
a reversal of what often happens, contributors were invited to submit
proposals for the panels for the conference with the understanding
that they would have the opportunity to write book chapters first and
then present the fruits of their labors in abbreviated form in Geneva.
Most accepted the invitation in this form; after a time, once it became
clear who would present only a conference paper and who would

provide both a chapter and a paper, a few others were invited to contribute to the volume. Thus, much of this book owes its genesis to the occasion of the conference and the invitation extended to me by ASCH. I extend thanks to both the conference organizers and to the leadership of ASCH.

As matters progressed, others provided encouragement and support for the panels I had arranged for the Geneva conference. I happily acknowledge them here, all within Indiana University–Purdue University Indianapolis: the Center for the Study of Religion and American Culture and its director, Philip Goff, along with the center's journal, *Religion and American Culture: A Journal of Interpretation;* and the Department of Religious Studies and its chair, Peter J. Thuesen.

My daughters, Mave and Gwynne, listened with good cheer as I rambled on (and on and on) about how the conference/book was going. They were also a constant reminder that, as legacies go, the most important ones often are not the subjects of scholarly works.

Finally, my dear wife, Terry, provided not only support and understanding during the editing of this book, but she also helped with the final manuscript preparation. For that, and for other things too numerous to list, I thank her. She is a constant reminder of the goodness of grace.

May 2009

Contents

Contributors, xi

Introduction, 3
Thomas J. Davis

Part I Society

1. Calvin and the Social Order in Early America: Moral Ideals and Transatlantic Empire, 19
Mark Valeri

2. Calvinism and American National Identity, 43
David Little

3. Implausible: Calvinism and American Politics, 65
D. G. Hart

Part II Theology

4. Practical Ecclesiology in John Calvin and Jonathan Edwards, 91
Amy Plantinga Pauw

5. "Falling Away from the General Faith of the Reformation"? The Contest over Calvinism in Nineteenth-Century America, 111
Douglas A. Sweeney

6. Calvin and Calvinism within Congregational and Unitarian
Discourse in Nineteenth-Century America, 147
David D. Hall

7. Whose Calvin, Which Calvinism? John Calvin and the Development
of Twentieth-Century American Theology, 165
Stephen D. Crocco

Part III   Letters

8. "Strange Providence": Indigenist Calvinism in the Writings of Mohegan
Minister Samson Occom (1723–1792), 191
Denise T. Askin

9. Geneva's Crystalline Clarity: Harriet Beecher Stowe and Max Weber on
Calvinism and the American Character, 219
Peter J. Thuesen

10. "Jonathan Edwards, Calvin, Baxter & Co.": Mark Twain and the Comedy
of Calvinism, 239
Joe B. Fulton

11. Cold Comforts: John Updike, Protestant Thought, and the Semantics
of Paradox, 257
Kyle A. Pasewark

Conclusion: John Calvin at "Home" in American Culture, 267
Thomas J. Davis

Index, 273

Contributors

Denise T. Askin is professor emerita of English and a former executive vice president of Saint Anselm College. She has taught on Calvin and American literature and on Native American literature. She has published a range of articles on Flannery O'Connor, Walt Whitman, T. S. Eliot, and William Styron. Her current research focuses on Samson Occom.

Stephen D. Crocco is the James Lennox Librarian at Princeton Theological Seminary. He is the author of numerous articles on American theology and ethics, writing on Jonathan Edwards, Karl Barth, Paul Ramsey, H. Richard Niebuhr, and Joseph Haroutunian. He has also served as editor of the *Princeton Seminary Bulletin*.

Thomas J. Davis is the Thomas H. Lake Scholar in Religion and Philanthropy and a professor of religious studies at Indiana University–Purdue University Indianapolis. He has authored several books, including *This Is My Body: The Presence of Christ in Reformation Thought* (2008), and he has served, since 1989, as managing editor of *Religion and American Culture: A Journal of Interpretation*.

Joe B. Fulton is a professor of English at Baylor University, where he has been honored as an "outstanding professor for scholarship" and as a "Baylor University Class of 1945 Centennial Professor." He is the author of three books, the latest of which is *The Reverend Mark Twain: Theological Burlesque, Form, and Content* (2006).

David D. Hall is the John Bartlett Research Professor of New England Church History at Harvard Divinity School. His books include *The Faithful Shepherd: A History of the New England Ministry in the Seventeenth Century* (1972; repr., 2006) and *Worlds of Wonder, Days of Judgment: Popular Religious Belief in Early New England* (1989).

D. G. Hart is the author of several books on American religious history, including most recently *Seeking a Better Country: 300 Years of Presbyterianism in America* (with John R. Muether; 2007) and *A Secular Faith: Why Christianity Favors the Separation of Church and State* (2006). He is currently at work on a global history of Calvinism.

David Little served as a professor of the practice in religion, ethnicity, and international conflict at Harvard Divinity School. He is the author of several books, including *Religion, Order and Law: A Study in Pre-Revolutionary England* (1969; repr., 1986), and the co-editor (with Donald K. Swearer) of *Religion and Nationalism in Iraq: A Comparative Perspective* (2006).

Kyle A. Pasewark is an associate with Debevoise & Plimpton LLP, New York. He is the author of *A Theology of Power: Being beyond Domination* (1993) and *The Emphatic Christian Center: Reforming American Political Practice* (with Garrett E. Paul; 1999); he has also published on John Updike and religion.

Amy Plantinga Pauw is the Henry P. Mobley Professor of Doctrinal Theology at Louisville Presbyterian Seminary. She is the author of *The Supreme Harmony of All: The Trinitarian Theology of Jonathan Edwards* (2002), and she has co-edited *Feminist and Womanist Essays in Reformed Dogmatics* (with Serene Jones; 2006).

Douglas A. Sweeney is a professor of church history and the history of Christian thought at Trinity Evangelical Divinity School. He is the author or editor of several books on Christian history and theology, including *Nathaniel Taylor, New Haven Theology, and the Legacy of Jonathan Edwards* (2003).

Peter J. Thuesen is a professor in and the chair of the Department of Religious Studies at Indiana University–Purdue University Indianapolis. He is the author, most recently, of *Predestination: The American Career of a Contentious Doctrine* (2009) and editor of *The Works of Jonathan Edwards*, vol. 26, *Catalogues of Books* (2008).

Mark Valeri is the E. T. Thompson Professor of Church History at Union Theological Seminary in Virginia. He has written on Puritanism, early American economic practice, and the writings of Jonathan Edwards. His latest book, forthcoming from Princeton University Press, is titled *Heavenly Merchandize: Ministers, Merchants, and the Market in Puritan New England*.

John Calvin's American
Legacy

Introduction

Thomas J. Davis

The year 2009 is the 500th anniversary of John Calvin's birth. For some, it is an occasion for celebration as heirs of his legacy remember the man and his ministry. For others, it brings to mind negative images of dogmatic religion gone mad with power, an unholy union of church and state. The memory of Calvin often evokes strong feelings, and those feelings are tied not just to Calvin himself but also to everything Calvin is seen to represent. As with the "Puritans" in historical memory, "Calvin" is a stand-in for ideologies with which one either agrees or disagrees (usually vehemently).

The contributors to this volume have taken this anniversary as an opportunity to gauge Calvin and Calvinism's influence on American culture. Some engage Calvin directly; others do so more indirectly as he is mediated by the various traditions that look to him as a guide. Because Calvin's influence was contested almost from the start by opponents, the history of Calvin's and Calvinism's influence has been written either by unquestioning loyalists, on the one hand, or by implacable foes, on the other. Though Calvin's historical presence is large enough to warrant attention in works on U.S. history and culture, one would probably be safe in assuming that, on balance, the foes of Calvin and Calvinism, again from almost the start but particularly in the nineteenth century, have had the greatest success in shaping his image in the culture. Though the careful scholarly work of the specialist will portray a more balanced and layered treatment of Calvin's influence in America, such work does not often make its way into broader scholarship in such a way as to nuance the generally negative rhetoric associated with assessments of Calvin and his influence. Indeed, as David D. Hall will point out in his chapter, even those who take seriously Calvin's positive contributions still end up adopting the more broadly held negative tropes about him. As I will note below, for example, it has not been uncommon for scholars who study "anti-Calvinist" authors to adopt uncritically the language about Calvin that these anti-Calvinist authors employ.

It seems useful, therefore, to prepare for the reading of this volume's chapters with a quick look at Calvin's life and the stereotypes that arise concerning it. The usefulness of these stereotypes will be questioned, for they not only impede the study of Calvin the man, but they also can cloud one's understanding of Calvin in the culture. There follows a short narrative tracing the movement of Calvinism from Europe to the New World. Finally, a brief description of the chapters contained herein is provided.

Calvin was born and educated in France. As a young man, he saw himself joining the ranks of humanist scholars. He earned both bachelor's and master's degrees in Paris, after which he left for law school, studying at Orléans and then Bourges. After attending to family matters following his father's death in Noyon, the town of Calvin's birth, he found his way back to Paris and published a commentary on Seneca's *On Clemency*. It was, by almost every measure, a failure. It did not secure him a place among up and coming humanist writers, and it certainly did no favors to his finances (the book was self-published, and Calvin did not recoup the costs).

The next time he published a book, there resulted a very different outcome. The year 1536 saw the publication of Calvin's *Institutes of the Christian Religion* (which would undergo major revisions and be published in several editions in the years to come), and this work brought a great deal of recognition to the young Calvin. The work also witnessed to a Calvin who had undergone a conversion experience to the Protestant faith. So began a lifelong journey of applying the skills he had honed as a humanist (and a humanistically trained lawyer) to the foundational document of the Christian faith, the Bible. His work in languages and textual analysis and his concern for the fundamental documents of the faith (among humanists and Christian reformers—both Protestant and Catholic—that was the rallying cry: *Ad fontes!* To the sources!) were brought to bear on the interpretation and explication of scripture.

An exile from France because of his religious views, Calvin ended up, for most of his adult life, in the city of Geneva. He originally was employed by the city government as a reader in Holy Scripture in 1536, was forced out of the city in the spring of 1538 (for what became a very satisfying period of time in the city of Strassburg with Martin Bucer, the city's leading Protestant reformer), and then he was asked to come back to Geneva, which he did most reluctantly, in the fall of 1541. There he stayed until his death in 1564. Over the almost quarter century in the city, he was a resident alien for about nineteen years, only becoming a citizen in 1559, five years before his death.

Calvin worked to reform the church in Geneva at the behest of the city government. At times, he was influential with the council; at other times, he was at odds with it. The council members forced him from the pulpit on one occasion; on others, they dictated what today would appear to be religious policy—for example, the number of times the sacrament of communion would be celebrated in the churches of the city. This example indicates that his position as theocrat has, at times, certainly been overstated: how could a religious figure be said to run a town when, in fact, he could not even get his way on when to serve communion?

Of course, much of Calvin's reputation as theocrat comes from two items in particular: the execution of Servetus and the workings of the consistory of Geneva. Though the Servetus affair serves to underscore all of the bad qualities of the Reformation and Calvin in particular in today's world, in the environment of the sixteenth century, it was the Servetus affair that, in some ways, cemented Calvin's position of authority within the city, at least so far as to keep him from fearing for his position with the church of Geneva. This is simply to say, the world of the sixteenth century is not our world or, at least, how we think the world should be. (Many of our judgments about the past seem to involve a good deal of condescension; we are oblivious to the ways in which our actions in today's world will be judged by future generations.) In Calvin's own time, however, the execution of Servetus was lauded by Protestants and Catholics alike. Servetus's denial of the Trinity was not, in that time period, simply a religious offense; it violated civil law as well. And there were plenty of executions taking place, for religious and nonreligious reasons, so there is no real need to lay the blame for the entirety of sixteenth-century blood lust completely at Calvin's feet, although such a strategy has been undertaken often enough that it now seems a commonplace to blame Calvin for the bigotry and violence of that century. Certainly, such a strategy is an ingenious attempt to separate out the "good" part of the Reformation from the "bad" part, but such does not make for real historical study (nor for real life).[1]

The consistory in Geneva sought to oversee the morals of the citizens because, it was assumed, all citizens were also church members (the notion of Christendom, a Christian society, was still very much alive in the sixteenth century). Stories about the consistory's actions are the stuff of legend: the heinous activities of the hypocritical self-righteous. And, of course, no modern American would want to live under such a regime. It should go without saying, however, that the people of sixteenth-century Geneva were not modern Americans. Some obviously chafed under the eye of the consistory; others encouraged the work. But what is clear, now that there has been, over the last few decades, significant historical work on the consistory records—beginning with the daunting and painstaking task of transcription—is that the consistory, at least during Calvin's time, was as much a complex phenomenon as one would expect. One would miss this only if one were looking to skewer Calvin from the start. There is a lot of prying into what we would consider private affairs in these pages. There is also the attempt to encourage people to get along, to live civilly with one another. One reads, for example, of admonitions that seek to curb the level of abuse in the home: spouse on spouse, parents on children, adult children on aging parents.[2] It is a complicated picture that arises, and the words "theocrat" or "theocracy" only provide, to use a cliché, more heat than light.

Of course, the image of Calvin as theocrat becomes especially horrific when one adds another element to the picture: the fact that he was predestinarian in his theology. With that addition, one has not only the tyrant of Geneva as theocrat, but his ultimate authority is a God who seems even more tyrannical than his servant. The words "arbitrary" and "despotic" get bandied about, and such words have been burned into the American psyche by not only the treatises and sermons of people such as William Ellery Channing but in the domestic and sentimental fiction produced in the nineteenth century by such writers as Catharine Maria Sedgwick, Lydia Child, and Sylvester Judd.[3]

This is another case, however, of conveniently reworking history in such a way as to put the "blame" for predestination as a doctrine on Calvin in order to sort out the good from the bad in the Reformation heritage. Though it should be obvious, perhaps, it bears repeating (and perhaps repeating and repeating) that many of the earliest Protestant reformers were predestinarian in outlook— Calvin, yes, but also Martin Luther, Huldrych Zwingli, Heinrich Bullinger, Martin Bucer, and others. Luther, after all, wrote a volume entitled *On the Bondage of the Will*. Two things are at work: the first is that, in terms of the developing Protestant theology of *sola fides*, Augustine stands as a foundational figure. Predestination had a long history as a doctrine within the Christian tradition long before the early Protestants came along. They found Augustine persuasive on this point.

Perhaps even more to the point: just as in Augustine, the writings of the apostle Paul carried tremendous weight with many early Protestant reformers. Indeed, one established one's bona fides as a reformer usually by writing a commentary on Paul's letter to the Romans, the only letter of Paul's that has anything like a systematic intent; it was a statement of his faith, an explanation of himself to the Romans. His other letters were of a much more occasional nature, dealing with quite specific issues that had arisen in the congregations Paul had founded. Romans is different. And therein, one finds stated most explicitly Paul's emphasis on sin, its universal nature, and its consequences. One also finds an emphasis on election and God's sovereign choice, a choice that eliminates human merit as a basis for salvation. God has mercy on whom God will have mercy. Chapters 8 and 9 of Romans was read by the reformers as a very strong revelation of God's sovereignty in matters of salvation. In addition to Romans, the reformers read from books such as Ephesians (which the reformers considered a Pauline epistle, though current New Testament scholarship seems to think Paul's authorship is iffy at best), which talks, in chapter 1, explicitly about predestination and God's choice of the elect according to God's plan before the creation of the world. Though a mystery to them in many ways in terms of its working, the early Protestant exegetes—Calvin certainly included but not singular in this regard—bowed to the revealed Word (as they saw it).

One might perhaps wonder why any of this is important. For one thing, it is a matter of proper recognition so that, perhaps, one may move away from stereotypes that might be helpful for quick categorization but not for an examination of any real substance. Otherwise good and useful books are marred by this, perhaps unconscious, adherence to the easy narrative of old-time history textbooks. For example, in a very good 2009 book on religion in the transatlantic world from the Reformation to the American Revolution, nuanced and insightful in all sorts of ways, especially in its inclusion of previously excluded peoples, Calvin makes just a couple of appearances, with his special characteristic presented as "predestination" (read: the bad heritage of the Reformation), and he is set alongside Luther, whose special contribution is boiled down to "the priesthood of all believers" (read: the good heritage of the Reformation, with the assumption that this is a democratic nod in Luther's thought; it is not, at least in the way that it is often used).[4] The heritage of the Reformation is a very mixed bag, and the tares are not quite so easily removed from the wheat. And, of course, the assumption of what constitutes "tares" is open for discussion: one may disagree with the reformers' outlook on predestination, but the move from disagreement to condemnation comes quickly and easily, and along with that condemnation comes a caricature of the doctrine. But, though caricatured over the course of time in the United States, it does not simply go away.[5]

One may ask, so what if Calvin's reputation has been impugned? So what if the name "Calvin" bears the brunt of sensible reaction against the excesses of the Reformation? The matter of his reputation is not so important as the matter of his influence, a much more interesting project. One could juxtapose to this question a statement by Marilynne Robinson, who has been working to repair the image of Calvin and his heirs: "The profoundly negative reputation of John Calvin and his tradition, which has burgeoned in the modern period in an outpouring of tendentious historical and social interpretation, ought not to be allowed to stand." Of course, one may ask of this declaration, why not? I think the answer that would come from her (and does, though not directly in regard to Calvin in this particular instance), is that "[t]o be shamed out of the use of a word is to make a more profound concession to opinion than is consistent with personal integrity." Part of her assessment is that Calvin is not in favor and should not be spoken of in polite society. His name is sullied in the broader culture, she thinks, but she is not willing to let that stand as a final assessment of Calvin and his tradition. She will not concede to popular opinion. As is clear from the title of one of her works, historical reputation has consequences.[6]

And so to the second point that follows from the first: stereotypes must be guarded against because historical reputation does indeed have consequences, one of which, I would argue, is that a historical stereotype impedes investigation into historical influence. Take, for example, this characterization of Calvin from John Fiske, one of the greatest popularizers of history America has produced: "Among all the great benefactors of mankind . . . [Calvin is] the least attractive." In a particularly damning characterization, Fiske states that Calvin was "the constitutional lawyer of the Reformation, with vision as clear, with head as cool, with soul as dry, as any old solicitor in rusty black that ever dwelt in chambers in Lincoln's Inn. His sternness was that of the judge who dooms a criminal to the gallows." This last statement obviously brings to mind Calvin's involvement in the Servetus affair. Because of Calvin's role in the Servetus trial—and because of his predestinarian views—Fiske concludes that Calvin was not easy to like; indeed, that much in Calvin should be loathed "as sheer diabolism."[7] Of course, with diabolism as one's starting point, one wonders how the contributions to humankind will be weighed.

Thus, we come back to John Calvin the historical character, not the stereotype. He did preach predestination, but he also preached the love of God and saw God primarily in terms of *fons bonorum*—the fount of goodness. He *was* involved and certainly complicit in the execution of Servetus, serving as a theological witness in the trial after having alerted the authorities to Servetus's presence in the city. He did ask for a humane method of execution for Servetus; the council, as happened on occasion, ignored Calvin's request and opted for the much slower and more painful death of burning alive. But it is also clear from consistory records that he thought the poor should be cared for, that the well-to-do should not lord it over the not-so-well-to-do, and that the church was responsible not just for the spiritual well-being of its members but also for their physical well-being. He pastored, he visited the sick (and he himself suffered various painful maladies over a period of more than ten years), and he com-forted the bereaved. He taught, and he wrote. He preached thousands of sermons, developed catechisms for training in the faith, and helped to create ordinances for church order. His correspondence kept him connected to many parts of Europe. He had friends, and he had enemies. There were those who, in his own time, disliked him and his work in Geneva; a few wrote unflattering biographies (to put it mildly). But there were others who saw his work as inspired, with the most famous contemporary assessment coming from John Knox, when he said of Geneva that it was "the most perfect school of Christ that ever was in the earth since the days of the apostles."[8] At the end of his days, in 1564, Calvin left a will and testament that distributed what little he had of earthly goods and remarked that he had endeavored to preach the gospel "purely and chastely." He recognized, however, that he had failed "innumerable times to execute my office properly," and so he cast himself upon the mercy of God. He died on May 27 and, in accordance with his wishes, was buried in an unmarked grave.[9]

What, then, of his legacy? Some have thought it an altogether bad one, flowing from a bad life. As mentioned, there were unflattering biographies and an image of Calvin built by those who opposed him that developed into some of the negative stereotypes we have today. Such stereotypes are not limited to the United States: wherever Calvin's heirs have engaged in controversies with others, there arise complaints about the "pope of Geneva." A 2009 book exam-ines some of these negative images and how they have become part of collec-tive memory (though that is not all the book is about). Another case in point: though he wrote in the nineteenth century, Jacob Burckhardt's historiographic star rose dramatically in the United States in the 1940s and 1950s with the publication in English translation of two posthumously published books. The son of a Swiss minister, Burckhardt also studied for the ministry and then abandoned that study along with his public profession of the Christian faith. Burckhardt saw Calvin's role in the Reformation as a terrible misfortune, and he wrote against what he saw as Calvin's stranglehold on the city of Geneva. Strong feelings are evoked by Calvin and his legacy.[10]

These strong feelings, however can be positive as well as negative. Calvin had devoted followers, as witnessed by John Knox's statement above. His influ-ence spread with his followers—from Geneva to France, the Low Countries, and parts of what became Germany, to Eastern Europe, and, of course, to England and Scotland. Though he is not the only figure, certainly, in the crea-tion and early development of what now is often called the Reformed tradition, he does stand with others as a foundational figure (many, but not all, would argue that he was the central foundational figure). Certainly, much of the tradition that follows often will have the appellation Calvinist or Calvinistic. Other times, the movement is simply referred to as orthodoxy, or by some other nomenclature, such as Reformed. Still, it is clear that, in the minds of many—Catharine Sedgwick, for example—what is referred to as orthodoxy has a connection to Geneva as its source and is bound to the name of John Calvin.

Though we divide American history into interesting and discrete chunks of time, it is well for us to remember that, within less than sixty years of Calvin's death, people stood on the shores of the American continent who were heirs of Calvin (though other European Christian groups had preceded them). English separatists, Calvinist in their theology, came to the New World on the *Mayflower* in 1620 (these "Pilgrims," however, constituted only part of the voyaging party) and established a settlement at Plymouth. Other groups followed.

Within ten years, a ship named the *Arbella* brought another group of religiously minded people to what would become New England. While still aboard the *Arbella*, John Winthrop, a Puritan and later the first governor of the Massachusetts Bay Colony, composed a lay sermon that most students of American history know, "A Model of Christian Charity" (1630). In some ways foundational beyond the confines of the Puritan (and Calvinist) tradition in America, given its place in what is often called America's civil religion (one remembers Ronald Reagan's constant use of the "city upon a hill" language, though other presidents have used the imagery as well), the sermon was also foundational to the specific group of Puritans who crossed the Atlantic. It presented a vision, a Calvinist vision, of a godly society, where members are knit together into one body (the sermon has several references to the apostle Paul's First Letter to the Corinthians, chapter 12, where one finds Paul's fullest explication of the church as the body of Christ). And the sermon moves toward its conclusion with a reminder to the colonists that "we shall be as a city upon a hill. The eyes of all people are upon us." The first part of the quote comes from Jesus' Sermon on the Mount, found at Matthew 5:14. The second part of the quote mirrors the concern of John Calvin (and others, of course) that a Christian society should be a good and proper example to the world.[11]

These Calvinists thus engaged in an attempt to establish a "city upon a hill." As in Geneva, there were successes and failures; contestation—religious, moral, political, cultural—marked the years. Wars were fought with external enemies; cultural wars were fought within. Europeans extended their reach into the continent, finally extending from shore to shore. Almost from the start, there were more than just the Puritans in New England, though they dominated the story of origins for a very long time. And among those other historical actors were other Calvinists: the Dutch in what became New York, the Huguenots in South Carolina. As time passed, still other groups came: the German Reformed found themselves in Pennsylvania, for example.

Yet, the Calvinist vision of society did not prevail. The passage of time (even from very early on, in the seventeenth century itself) eroded strict adherence to orthodoxy; conflict over religious authority—again, from almost the start—kept homogeneity at bay; the size of the new land; wave after wave of new immigrants; the gradual appearance of real pluralism—these and so many other things doomed the vision. But still, the vision did not vanish completely, nor did the influence of strongly held religious beliefs and practices.

The point of this book is that, despite all of the changes and challenges; despite Calvinism's ultimate failure to hold the American consciousness; and despite an especially fervent effort to dismiss the Calvinist outlook from American culture by sermon (Channing and, after him, religious movements that numerically overwhelmed the old Puritan faith, such as Methodism) or by the art of letters and the novel (Sedgwick and others, yes, but also those deep within the tradition of Calvinism who brought their most anguished complaints against it to the light of day through their written work; one thinks of the Beecher children here) or by the sardonic newspaper column (H. L. Mencken), the fact remains that Calvinism in America has had an impact on American society and culture in every century, even if at times it has gone unrecognized. And behind Calvinism stands Calvin.

And so, at the time of the 500th anniversary of Calvin's birth, it seems appropriate to reckon with the breadth of his influence—both immediate and mediated—in American culture. It is not that Calvin's influence has not been examined before; it certainly has. In every broad area this book explores (though not the particular subjects of these chapters), there is an already existing body of literature. The value of this volume is in its approach: to look at the variety of ways that Calvin and Calvinism have been important across the centuries. While individual volumes may deal with Calvin and economics, or Calvin and politics, or Calvin and theology, or Calvin and literature—some very well and in-depth—this book gives acknowledgment to all of these areas and attempts to show that, consistently over time, Calvin has had a substantial impact on things American. Here is where reputation needs to be considered with influence: if, by reputation, Calvin is dismissed, then one is less likely to take his influence seriously. While it is funny that Garrison Keillor can declare in one of his standard mock commercials for A Prairie Home Companion—"Mournful Oatmeal! The breakfast cereal of Calvinists"[12]—it is also interesting that the people in the audience get the joke and laugh. Calvin lingers in the consciousness, through a variety of cultural and social avenues. It is hoped that this work can help to explain how that has come to be the case.

This book is divided into three broad areas of concern: (1) Calvin and American society, (2) Calvin and American theology, and (3) Calvin and American letters (looking at both fiction and nonfiction writers). Some of the chapters are synthetic in nature: these will explore Calvin's influence in regard to specific themes over the course of time. Others have more of a case study approach, situating Calvin's influence in a particular place and time, or in relation to a particularly influential person.

In part I, Mark Valeri details Calvinist attitudes and economic activity in colonial America in relation to changing circumstances and locales. David Little explores Calvin's contribution to American identity, to the American credo, tracing two divergent understandings of American society back to ambiguities in Calvin's own thought. To finish the section, D. G. Hart takes on the question of Calvin's influence on the U.S. political order, asking if the sort of positive claims made in this regard can bear the weight of evidence.[13]

In the second part, on Calvin and American theology, Amy Plantinga Pauw focuses on a comparison of Jonathan Edwards and John Calvin, arguing that there are "deep commonalities" in the way the two think about church practice, which certainly adds nuance to the standard line that Edwards represented a move away from Calvin in this regard. Douglas A. Sweeney counters the notion that the strife among various Calvinists concerning how best to read Calvin's theology revealed a weakening tradition with the argument that, instead, it represented the vitality of Calvinist theology in the nineteenth century. David D. Hall traces the contours of the Unitarian-Calvinist controversy of the same century, but then he moves into the twentieth-century historiography of Calvin and the Puritans through the works of Williston Walker and Perry Miller, underscoring the power (and ironies) of stereotype in historical study. Finally, Stephen D. Crocco ranges over the twentieth-century terrain of Calvin and American theology, looking back at the assessment of Calvin at the time of the 400th anniversary of his birth and then moving forward to examine the variety of ways in which Calvin's theology has been "quarried" for modern use.

The last part of the book, concerning Calvin and American letters, begins with Denise T. Askin's analysis of the sermons of Samson Occom, an eighteenth-century Mohegan, tribal representative, Presbyterian minister, missionary, and scholar, in whose language she finds an "indigenous" Calvinism. Peter J. Thuesen mines Harriet Beecher Stowe's work, starting with her recollections of her trip to Geneva, to discover that, well before Max Weber, she had arrived at judgments about Calvin and Calvinism that were later hallmarks of Weber's thought about Calvinism and the way it worked in the world. Joe B. Fulton takes the reader through the writings of Mark Twain, turning much of the standard thinking about Twain's relation to Calvinism on its head and suggesting that the evidence leads one to realize that Twain's genius came not insofar as he was able to disentangle himself from the tradition but, rather, insofar as he wrestled with it. Kyle A. Pasewark, in the final chapter, presents a thoughtful reflection, in conversation with the work of John Updike, on the notion of freedom in the contemporary United States and what is lost when Calvin's understanding of the relationship between grace and freedom is removed from consideration.

My short conclusion considers the work of Marilynne Robinson in its attempt to restore to Calvin a place in the American consciousness free from stereotypes. Perhaps this book will help in that regard, too.

NOTES

1. I have analyzed elsewhere the way this dichotomy of good and bad parts of the Reformation played out in nineteenth-century world history textbooks used in the United States. See Thomas J. Davis, "Images of Intolerance: John Calvin in Nineteenth-Century History Textbooks," *Church History* 65, no. 2 (Summer 1996): 234–48. In most of these textbooks, Calvin epitomizes the problems and excesses of the Reformation, with the Servetus affair being the prime example. One author blamed Calvin not just for the death of Servetus, but also for the deaths of hundreds of thousands of people. See Willis Mason West, *The Story of Modern Progress: With a Preliminary Survey of Earlier Progress* (Boston: Allyn and Bacon, 1920), 148. Because nineteenth-century textbooks used foils as a standard practice to illustrate good versus bad in history, Luther stands for the good things—regardless of whether or not Luther actually represented those good things. Among the many "benefits" of the Reformation was freedom of thought, according to this nineteenth-century historiography (though such an appraisal is not confined to that century; it is a legacy from an Enlightenment way of speaking about the Reformation, as shown by A. G. Dickens and John M. Tonkin with Kenneth Powell, *The Reformation in Historical Thought* [Cambridge, Mass.: Harvard University Press, 1985], chap. 6 and esp. 130). Luther's stand before the Diet of Worms in 1521 is often used as a stirring narrative to underscore the evidence for his breakthrough into the enlightened world of freedom—a literal stand against the highest authorities of church and state. Of course, what he actually said is often overlooked: "My conscience is held captive by the Word of God."

2. In terms of the picture the consistory records paint, the first place to look is the work of Robert Kingdon (with a second look at the corpus of work produced by the Ph.D. students he has mentored at the University of Wisconsin History Department). See, in particular, regarding the limits the consistory tried to place on physical violence in the family, Robert M. Kingdon, "Calvin and the Family: The Work of the Consistory of Geneva," *Pacific Theological Journal* 17 (1984): 13; for an assessment of how the consistory functioned during the time of Calvin, see Kingdon, "A New View of Calvin in Light of the Registers of the Geneva Consistory," in *Calvinus Sincerioris Religionis Vindex: Calvin as Protector of the Purer Religion*, ed. Wilhelm H. Neuser and Brian Armstrong (Kirksville, Mo.: Sixteenth Century Journal Publishers, 1997), 21–34,

wherein Kingdon examines the role of the consistory in the work of reconciliation, describing that work as being "closer to an obligatory counseling service than to a court" (23).

3. The literature on Channing is substantial, but perhaps one would do well to start with David D. Hall's chapter in this volume. On the fiction writers who have protested Calvinism's emphasis on predestination, see Thomas J. Davis, "Rhetorical War and Reflex: Calvin and Calvinism in Nineteenth-Century Fiction and Twentieth-Century Criticism," *Calvin Theological Journal* 33, no. 2 (November 1998): 443–56. One important point of this latter essay is the way the critics seem uncritically to adopt the attitudes toward Calvinism that the nineteenth-century writers carried; indeed, they (wittingly or unwittingly, perhaps depending on the critic) continued the culture war started (and, on the level of cultural images, won) by writers such as Sedgwick, who was explicit in her desire to see Calvinism displaced. She saw such displacement to be a moral task, as she explained to William Ellery Channing. See Sedgwick, *The Power of Her Sympathy: The Autobiography and Journal of Catharine Maria Sedgwick*, ed. Mary Kelley (Boston: Massachusetts Historical Society, 1993), 31 and 30, 36–37. Sedgwick connected "the horrors of Calvinism" and its "monstrous" teachings to "the cruel doctrines of Geneva" (86).

4. See Carla Gardina Pestana, *Protestant Empire: Religion and the Making of the British Atlantic World* (Philadelphia: University of Pennsylvania Press, 2009), 35.

5. See Peter J. Thuesen, *Predestination: The American Career of a Contentious Doctrine* (New York: Oxford University Press, 2009).

6. Marilynne Robinson, "The Polemic against Calvin: The Origins and Consequences of Historical Reputation," in *Calvin and the Church: Papers Presented at the 13th Colloquium of the Calvin Studies Society, May 24–26, 2001*, ed. David Foxgrover (Grand Rapids, Mich.: CRC Services for the Calvin Studies Society, 2002), 122; Robinson, *The Death of Adam: Essays on Modern Thought*, paperback ed. (New York: Picador, 2005; first published 1998), 260.

7. John Fiske, *The Beginnings of New England; or, The Puritan Theocracy in Its Relation to Civil Liberty* (Boston: Houghton Mifflin, 1889), 57–59.

8. John Knox to Mrs. Locke, December 9, 1556, in *The Works of John Knox*, vol. 4, ed. David Laing (Edinburgh, 1855), quoted in Robert M. Kingdon, "Calvin and the Establishment of Discipline in Geneva: The Institution and the Men Who Directed It," *Nederlands Archief voor Kerkgeschiednis* 70 (1990): 167.

9. John Calvin, *John Calvin: Selections from His Writings*, ed. John Dillenberger (Garden City, N.Y.: Doubleday, 1971), 35–36.

10. On Calvin as the Protestant pope, see Davis, "Images of Intolerance." For proof that the image still exists, see Philip Pullman's fantasy series *His Dark Materials*, a trilogy wherein the notion of Calvin as a pope figure is taken literally (in the world Pullman has created, John Calvin became the pope in the sixteenth century), and I assume he uses the case of Servetus to extrapolate what would have happened if Calvin had gained real power. In Pullman's fiction, Calvin sets up a system whereby one can become a religious assassin, and the fictional Calvin also orders the deaths of children. See Philip Pullman, *The Amber Spyglass: His Dark Materials*, book 3 (New York: Laurel

Leaf, 2000), 64, 184. A work that looks at images of Calvin that have arisen over the last 200 years in a variety of countries is Johan de Niet, Herman Paul, and Bart Wallet, eds., *Sober, Strict, and Scriptural: Collective Memories of John Calvin, 1800–2000* (Leiden: Brill, 2009). For Burckhardt's views on Calvin, see Jacob Burckhardt, *Judgments on History and Historians*, trans. Harry Zohn (Boston: Beacon, 1958), 131, 134–35.

11. Though many abbreviated versions of Winthrop's "A Model of Christian Charity" (1630) can be found in print and on the Web, the work in its entirety is easily accessed at http://religiousfreedom.lib.virginia.edu/sacred/charity.html. The material quoted from this site is obviously in contemporary English. Something closer to the original can be found at http://history.hanover.edu/texts/winthmod.html, which contains a scan of the Winthrop sermon taken from the *Collections of the Massachusetts Historical Society*, 3rd ser. (Boston, 1838), 7:31–48. Winthrop's assertion that "the eyes of all people are upon us" echoes not just Calvin's general concern about the example of Christian society before the world, but the words themselves are close to Calvin's comments on Matthew 5:14, as found in the English translation of that commentary in print during Winthrop's time: "By which woordes he [Jesus] woulde signifie that they should so liue, as if they were sette oute to be looked vppon of all menne" and "because that all mennes eyes were sette vppon them as vppon lanternes" (the passage contains a reference to the light of the world). John Calvin, *A harmonie vpon the three Euangelists, Matthew, Mark and Luke with the commentarie of M. Iohn Caluine: Faithfully translated out of Latine into English, by E. P. Whereunto is also added a commentarie vpon the Euangelist S. Iohn, by the same authour* (London: Printed by Thomas Dawson, 1584; repr., 1610), 165.

12. This line—and its variants—has appeared often over the years. Garrison Keillor, *A Prairie Home Companion*, broadcast July 1996, WFYI radio, Indianapolis, Indiana (originally aired live from Savannah, Georgia, June 22, 1996).

13. One view of Calvin's contribution to Western notions of representative government may be found in Robert M. Kingdon, "John Calvin's Contribution to Representative Government," in *Politics and Culture in Early Modern Europe: Essays in Honor of H. G. Koenigsberger*, ed. Phyllis Mack and Margaret C. Jacobs (Cambridge: Cambridge University Press, 1987), 183–98, which is about Geneva as a political model; for a view of Calvin's, and then Calvinism's, contribution to resistance theory, see Quentin Skinner, "Calvinism and the Theory of Revolution: The Right to Resist," part 3 of Skinner, *The Foundations of Modern Political Thought*, vol. 2, *The Age of Reformation* (Cambridge: Cambridge University Press, 1978), 186–348.

PART I

Society

I

Calvin and the Social Order in Early America: Moral Ideals and Transatlantic Empire

Mark Valeri

The subject of John Calvin's influence on social and economic orders in America has evoked a long and distinguished commentary, marked by contrasting opinions about the supposed modernity or antimodernity of the Puritan social conscience. Most of the debate, focused on early New England, follows from two common observations. First, the Calvinist settlers of Massachusetts Bay condemned many aspects of England's nascent market economy and initially instituted severe restrictions on overseas merchants. Second, by the end of the seventeenth century, most New Englanders had embraced the dictates of the transatlantic market as a moral good and social mandate. Historians, however, have given various reasons for this commonly recognized transformation. Their answers reflect quite different perspectives on the influence of Calvin in America.

To simplify the historiography, we can gather the literature into two groups. The first asserts, in a rather commonsense fashion, that secular, material forces—that is, the market itself—simply overwhelmed religious tradition over the course of the seventeenth century. Not surprisingly, this has been the major theme of historians more interested in questions of economic power than in cultural forces such as religion. Social and political historians writing during the mid-twentieth century frequently pitted Puritanism against commerce and decreed a quick victory for the latter. Bernard Bailyn maintained that most of Boston's merchants had little sympathy with the farmers and preachers who cherished old-fashioned communal ideals and moral hedges against the emergent market economy. Darrett Rutman contended that economic interests prevented any cohesive social polity for New Englanders from the moment settlers stepped ashore at the cold edges of Massachusetts Bay. He described a contest between ministers and merchants and the inevitable triumph of the latter over the former by the middle of the century. Providing close studies of New England towns, Kenneth Lockridge and Michael Zuckerman argued that New Englanders out-side of Boston held to a communal and anticommercial ethic until the eight-eenth century, when material forces eclipsed the original moral vision for New England. John Frederick Martin reduced the whole enterprise of New England to a speculative venture designed for investors' profits. Were we to take this line of argument, then, our conclusion about the influence of Calvin on the early American economy would be short and none too interesting, fleeting at best.[1]

The second group of studies clusters around the influential thesis of Max Weber's *The Protestant Ethic and the Spirit of Capitalism*. Taking their cue from Weber's assertions about the unintended consequences of the Calvinist theol-ogy, American intellectual historians from Perry Miller through Stephen Foster have probed for deep-rooted tensions within the Puritan movement between a traditional social ethic and economic innovation. Adherents of Calvinism, as this narrative goes, stressed the glorification of God through labor and thus promoted the capitalistic virtues of diligence, frugality, and economic rational-ity. Miller held that the first generation of Puritan settlers linked such virtues to communal and antimodern social patterns, but he concluded that this synthe-sis disintegrated under the force of political and demographic changes during the second generation. Freed from customary restraints and Calvinistic dogma, the Puritan personality developed into a full-fledged Yankee disposition toward hard bargains and individual profits. Foster argued that, after the imposition of royal control over trade in New England during the 1660s and the revocation of Massachusetts's charter in 1684, the potential individualism of Puritanism was manifested in a widespread concession to market ethics. Charles Cohen has echoed this claim of Puritan ambiguity in an important programmatic essay.[2]

A more recent generation of economic and cultural histories has refur-bished the Weber thesis for New England, producing what Darren Staloff has called "a new 'commercial' paradigm for puritan development in New England." Modifying Weber and drawing on R. H. Tawney, Stephen Innes portrayed an essential and determinative link between Puritan ethics and capitalism. Puritan moral ideas, by his account, eventuated in the rejection of external, corporate measures against market economies soon after the initial decade of settlement in Massachusetts Bay—a short period when economic exigencies compelled only temporary and aberrant discipline over merchants. Margaret Newell maintained that Puritans sought to develop New England economically through investment in manufacturing, overseas trade, and other entrepreneurial ventures. She contended (again, Weber looms large) that Puritanism provided a rational and even economically scientific world view that freed New Englanders from regressive policies. Mark Peterson argued that most Puritans sought to use the market as a means for profits to be used for the spread of religion. Puritanism, by his reading, was evangelistic; what is more, its most alert adherents took economic expansion as a corollary to religious growth.[3]

This assertion of a Calvinist-capitalist nexus has entered into more popular studies as well: it now appears as a commonplace for commentators to posit the progressive, rational, modern, and even liberal inheritance of Calvinism. Distinguished social commentators such as Walter Russell Mead, economists such as Benjamin Friedman, and business historians such as Kenneth Hopper and William Hopper have all, in the early twenty-first century, given forceful variations on the Weber thesis. From their perspectives, Calvin bequeathed to his followers in early America a drive to economic development, reliance on scientific economic analyses, confidence in markets, and optimism that commercial success served God, the social order, and the human community at the same time. (No telling what the 2008–2009 economic crisis—and the collapse of financial markets—portends for this sanguine reading of Calvin.) The port towns in which commerce developed earliest and most fully were, after all, heavily populated by Calvinists: Puritan Boston, Dutch Reformed New York, Presbyterian Philadelphia, and Huguenot Charleston.[4]

These interpretations of Calvin's influence all engage a cluster of issues concerning the modernity or antimodernity of the Reformed tradition in America and raise a crucial question. How should we account for their polarized interpretation of Calvin's influence on American economic life? Much of the discussion assumes that Calvinist dogma—logically interconnected doctrines such as divine sovereignty, human depravity, predestination, and sanctification—expressed an affinity for one economic ideology or another. This highly systematized reading of Calvin implies that Calvinists must have formed a single social teaching, either antimodern and regressive or rational and proto-capitalist. It has produced overly simplified assessments on both sides: Calvinists as retrograde critics of a modern economy, doomed to irrelevance, or Calvinists as proto-Yankees, nudging American society into a bureaucratic and capitalist age.[5]

Late twentieth- and early twenty-first-century scholarship on Calvin's method for using the Bible as a guide to social problems offers a way out of this interpretive impasse: an alternative reading that suggests neither capitulation to pure material interests nor an elective affinity of Calvinist creed for capitalism. Calvin promulgated a flexible and pragmatic approach to scripture that allowed his adherents to adapt economic instruction to the needs of their religious communities. Early American Calvinists followed this method when they transformed their teaching about commerce and the nascent market economy in the context of colonization. They inherited a relatively conservative, which is to say, highly critical, platform on market systems. They changed their position in response to the transatlantic contest for empire, that is, the struggle between Protestant and Catholic regimes during the second half of the seventeenth century. Calvin's influence on early American society thus follows a pattern of creativity and adaptation. This chapter illustrates that pattern with a comparative sketch of three Reformed communities in colonial America: Puritan in Boston, Dutch Reformed in New York, and Huguenot in Charleston, South Carolina.[6] Their stories show that Calvinists had profoundly religious reasons, having little to do with a Weberian list of Reformed doctrines, for aligning their morality with the new economy.

Our first task, however, is to reconsider the very approach that Calvin took to moral and social problems. Calvinist settlers in American colonies inherited from English and European authorities a moral method that Stephen Toulmin has described as humanistic pragmatism.[7] "Humanistic" refers not to optimism about human nature but to Renaissance humanism: a trust in the authority of the ancient text. Calvin modeled for his followers a highly disciplined moral method grounded in the Bible. His vision for social order was breathtakingly rigorous and demanding in such terms. Calvinists applied the Bible to everything. They attempted to shape civil law, secular jurisprudence, politics, national policy, domestic affairs such as marriage and divorce, and economic matters such as personal consumption and commercial exchange to the Old and New Testaments. The notion of a Bible commonwealth, which scholars apply to early New England, hints at the power and scope of this ideal.[8]

Yet Calvin's deployment of the Bible as an absolute rule for social behavior had a rather ironic consequence: it deflated the Calvinist's enthusiasm for ideology. For Calvin, scripture stood over and sometimes against the political or economic philosophies that hold sway at any moment. As William J. Bouwsma, Serene Jones, and others have argued, Calvin applied the Bible in an almost ad hoc fashion to public dilemmas as they presented themselves. Just as he avoided systematic doctrinal formulations, he rebuffed elaborate social theories. He addressed local and immediate problems in their particular contexts. His pragmatism made it difficult to fix a Calvinist politics or economics but easier to identify Calvinism's chief appeal: it was mobile, practical, and flexible. It was untethered to any theory: absolutism or republicanism, free markets or state control over exchange, capitalism or socialism. It avoided theoretical abstractions and absolute claims for any one set of social ideals. It settled moral rules on the needs of particular Reformed communities at a given time.[9]

Perhaps we can best illuminate Calvin's social teaching by way of a single instance. On Friday, December 20, 1555, he delivered one of his 200 lectures on the Old Testament book Deuteronomy. His text, Deuteronomy 20:19–20, contains a command for the invading armies of Israel to refrain from cutting down fruit trees in conquered territory. Calvin explained the passage in this way: the Lord commanded Israel to preserve such gifts as expressions of his favor to humanity in general. Calvin then spoke quite directly to economic conditions and activities in his city. Many of his auditors that afternoon were refugees from France or exiles from England, who had fled to Geneva during the past year. They crowded Geneva's streets and precincts, taxing the city's supplies of food, housing, and other necessaries. Calvin noted how native merchants had responded. They took advantage of food shortages by buying up wheat, storing it until demand was at its peak, and then selling it at inflated prices. They even let the grain sit unused over the summer, when it often spoiled (here, according to his reading, was the link to wasting fruit trees). Grain speculators acted like brutes. They disregarded their "common humanity" with other inhabitants of Geneva. The text compelled them "to communicate one with another in peace and fraternity" and to "bring [their] neighbors into partnership" with them. In practical terms, Calvin demanded that merchants put their grain on the market immediately and price it at the customary, affordable rates.[10]

Calvin's occasional letters, biblical commentaries, other sermons, and treatises reveal the consistency of this approach, what specialists have described as his appropriation of Renaissance rhetorical techniques, or a rhetorical logic. As he moved from text to application, he did not engage in scholastic discussions of the essences or universal meanings of moral terms. He eschewed metaphysical claims and sweeping generalizations of the sort that produced social or political ideology. He participated in what Bouwsma has called the "instrumentalism of Renaissance culture," the conviction that the text served as a practical guide for particular moral dilemmas.[11]

Taken together, Calvin's economic ideas amounted to no consistent theory but, rather, to a case-by-case application of the biblical text to local conditions. He warned well-to-do citizens against pursuing impoverished debtors in civil courts and railed against almost all forms of usury (turning credit into a commodity for profit). He furthermore scolded cash-holding residents who refused to give alms or offer jobs to the needy. He strengthened institutionalized poor relief in the city. Yet Calvin just as readily supported business institutions in Geneva. He urged an active pursuit of economic abundance, recommended a modest level of personal consumption, sought public funding for the development of new manufactures, and encouraged the establishment of a public bank to assist new entrepreneurs. He advised his followers outside of Geneva to practice business in ways that enhanced social life in their respective locales, even prompting a German merchant with business overseas to exchange credit for a profit, the very tactic that Calvin had condemned in Geneva's tight credit market. Whatever served the community of the faithful, for Calvin, served the cause of godliness in the world.[12]

The mobility of Calvin's social ideas rested on their non-ideological nature; they could be applied in different situations according to local needs and problems. This partly explains the appeal of Calvin to the English Puritans who made the Great Migration to New England. English Calvinists had made quick work of publishing Calvin's social commentary and ethics, beginning with the return of the Marian exiles in the late 1550s. English printers favored Calvin's sermons on Deuteronomy and commentary on the Ten Commandments. Shorter selections of Calvin's work, especially his scattered sermons on social issues such as usury, appeared in the numerous English tracts on that subject throughout the late sixteenth and early seventeenth centuries. The godly party drew on these writings to address a series of severe economic dislocations in England at the turn of the seventeenth century: a decline in the cloth trade, rising unemployment and poverty, price inflation, and a dearth of credit. From the 1580s through the 1620s, English moralists complained about parliamentary malfeasance, corruption in the courts, royal preferment for large overseas trading companies over middling merchants, aggressive enclosure (removing tenants from agricultural fields for the sake of more lucrative ventures), and the rise of a class of financiers who practiced usury on previously unimaginable levels.[13]

Instructed by Calvin's moral pragmatism, Puritans criticized this bundle of market practices as inhumane and fractious, usurious and oppressive. In the isolated cases where they gained control of local parishes and county ecclesiastical tribunals, they instituted Geneva-like discipline over usurers. They also hounded credit brokers, price gougers, and especially wealthy landowners who, through enclosure, impoverished land-poor farmers. Puritans in London focused on the plight of small and middling merchants. They denounced shifty creditors with their inflated fees, high-priced lawyers in the service of wealthy overseas traders, and members of Parliament eager to line their pockets with bribes.[14]

Puritan colonists carried this moral perspective to Massachusetts. The founders of the Bay Colony framed their venture as an opportunity to enact biblical rules in local communities that faced daunting economic challenges: a dearth of labor and a scarcity of goods, competition from Dutch traders and threats of privateering, the constriction of transatlantic trade and the outbreak of civil war at home, the opportunities and dangers of exchange with Native Americans, and a complete dependence on English specie or credit issued from London. New England afforded Puritans an opportunity to establish and institutionalize religious discipline over this economic disorder.

The colonists drew on their Calvinist training to address such problems. Governor John Winthrop and John Cotton, pastor of Boston's First Church, along with their colleagues, brought biblical teaching to bear on nearly every public institution, including schools, law courts, the legislative body, and government. Massachusetts legal procedures, for example, were famous for their simplified language, personal protocols, and arguments based on biblical passages. Echoing Calvin, Bay Colony pastors decreed in 1635 that the "general rules of the Word [of God]" ought to be applied to "the state of the people," by which they meant the practical and political conditions that demanded flexibility in matters of social policy.[15]

In economic terms, these early Puritan settlers understood the New Testament mandate for social solidarity and mutual affection to mean a strict oversight of trade, especially low ceilings on prices, restraints on imports, the development of manufactures such as iron foundries, and minimal interest rates on loans given to fellow colonists—policies that bore a remarkable resemblance to Genevan affairs under Calvin's sway. Most famously, Winthrop and Cotton turned against one of Boston's most respected overseas traders and church members, Robert Keayne, for the sins of high price margins and usury. The civil court fined Keayne, and the church censured him. During these first decades, Boston's First Church issued dozens of censures and excommunications on wayward members for commercial transgressions: inflated prices, deceptive business practices, hidden loan fees, and general disregard for poor neighbors.[16]

The story of Calvin and the economy in early New England, however, moves along a line of change. After the initial decades of settlement, Puritan leaders in Massachusetts adjusted their economic teachings. They did so in the midst of New England's increasing integration into an Atlantic economy and the growth of a class of moderately successful overseas merchants in Boston. Building networks of exchange after the most disruptive years of the English Civil War, they exported timber and fish to England, imported European and English goods back to Massachusetts, and engaged in trade with partners in the Caribbean, the Chesapeake, and New England. As they extended their business contacts and developed long-term market strategies, they began to adopt innovative techniques and protocols: exchanging securities and promissory notes across great distances; deploying credit as a commodity, that is, as a means to profit in and of itself; and using civil courts to adjudicate disputes over debt and credit. Furthermore, they adopted the analytical language of their London counterparts, learning accounting techniques and even an epistolary style grounded in formality, legal propriety, and mathematical precision.[17]

Pious Calvinist merchants and their pastors did not applaud all of these developments, but they did deem many of them to be moral goods. They did so because changing social and political conditions from the 1650s through the 1680s compelled them to different readings of scripture than the ones that had captured previous generations. The restoration of the Stuart monarchy brought London's power to bear on Massachusetts politics in unprecedented measure, from the imposition of royal officials to the revocation of the colony's charter to the establishment of an Anglican church in Boston. Hostilities with Native Americans erupted into terrifying warfare, most notably in King Philip's War from 1675 to 1676. Taken together, these threats to New England provoked a sense among the clergy of collective danger.[18]

Preachers responded by encouraging New Englanders to read the calamities of the day through the lenses of scriptural narratives that imputed providential purpose to public events. This gave rise to the jeremiad, a sermonic form that lamented the sins of New England in rich and depressing detail and explained political and economic misfortune as instruments of divine punishment. If New Englanders did not repent from their worldliness, avarice, selfishness, and unbelief, preachers warned, then the Lord would deliver more Indian raids, harsher weather, meaner pirates off the coast, and more humiliating submission to a corrupt court in London.

Such preaching, of course, gave material for later critics to deride Puritans as gloomy prigs, but it also could be read as a strangely liberating code because it implied that God had special purposes for New England. As the foremost preacher of the jeremiad, Increase Mather, put it, "This is Immanuels Land." "Christ by a wonderful Providence" had "caused as it were *New Jerusalem* to come down from Heaven." So, "the dealings of God with our Nation" were "different than with other" nations and colonies. If this were the case—if the Lord promised prosperity for obedience as a counterpoint to disobedience and poverty—then commercial expansion and economic prowess could be understood as divine mandates. God wanted New England to flourish economically because it was the vanguard of the English Reformed movement.[19]

Second-generation Puritans were as tied to biblical principles as were their predecessors. They reiterated Calvinist rules of charity, prohibitions against usury, demands for almsgiving, and warnings against avarice and ostentatious consumption. Puritan pastors and their most devoted parishioners nonetheless determined that many older restrictions on overseas trade were anachronistic.

God had chosen New England, and New England depended on overseas trade for its very survival. The churches of Boston stopped bringing merchants before disciplinary tribunals. Preachers subtly shifted the meaning of the sin of usury from any exchange of credit for a profit to mean-spirited lawsuits against impoverished debtors. They complained about a litigious spirit that clogged courts with commercial cases but allowed that New England merchants ought to pursue their cases against delinquent commercial partners. They railed against the importation of costly luxury goods but did so by indicating the baneful effects of an imbalance in trade. In sum, they began to legitimate the very exchange techniques once denounced as vile and inhumane: using credit as a commodity, the determination of prices by market forces, and adjudicating commercial disputes in law courts rather than in church meetings. None of this revealed an abandonment of essential Calvinist tenets or piety. One could hardly accuse Increase Mather or his merchant parishioners of secularization. It revealed instead the malleability and pragmatism of the Calvinist inheritance.[20]

Puritan moral teaching in New England underwent yet another transformation during the provincial era, from the late 1680s through the 1730s. A remarkable set of political changes marked that period. The most important was the Glorious Revolution in England, which ended the reign of the crypto-Catholic Stuarts and brought to the throne a line of monarchs widely perceived to hold strong Protestant sympathies: William of Orange, George I, and George II. In Massachusetts, Calvinist ministers from across the spectrum—rationally oriented progressives such as Benjamin Wadsworth and Ebenezer Pemberton, proto-evangelicals such as Benjamin Colman and Thomas Prince, and moderates such as Cotton Mather—all revered the Hanoverian monarchy. As war with Catholic France spread throughout the Atlantic world, including New England and Canada, New Englanders injected the language of providence and divine sovereignty into imperial politics. They detected the hand of God in Protestant and English triumphs over French Catholic absolutism and superstition.[21]

Political conflict also demanded new economic strategies to abet England's Protestant empire. To sustain its dynastic program and fund imperial warfare, the British monarchy and Parliament increasingly co-opted commercial interests. They promoted a regularized system of national debt through the Bank of London, worked in concert with new trading companies to contest especially French colonial ventures, promoted the African slave trade, issued lucrative monopolies to manufacturing and mercantile firms, and attempted to control trade with the British colonies through navigation laws and ever-mounting tariffs and regulations.[22]

Commentators developed an economic science—political economy—to track the interdependence of political stability, military strength, and invigorated trade between the metropolis and its colonial extensions. A cadre of political economists described commerce not as a matter of private concern but as a platform for the affairs of state. As they did so, they developed increasingly sophisticated methods to measure the nation's productivity and wealth. They contended that free-floating prices and interest rates, increased domestic consumption, low tariffs, and free trade all enhanced Britain's wealth and, therefore, served patriotic duty.

This imperial economic agenda, often discussed under the rubric of mercantilism, transformed a modern economic science into a tool for Protestant hegemony in a worldwide battle with Catholic tyranny. It inflected commercial sagacity with moral mandate. Decidedly oriented to a market culture and commercial innovation, mercantilism was imported to New England through newspapers and magazines, taken up in debates in Massachusetts about provincial finances, and reflected in the private correspondence and public declarations of leading merchants in Boston.

Calvinist preachers accordingly applied scriptural rules about trade to this transatlantic market by showing how the Bible legitimated the honest, diligent, assiduous, and rational merchant. So, in his 1710 *Theopolis Americana*, Cotton Mather deemed Boston merchants to be instruments of providence. He imagined the golden streets of heaven to adumbrate the economic prowess of Protestant empires: wealthy Britain and its American colonies would surpass Spanish and French regimes with their dwindling supply of gold from Mexico and silver from Peru. In sermons such as "Heavenly Merchandize" and in 1704 lectures published as *A Compleat Body of Divinity*, the fullest theology written in colonial New England, Boston's Samuel Willard refrained from eschatological surmises and made the Calvinist-mercantilist connection more directly. He argued that the customary prohibitions against usury amounted to old Catholic superstitions long made anachronistic; that merchants who set their prices by the market merely followed the laws of providence; and that the host of new techniques for making a profit in the market, from using lawyers and factors to trading bonds and securities, were godly practices.[23]

The Dutch Reformed settlers of New Amsterdam offer strikingly similar cases of the flexibility of a Calvinist moral perspective with their readiness to transform economic mores to meet shifting religious needs and perspectives in the transatlantic context. Like the Puritans, Dutch Reformed believers inherited a body of Calvinist teachings often set against market mandates. A fragile republic, consisting of seven provinces and surrounded by hostile Catholic states, the Netherlands depended on a cohesive cultural and religious order to sustain national identity. For Dutch Calvinists, patriotic affiliation often trumped international commercial agendas at the close of the sixteenth and start of the seventeenth centuries, leading ministers to emphasize biblical rules for neighborly obligations and personal frugality. In Amsterdam, Reformed ministers preached against usury and the whole stock and trade of the city's central financial exchange, the Bourse, where merchants and financiers made alliances with foreign partners, speculated in bonds and bills, gambled on risky ventures, and used spies and informers to track the latest international trends in the market. Academic divines such as Gisbert Voetius drew on English Calvinists such as William Ames to construct a moral theology that hedged new market activities with biblical principles. City preachers such as Jacobus Triglund and Jacobius Lydius were known for their denunciations of Amsterdam's merchants who made a killing in the exchange and displayed their avarice and cupidity through ostentatious consumption.[24]

Just as English Puritans attempted to institute Calvinist moral ideals through church discipline, so, too, did Dutch church authorities through the mid-1620s. A hierarchy of ecclesiastical organizations of the Reformed Church—parochial consistories, local classes, regional synods, and national synods—promulgated Calvin's instructions on social issues with special attention to the power of overseas traders and bankers. Leading spokesmen such as Leiden's Johannes Cloppenburg urged the synods to ban bankers—so-called lombards, who made their livings from usurious practices—from communion. The first national synod, which met at Emden in 1571, and subsequent synods through 1620 decreed that lombards fell under censure. In 1604, the Amsterdam consistory suspended high-flown merchants in the East India Company, such as Isaac LeMaire, under this rubric.[25]

The reform efforts of the Dutch church in New Amsterdam also mirrored developments among Calvinist settlers in New England, albeit in a more heterogeneous cultural milieu. New Amsterdam was settled almost exclusively as a mercantile venture of the Dutch West India Company, and its early years reflected the dominance of the overseas traders on whom the economy of the town depended. Shipping pelts and other goods from the Hudson River valley to Europe, its small collection of merchants hewed closely to the agenda of a colonial administration composed of company officials who reported to the headquarters in Amsterdam. During the first years of settlement, the company hired "comforters of the sick," that is, chaplains, who chiefly served to validate the virtues of hardscrabble merchants whose practices, including privateering, served political purposes but hardly accorded with standard Calvinist moral teachings. In 1628, the company settled Jonas Michaelius, a genuine Calvinist (in Dutch terms, anti-Remonstrant), as a regular minister over the first

Reformed Church congregation, but his attempts to shape the church into a disciplinary regime over trade—to inhibit dissolute social behaviors, restrict the influence of non-Protestants in the town, and control exchange practices— earned him the disfavor of the directors. He returned to Amsterdam after four miserable years.[26]

The appointment of Pieter Stuyvesant as director general over New Netherland from 1647 to 1664, however, allowed Dutch Reformed preachers in New Amsterdam the opportunity to enact reform along Calvinist lines. Although often opposed by West India Company officials, Stuyvesant supported pastors who brought the economically conservative mores of their Amsterdam supervi- sors to church discipline in the town. They initiated a partly successful campaign to use the local consistory to close brothels, enforce Sabbath regula- tions, and warn merchants against usurious practices and harsh debt litigation. They also brought itinerant preachers, wayward Dutch pastors, and trespassing Lutherans under confessional regulation and attempted to prohibit trade with enemies of the Reformed cause.[27]

Yet, just as New Englanders encountered social conditions that brought new threats to the church and embraced theological ideas that legitimated the latest commercial techniques as a result, so, too, did Dutch Reformed minis- ters. Stuyvesant's directorship ended when the English Crown annexed New Amsterdam (and renamed it New York) in 1664. As a result, New York's mer- chants came to rely on patronage and political support from London. The Dutch Reformed Church also came to depend on the political freedoms granted by English officials. Wary of royal incursion into the region's ecclesiastical affairs, Reformed ministers curried favor with English officials and Crown appointees and gave public approval to mercantilist policies that linked overseas commerce to England's interests. These measures protected the reputation of the Reformed Church as an ally of the kingdom. Dutch ministers had compel- ling religious reasons to transform their economic teaching and align it with mercantilism.[28]

Subsequent statements by the Dutch church in New York supported poli- cies that favored city merchants in competition with inland traders. The church also embraced commercial protocols that implied patriotic loyalties. The New York consistory issued no censures against merchants for common credit prac- tices; Dutch financiers faced no threat of excommunication in the New World. Indeed, by the mid-1680s, Reformed preachers in New York celebrated what appeared to them to be a holy alliance among Reformed piety, civic stability, and commercial prosperity. "The Lord," according to a 1685 decree of the church, had preserved "this land in piece and quiet" and blessed "this City" with "negotiation and commerce" in unusual measure. Rather than condemn market measures such as usury and market pricing, the church itself practiced them. A large landowner and renter in the city, the congregation often received bonds for payment and repeatedly warned debtors that it would sue them in court if the bonds went unpaid past their due date. The Dutch Reformed Church did not begin as an ally of mercantilist agendas, but it evolved into one in complete congruence with its religious identity.[29]

Dutch Calvinists, unlike New Englanders, also depended quite heavily on theological instruction from the Old World, which provided even further rationales for adopting new economic ethics. The Amsterdam classis maintained disciplinary oversight of the Dutch church in the New World and supplied the ministers, doctrinal regulations, and publications that secured a Dutch Calvinist identity across the Atlantic. Tellingly, the Amsterdam classis, along with the Synods of Leiden and Gouda, adopted progressive versions of Reformed theology during the 1650s. Theologians such as Johann Kriex and Claude de Saumaise rejected the teaching of conservatives such as Voetius and gradually adopted rationalist theological ideas that, on the one hand, aligned Reformed doctrine to the latest philosophical and scientific knowledge and, on the other, conformed moral instruction to theories of natural law that legitimated progressive economic standards. After Saumaise produced a lengthy treatise that defended usury and trading in securities, the Synods of Amsterdam and Leiden removed restrictions on lombards, effectively giving religious sanction to the new class of financiers and transatlantic merchants. The church in New York depended on an Amsterdam classis that identified Reformed teachings with the most progressive, mercantilist agendas.[30]

A similar pattern of transmission and adaptation can be detected in the early history of the French Reformed Church in South Carolina. Huguenot merchants immigrated across the Atlantic during the decade immediately before and two decades following the revocation of the Edict of Nantes in 1685. The revocation, which reestablished a policy of royal intolerance toward Protestantism, produced a great diaspora of French Calvinists. A few families settled in French Canada and the French West Indies. The most durable communities were established in major ports on the North American mainland. Eight hundred immigrants settled during this period in New York City, 400 in Charleston and surrounding enclaves in South Carolina, and 200 in Boston and nearby towns. French exiles to Charleston included many artisans and aspiring plantation farmers, yet merchants comprised a significant portion of the immigrant community and a powerful bloc in South Carolina's commercial trade. Sixty-five percent of the exiles came from port towns in France, especially La Rochelle. Thirty percent of the colony's merchants were French.[31]

These merchants led the formation of the Reformed French Protestant Church in Charleston. While many of their compatriots in other regions, including the influential Bowdoin and Faneuil families in Boston, joined the Anglican church during the eighteenth century, the group in Charleston maintained its Calvinist confession throughout the colonial period. The members traced their origins to a French church that adhered closely to Calvin's teachings and adopted Calvin's Ecclesiastical Ordinances nearly wholesale. Prefaced by a letter from Calvin, the 1559 national constitution of the French Protestants, the Gallican Confession (also called the Gallic Confession), and subsequent acts of French national synods, sometimes included by printers in French editions of the Bible, incorporated Calvin's guidance on commercial matters such as usury, almsgiving, fraud, price gouging, and honesty in business contracts. The first national synod of the church deliberated whether bankers, who made their livings from interest on credit, ought to be allowed to be elders. While the French did not go so far as the Dutch Reformed, who in this period excluded all bankers from communion, they did bar them from church office. The synod also warned Calvinists that "they shall be forthwith Excommunicated" if they dealt with Catholic benefices or other institutions of the Roman church. The Reformed consistory at Nîmes threatened similar censures. The immigrant church in Charleston and its pastor, Elias Prioleau, certified this Calvinist creed by including the Gallican Confession as the founding document of the congregation.[32]

Yet, just as English Puritans and Dutch Calvinists reconfigured their moral teachings in the process of colonization, so, too, did French Calvinists. Quickly abandoning Old World Calvinist proscriptions against usury and slave trading, Huguenot merchants were the core of the financier class in Charleston, serving as the most important creditors in the growing exportation of rice, tobacco, and indigo and the importation of slaves. Massive amounts of credit flowed through Huguenot hands, including an energetic trade in mortgages, bonds, and indentures. Their interest rates matched the highest levels in the American colonies and funded a small class of large-scale traders such as Benjamin Godin and Solomon Legare; the latter's estate of some £18,500 consisted largely of notes, securities, and mortgages. Not surprisingly, these financier-merchants opposed planters and credit-needy inland merchants who lobbied for liberal currency policies (abundant emissions of notes) that favored debtors over creditors but hampered overseas merchants.[33]

Huguenot merchants and their pastors had peculiar reasons—albeit deeply religious ones—for their participation in the Atlantic market. French Protestants had long secured their Calvinist identities through cohesive kinship connections. Family lines maintained a Protestant confession in the midst of hostile social and political powers. So, too, they maintained their Calvinism while dispersed in America through extended networks of Francophone and Protestant relations. They identified with a society of Protestant exiles centered in London with outposts throughout the Atlantic world.[34]

Overseas trade through these very same networks, then, reinforced not only commercial partnerships but also religious community. Charleston merchants, from great trading houses headed by Marie de Rouchefoucauld, dame de Champagné, to modest firms that made money chiefly through financing trade between inland plantations and other colonies, did business through a Huguenot network connecting New York, Boston, the West Indies, and London. Historians of those firms have described them as "the Protestant International" and a "cosmopolitan trading community of [French] Protestants."[35] In contrast to Calvinist traders in Boston and New York, however, these French merchants never embraced the mercantilist agendas of the English metropolis. Their affinities for an international Calvinism suggested, in fact, an anti-imperial bias, reinforced by resentment toward English policies that prohibited direct trade with France and that channeled tariffs to London and by royal statutes from Paris that prohibited the export of French currency. Such differences from Calvinists to the north aside, South Carolinian Huguenots equally infused commerce with theological conviction and religious identity.[36]

These narratives of the Puritan, Dutch, and Huguenot communities in America, greatly simplified as they are, help us to situate the Calvinist turn in economic teaching during the transatlantic contest for empire at the end of the seventeenth century, setting the narrative of Calvinism and commerce in the context of Atlantic history.[37] The cases given here represent permutations of that history: New England Puritans who identified quite directly with a Protestant empire in conflict with Catholic regimes; Dutch Calvinists in New York who attempted to certify their loyalties to that empire as a means of self-preservation and who followed mercantilist ideas coming from Amsterdam's religious authorities; and Huguenots in Charleston who maintained their Calvinist confession through widespread networks of commercial exchange. The transformation of Calvinist economic discipline, from resistance to new market practices at home to the legitimization of those practices in America, did not represent a capitulation to secular market agendas. It instead reflected moral pragmatism for the sake of the church. As such, it derived from a Calvinist method that elevated scriptural mandates to protect the godly community above any one economic ideology.

We also might evoke later instances of the pragmatism and flexibility of a Calvinist economic morality in early America. To return to New England for one last example, we can scan developments at the end of the colonial period, when a revolutionary generation of Calvinist preachers argued that Britain's imperial agendas had begun to tyrannize and oppress its colonial children. After the 1763 Treaty of Paris, which ended the colonial wars between France and Britain, many commentators noted a remarkable stratification of wealth among merchants, including the growth of hugely wealthy trading houses and the failure of many smaller firms. Several economic thinkers of this period, most famously Adam Smith but also his intellectual predecessors in London and Edinburgh, broke with the imperial-mercantile ideology because they foresaw a vicious trend toward monopoly, dynasty, slavery, and widespread starvation. They proposed, of course, what has become known as a free market, or laissez-faire, economic system: individuals seeking profits and commodities according to their internal desires and rational acumen without state intervention.

For the most part, American Calvinists, along with other moralists during the second half of the eighteenth century, embraced this critique of the mercantilist system and accepted many of the assumptions of a free market. As colonials, they were subject to unfavorable trade policies and political malfeasance. More tellingly, they chafed against an imperial program that, they feared, threatened to impose Anglicanism over local ecclesiastical traditions with Calvinist leanings. Defending the interests of the congregational and Presbyterian churches in North America, they used the language of freedom and liberty to resist Parliament. Following the Calvinist method, they rooted their arguments in biblical texts: the prophets' call for justice, the psalmists' cry for deliverance, Paul's exhortations for the children of God to exercise Christian freedom. They stressed the humane, even benevolent, agendas implied in unrestricted trade. Citing the very scriptural passages that previous Calvinists had used to condemn the market, they emphasized the capacity of the market to humanize exchange, ameliorate poverty, and sustain Calvinist liberties. Evangelicals such as Thomas Prince (a devotee of Jonathan Edwards), severe Calvinists such as Samuel Hopkins (who denounced the slave trade), liberal Bostonian clergy such as Jonathan Mayhew, and Presbyterian leaders in the Philadelphia region such as John Witherspoon condemned imperial economics as oppressive, impoverishing, and inhumane. In their view, a free market offered the possibility of economic exchange and prosperity without political favoritism, slavery, dynastic ambition, and artificial restrictions against social mobility. They hoped that wide commercial channels would speed the diffusion of wealth, prevent widespread economic calamity, and protect the civil prerogatives of a genuine Reformed piety.[38]

Nothing in this shift of economic opinion evidenced the abandonment of a Calvinist ethos. The Calvinists of the 1770s cited the Bible just as fervently as did their predecessors and confided in divine sovereignty equally as well, but they took the meaning of scripture to confirm the necessity of American independence. Indeed, the Congregationalist and Presbyterian pastors who combined free market arguments with revolutionary fervor fastened on biblical exhortations to charity and social union. They alerted parishioners and political leaders to the dangers of a purely self-serving mode of exchange. Edwards and other evangelicals denounced high fashion, the emergent consumer culture, unbridled material ambition, financial speculation, and the inattention to private poor relief. Moral thinkers such as Witherspoon challenged the assumption made by more extreme market advocates who urged people to pursue their private passions and self-interests without restraint from customary moral teachings. Their attention to the Bible formed a hedge against a complete devotion to laissez-faire economics. Yet these same Calvinists valued the benefits of transatlantic trade and promoted the dismantling of imperial restrictions on international commerce as a means to support their congregations. They hoped that the sort of exchange defended by the likes of Smith would redress the more oppressive effects of the old imperial system, from its implied political tyranny to its threats against religious liberty in America.[39]

The twentieth-century American theologian H. Richard Niebuhr captured something of the malleability of Calvinist social ethics when he argued that the reformers bequeathed to the Puritans an antiauthoritarian and antitraditional mindset.[40] For him, as for his theologian brother, Reinhold Niebuhr, the genius of Calvinism consisted, in part, of a biblicism that freed the confessing community from temporal ideologies. As historians, we can moderate such claims. The transformation of Puritans, Dutch Calvinists, and Huguenots from critics of market culture to devotees of Protestant commercial empire represents a variation of social loyalties rather than the total eclipse of such loyalties by visions of the kingdom of God. Yet the Niebuhrs nonetheless located an essential element of a Calvinist religious mindset: a willingness to reformulate practical moral teachings in response to shifting communal needs.

Calvin's method allowed early American Calvinists to maintain their claims to piety and true doctrine while changing their economic teachings during a crucial period in the development of a market culture in early America. Britain's transatlantic empire and the colonial wars between England and France framed the growth of an American provincial society shaped by commercial agendas. The market took shape as a permanent force and moral mandate in this context. From this perspective, we can project Calvin's influence through his late seventeenth-century adherents onto the very origins of the transatlantic market culture. We would miss the whole point, however, if we assumed that this amounts to a fixed association between Calvinism and capitalism. As the later history of Calvinist moral reform indicates, the very sort of freedom that colonial Calvinists held to embrace the market led their heirs to set the Bible against capitalism under different social circumstances.[41] Such a readiness to replace economic ideology with a practical application of the Bible to local circumstances has amounted, in the long run, to the Calvinist legacy in America.

NOTES

1. Bernard Bailyn, *The New England Merchants in the Seventeenth Century* (Cambridge, Mass.: Harvard University Press, 1955); Darrett B. Rutman, *Winthrop's Boston: Portrait of a Puritan Town, 1630–1649* (Chapel Hill: University of North Carolina Press, 1965); Kenneth A. Lockridge, *A New England Town: The First Hundred Years: Dedham, Massachusetts, 1636–1736* (New York: Norton, 1970); Michael Zuckerman, *Peaceable Kingdoms: New England Towns in the Eighteenth Century* (New York: Knopf, 1970); John Frederick Martin, *Profits in the Wilderness: Entrepreneurship and the Founding of New England Towns in the Seventeenth Century* (Chapel Hill: University of North Carolina Press, 1991).

2. Perry Miller, *The New England Mind: From Colony to Province* (Cambridge, Mass.: Harvard University Press, 1953), esp. 19–57; and Miller, *Nature's Nation* (Cambridge, Mass.: Belknap Press of Harvard University Press, 1967), esp. 14–49. See Stephen Foster, *Their Solitary Way: The Puritan Social Ethic in the First Century of Settlement in New England* (New Haven, Conn.: Yale University Press, 1971); and Foster, *The Long Argument: English Puritanism and the Shaping of New England Culture, 1570–1700* (Chapel Hill: University of North Carolina Press, 1991). Along these lines, see also T. H. Breen and Stephen Foster, "The Puritans' Greatest Achievement: A Study of Social Cohesion in Seventeenth-Century Massachusetts," *Journal of American History* 60 (1973): 5–22; and Charles L. Cohen, "Puritanism," in *Encyclopedia of the North American Colonies*, 3 vols., ed. Jacob Ernest Cooke et al. (New York: Scribner's, 1993), 3:577–93.

3. Darren Marcus Staloff, "'Where Religion and Profit Jump Together': Commerce and Piety in Puritan New England," *Reviews in American History* 27 (1999): 8–13, quote from 8; Stephen Innes, *Creating the Commonwealth: The Economic Culture of Puritan New England* (New York: Norton, 1995); Margaret Ellen Newell, *From Dependency to Independence: Economic Revolution in Colonial New England* (Ithaca, N.Y.: Cornell University Press, 1998); Mark A. Peterson, *The Price of Redemption: The Spiritual Economy of Puritan New England* (Stanford, Calif.: Stanford University Press, 1997).

4. Walter Russell Mead, *God and Gold: Britain, America, and the Making of the Modern World* (New York: Knopf, 2007), 234–47; Benjamin M. Friedman, *The Moral Consequences of Economic Growth* (New York: Knopf, 2005), esp. 15–47; Kenneth Hopper and William Hopper, *The Puritan Gift: Triumph, Collapse and Revival of an American Dream* (New York: Tauris, 2007), esp. 1–45. For one critique of this use of the Weber thesis, see Rodney Stark, *The Victory of Reason: How Christianity Led to Freedom, Capitalism, and Western Success* (New York: Random House, 2005).

5. A twenty-first-century set of essays by American and European writers rightly moves beyond the old paradigm. Even though it contains several contributions misshaped around the question of Calvin and Weber, it raises new questions about Calvin on creation and stewardship and on moral discipline: Edward Dommen and James D. Bratt, eds., *John Calvin Rediscovered: The Impact of His Social and Economic Thought* (Louisville, Ky.: Westminster John Knox, 2007). I, too, misframed Calvin with a discussion of Weber in Valeri, "Religion, Discipline, and the Economy in Calvin's Geneva," *Sixteenth Century Journal* 28 (1997): 123–42.

6. For a suggestive essay that takes a similarly comparative approach but applies it to moral reform, confessional identity, political agendas, and especially legal institutions in the seventeenth-century American colonies, see Richard J. Ross, "Puritan Godly Discipline in Comparative Perspective: Legal Pluralism and the Sources of 'Intensity,'" *American Historical Review* 113 (2008): 975–1002.

7. Stephen Toulmin, *Cosmopolis: The Hidden Agenda of Modernity* (Chicago: University of Chicago Press, 1990).

8. For the idea of a Bible commonwealth, see the various essays in James Turner Johnson, ed., *The Bible in American Law, Politics, and Political Rhetoric* (Philadelphia: Fortress, 1985).

9. William J. Bouwsma, *John Calvin: A Sixteenth-Century Portrait* (New York: Oxford University Press, 1988); Serene Jones, *Calvin and the Rhetoric of Piety* (Louisville, Ky.: Westminster John Knox, 1995); and Olivier Millet, *Calvin et la dynamique de la parole: Étude de rhétorique réformée* (Paris: Champion, 1992). An earlier study in this vein was Quirinus Breen, *John Calvin: A Study in French Humanism* (Grand Rapids, Mich.: Eerdmans, 1931).

10. Calvin, "Sermons sur le Deuteronome," sermon number 119, in *Ioannis Calvini opera quae supersunt omnia*, 59 vols., ed. G. Baum, E. Cunitz, and E. Reuss (Braunschweig: Schwetschke, 1863–1900), vol. 27, cols. 639–40. All subsequent references to this edition of Calvin's works are cited in the following form: CO vol. no.:col. nos. Subsequent references to the Deuteronomy sermons are cited as Serm. Deut. (So, the above citation would read: Calvin, Serm. Deut. 119, CO 27:639–40.)

11. Bouwsma, *John Calvin*, 159.

12. I have summarized here material from many of Calvin's sermons (for example, Calvin, sermons and commentaries on Ephesians, in *Commentarius in Epistolam ad Ephesios*, CO 51:231–32, 639–40; commentary on Psalm 41:2, CO 31:418; Serm. Deut. 137, CO 28:150–63; Serm. Deut. 139, CO 28:175–87; Serm. Deut. 94, CO 27:333–36; Serm. Deut. 95, CO 27:339); and from the *Institutes of the Christian Religion* (1559), ed. John T. McNeill, trans. Ford Lewis Battles (Philadelphia: Westminster, 1960), 2.8.13–50, 3.3.17–18, and 3.10.2–4 (cited here in the standard format of book, chapter, and section). For Calvin's pragmatic and non-ideological approach to economics, see esp. Bouwsma, *John Calvin*, 192–203. For Calvin's practical recommendations, see also Ernst Troeltsch, *The Social Teachings of the Christian Churches*, 2 vols., trans. Olive Wyon (London: Allen and Unwin, 1931), 2:641–48, 903–11; André Biéler, *La pensée économique et sociale de Calvin* (Geneva: Librairie de l'Université, 1959), 156–57; and W. Fred Graham, *The Constructive Revolutionary: John Calvin and His Socio-Economic Impact* (Richmond, Va.: John Knox, 1971), 80–84, 116–33.

For Calvin's different opinions of usury or, rather, his criticism of usury yet pragmatic allowance for interest-earning commercial loans, see especially his "De Usuris," CO 10:246, 249, and his letter to the Reformed Churches of France, annexed to the "Acts, Decisions, and Decrees" of the Reformed Churches of France, Fourth National Synod (Lyon, 1563) and to the "Acts, Decisions, and Decrees" of the Reformed Churches of France, Sixth National Synod (Vertveil, 1567), reprinted in John Quick, *Synodicon in Gallia Reformata; or, The Acts, Decisions, Decrees, and Canons of Those Famous National Councils of the Reformed Churches in France*, 2 vols. bound in one (London, 1692), 79–80. For welfare in Geneva, see Robert M. Kingdon, "Social Welfare in Calvin's Geneva," *American Historical Review* 76 (1971): 50–69; Elsie Anne McKee, *John Calvin on the Diaconate and Liturgical Almsgiving* (Geneva: Droz Librairie, 1984); and Jeannine E. Olson, *Calvin and Social Welfare: Deacons and the Bourse Française* (Selinsgrove, Pa.: Susquehanna University Press, 1989).

13. For example, Calvin, *De vita hominis*, trans. T. Broke (n.p., 1549); *Le Catechisme de Gèneve* (London, 1552), 69–70; *The Laws and Statutes of Geneva*, trans. Robert Fills (London, 1562); and James Spottswood, *The Execution of Neschech . . . Whereunto There Is Subjoyned an Epistle of . . . John Calvin* (Edinburgh, 1616). For publishing patterns, see P. G. Lake, "Calvinism and the English Church, 1570–1635," *Past and Present* 114 (1987): 32–76.

14. See David Underdown, *Fire from Heaven: Life in an English Town in the Seventeenth Century* (New Haven, Conn.: Yale University Press, 1992); and especially William Hunt, *The Puritan Moment: The Coming of Revolution in an English County* (Cambridge, Mass.: Harvard University Press, 1983).

15. The quotation, from an anonymous manuscript later quoted by Roger Williams, "Model of Church and Civil Power," is cited in Ross, "Puritan Godly Discipline," 984. For Puritan legal procedures, see Cornelia Hughes Dayton, *Women before the Bar: Gender, Law, and Society in Connecticut, 1639–1789* (Chapel Hill: University of North Carolina Press, 1995), 29–30; and David Thomas Konig, *Law and Society in Puritan Massachusetts: Essex County, 1629–1692* (Chapel Hill: University of North Carolina Press, 1979).

16. See Mark Valeri, "Religious Discipline and the Market: Puritans and the Issue of Usury," *William and Mary Quarterly*, 3rd ser., 54 (1997): 747–68.

17. Bailyn, *New England Merchants*.

18. For this and the following paragraph, see Mark Valeri, "Providence in the Life of John Hull: Puritanism and Commerce in Massachusetts Bay, 1650–1680," *Proceedings of the American Antiquarian Society* 117 (2008): 57–118.

19. Increase Mather, *The Day of Trouble* (Cambridge, Mass., 1674), 26–27. The classic study of the jeremiad is Sacvan Bercovitch, *The American Jeremiad* (Madison: University of Wisconsin Press, 1978).

20. Valeri, "Providence in the Life of John Hull."

21. See Thomas S. Kidd, *The Protestant Interest: New England after Puritanism* (New Haven, Conn.: Yale University Press, 2004).

22. For this and the next two paragraphs, see Joyce Oldham Appleby, *Economic Thought and Ideology in Seventeenth-Century England* (Princeton, N.J.: Princeton University Press, 1978); Istvan Hont, *Jealousy of Trade: International Competition and*

the Nation-State in Historical Perspective (Cambridge, Mass.: Belknap Press of Harvard University Press, 2005); and David Armitage, *The Ideological Origins of the British Empire* (Cambridge: Cambridge University Press, 2000), esp. 146–69.

23. Cotton Mather, *Theopolis Americana* (Boston, 1710); Samuel Willard, *A Compleat Body of Divinity* (Boston, 1726), e.g., 685, 689, 706, 720.

24. Simon Schama, *The Embarrassment of Riches: An Interpretation of Dutch Culture in the Golden Age* (Berkeley: University of California Press, 1988), esp. 51–125 (for patriotic mandates) and 331–38 (for Amsterdam preachers in this period). For Voetius, see his *Selectae Disputationes Theologicae*, in *Reformed Dogmatics*, ed. and trans. John W. Beardslee III (New York: Oxford University Press, 1965), 269–75. For other academic theologians, see Jelle C. Riemersma, *Religious Factors in Early Dutch Calvinism, 1550–1650* (The Hague: Mouton, 1967), esp. 77–79.

25. Johannes Cloppenburg, *Christelijcke onderwijsinge van Woecker, interessen, coop van renten, en allerlei winste van gelt met gelt* (Amsterdam, 1637). For the synodical deliberations, see J. Reitsma and S. D. van Veen, eds., *Acta der Particuliere Synoden van Zuid-Holand, 1572–1620*, 8 vols. (Groningen: Wolters, 1892–1899), esp. 1:273; 2:148; 3:155, 252, 271–72, 284; 4:92, 96, 345; 5:236, 246; and W. P. C. Knuttel, ed., *Acta der Particuliere Synoden van Zuid-Holand, 1621–1700*, 6 vols., published as vols. 3, 5, 8, 11, 15, 16 of *Rijks Geschiedkundige*, short series (The Hague: Nijhoff, 1908–1916), esp. 5:30, 36, 178, 220–21, 225, 265, 273, 318, 382–84, 507. For background, see Albert Hyma, "Calvinism and Capitalism in the Netherlands, 1555–1700," *Journal of Modern History* 10 (1938): 321–43.

26. See especially Willem Frijhoff, "The West India Company and the Reformed Church: Neglect or Concern?" *De Halve maen* 70 (1997): 59–68.

27. George L. Smith, *Religion and Trade in New Netherland: Dutch Origins and American Development* (Ithaca, N.Y.: Cornell University Press, 1973), esp. 114–41; Jaap Jacobs, *New Netherland: A Dutch Colony in Seventeenth-Century America* (Leiden: Brill, 2005), 263–325; and Oliver A. Rink, "Private Interest and Godly Gain: The West India Company and the Dutch Reformed Church in New Netherland, 1624–1664," *New York History* 75 (1994): 245–64.

28. For the Reformed Church in New York and its alliances with English officialdom, see Randall H. Balmer, *A Perfect Babel of Confusion: Dutch Religion and English Culture in the Middle Colonies* (New York: Oxford University Press, 1989).

29. Records of church censures and decrees are available in the Dutch Reformed Church, City of New York, "Records of the Reformed Protestant Church, City of New York," transcribed and translated by Talbot Chambers, housed under "Collegiate Church Consistory Minutes and Related Records" at the Collegiate Reformed Protestant Dutch Church, City of New York; the quotation is from 46. For city merchants and inland traders, see Oliver A. Rink, *Holland on the Hudson: An Economic and Social History of Dutch New York* (Ithaca, N.Y.: Cornell University Press, 1986); for mercantilist ideas in the city, see Cathy Matson, *Merchants and Empire: Trading in Colonial New York* (Baltimore, Md.: Johns Hopkins University Press, 1998), 13–91.

30. See especially Claude de Saumaise, *De Usuris Liber* (Leiden, 1638), a 700-page defense of usury against the likes of Voetius and Cloppenburg. For the

synods, see Knuttel, ed., *Acta*, 4:13; and for the complete lack of prohibitions against usury thereafter, see vols. 6–7. For the liberal-rationalist turn in the Dutch church, see Riemersma, *Religious Factors*, 79–80; and Hyma, "Calvinism and Capitalism."

31. See Jon Butler, *The Huguenots in America: A Refugee People in New World Society* (Cambridge, Mass.: Harvard University Press, 1983), esp. 42–49; and R. C. Nash, "Huguenot Merchants and the Development of South Carolina's Slave-Plantation and Atlantic Trading Economy, 1680–1775," in *Memory and Identity: The Huguenots in France and the Atlantic Diaspora*, ed. Bertrand Van Ruymbeke and Randy J. Sparks (Columbia: University of South Carolina Press, 2003), 208–40.

32. French Reformed Church, "Canons of Church Discipline," in *Confession of Faith of the First National Synod* (Paris, 1559), in Quick, *Synodicon in Gallia Reformata*, xii, liv, lvi, xv, 8–9, 79–80. For background, see Raymond A. Mentzer, "*Disciplina nervus ecclesia*: The Calvinist Reform of Morals at Nîmes," *Sixteenth Century Journal* 18 (1987): 89–115; Mentzer, "Morals and Moral Regulation in Protestant France," *Journal of Interdisciplinary History* 31 (2000): 1–20; and Glenn S. Sunshine, "Reformed Theology and the Origins of Synodical Policy: Calvin, Beza, and the Gallican Confession," in *Later Calvinism: International Perspectives*, ed. W. Fred Graham (Kirksville, Mo.: Sixteenth Century Journal Publishers, 1994), 141–58. On the establishment of the church in Charleston, see Arthur Henry Hirsch, *The Huguenots of Colonial South Carolina* (Durham, N.C.: Duke University Press, 1928), 52–53; for conversion to Anglicanism, see Robert M. Kingdon, "Pourquoi les réfugies huguenots aux colinies américaines son-ils devenus épiscopaliens?" *Bulletin de la Societé de l'Histoire du Protestantisme Français* 115 (1969): 487–509.

33. Hirsch, *Huguenots of Colonial South Carolina*, 131–91; and Nash, "Huguenot Merchants."

34. J. F. Bosher, "Huguenot Merchants and the Protestant International in the Seventeenth Century," *William and Mary Quarterly*, 3rd ser., 52 (1995): 77–102.

35. Bertrand Van Ruymbeke, *From New Babylon to Eden: The Huguenots and Their Migration to Colonial South Carolina* (Columbia: University of South Carolina Press, 2006), 80; Bosher, "Huguenot Merchants and the Protestant International." For merchant kinship networks, see especially Carolyn Lougee Chappell, "Family Bonds across the Refuge," in *Memory and Identity*, ed. Ruymbeke and Sparks, 172–93.

36. Hirsch, *Huguenots of Colonial South Carolina*, 139–52 and 186–87.

37. For one example of Atlantic history, see J. H. Elliott, *Empires of the Atlantic World: Britain and Spain in America, 1492–1830* (New Haven, Conn.: Yale University Press, 2006).

38. See Patricia U. Bonomi, *Under the Cope of Heaven: Religion, Society, and Politics in Colonial America* (New York: Oxford University Press, 1986); Carol Bridenbaugh, *Mitre and Sceptre: Transatlantic Faiths, Ideas, Personalities, and Politics, 1689–1775* (New York: Oxford University Press, 1962); and the text and notes in Mark A. Noll, *America's God: From Jonathan Edwards to Abraham Lincoln* (New York: Oxford University Press, 2002), 53–157.

39. Mark Valeri, "The New Divinity and the American Revolution," *William and Mary Quarterly*, 3rd ser., 46 (1989): 741–69.

40. See, for example, H. Richard Niebuhr, *The Kingdom of God in America* (New York: Harper, 1937).

41. One could point here to the Niebuhrs' critiques of capitalism, the earlier criticisms made by proponents of the Social Gospel, or debates among nineteenth-century reformers. See, for the last, Stewart Davenport, *Friends of Unrighteous Mammon: Northern Christians and Market Capitalism, 1815–1860* (Chicago: University of Chicago Press, 2008).

2

Calvinism and American National Identity

David Little

In 2004, the late Samuel P. Huntington, a distinguished American
political scientist, published a provocative book arguing that
American national identity was and still is profoundly influenced by
what he called "Anglo-Protestant culture, tradition, and values"
(xvii),[1] even though that identity is, in his view, sorely tested at
present by disaffected American elites and growing numbers
of Mexican immigrants. While Huntington did not specifically
mention John Calvin, he attributed the major part of that influence to
Calvin's heirs, the New England Puritans, whom he associated with
what he called "dissenting Protestant culture." "In some measure,"
wrote Huntington, quoting Tocqueville, "'the entire destiny of
America' was shaped by the Puritans" (64).

In particular, Huntington drew a connection between the
Puritans and what is known as the American creed. The creed is a
collection of legal and political ideals associated with American
constitutionalism, namely, constitutional limits on governmental
power, including the separation of powers, judicial review, guarantees
of equal inherent and inalienable rights for all citizens, and respect
for "the people" as the ultimate source of political authority (67).
"The American creed," said Huntington, "is the unique creation
of a dissenting Protestant culture" (68).

While American constitutionalism eventually ensured freedom
of religion, according to which all religious groups, Christian and
non-Christian, came to be allowed "freely to practice and promulgate

their beliefs" (101), Huntington believed that the framers designed the Constitution, including the separation of church and state, "not to establish freedom
from religion, but to establish freedom *for* religion" (85). This means that,
despite allowance for the diversity of American religious expression, Americans
are inescapably a "Christian people," a "Christian nation," as Huntington kept
repeating (98; see also 15, 354–55).

This theme has significant consequences. However free non-Christian
groups are to avow and practice their religions, "non-Christian faiths have little alternative but to recognize and accept America as a Christian society"
(101). Huntington illustrated the depth of his commitment to this proposition
by reviewing two legal cases concerning non-Christians. The first involved a
legal initiative, undertaken in 2002 by Dr. Michael Newdow, an avowed atheist,
to withdraw the words "under God" from the Pledge of Allegiance. The initiative was upheld in a lower California court and then later overturned by a
higher court on the grounds that Newdow did not have legal standing. The
second case concerned Brian Cronin who, in 1999, sought the removal of a
sixty-foot cross that had stood on public land in Boise, Idaho, for forty-three
years.

In response to the first case, Huntington commented on Newdow's claim
that the words "under God" in the pledge made him feel "like an outsider," a
claim with which the lower court agreed:

> Dr. Newdow and the court got it right: atheists are "outsiders" in the
> American community. As unbelievers they do not have to recite the
> Pledge or to engage in any religiously tainted practice. They also,
> however, do not have the right to impose their atheism on all those
> Americans whose beliefs now and historically have defined America
> as a religious nation.
>
> Is America also a Christian nation? The statistics say yes; 80
> percent to 85 percent of Americans regularly identify themselves as
> Christians. (82)

As to Cronin's case, Huntington took the same position. In response to Cronin's
claim that, "[f]or Buddhists, Jews, Muslims, and other non-Christians in Boise,
the cross only drives home the point that they are strangers in a strange land,"
Huntington wrote:

> Like Dr. Newdow, Mr. Cronin was on target. America is a
> predominantly Christian nation with a secular government.
> Non-Christians may legitimately see themselves as strangers because
> they or their ancestors moved to this "strange land" founded and

peopled by Christians, even as Christians become strangers by moving to Israel, India, Thailand or Morocco. (83)

Huntington's thesis that, since America is a Christian nation, Christian identity is and ought to remain an essential defining characteristic of authentic citizenship has, predictably, provoked sharp controversy. Critics charge that Huntington's account of a consistently uniform, historically stable "Anglo-Protestant" American culture is grossly oversimplified. Even during the colonial period, the religious and ethnic makeup was much more complex than Huntington admitted. Along with the English, colonists included Dutch and Germans, and the mix included Catholics, Anglicans, and various other non-Puritans; the complex of national and religious groups only increased and further diversified as the country matured and expanded. It may be true that, during the nineteenth and early twentieth centuries, non-Protestant immigrants, like Catholics and Jews, became "Protestantized" in various ways. Nevertheless, "Huntington fails to appreciate the degree to which immigrants shaped American culture even as they assimilated." Already the largest Christian denomination by the second half of the nineteenth century, Catholicism "changed the way Americans celebrate Easter, attend school, play sports, and conduct foreign policy," and "the paradigmatic embodiment of American culture, the motion picture, was from its early days shaped by a distinctly Jewish sensibility."[2]

Moreover, Huntington was clearly mistaken to suggest that removing the words "under God" from the Pledge of Allegiance would be the same as imposing atheism. That would happen only if words such as "*not* under God (since God does not exist)" were substituted, which is most unlikely. Nor did Huntington pause to recall that the reference to a deity in the pledge is a very recent innovation, added in 1954 in the thick of the Cold War as a response to the perceived threat of "godless Communism."[3] Finally, his assertion that members of religious minorities, whether in the United States or in Israel, India, Thailand, or Morocco, should cheerfully resign themselves to the status of "outsiders" or "strangers" was a serious lapse in the light of the troubling record of minority discrimination at the hands of majorities in all of those countries.

Still, despite these and other telling objections,[4] Huntington did get one important point at least partly right: the connection between Puritanism and the American creed, meaning the ideals of American constitutionalism. Even there, however, the connection turns out to be more complicated than Huntington understood.

In his 2007 book on the influence of Calvin's thought and practice on ideas of law, religion, and human rights in France, Britain, Holland, and colonial America, John Witte—perhaps inadvertently—hints at an issue that became a source of division among American Puritans, as it would among the founders in the eighteenth century, and, indeed, as it has remained for Americans ever since. At bottom, the point of contention is whether or not the United States, according to its constitutional creed, ought to be thought of as a Christian nation:

> [New England] Puritan teachings on liberties of covenant and
> covenants of liberty were one fertile seedbed out of which later
> American constitutionalism grew. Many of the basic constitutional
> ideas and institutions developed by the Puritans in the seventeenth
> century remained in place in the eighteenth century . . .
> Enlightenment liberals of various sorts found in the Puritan ideas of
> natural man and natural law important sources and analogies for
> their ideas of the state of nature and natural liberty. They found in
> the Puritan ideas of a social covenant and a political covenant
> prototypes for their theories of a social contract and a governmental
> contract. They found in the doctrine of separation of church and state
> a foundation for their ideas of disestablishment and free exercise of
> religion. In turn, Civic Republican writers of various sorts
> transformed the Puritan idea of the elect nation under "solemn
> divine probation" into a revolutionary theory of American
> nationalism under divine inspiration.[5]

Witte's comment correctly calls attention to the common commitment among seventeenth-century New England Puritans to constitutional government and to the important influence that commitment would have on the formulation of the founding document of the republic a century later. But, just as importantly, it also indicates in passing a point of deep tension in the interpretation of American constitutionalism going back to the Puritans themselves, a point Huntington utterly overlooked in his description of "dissenting Protestant culture" and a point that continues to be of the utmost importance in sorting out the meaning of American national identity.

Puritans, in their way, generally shared a belief in some of the ideals of constitutionalism that Witte associates with eighteenth-century Enlightenment liberalism: natural liberty, the centrality of social and political contracts, the separation of church and state, and some allowance for religious freedom. At the same time, they divided sharply over the interpretation and implementation of those ideals, most specifically in regard to the notion Witte attributes to the civic Republicans, "a revolutionary theory of American nationalism under divine inspiration." How, to be precise, was a theory of America as a Christian nation to be accommodated to a doctrine of church and state separation and the disestablishment and free exercise of religion?

In short, some Puritans were close to Huntington; others, most emphatically, were not. For the former group, a clear majority, the essential constitutional ideals they embraced were not only compatible with a notion of national identity under divine inspiration, but they were also believed to be thoroughly deficient without it. Though the majority drew the limits on religious freedom much more tightly than did Huntington, they shared with him the idea of America as a Christian nation. For the latter group, a distinct dissenting minority, the constitutional ideals pointed in a radically different direction. They were seen to oppose any religious community or group of communities from acquiring special status or preeminence in defining national identity or membership.

My thesis in what follows is that the deep division over religion and national identity did not originate with the New England Puritans, however much they exhibited the division. Rather, that ambivalence is at the root of the Calvinist tradition of which they were a part, going back to the founder, John Calvin himself. It remains to elaborate this division, first in respect to the Puritans and then in Calvin's own thought.

The Puritan Dilemma

The fact, according to a leading historian of the subject, that the critical precedent for modern constitutionalism was established by the "North American colonies of Great Britain" makes all the more significant the Puritan contribution. Clearly, the idea of "written constitutions creating, defining, and limiting governments," which subsequently became "the general rule in almost the whole of the constitutional world,"[6] found strong, early expression in the founding documents of Puritan New England. Several of the key features of constitutionalism were there:[7]

1. A written code understood as "fundamental" in being antecedent to the government and subsequently "unalterable by ordinary legal process."
2. Attribution of political and legal authority, including limits on and division of power, by means of a "self-conscious," "direct and express" act by "the people" whom the government is taken to represent.
3. The conviction that any exercise of government outside the enumerated limits is an exercise of "power without right."

In addition, Puritans devised an important innovation in the development of the U.S. system of government: the codification of a set of individual rights that were partly based, to be sure, on traditional English law but were also critically reconceived in constitutional terms and were believed to rest on foundations supplementary to, and occasionally at odds with, English law, custom, and other traditions.

Above all, the special Puritan idea of covenant—a decisive aspect of the Calvinist legacy—was at the heart of things. "The transition from medieval to modern times . . . was marked by a transformation in which one [person's] relationship to another ceased to depend so much on the estate or station in life occupied by each and came to be based more on whatever covenant, that is, contract or agreement, might exist between them."[8] The sacred history of which the Puritans saw themselves a part was defined by a series of covenants between God and human beings and, subsequently, among human beings themselves. This notion would exert an important influence on American politics.

First, there was God's "covenant of works" with Adam, who, though created in the image of God, fatefully defaulted, only to have the divine-human relationship redefined by a second "covenant of grace" between God and Abraham. That covenant, initially limited to the people of Israel, was again renegotiated with the coming of Christ and, thereby, opened to "all peoples and nations" on the basis of their personal commitment to accept and live out the terms of the "new covenant." This revised understanding, in turn, revolutionized the foundations of human government, which were no longer determined exclusively by custom and tradition, nor by ethnic or other ascribed attributes, but by "self-conscious," "direct and express" acts of the people designed to control political power in accord with the "public welfare," as individually and collectively understood.

For example, incipient constitutionalism was at work from the earliest origins of the government of the Massachusetts Bay Colony, well before the eventual founders had left for the New World. The charter of the Massachusetts Bay Company, which elaborated the form of government for the new colony, including elected officials such as the governor and assistants and members of a Great and General Court, was modified by the Cambridge Agreement, adopted on August 26, 1629, in Cambridge, England, by the stockholders or "freemen" of the company. The agreement, calling as it did for the founders to expand control over their own affairs, gave considerable impetus to the notion of constitutional self-government:

> It is fully and faithfully agreed amongst us . . . that . . . we will be
> ready in our persons . . . to embarke for the said plantation by the

first of March next, . . . to the end to passe the seas (under God's
protection) to inhabite and continue in New England. *Provided always,*
that before the last of September next the whole government together
with the patent for the said plantation be first by an order of court
legally transferred and established to remain with us and others
which shall inhabite upon the said plantation.[9]

Though the government in Massachusetts Bay took time to evolve from
corporation to commonwealth and, when completed, was more oligarchy than
democracy—given the fear on the part of some of untrammeled popular
control[10]—the Puritan authorities nevertheless "left out of their foundations
two principles of government, the feudal and the hereditary, upon which
democracy had always found it difficult to [develop]." Moreover, even the religiously limited franchise had a democratic side to it because "it made no
account of social standing or estate." "Narrow as the franchise was, it cut
through the community vertically, not horizontally."[11] Beyond that, the appre-
hensions about democracy of some leaders were partially counterbalanced by
other leaders who affirmed the merits of elections as a necessary restraint on
arbitrary government.[12]

Of particular importance was the Body of Liberties of the Massachusetts
Colony in New England, which was adopted into law by the General Court in
1641 and which amounted to an exceptionally lengthy bill of rights. Though its
author, Nathaniel Ward (1578–1652), a prominent pastor and lawyer, incorporated provisions drawn from English statutes and precedents, including the
Magna Carta (1215) and the Petition of Right (1628), the Body of Liberties was
anything but a simple reiteration of tradition and custom. It redefined and
restructured the traditional rights of English subjects in the light of Puritan
Christianity, adding modified portions of biblical law and some "daring rights
proposals"[13] from left-wing English Puritan pamphleteers.

It is true that there was a diversity of opinion among the Bay Colony leadership over the Body of Liberties. Governor John Winthrop (1587?–1649) opposed
on principle the codification of rights since magistrates ought, he thought, to
retain wide discretion in interpreting and applying them, and he revealed a
strong traditional English bias in expressing worries about elevating rights over
the obligations and responsibilities of the subject. For his part, John Cotton
(1585–1652), an eminent pastor and church leader, preferred a code more
strictly based on biblical law. However, such reservations did not prevail:

> [Above all,] what was new . . . was to have these widely scattered
> traditional common law rights (and many rights besides) compiled in
> a single source, generally available to all subjects of the community

regardless of the court in which they appeared, and generally binding on all officials and citizens at once.[14]

While the code incorporates familiar principles and prescriptions of English law, the biblical and other additions frequently render its provisions more humane as compared with contemporary common law, for example, in regard to punishment and the use of torture in treating prisoners. Furthermore, "feudal dues [were] prohibited, complete testamentary liberty . . . provided, and foreigners [were] assured the equal protection of the laws."[15]

In addition to humanizing interrogation techniques and forms of punishment, the Body of Liberties expanded the number of criminal procedural rights and protections, including the use of grand juries and bail (except in capital crimes), the right to indictment only for crimes prohibited by statute, the right to an impartial hearing and a speedy trial, and conviction by "clear and sufficient evidence." In civil cases, defendants could choose to be heard by a judge or a jury and would be imprisoned for fines or debts only if sufficient payment could not otherwise be secured, and, even then, the defendant (absent a specific court order) "shall be kept at his own charge, not the plaintiff's till satisfaction be made."

It also protected private property against unauthorized government intrusion, "fraudulent conveyances" of any sort, monopolies (except "such new inventions that are profitable to the country, and that for a short time"), and disproportionate rates of interest. It enumerated special provisions for the protection of women, children, and servants and even legislated against "any tyranny or cruelty towards any brute creature[s] which are usually kept for man's use." In addition, it listed a number of public or civil rights, including the right of "freemen" (male church members, twenty-one years of age or more) to vote and stand for office, along with the "liberty to come to any public court, council, or town meeting, and either by speech or writing to move any lawful, seasonable, and material question, or to present any necessary motion, complaint, petition, bill or information," and the "free liberty to search" and obtain copies of public records.[16]

Although the grounds on which these rights were believed to rest are not mentioned in the document itself, Ward made clear in a pamphlet written four years later that, in his view, the enumerated rights were founded on a combination of "God's rule," experience, tradition, and the "light of nature," all of which assume a universal set of moral "essentials" where, beyond local differences and variations in the form of government, "rule and reason will be found [to be] all one."[17]

There was, however, one part of the Body of Liberties that generated a particularly strong division of opinion: the rights pertaining to religious belief and practice, namely, section 95, articles 1–11, identified as "A Declaration of the Liberties the Lord Jesus Hath Given to the Churches." According to these articles, all members of the colony have "full liberty" to "gather themselves into a church estate" of their choosing, though only so long as they "be orthodox in judgment" and practice their religion "in a Christian way, with due observation of the rules of Christ revealed in his word"; similarly, "every church has full liberty to exercise all the ordinances of God," if they do so "according to the rules of scripture"; and, again, they may elect church officers, "provided they be able, pious and orthodox," or may admit, discipline, and expel whom they will, but only "according to the rules of [Christ's] word."

The special conditions on religious rights, permitting free exercise but only in conformity with orthodox Christian scriptural and doctrinal interpretation, points to what Cotton called the "theocratic" character of the Massachusetts Bay Colony, namely, it was a state governed by officials regarded as divinely guided.[18] In his aforementioned pamphlet, Ward summarized the strong opposition of officials of the colony, like John Winthrop and John Cotton, to ideas of "toleration" and "liberty of conscience":

> [As between] persecution of true religion, and toleration of false, . . .
> the last is far the worst. . . . He that is willing to tolerate any religion,
> or discrepant way of religion, that his own may also be tolerated,
> though never so sound, will [in effect] hang God's Bible [on] the
> Devil's girdle. . . . That state that will give liberty of conscience in
> matters of religion, must give liberty of conscience . . . in their moral
> laws, or else the fiddle will be out of tune, and some of the strings
> crackle.[19]

While leaders like Cotton argued that church and state should not be "confounded," as they serve different ends and jurisdictions,[20] the two spheres should nevertheless be "close and compact and co-ordinate one to another,"[21] precisely so as to prevent the kind of heterodoxy in thought and practice and the consequent disruption of civil and moral order of which Nathaniel Ward warned. As one contemporary divine put it, "the interest of righteousness in the commonwealth and holiness in the churches are inseparable. The prosperity of church and commonwealth are twisted together. Break one cord, you weaken the other also."[22]

"Twisted together" church and state most certainly were. Although magistrates were precluded from holding church office and church officials from holding civil office, only church members could vote in civil elections. In addition, churches and clergy received direct public support through taxes and other donations, and religious beliefs and practices were extensively and harshly regulated by laws covering blasphemy, irreverence, profanity, idolatry, and "schismatic" activity. Ministers were regularly called upon to provide instruction on the pertinence of God's law to new legislation.[23]

However, by no means did all Puritans agree with the official Massachusetts Bay position on religious rights and especially with the meaning of "full liberty" when it came to avowing and practicing one's faith, as mentioned in section 95 of the Body of Liberties. Article 7 of that section was the focus of particular problems. It permitted the elders of the churches "free liberty" to consult at their discretion on matters of church concern and was interpreted by a group of recent arrivals from England to mean that the elders might do so without the concurrence of the civil authority. The group supported its claim by referring to what it spoke of as a growing appreciation in England of freedom of conscience, which was gathering momentum, they implied, toward the untwisting of religious and civil affairs.

True to form, John Winthrop tried to combat these liberalizing tendencies, claiming that elders might properly meet on their own motion only in cases of emergency, lest state and church come to oppose each other with the result that civil authorities could no longer carry out their all-important obligations as "nursing fathers to the churches."[24] But the cat was out of the bag, and this facially minor conflict over the interpretation of one of the provisions of the Body of Liberties concerning the rights of church authorities symbolized a much deeper and wider challenge to the "theocratic" structure of Massachusetts Bay and to the assumption that the American creed, as constitutionally expressed, should be governed by special religious preferences.

The task of articulating and mobilizing that challenge, and thus giving effective voice to the other side of Puritan thinking on religious freedom, fell to Roger Williams (1603–1683?), who had been in trouble with the colony's authorities almost from the time he set foot in New England in 1631. Upon arrival, Williams was assigned to be pastor of a prominent Boston church, but he declined because it had not, in his view, sharply enough differentiated itself from the Church of England. Thereupon, he was sent to a pastorate in Plymouth, where he interacted with local Narragansett Indians and learned their language. He was, however, soon removed for publicly opposing laws that punished idolatry, Sabbath breaking, false worship, and blasphemy—all of which were provisions in the Body of Liberties bearing on the civil supervision of religion—and for arguing that all individuals should be free to follow their conscience in religious affairs.

Next, he was assigned to a church in Salem, where, eventually, legal charges were brought against him for continuing to oppose laws enforcing religion as well as other official beliefs and practices he found offensive, such as the assumption that colonial lands belonged to the English monarch and not, as he thought, to the Native Americans, or that the English flag was legitimate even though it prominently displayed a Christian cross at its center, thereby, in Williams's view, hopelessly confusing the civil and spiritual spheres. Predictably, Williams was found guilty as charged and condemned to be transported back to England for punishment. However, he eluded the authorities and, with the help of Narragansetts he had befriended, found his way to territory that, under his leadership, would eventually become the Rhode Island colony. In accord with his respect for the rights of Native Americans to their own territory, Williams and his confreres were careful to purchase the land that would make up the colony, thus continuing his amicable relations with the Native Americans. The colonists then proceeded to establish a government analogous, in some respects, to Massachusetts Bay and the other colonies, but distinctively different in others.

In 1643, Williams acquired a minimal patent for the towns of Providence, Portsmouth, and Newport from Parliament which, by 1647, was expanded into a fuller constitutional document that "gives us power to govern ourselves and such others as come among us, and [to establish] such a form of civil government as by the voluntary consent, etc., shall be found most suitable to our estate and condition." In words somewhat to the left of the Bay Colony's view, the document goes on to specify without apology and without reservation that the form of government will be "democraticall," which is to say, "a government held by the free and voluntary consent of all, or the greater part of the free inhabitants," assuring "each man's peaceable and quiet enjoyment of his lawful right and liberty." And it continues in language largely reminiscent of the Massachusetts Bay charter and the Body of Liberties to outline a representative political system together with legal institutions carefully regulated by due process, including extensive rights against arbitrary injury, unfair trial, imprisonment, loss of property, and so on.[25]

Where the Rhode Island colony differed most sharply from Massachusetts Bay and other colonies was in the treatment of religion, a point articulated most eloquently in the charter of 1663 that Williams and his associate, John Clarke, were able to acquire from King Charles II. The charter commends the aspirations of the colonists "to hold forth a lively experiment, that a most flourishing civil state may stand and best be maintained . . . with the full liberty in religious concernments . . . and . . . in the free exercise and enjoyment of all . . . civil and religious rights." It then declares, in a radical departure from the Bay Colony's understanding of "full liberty":

[N]o person within said colony, at any time hereafter, shall be [in] any wise molested, punished, disquieted, or called into question, for any

difference of opinion in matters of religion, and do not actually
disturb the civil peace, . . . but . . . all and every person and persons
may . . . freely and fully have and enjoy . . . their own judgments and
consciences in matters of religious concernments, . . . they behaving
themselves peaceably and quietly.[26]

For Williams and the Rhode Islanders, the Massachusetts Bay authorities,
while expressing commitment to the ideas of freedom of conscience and separation of church and state, had grossly distorted the meaning of those terms.
The conscience and the civil authority—the "inner forum" and the "outer
forum," to use the accepted terms of reference—are, at bottom, different realms
governed by different laws, the one by the "law of the spirit," the other by the
"law of the sword."

As with Nathaniel Ward and his sympathizers, Williams's judgments about
the constitution and character of government, including the basic rights it was
created to protect, rest upon several grounds, namely, tradition, experience,
reason, the "light of nature," and God's Word, all of which are seen to converge
around a common set of moral "essentials," as Ward put it. Williams simply
read the essentials differently. For him, the law of the sword, administered by
temporal governments and backed by physical coercion, applies to "the bodies
and goods" of human beings, to their "outward state," while the law of the
spirit applies to the inner life, a life that operates according to the standards of
reason and sentiment. To try to convince a person of the truth of something by
threatening injury or imprisonment is to make a mistake about how the mind
and spirit work. It is futile, wrote Williams, to try "to batter down idolatry, false
worship, and heresy" by employing "stocks, whips, prisons, [and] swords"
because "civil weapons are improper in this business and [are] never able to
effect anything in the soul." Instead, "only let it be their soul's choice, and no
enforcing sword, but what is spiritual in their spiritual causes. . . . I plead [to the
civil authority] for impartiality and equal freedom, peace, and safety to [all] consciences and assemblies, unto which the people may as freely go, and this
according to each conscience, [in keeping, of course, with the requirements of
civil order]."[27]

Williams believed that confusing spirit and sword, after the fashion of
Massachusetts Bay, is a violation of the clear lessons of reason and experience,
and it is also a fundamental offense to the example of Jesus Christ and the
teachings of scripture. Endorsing a Christian political theory deeply at odds
with that of Winthrop and Cotton, Williams wrote:

I affirm that that state policy, which for the peace of the state and
preventing . . . rivers of civil blood permits [true freedom of conscience],

will be found to agree most punctually with the rules of the best
politician that ever the world saw, the king of kings, and lord of lords.

How much at odds Williams's views were with the prevailing colonial political
theory cannot be overestimated:

> All lawful magistrates in the world, both before the coming of Christ
> Jesus, and since (excepting . . . the church of Israel) are but derivatives
> and agents [of the people who appointed them] immediately derived
> and employed as eyes and hands, serving . . . the good of the whole.
> Hence they have and can have no more power than fundamentally
> lies in [the people] themselves, *which power, might or authority is not
> religious, Christian, etc., but natural, humane, and civil.*[28]

Here is an unqualified endorsement of a secular, religiously tolerant theory
of government justified on multiple grounds: biblical, rational or natural, and
experiential. And Williams meant what he said. All of these sources point to a
set of "common rights" that assure the "peace and safety of all citizens," even
atheists and people altogether indifferent or hostile to religion. Such an outcome, he conceded, runs a risk: "however it is infinitely better, that the profane
and loose be unmasked, than to be muffled up under the veil and hood as of
traditional hypocrisy, which turns and dulls the very edge of all conscience
either toward God or man."[29] Beyond that, he was fully prepared to grant equal
freedom to religions like Judaism, Islam, and Roman Catholicism, so long, of
course, as their adherents were willing to accept citizenship on Williams's general terms. It is "known by experience," he said, that "many thousands" of
Muslims, Roman Catholics, and pagans (meaning: Native Americans) "are in
their persons, both as civil and courteous and peaceable in nature, as any of the
subjects in the state they live in."[30] Such people, whatever their religious identity, may be trusted because there exists a "natural" moral law universally available as the proper basis for protecting the "common rights, peace and safety"
of all citizens.[31] In fact, because of such widely distributed common moral
essentials, "civil places need not be monopolized [by] church members, (who
are sometimes not fitted for them), and all other [people] deprived of their natural
and civil rights and liberties."[32]

Calvin as Background

While the specifics of Calvin's relationship to American Puritanism have been
debated, there is strong agreement that, although American Puritans across the

spectrum from John Cotton to Nathaniel Ward to Roger Williams by no means refrained from taking issue or disagreeing with Calvin, they nevertheless all regarded him "as the pioneering force behind their Reformed faith" and, generally, "adhered to the theological framework they inherited from him."[33]

This is abundantly clear in relation to the ideas we have been considering. Despite some minor differences on the subject,[34] Calvin anticipated the heavy emphasis on the concept of covenant as the background for constitutional government in both church and state, entailing written documents designed to limit political and ecclesiastical authority that are endorsed "by the free and voluntary consent" of "the people" and that enshrine their basic rights and liberties. Of special interest is the fact that the profound division of opinion among the New England Puritans over how to interpret, for constitutional purposes, the meaning of "full liberty" in matters of religion and conscience also lies at the heart of Calvin's thought.

Calvin devotes extensive attention in the *Institutes of the Christian Religion* and elsewhere to the idea of covenant as a divine gift to human beings that provides the basis for free and loving interactions with God and among human beings. As a model of reciprocal voluntary benevolence, it comprises the ultimate standard of divine and human authority. The model has important consequences for distinguishing the constitutions of church and state. There is, wrote Calvin, "a great difference and unlikeness . . . between ecclesiastical and civil power." Unlike the state, the "church does not have the right of the sword to punish or compel, not the authority to force; not imprisonment nor the other punishments which the magistrate commonly inflicts." "The church does not assume what is proper to the magistrate; nor can the magistrate execute what is carried out by the church."[35] In an arresting passage, Calvin leaves no doubt about what he means:

> There is a twofold government: one is spiritual, whereby the
> conscience is instructed in piety and reverencing God; the second is
> political, whereby [people are] educated for the duties of humanity
> and citizenship that must be maintained. . . . These are usually called
> "spiritual" and "temporal" jurisdiction[s] . . . by which is meant the
> former pertains to the life of the soul, while the latter has to do with
> the concerns of the present life—not only with food and clothing but
> with laying down laws whereby [one] may live among [others] . . .
> honorably and temperately. For the former resides in the inner mind,
> while the latter regulates outward behavior. . . . Now these two, as we
> have divided them, must always be examined separately; and while
> one is being considered, we must call away and concern the mind

from thinking about the other. There are . . . , so to speak, two worlds over which two kings and different laws have authority.[36]

So understood, the church is the context of the "liberation of the conscience,"[37] where regenerated persons no longer need be coerced or compelled to do the right thing but, inspired and guided by the "law of the spirit" as manifest in scripture, are able to grasp and to do the will of God of their own accord. By implication, the church would be sharply set apart from the civil authority and, as such, would assume control over its own affairs based on an ideal of active membership participation and on the principle that individuals must be able, free of all civil restraint or liability, to exercise their conscience by choosing whether or not to associate themselves with the church and its mission. According to this line of thinking, civil identity and religious identity are sharply differentiated from each other.

Calvin says as much in an extraordinary comment on Romans 13:10, expressing a view on the essential responsibilities of temporal government:

> Since magistrates are the guardians of peace and equity, those who
> desire that every individual should preserve [one's] rights, and that all
> [persons] may live free from injury, must defend to the utmost of their
> power the order of magistrates. . . . Paul's repetition of the statement
> that love is the fulfillment of the law is to be understood, as before, as
> that part of the law that refers to human society. *There is no allusion at
> all here to the first table of the law, which deals with the worship of God.*[38]

It is of no little interest that Roger Williams himself, in referring to "that excellent servant of God, Calvin," invokes this very passage in defense of his theory, outlined above, that the appropriate jurisdiction of the state concerns only the second table of the commandments and *not* the first.[39]

In practice, however, Calvin gave little aid and comfort to Williams's position. Over time, his policies in Geneva came to resemble much more closely the policies of John Winthrop and John Cotton in Massachusetts Bay than Williams's in Rhode Island. Partly because of the strong influence of the Genevan political authorities and partly because of Calvin's own experience with an unruly populace and his worries about social disorder, he went back on his claim in the Romans commentary that civil government should have nothing to do with the first table of the Decalogue and wound up encouraging the political authorities to enforce across the city "the outward worship of God" and a "sound doctrine of piety and the position of the church."[40]

The consolidation of Calvin's position in favor of explicitly enforcing religious orthodoxy was influenced by the trial of Michael Servetus in 1553, in which Servetus was condemned to death for heretical views regarding the doctrine of the Trinity. The trial raised for Calvin the question of "whether Christian rulers had the right and duty to punish heretics and to support pure religious doctrine, a question that he believed had to be answered in the affirmative." It also reinforced his inclination to narrow stringently the limits on freedom of conscience, in opposition to more liberal expressions, which were also retained—rather inconsistently—in the final version of the *Institutes*. According to the policies Calvin endorsed in the latter years of his life, "freedom of faith and confession does not mean that everyone may be allowed to confess any old view, including atheism, without legal penalty." Indeed, for Calvin, the great enemy of all political and social order became the idea of atheism. True freedom exists only in a true belief in God.[41]

Calvin's Ecclesiastical Ordinances of the Church of Geneva, adopted in 1541, which laid out the constitution of the church, including church-state relations, did succeed in preserving some features of the freedom of the church he espoused, such as provisions for the "common consent of the company of the faithful" in selecting church officials and for assuring that the church might exercise "no compulsive authority or jurisdiction." Nevertheless, the document as finally agreed to "offered numerous departures from Calvin's ideal"[42] and wound up confirming the judgment that one of the reasons for "Calvin's later influence [was] that he claimed for the church more independence than he obtained."[43]

As to the organization of civil authority, Calvin clearly anticipated developments in New England. He endorsed unequivocally the basic features of modern constitutionalism:

1. "Every commonwealth rests upon laws and agreements," preferably written, that are regarded as fundamental to the protection of the "freedom of the people." Written law is "nothing but an attestation of the [natural law], whereby God brings back to memory what has already been imprinted in our hearts."[44]

2. The structure of government should be polyarchic rather than monarchic. "It is very rare for kings so to control themselves that their will never disagrees with what is just and right, or for them to have been endowed with such great keenness and prudence, that each knows how much is enough. Therefore, men's fault or failing causes it to be safer and more bearable for a number to exercise government."[45]

3. "Certain remedies against tyranny are allowable, for example when magistrates and estates have been constituted, to whom has been committed the care of the commonwealth; they shall have power to

keep the prince to his duty and even to coerce him if he attempt anything unlawful."[46]

4. A set of basic rights and freedoms are taken to undergird the founding agreement and to comprise an imprescriptible limit on governmental power. They are a collection of what can be described as "original natural rights of freedom."

Under the rights of personal freedom, liberty and property stand out. . . . God has equipped rulers with full authority that the rights of each individual to person and property not be denied, for these rights are goods bestowed by God. The authorities protect these rights through laws, which therefore must be made firm and durable; continually changing established public law is a mark of arbitrariness, which every form of reasonableness rules out. In short, the subjective rights of freedom have no strong security if they are not supported by the authorities and legislation. This individual sphere of freedom . . . yet belongs to the enjoined rights and duties associated with the second table of the Decalogue.[47]

Conclusion

While Samuel Huntington was right that Puritanism made a distinctive contribution to the American creed, thought of as a set of constitutional ideals, and, consequently, to the understanding of American national identity, he seriously oversimplified that contribution. The idea that Puritanism stood solidly and without reservation on the side of a notion of America as a Christian nation, of a place where atheists and non-Christians should think of themselves as outsiders and strangers, is grossly one-sided.

As we have seen, Puritans were deeply divided over the relation of religion and constitution. However unified they were about the general principles of modern constitutionalism, they differed unalterably as to the legal and political meaning of "full liberty" when it came to religion. For Winthrop, Cotton, and Ward, Christian belief and practice, as they conceived of them, were indeed indispensable to national health and prosperity. Without a uniform religious foundation, society could not endure. For Roger Williams, on the contrary, citizenship and national identity rested only on "natural" civil and moral essentials shared by human beings regardless of their religious beliefs and practices. So long as they conformed to the demands of common moral and civil standards, they were all free to consult and observe their conscience as they saw fit, outside the surveillance or supervision of the civil authority. In Williams's memorable words, governmental "power, might or authority is not religious, Christian, etc., but natural, humane, and civil." So much for the idea of a Christian nation.

I have contended that the foundations of this division lie deep within the thought of John Calvin, a figure of great influence on American Puritanism, so that it would be as incorrect to reduce Calvin's views to those of Winthrop, Cotton, and Ward as it would be to reduce them to those of Williams. In many ways, American Puritanism exemplifies conflicting propensities within Calvin himself.

If Calvinism is as divided as I say, then it is no longer possible to speak unequivocally about its contribution to American national identity.

NOTES

1. Samuel P. Huntington, *Who Are We? The Challenges to America's National Identity* (New York: Simon and Schuster, 2004). Page numbers for cited material from this book will be given parenthetically in the text.

2. Alan Wolfe, "Native Son: Samuel Huntington Defends the Homeland," *Foreign Affairs* 83, no. 3 (May–June 2004): 120.

3. See T. Jeremy Gunn, *Spiritual Weapons: The Cold War and the Forging of an American National Religion* (Westport, Conn.: Praeger, 2009), 64–69.

4. See Louis Menand, "Patriot Games: The New Nativism of Samuel P. Huntington," *New Yorker*, May 17, 2004, 96–97; and David Brooks, "The Americano Dream," *New York Times*, February 24, 2004, A27, for objections concerning Huntington's alarmist rhetoric about the supposed threat to American identity posed by Mexican immigrants. These objections were confirmed and developed by my Harvard colleague, Professor Davíd Carrasco, in a public discussion of *Who Are We?* that he and I had with Professor Huntington at Harvard Divinity School in the fall of 2004. It must be added that the evidence Huntington himself supplies (on 254–56) to support the explosive claim that Mexican Americans are "often contemptuous of American culture" is surprisingly weak.

5. John Witte Jr., *The Reformation of Rights: Law, Religion, and Human Rights in Early Modern Calvinism* (Cambridge: Cambridge University Press, 2007), 318.

6. Charles Howard McIlwain, *Constitutionalism: Ancient and Modern* (Ithaca, N.Y.: Cornell University Press, 1966), 14.

7. Ibid., 9, 14, 21. There is a question about how much modern constitutionalism was anticipated by the Roman constitution. Certainly, the Roman example was in the background of Puritan thinking and, for that matter, of Calvin's thinking, as we shall see. The emphases on division of powers and popular consent were important for Calvinist constitutional theories. In contrast to modern constitutions, however, the Roman constitution was unwritten and was justified on traditional grounds, being thought of as the "customs of the ancestors" (*mos maiorum*), and it is doubtful that there existed in classical Roman law any doctrine of individual natural rights

(Brian Tierney, *The Idea of Natural Rights* [Atlanta, Ga.: Scholars Press, 1997], 45–46). Moreover, the Roman constitution proved a weak reed against the rise of autocracy, which eventually overwhelmed the Roman republic. On this last point, see Quentin Skinner, *The Foundations of Modern Political Thought*, 2 vols. (Cambridge: Cambridge University Press, 1978), 2:123–24.

8. Edmund S. Morgan, ed., *Puritan Political Ideas, 1558–1794* (Indianapolis, Ind.: Bobbs-Merrill, 1965), xxii.

9. Cited in Samuel Eliot Morison, *Builders of the Bay Colony* (Boston: First Northeastern Edition, 1981), 69 (emphasis in original).

10. As one leader, John Cotton, put it: "If the people be governors, who shall be governed?" John Cotton, "A Letter from Mr. Cotton to Lord Say and Seal" (1636), in *Puritan Political Ideas*, ed. Morgan, 163. See also John Winthrop's opposition to democracy, cited in Francis J. Bremer, *John Winthrop, America's Forgotten Founding Father* (Oxford: Oxford University Press, 2003), 355.

11. Morgan, ed. *Puritan Political Ideas*, 86.

12. See Witte, *Reformation of Rights*, 317.

13. Ibid., 280.

14. Ibid., 286.

15. Morison, *Builders of the Bay Colony*, 231–32.

16. The liberties are usefully summarized by Witte, *Reformation of Rights*, 281–87.

17. Nathaniel Ward, "The Simple Cobler of Aggawam" (1645; first published 1647), in *The Puritans: A Sourcebook of Their Writings*, 2 vols., ed. Perry Miller and Thomas H. Johnson (New York: Harper Torchbook, 1963), 1:236. (I have modernized and here and there "translated" some of the archaic words and forms of speech.)

18. Cotton actually uses the term to describe what, in his mind, is "the best form of government in the commonwealth, as well as the church," in *Puritan Political Ideas*, ed. Morgan, 163.

19. Miller and Johnson, eds., *The Puritans*, 1:230.

20. Morgan, ed., *Puritan Political Ideas*, 162–63, 164–65.

21. Ibid., 163.

22. The statement is by Urian Oakes, pastor and president of Harvard, cited by Witte, *Reformation of Rights*, 310.

23. I am drawing here on Witte's excellent summary of the church-state arrangement in the Bay Colony; see ibid., 310–12.

24. Williston Walker, ed., *The Creeds and Platforms of Congregationalism* (Boston: Pilgrim, 1960), 171–72.

25. See http://oll.libertyfund.org/index.php?option=com_content&task=view&id=1040S&Itemid=264, p. 7.

26. See http://avalon.law.yale,edu/17th_century/ri04.asp, p. 1.

27. Roger Williams, *Complete Writings of Roger Williams*, 7 vols. (New York: Russell and Russell, 1963), 3:148, 7:154–55.

28. Ibid., 7:178, 3:398.

29. Ibid., 7:181.

30. Cited in James Calvin Davis, *The Moral Theology of Roger Williams: Christian Conviction and Public Ethics* (Louisville, Ky.: Westminster John Knox, 2004), 94. It is true that Williams, worryingly, advocated that Catholics should wear some overt identification. Nevertheless, Williams's commitment to an extraordinary degree of tolerance for Catholics should not be overlooked. As Davis says:

> [B]esides this method of public identification, Williams rejects any arguments for the restriction of Catholic freedoms that depend on the mistaken belief that they are less capable of civility and moral citizen[ship] than their Protestant counterparts. He even goes so far as to blame the instances of Catholic insurrection in seventeenth-century Britain not on Catholic ignorance of civility but on the suppression of their consciences and religious practices by the Protestant political authorities. (Ibid., 159n7)

31. Ibid., 363.

32. Williams, *Complete Writings of Roger Williams*, 4:365.

33. Davis, *The Moral Theology of Roger Williams*, 18 and 17.

34. The belief of the American Puritans in a covenant of works prior to a covenant of grace is not to be found in Calvin's thought.

35. John Calvin, *Institutes of the Christian Religion*, ed. John T. McNeill, trans. Ford Lewis Battles (Philadelphia: Westminster, 1960), 4.11.3. This is the standard English translation of the last Latin edition of the *Institutes* (1559).

36. Calvin, *Institutes*, 3.19.15. I have edited this passage for felicity of expression. At one point, however, I have taken special (possibly impeachable) liberties. Before the words "honorably and temperately" in the original text, the word "holily" appears. I have removed the word, not only because the translation is bad English, but also, more important, because the reference to religious practice in this context confuses the otherwise clear distinction Calvin is *himself* endeavoring to draw.

37. Words contained in the heading to Calvin, *Institutes*, 2.7.14.

38. John Calvin, *Epistles of Paul the Apostle to the Romans and the Thessalonians*, ed. David W. Torrance and Thomas F. Torrance, trans. Ross MacKenzie (Grand Rapids, Mich.: Eerdmans, 1973), 286 (italics added). There is reason to wonder how secure Calvin is in this unequivocal statement, since, in a preceding comment on Romans 13:8, having admitted that Paul "makes no mention of the worship of God," Calvin adds, "although he should not have omitted this." This countervailing comment suggests a rather deep ambivalence in Calvin's position (which I suspect is there).

39. Williams, *Complete Writings of Roger Williams*, 3:153–55.

40. Calvin, *Institutes*, 4.20.2.

41. Josef Bohatec, *Calvins Lehre von Staat und Kirche mit besonderer Berücksichtigung des Organismusgedankens* (1937; repr., Aalen, Germany: Scientia, 1961), 95–96, 96 (translations are mine).

42. John T. McNeill, *The History and Character of Calvinism* (Oxford: Oxford University Press, 1954), 161.

43. Lord Acton, *Lectures on Modern History* (New York: Meridian, 1961), 134.

44. John Calvin, *Homilies on I Samuel*, 10, cited in Herbert D. Foster, "Political Theories of Calvinists," in *Collected Papers of Herbert D. Foster* (privately printed, 1929), 82; Calvin, *Institutes*, 4.20.31; Calvin, *Commentary on the Psalms*, Ps. 119, cited in Foster, *Collected Papers*, 82.

45. Calvin, *Institutes*, 4.20.8.

46. Calvin, *Homilies on I Samuel*, 8, cited in Foster, *Collected Papers*, 82.

47. Bohatec, *Calvins Lehre von Staat und Kirche*, 94–95.

3

Implausible: Calvinism and American Politics

D. G. Hart

At the opening of his third lecture on Calvinism, delivered in 1898 at Princeton Theological Seminary to a largely Presbyterian audience, Abraham Kuyper asserted with characteristic confidence the relationship between the Reformed faith and political liberty that was typical of a time when Protestantism appeared to be responsible for most of the blessings of modernity. The Dutch theologian, who performed a remarkable degree of sphere sovereignty in politics, church life, economics, and higher education, believed that "every competent historian" understood that "Calvinism has led public law into new paths, first in Western Europe, then in two Continents, and today more and more among all civilized nations." One of those historians was the American George Bancroft, whom Kuyper quoted glowingly on Calvinism's wonder-working power: "The fanatic for Calvinism was a fanatic for liberty, for in the moral warfare for freedom, his creed was a part of his army, and his most faithful ally in the battle."[1]

By the end of his lecture, after developing the specific reasons for Calvinism's support for liberty and qualifying the nature of such freedom, Kuyper was no less confident of the link between Reformed theology and personal liberty. He did concede that Reformed magistrates had, in practice, "made a desperate effort to hinder the spread of literature which they disliked, by censure and refusal of publication." But these breaches in executing statecraft could not alter the necessary affinity between Calvinism and liberty. The

Netherlands was a case in point, a nation where "the free expression of thought, by the spoken and printed word . . . first achieved its victory." In fact, "the logical development of what was enshrined in the liberty of conscience, as well as that liberty itself, first blessed the world from the side of Calvinism."

Indeed, Kuyper was not even content with ascribing to Calvinism the political advances of his own nation, Great Britain, or the United States, which he did in one of his lectures on Calvinism and politics. He set his sights even higher:

> The fact remains that the broad stream of the development of our
> race runs from Babylon to San Francisco, through the five stadia of
> Babylonian-Egyptian, Greek-Roman, Islamitic [sic], Romanistic, and
> Calvinistic civilization, and the present conflict in Europe as well as
> in America finds it main cause in the fundament[al] antithesis
> between the energy of Calvinism which proceeds from the throne of
> God . . . and its caricature in the French Revolution, which
> proclaimed its unbelief in the cry of "No God no master."[2]

Lest cynics think that Kuyper was merely tickling the ears of his Presbyterian hosts, other nineteenth-century Europeans had registered similarly positive estimates of Calvinism's influence on the modern world and its social institutions. One of them was James Anthony Froude (1818–1894), an unlikely candidate to defend Calvinism if only because of his youthful involvement with the Oxford movement while a student at Oriel College at Oxford University. Once he became frustrated with the Oxford movement, Froude resigned his fellowship at Oriel and began duties as the editor of *Fraser's Magazine*, a post that also allowed him to write a massive and popular history of England. This achievement, in turn, earned Froude an appointment in 1868 as rector of the University of St. Andrews.

Almost three decades before Kuyper's lectures at Princeton, Froude anticipated many of the Dutch statesman's arguments in a public address given at St. Andrews entitled, simply enough, "Calvinism." Froude started from the premise that the Protestant Reformation was "the root and source of the expansive force which has spread the Anglo-Saxon race over the globe." He conceded that its teachings on predestination and freedom of the will could be interpreted as undermining morality. But, in point of fact, Calvinism possessed "singular attractions" for some of the "greatest men that ever lived," including Martin Luther, John Knox, Andrew Melville, Oliver Cromwell, John Milton, and John Bunyan. These were men "whose life was as upright as their intellect was commanding and their public aims untainted with selfishness . . . frank, true, cheerful, humorous, as unlike sour fanatics as it is possible to imagine any one, and able in some way to sound the key-note to which every brave and faithful heart in Europe instinctively vibrated." If Calvinism could produce the likes of these figures, Froude deduced, then its genius could not be reasonably denied. It was, in fact, the religion that "overthrew spiritual wickedness, and hurled kings from their thrones, and purged England and Scotland, for a time at least, of lies and charlatanry." "Where we find a heroic life appearing as the uniform fruit of a particular mode of opinion, it is childish to argue in the face of fact that the result ought to have been different."[3]

If these respectable European academics could take such a rosy view of Calvinism's contribution to the modern world, American Presbyterians were not committing any significant breach of Western intellectual etiquette if they were similarly boastful about the influence of Reformed Protestantism on U.S. political traditions. Indeed, the consensus of many nineteenth-century students of the West was that Calvinism deserved a great deal of credit (by the 1960s, it would turn to blame) for the political liberties and social capital of civil society in the West generally and in the United States specifically. Presbyterian dissent from this understanding would be not only self-destructive but also unfitting. And yet, some Presbyterians were not convinced of the links that many tried to establish between Calvinism and American politics. These critics knew the political background and held on to the theological affirmations that had shaped the Scottish Reformation and informed the Westminster Assembly. These Presbyterians also understood the inherent tensions between the liberties that Americans celebrated and the duties that sixteenth- and seventeenth-century Calvinists believed to be required of the civil magistrate.

What follows is a survey of Presbyterian advocates and critics of the liberties that became the standard fare of modern statecraft in the West. The particular aspect of modern politics that divided Presbyterians, for lack of better terms, into libertarian and authoritarian camps was the relationship of Calvinism to religious and civil liberties. As it turned out, both sides had a point about Calvinism's political implications. On one side, the proponents of Calvinism's political blessings, who are invariably from the mainstream denomination, the Presbyterian Church (U.S.A.) (PCUSA), or its distant cousins, could point to certain forms of Reformed political arguments and practices that had contributed to the kind of civil society enjoyed by most of the West, which, in turn, had secured the kind of religious freedom unknown in the West prior to the revolutions of the late eighteenth century. On the other side, primarily composed of Presbyterians with ties to Scottish Presbyterian denominations, links that nurtured expectations about the magistrate's duty to maintain the true religion, faultfinders have argued that the modern state was delinquent in carrying out its divinely ordained responsibilities to promote religious fidelity. What these perspectives reveal is that the effort to correlate politics with theology is never easy and that the relationship between Calvinism and liberty, like that between Christianity and politics more generally, is fundamentally paradoxical. In other words, as much as interpreters of the Reformed tradition have attributed to Calvinism a coherent political vision, the historical record indicates that Reformed theology was always easier to understand as a religion than as a political philosophy, and Calvinists themselves more often than not appealed to different strands of their tradition to justify their differing views of practical political realities.

Libertarian Calvinists

Anglo-American Protestants, especially those with ties to Calvinism, have been convinced that their faith and political liberty went hand in hand since the heady debates over independence from Great Britain, when Presbyterians and Congregationalists overwhelmingly supported the American Revolution. John Witherspoon's sermon "The Dominion of Providence over the Passions of Men" was a notable and famous expression of this synthesis of faith and politics. Based on Psalm 76:10 ("Surely the wrath of men shall praise thee; the remainder of Wrath shalt thou restrain") and delivered on Friday, May 17, 1776, a day designated by the Continental Congress to be set aside for prayer, the sermon proved to be so useful for the purposes of American independence that it was published the next month in the city where the Continental Congress met. Its popularity also accounts for Witherspoon's election in late June 1776 to serve in Congress as a representative from New Jersey, a post that placed him in good stead to sign the Declaration of Independence. The logic of Witherspoon's devotional discourse was powerful in giving voice to a conception of liberty that would prove to be enduring among American Calvinists.[4]

In the second part of the sermon, where he applied the meaning of the text to the political situation in the colonies, Witherspoon attempted to inspire his listeners to patriotic greatness by exhorting them to trust in God and hope "for his assistance in the present important conflict." The patriots could, he believed, have confidence in divine assistance if their cause was just, their principles pure, and their conduct prudent. Although he ended the sermon with exhortations to greater moral integrity, a signal that Witherspoon was worried about spiritual degeneracy among his contemporaries, he had little doubt about the justice of their grievance with England. "The cause in which America is now in arms," he declared, "is the cause of justice, of liberty, and of human nature."

Witherspoon explained that the colonists had not been motivated by "pride, resentment, or sedition." Instead, the desire for independence from England arose from "a deep and general conviction" that religious and civil liberty, as well as "the temporal and eternal happiness of us and our society," depended on political autonomy. Here, Witherspoon had a precise conception of the relationship between civil and religious liberty. "The knowledge of God and his truths," he elaborated, "have from the beginning of the world been chiefly, if not entirely, confined to those parts of the earth, where some degree of liberty and political justice were to be seen." In effect, Witherspoon was articulating the fundamental Protestant logic that assumed that true religion, namely, Protestant Christianity, only flourished where civil magistrates protected civil liberties. The flip side of this assumption was the similar belief that Protestantism was the best soil from which civil liberty naturally grew. Witherspoon made this relationship crystal clear when he asserted that "there is not a single instance in history in which civil liberty was lost, and religious liberty preserved entire." For this reason, if the colonists were to "yield up our temporal property" to Parliament through unfair taxes, they would also be delivering their consciences "into bondage."[5]

To say that Witherspoon's argument was distinctly Presbyterian would be an overstatement. Other Protestants appealed to the same sort of affinities between American freedom and Christianity, as they understood the faith within their own theological tradition. The American framers, from George Washington and Ben Franklin to Thomas Jefferson and John Adams, could marshal arguments for American political ideals from decidedly heterodox positions, so powerful were the intellectual ties among republicanism, liberalism, and Christianity in the debates that forged American independence. Even so, Protestants in the Reformed tradition spoke forcefully and often about the Puritan and, hence, Calvinist origins of American liberty. And because Calvinistic clergy supported overwhelmingly the cause of independence, the Reformed arguments for political liberty nurtured among Presbyterians and Congregationalists a sense of entitlement in defending the achievement of the revolution and the unique character of America's cultural ideals.[6]

Indeed, the defenders of Presbyterianism after Witherspoon rarely missed a chance to affirm the continuities between either their own form of church government or Calvinistic theology and the American form of government and the liberties it protected. Charles Hodge, for instance, arguably the most important Presbyterian theologian of nineteenth-century America, echoed the Witherspoonian syllogism that began with the major premise of Reformed Protestantism and concluded with America's contribution to political liberty. At an 1855 lecture on the nature of Presbyterianism for the Presbyterian Historical

Society, Hodge traced the connections between Calvinism and liberal representative societies. He conceded that democracy itself was not consistent with Presbyterianism. "The Church," he wrote, "is not a vast democracy, where everything is decided by popular vote." Even so, the idea that "all civil power vests ultimately in the people" was not opposed to delegated authority in the hands of "legitimate officers, legislative, judicial, and executive," to be exercised in accordance with the law. In the same way, the doctrine that vests church authority in the church itself was compatible with a Presbyterian form of government that placed rule within the church in "a divinely appointed class of officers." Consequently, Presbyterianism was not hierarchical or egalitarian but a mixed form of government in which "the principle of liberty and the principle of order are perfectly harmonious." In fact, the ability to rule that elders possessed within the Presbyterian system was directly comparable to a republican form of government. In the same way that members of Congress "can exercise only those powers which are inherent in the people," so Presbyterian elders exercised "the powers which radically inhere in those for whom they act."[7]

These parallels led Hodge to conclude that the "combination of the principles of liberty and order in the Presbyterian system, the union of the rights of the people with subjection to legitimate authority," was, not surprisingly, the "parent and guardian of civil liberty in every part of the world." He conceded that Calvinism's purpose was higher than the establishment of secular government; such government was only "an incidental advantage" for this variant of Protestantism. But even for a theologian less inclined to derive social programs from theological reflection, Hodge believed that the success of Presbyterian government was dependent on the same sorts of virtues that made republicanism tick. "If the people possess the gifts and graces which qualify and entitle them to take part in the government," he deduced, "then the exercise of that right tends to the development of those gifts and graces." In other words, Hodge thought that political and ecclesiastical liberty, that is, republicanism and Presbyterianism, stem from a common basis of "scriptural liberty." As such, in the same way that "republican institutions cannot exist among the ignorant and vicious," so Presbyterianism needs people who are "enlightened and virtuous."[8]

Hodge's nemesis in the Old School–New School controversy (which eventually divided mainstream American Presbyterians into four different denominations after the sectional crisis of the mid-nineteenth century), Albert Barnes, was on the same page with his Old School opponent when it came to religion and politics. In the short pamphlet *Presbyterianism: Its Affinities* (1863), the Philadelphia pastor observed that one of Calvinism's chief contributions was a representative system of government. Presbyterianism, in effect, represented

a middle course, "distinguished, on the one hand, from the monarchical principle, and on the other from strict and radical democracy." "All just notions of
liberty in modern times" were connected with the fundamental principles
taught by Presbyterian understandings of government.[9] A representative form
of government was, for Barnes, only one of six (and the fifth one, at that) material principles of Presbyterianism considered as a system of church government. Reconciling this mediating position between monarchy and democracy
with other Presbyterian principles that located all power in Christ, who was not
only the head of the church but also the king, was a task that Barnes did not
carry out. For him, it was enough to assert the failure of experiments with monarchy and radical democracy, point to Presbyterianism as the successful alternative, and still affirm the kingship of Christ.

One reason for Barnes's apparent nonchalance about the tension between
divine monarchy and earthly republicanism was that he conceived of America's
political traditions in orderly as opposed to libertarian terms. The United States,
from Maine to California, had developed precisely as the product of minds
schooled in the teachings of Calvinism and dedicated to perpetuating these
ideals in institutions and associations. "The Puritan mind, to which our country owes so much in its character, and in the form of its civil institutions, is
essentially Calvinistic," Barnes insisted. But the Puritans had help from the
"Huguenot mind," the "Scotch mind," and the "Scotch-Irish mind." For Barnes,
these "classes of mind" had a uniform set of characteristics: "They are firm,
resolute, decided; they act more from principle than from impulse; they are
friendly to law and order, they are friends of sound learning and science; they
will be certain to found and patronize schools and colleges; they will be reliable
in all times when great principles are at stake."[10]

Barnes increased the affinities between Calvinism and American political
customs when he argued that Reformed Protestants were an especially loyal set
of Christians—loyal to "just government" and "to our country." At the time of
the revolution, Presbyterian ministers were distinguished and deserved "a
noble place" among the patriots for their advocacy of "our principles as related
to human rights, to patriotism, to civil liberty." In fact, "whoever among the
clergy of the land, in the time of the Revolution, were disloyal, Presbyterians
were not." This stemmed from Presbyterianism's inherent tendency toward
"loyalty to a government administered in conformity to a constitution; loyalty to
the principles of liberty; loyalty to a country as such; loyalty to the powers that
be." Again, Barnes failed to notice the discrepancy between this account of
Presbyterianism and the reality of American Calvinists' disloyalty to British
political sovereignty or its constitutional order. And the reason was his haste
to affirm that Calvinism was on the side of law and order rather than chaotic

freedom. For Barnes, "the sum of all our doctrines, and all our efforts, is to bring men back to allegiance to the laws and government of our Maker." Indeed, the ties between Calvinism and American politics were so close that Barnes could attribute to Calvinism political forms of a distinctly American character: "security against any usurpation of power," "absolute security against any invasion of right," and "checks and safeguards appointed for securing the permanency and the wise administration of government forever."[11]

At the end of the nineteenth century, the antebellum Presbyterian synthesis of Calvinism and American liberty was still in force. William Henry Roberts, the clerk of the northern PCUSA, continued to highlight the ties between Calvinism and liberal society. Again, the ties between religion and politics resulted in a curious mix of restraint and freedom. On the one hand, Roberts insisted that the "controlling idea" of Presbyterianism was the "doctrine of divine sovereignty." In addition, the "organizing principle" of Calvinism was "the sovereignty of the word of God." These two features prompted Roberts to stress that Presbyterianism was a faith that did justice to the "perpetual binding obligation" that God and scripture placed on every person. On the other hand, Calvinism promoted freedom as much as it advocated subjection to the will of God. The key to the libertarian side of Presbyterianism was the doctrine of liberty of conscience. The syllogism ran something like this: God is sovereign; God as the author of scripture means that the Bible is "the supreme rule of faith and practice;" therefore, "every Christian is entitled to interpret the Scripture for himself."[12]

Although Roberts was writing about Presbyterianism more as a form of faith than as a social entity, he could not resist noting the political benefits and civil implications of Calvinism. Recognizing the divine-command contribution of Presbyterianism was a fairly simple enterprise. "True Calvinism has been and is a most potent source of good to both the individual and the State," Roberts explained, "in the one of right conduct, and in the other of social order." Presbyterianism's "choicest products are the God-fearing believer and the law-abiding citizen." But the stress on divine rule was still a source of political freedom. The application of Presbyterianism in civil affairs was "a free Church in a free State." Consequently, even if Calvinism emphasized submission and obedience, its direct implication for politics was freedom—that is, a state where political freedom was the ideal. Roberts asserted that Presbyterianism was "the bulwark of civil and religious liberty" both in the past and in the present.[13]

Most of these Presbyterian arguments were situated north of the Mason-Dixon Line and could readily be traced back to the vicinity of Princeton, where Witherspoon had initially offered a Presbyterian rationale for American independence. Still, southern Presbyterians were equally convinced of Calvinism's contribution to civil liberty and representative forms of government. One sign of southern agreement was Francis R. Beattie's series of lectures around the turn of the twentieth century, published as *Calvinism and Modern Thought* (1901). A professor of theology at Louisville Presbyterian Theological Seminary, Beattie's aim was to address Calvinism's ongoing intellectual vitality even in the context of new ideas in history, philosophy, science, and society that, on the surface, might seem to discredit this branch of Protestantism. Without surprise, he showed that Calvinism was by no means antiquated and possessed the resources to adapt—and, in some cases, actually contribute—to the advance of modern thought. Beattie likely reassured his hearers with the conclusion: "On the one hand, we need not fear modern thought. All that is good and true in it will be found in harmony with Calvinism. . . . On the other hand, Calvinism, in its essential principles will ever abide, and always keep pace with all that is true and good in modern thought."[14]

En route to this comforting assessment, Beattie could not resist pointing out Calvinism's contribution to modern politics. The influence was a curious combination of freedom and restraint, with apparently little attention given to the tensions between the two. For instance, Beattie asserted that Calvinism's view of civil government was that the state is "God's ordinance for the proper regulation of human affairs." The church was a similar mixture of divine sovereignty and human freedom. The church, according to Beattie, is a "great, free, spiritual commonwealth of which Jesus Christ is the only King and Head." The relationship between church and state could be summarized with the slogan "A free Church in a free State." This indicated that Calvinism stood "everywhere" for civil and religious liberty. Somehow, this stand also involved subjection to Christian truth because, according to Beattie, "the battle cry of Calvinism is the conquest of the world for Christ, so that he may see the travail of his soul and be satisfied." Still, the apparent discrepancy between liberty for all and subjection to Christ everywhere was not a misprint. Beattie reiterated that Calvinism has "always stood for freedom of thought and the right of private judgment, as she stands everywhere for civil and religious liberty."[15] As much as this made sense of a rationale for Calvinism's capacity to adjust to modern thought, it appeared to leave little room for the thought, especially the doctrines, of other religions or even non-Protestant Christianity.

By the era of World War I, the self-consciously Presbyterian argument about Calvinism's contribution to liberal society had evaporated considerably. Part of the reason was much less confidence about Presbyterianism as a unique branch of Protestantism. Both Protestant modernism and fundamentalism contributed to a loss of denominational identity as both sides of the emerging controversy began to assert the importance of generic truths on either the left (for example, the fatherhood of God, the brotherhood of man, and the Golden Rule) or the right (for example, creation, inerrancy, the virgin birth, and the imminent return of Christ).[16] An example of Presbyterian loss of nerve is Hugh T. Kerr's booklet *What the Presbyterian Church Stands For* (1919). A professor at McCormick Theological Seminary in Chicago, a pastor, a popular radio preacher, and the executive of the northern Presbyterian church's Department of Christian Education, Kerr was well situated in trends that were responsible for broadening the theological orientation of the PCUSA. For this reason, he seemed to show little awkwardness in admitting that the old controversies between Calvinism and Arminianism, along with the associated rivalries between Presbyterians and Methodists, had "now almost disappeared." Even so, Kerr, a native of Canada, could not help noting the overlap between Presbyterianism and the polity of the United States under the heading "Presbyterian Point of View," namely, "The Right of the People to Rule Themselves." Kerr observed that Presbyterianism itself had a republican form of government and that many historians of the United States, such as George Bancroft, had commented on the similarities between the Presbyterian polity and America's governing structures. Presbyterians themselves had a "great influence" on the writing of the Constitution, and two-thirds of the American people at the time of the revolution were "of a Calvinistic sentiment." "Presbyterian government," Kerr insisted, "is responsible." "It has the power to appeal from the lowest court to the highest. It is a government 'of the people, by the people, and for the people.'"[17]

Even if a declining denominational self-consciousness diminished Presbyterian boasts about the origins of America's political tradition, the practice of church history enabled scholars teaching at denominational seminaries to keep alive the logic of America's debt to Calvinism. For instance, Leonard Trinterud, who taught during the middle decades of the twentieth century at McCormick Theological Seminary, published a path-breaking book on colonial Presbyterianism in 1949 entitled *The Forming of an American Tradition*. Trinterud's subject was a natural place to consider the contribution of Witherspoon and other ministers to the American founding. While the work was not as jingoistic as it might have been, Trinterud did not hesitate to identify Calvinism with the cause of liberty; he declined to call it "sacred" but did use the synonym "holy." Fears regarding the establishment of an Anglican bishop in North America were a natural starting point for Presbyterians to endorse the liberties, both civil and religious, that animated American patriots. "The most important result of the controversy over the episcopate," Trinterud wrote, "was that the Presbyterian and Congregationalist Churches had become fully convinced that religious liberty for them stood or fell with the civil liberties of the colonies." But the affinities between Presbyterianism and American independence ran deeper than political circumstances. According to Trinterud, "the idea that a people suffering under a tyrant had the right to resist him through their legally consti-tuted representatives was traditional Calvinism." On top of this basic insight came developments among the British Whigs and the work of John Locke so that, when Thomas Jefferson penned the Declaration of Independence, "Pres-byterians recognized at once their Calvinistic theology and their Whig political theory." This recognition intensified opposition to an Anglican bishop, and Presbyterians understood that "the cause of American independence had become a holy cause."[18]

Only a few years later, in his contribution to *They Seek a Country*, H. Gordon Harold underscored Trinterud's argument about Presbyterianism's contribution to the polity of the United States. Harold's essay was part of a historical conference in which the PCUSA and the United Presbyterian Church of North America were gearing up for their 1958 merger. Perhaps the excite-ment of uniting these two denominations accounted for Harold's much more immodest claims about Calvinism's place in American independence. Not only did the political and ecclesiastical circumstances of the British colonies prompt Presbyterians to support political liberty, but Calvinist theology also supplied a theological rationale for the new nation's political ideals. According to Harold, the sovereignty of God, the rights of laypeople, and "the solidarity of human-kind" all added up to a theory of "the divine right of man set over against the obnoxious and iniquitous idea of the divine right of kings." And because Cal-vinism was the widespread teaching of practically all colonial Protestant denominations, it was "fertile soil to bear fruit in a Christian democracy." Even so, Presbyterians played a unique role in the shaping of the United States. The polity of the Presbyterian Church set an example of an "ecclesiastical republic" for the nation to follow. Consequently, "it fell to the Presbyterian Church's lot, as the only fully developed federal republican institution, to lead the way." The United States, he concluded, "owes much to that oldest of American republics, the Presbyterian Kirk."[19]

The most recent notable expression of libertarian Presbyterianism, some two centuries after Witherspoon's initial iteration, was the pastiche of argu-ments proposed by Francis Schaeffer, the so-called father of the religious right. A student at Westminster Seminary and at Faith Seminary and then a protégé of the militant anticommunist Carl McIntire, Schaeffer worked for much of his career as a missionary to children in Switzerland after World War II. During this time, he opened his home to many European and American college stu-dents who were traveling through the Alps looking for themselves and for answers to the meaning of life. His answers attracted the interest of evangelical colleges during the 1960s; his lectures were published as *The God Who Is There* (1968), *The Pollution and Death of Man* (1970), and *He Is There and He Is Not Silent* (1972). Schaeffer's critique of secular humanism and the cultural decadence of the West and its American outpost led to political arguments by the end of his life that were crucial to the religious right's engagement in the culture wars of the 1980s and 1990s. As Garry Wills described Schaeffer's influence in *Under God: Religion and American Politics*, although non-evangelicals "would consider Schaeffer's art criticism philistine," the apologist "deserves more credit than anyone else" for galvanizing evangelicals, specifically through anti-abortion activism and generally through an effort to recover America's Christian roots.[20]

The older Presbyterian arguments about the links between Calvinism and American politics were harder to appreciate under Schaeffer's critique of medieval philosophy and unrelenting pessimism about Western civilization. Even so, to the extent that the United States achieved a proper balance of civil liberty and political stability, Reformed Protestantism, according to Schaeffer, deserved credit. In his popular book *How Should We Then Live?* he mingled theological and philosophical history with political activism. Rather than citing Calvinism generally or referring to the Presbyterian polity, Schaeffer went directly to Scotland and the influence of Samuel Rutherford, whose arguments in *Lex Rex* (1644) provided a model for a "government of law rather than of the arbitrary decisions of men—because the Bible as the final authority was there as a base." Schaeffer detected the influence of Rutherford, mediated first through Witherspoon and then through John Locke, on the American Constitution. Even if Locke did not have Rutherford's theology, the English political theorist did articulate "the results which come from biblical Christianity." Schaeffer lamented that Locke and, later, Jefferson secularized the political insights of Presbyterianism. Yet, enough of a Calvinist foundation was still undergirding the American experiment to allow its Constitution to bring forth from the Bible its political conclusions, which were to achieve "form and freedom in society and government." As such, from the Reformation came the United States' political achievement. This understanding of the reformational basis of the U.S. government shaped Schaeffer's contribution to the culture wars of the 1980s, namely, convincing conservative Christians to recover their republic's Christian origins.[21]

Schaeffer's arguments about the debt the American founding owed to the Reformation had clearly changed from Witherspoon's original claims regarding the ties between true religion and political liberty. But even if the particulars differed, the point remained. Protestantism in general and Calvinism in particular provided the only adequate basis for the American experiment of a republic based on limited government and civil liberty. Because other observers with less of a vested interest in Presbyterianism discerned this same affinity, Presbyterian boosters of American liberty could be forgiven for parts of their denominational chauvinism. Still, for Presbyterians in the United States with a different political experience, the mainstream Presbyterian arguments for Calvinism as a bulwark of political liberty likely sounded overly sanguine and not very Calvinistic.

Authoritarian Calvinists

As much as the mainstream of American Presbyterianism, including both the mainline and sideline denominations, took the affinities between American freedoms and Calvinism for granted, Reformed Protestantism was historically not so liberal or Whiggish. Practically every major confession from the sixteenth-century Reformed or Presbyterian churches affirmed that the civil magistrate was responsible for enforcing the true religion and had a duty to protect the true church. For instance, the Gallic Confession of Faith (1559), which received a heavy dose of John Calvin's insights, affirmed in article 39 that God "has put the sword into the hands of magistrates to suppress crimes against the first as well as the second table of the Commandments of God." This power required believers to hold the magistrates "in all reverence" as those officers who execute a "legitimate and holy authority." The Scottish Confession of Faith (1560), shaped to a large degree by John Knox, declared in chapter 24 that "the preservation and purification of religion is particularly the duty of kings, princes, rulers, and magistrates." As such, God appointed the civil authority not only for the affairs of state but also "to maintain true religion and suppress all idolatry and superstition." One more example of the magistrate's duty to enforce the true religion comes from the Belgic Confession (1561), a creed written by Guido de Bres for Protestants in the Netherlands. Article 36 echoed the Reformed consensus that the magistrate's duties pertained not only to public welfare but also involved protecting "the sacred ministry," removing and preventing "all idolatry and false worship." These were hardly a confessional basis from which to derive either religious or civil liberty, especially as Americans came to construe such freedoms. American Presbyterian notions of the relationship between Calvinism and civil polities, then, were generally foreign to the original teachings of the Reformed churches. The first Protestants did not have any conception of a religiously mixed society, few countenanced republicanism as a viable form of government, and practically no one linked civil and religious liberty the way that American Presbyterians did.[22]

Early in the reception of Presbyterianism in North America, first in the British colonies and then in the United States, the theological heirs of John Calvin were aware of the tension. The Westminster Confession of Faith and Catechisms, to which American Presbyterians subscribed, was clear in maintaining the older sixteenth-century view of a state church backed up by a magistrate committed to the faith of the Reformation. Chapter 23 reads:

> The civil magistrate may not assume to himself the administration of
> the Word and sacraments, or the power of the keys of the kingdom of
> heaven: yet he hath authority, and it is his duty, to take order, that
> unity and peace be preserved in the Church, that the truth of God be
> kept pure and entire; that all blasphemies and heresies be
> suppressed; all corruptions and abuses in worship and discipline
> prevented or reformed; and all the ordinances of God duly settled,
> administered, and observed. For the better effecting whereof, he hath
> power to call synods, to be present at them, and to provide that
> whatsoever is transacted in them be according to the mind of God.[23]

Consequently, when, in 1729, American Presbyterians considered their first constitution and the adaptability of the Westminster standards to the colonies, the Synod of Philadelphia collectively decided to note reservations about the Westminster Confession's teaching on the magistrate. They even regarded this as not "essential and necessary" to biblical teaching.[24]

American uneasiness with the Old World church-state arrangements implied in their tradition generally and taught in the Westminster standards specifically led the PCUSA, in 1787, to begin the process of revising its confession and catechisms.[25] Interestingly, Witherspoon's fingerprints were on the confessional revisions, thus adding a measure of irony to the indifference that American Presbyterians who embraced his views on religious and civil liberty showed toward the American Calvinist departure from the old Reformed understanding of religion and the state. The most obvious part of the revisions occurred in the twenty-third chapter of the confession on the civil magistrate. In paragraph three of the original, the Westminster divines asserted that the civil magistrate has "authority, and it is his duty, to take order, that unity and peace be preserved in the Church, that the truth of God be kept pure and entire, that all blasphemies and heresies be suppressed, all corruptions and abuses of worship and discipline prevented or reformed, and all the ordinances of God duly settled, administered, and observed." In addition, the magistrate's authority extended to calling synods, being present at them, and ensuring that "whatsoever is transacted in them be according to the mind of God."[26] In 1640s England, with a state church still the rule and Christendom the assumption, granting the state such broad power within the church made sense. To have thought otherwise would have meant siding with the Anabaptists and other radicals.

Obviously, this outlook made no sense in Philadelphia after the war for independence, when a national state church did not exist and none of the local ecclesiastical establishments were Presbyterian. Consequently, American Presbyterians downgraded the magistrate to a "nursing father" whose duty was "to protect the church of our common Lord, without giving the preference to any denomination of Christians above the rest in such a manner, that all ecclesiastical persons whatever shall enjoy the full, free, and unquestioned liberty of discharging, every part of their sacred functions, without violence or danger." In addition, the Americans held that the magistrate should not "interfere with, let, or hinder, the due exercise" of any Christian denomination. This was not simply tolerance for Protestant churches because the magistrate's duty included protecting "the person and good name of all their people" such that no one, "upon pretense of religion or of infidelity," should endure any "indignity, violence, abuse, or injury." This sentiment clearly pointed in the direction of religious liberty for all citizens. From this confessional amendment on the magistrate followed other smaller ones in chapters 20 and 31 to make sense of the larger change in chapter 23. The revision to chapter 20, "Of Christian Liberty and Liberty of Conscience," deleted the last phrase from paragraph four, which granted the state the right to discipline church members who abused their freedoms to upset the peace of the church. The modification of chapter 31, "Of Synods and Councils," was a little more drastic since it eliminated all of the second paragraph, which was another assertion of the magistrate's right to call assemblies combined with counsel on what to do if the governor were an "open" enemy of the church.[27]

Many scholars of the Westminster Assembly note that the divines rejected Erastianism. What this typically means is that they affirmed that the church has the sole power of determining who should be admitted to communion (or, conversely, who might be excommunicated). But while Erastianism technically involved disputes about admission to the Lord's Supper, it also became synonymous with a view of church-state relations that granted the state powers of surveillance within the ecclesiastical sphere. In this sense, the original Westminster Confession leaned Erastian. It may be even harder to imagine how a group of ministers, called by Parliament to draft the norms for England's church, could have asserted any position other than the magistrate possessing the power to maintain, protect, and intervene within the church. If said clergy had denied the power of the magistrate to supervise the church, then they would have undermined the very legitimacy of the Westminster Assembly, in addition to risking their own law-abiding status.

But the Westminster Assembly's teaching on the power of the magistrate, later rejected by American Presbyterians, was not peculiar to the English and the few Scots who gathered during the 1640s in London to undertake a new ecclesiastical establishment for the United Kingdom. Presbyterians themselves had a fairly strong record before the Westminster Assembly of insisting that the magistrate had a duty to promote true religion, even if they also insisted that they could instruct the magistrate about the content of religious truth. In 1580, the Scottish King's Confession, as reaffirmed in the National Covenant (1638), required the monarch, then James VI, to "maintain the true religion of Christ Jesus, the preaching of His holy word, the due and right administration of the sacraments now received and preached within this realm, (according to the Confession of Faith immediately preceding) and shall abolish and gain-stand all false religion contrary to the same."[28] The design of this confession clearly was to root out any trace of Roman Catholicism in Scotland and to establish Presbyterianism as the religion of the realm. The King's Confession in turn became the foundation for the National Covenant of 1638 by which Presbyterians from Scotland attempted to undermine Charles I's religious policies. Although it constituted an appeal to the people against the king, it was also a reminder to the Crown of the monarch's vow, taken in 1580, to uphold and defend Reformed Christianity in Scotland. Five years later, the Westminster Assembly ratified the Solemn League and Covenant (1643), which took the same tack as the National Covenant, except in this iteration it also included the English and Irish in the Scots' efforts to force the king to honor his obligations to protect and defend Reformed Christianity. As much as the Solemn League and Covenant was implicated in the growing political antagonisms between the Crown and Parliament, and so a religious document with a not quite so covert political subtext, it, too, like the King's Confession and the National Covenant, reiterated the Presbyterian desire for a magistrate who would support the true faith. With a king ready if not willing to support Presbyterianism, the original Westminster Confession's construction of the magistrate's ecclesiastical powers made much sense.[29]

But, in one fell swoop, the American Presbyterian church swept away almost two centuries of Presbyterian politics with its 1788 revisions. The American version of the Westminster standards revealed that Presbyterians in the United States were not only breaking with the political struggles of Great Britain that had prompted Old World Presbyterians to seek the protection of a Reformed monarch and Parliament, but it also demonstrated that New World Presbyterians now conceived of religion and the state in different categories. On the one hand, religion constituted a sphere distinct from politics and best flourished without the threat or assistance of the magistrate. On the other hand, the function of the state was at least not overtly spiritual, and its assistance could do more harm than good to the church's ministry.

Nevertheless, the American revisions to the Westminster standards did not speak for all Presbyterians in the United States. Periodically throughout American Presbyterian history, minority groups in the mainstream denominations have objected to either the United States' moral decline or its secularization and so expressed arguments similar to the understanding of the magistrate taught by Reformed churches during the sixteenth and seventeenth centuries. One example would be those southern Presbyterians who insisted that the Confederacy insert an affirmation of the lordship of Christ in its constitution. Another is the more recent expression of Christian reconstruction, or theonomy, which uses Old Testament political arrangements as foundational for statecraft in all times and places. This is not to say that early modern Reformed teachings on the state were theocratic, especially since the assertion that God's law is the basis for all legislation does not settle whether clergy or magistrates administer divine law. But theonomists do look back to older Reformed understandings of the magistrate as much more congenial to their views than to the new political and ecclesiastical realities of liberal democracy.[30]

Aside from dissenting groups in mainstream American Presbyterian circles, one Reformed community has tried to maintain the Calvinistic teaching that informed the original Westminster Confession of Faith. By their very name, the Covenanters, also known as Reformed Presbyterians, show an allegiance to the covenanting tradition in Scotland that had originally prevailed at the time of the Scottish Reformation. By implication, the Stuart monarchy extended to the United Kingdom at large when James VI of Scotland became James I of England in 1603. He was the king with whom the Scottish kirk had originally covenanted to maintain the true religion in Scotland, and his successor, Charles I, was the monarch whom Parliament expected to uphold the Solemn League and Covenant. The Covenanters continued to insist on the validity of these covenants well after civil war, regicide, an experiment with republicanism, and the restoration of monarchy showed to many British Protestants that the tradition of covenanting was unstable. After maintaining and suffering heroically for their faith, the Covenanters refused to join the reestablishment of the kirk in 1690. Not until 1743 did they form their own official presbytery. In North America, the Covenanters had one congregation as early as 1738 but did not form a presbytery until 1774. Although it has always remained a small denomination, the Reformed Presbyterian Church of North America (RPCNA) has also been a steady reminder of ideas about the magistrate that libertarian Presbyterians conveniently buried in their paeans to civil and religious liberty.[31]

In 1871, for instance, after roughly a century of libertarian Presbyterian support for America's political traditions, the RPCNA affirmed a new covenant between themselves and God that tapped the old Covenanter convictions about the duties of the magistrate. In addition to affirming the true Presbyterian faith, both in theology and church government, and rejecting all forms of infidelity, from atheism to popery, the RPCNA confessed its belief that "God is the source of all legitimate power," that Christ is the head of the nation, and that the Bible "is the supreme law and rule in national as in all other things." As such, all nations were obligated to regulate all "civil relations, attachments, professions, and deportment" by allegiance to Christ, "our King, lawgiver, and Judge." These beliefs did not require direct and explicit opposition from Covenanters to governments like the United States that did not acknowledge the kingship of Jesus Christ in its Constitution. The RPCNA pledged that it would "pray and labor for the peace and welfare of our country." But part of this prayerful support also included petitions for America's "reformation by a constitutional recognition of God as the source of all power, of Jesus Christ as the Ruler of Nations, and of the Holy Scriptures as the supreme rule, and of the true Christian religion."[32]

This American national covenant was part of the RPCNA's constitution from the late nineteenth century until 1989, when it was relegated to the historical section of official documents, along with the denomination's "Declaration and Testimony," a running commentary on the Westminster Confession that applied in a binding manner the teachings of the Westminster Assembly to contemporary society. The 1949 version of the "Declaration and Testimony" explained the propriety of church members dissenting from a duly constituted civil government. Because no nation was neutral in its allegiance to Christ—either "the spirit of Christ was in control of national life" or the "powers of this world have the ascendancy"—the RPCNA held that a Christian was bound to dissent from the rule of nations that did not acknowledge Christ as king. Specifically, a Christian would have to "separate from the government at the point where the government separated from Christ," that is, a Christian should dissent from any constitution or form of civil government that "neglects to own allegiance to Jesus Christ, the Prince of the kings of the earth." The RPCNA's account of rightful dissent insisted that such resistance was not a form of disloyalty and so should not be punished. In fact, those who dissented for Covenanter reasons deserved protection by non-Christian or secular states because "they not only pay taxes, obey the laws and in cases of emergency serve in the defense of their country, but by their consistent loyalty to Jesus Christ in dissenting from that which dishonors Him are contributing also, by a personal sacrifice, to the nation's highest welfare."[33] Teachings like this were responsible for Covenanters refusing to vote, hold public office, or serve in the military except in cases of emergency.

Similar convictions are still part of the contemporary Covenanter constitution and formal doctrines. For instance, the current "Testimony" of the Reformed Presbyterian Church (2004) allows church members to run for political office in the United States even though the nation's Constitution still does not recognize Jesus Christ as king. Even so, the church offers the following directions about participating in the electoral process:

> When participating in political elections, the Christian should support and vote only for such men [sic] as are publicly committed to scriptural principles of civil government. Should the Christian seek civil office by political election, he must openly inform those whose support he seeks of his adherence to Christian principles of civil government.[34]

Although a minority perspective within the history of American Presbyterianism, the Covenanters' allegiance to the original confessional content of the Reformed churches is a reminder to other Calvinists of the way their faith needed to be and was adapted for the political circumstances of the United States. What is more, the Covenanter tradition raises important questions about a religious and scholarly consensus that has generally stressed continuity between Reformed Protestantism and the political lineaments of liberal democracy.

Calvinism and America

The contrast developed here between the libertarian and authoritarian wings of Reformed Protestantism may be stronger on paper than it has been in practice. Mainstream American Presbyterians and Covenanters have used different versions of the Westminster Confession and remained in separate communions thanks to significant tensions within Calvinism regarding the nature of politics and the duties of the magistrate. On the surface, Calvinist teachings about human depravity and the bondage of the will to sin would seem to be strange bedfellows with liberal individualism or even classical republicanism. The lessons that the Calvinist account of sin would teach libertarians or republicans is either that humans cannot be trusted with freedom or that men and women are incapable of the public virtue required for the well-being of the republic.

But Calvinism's bleak view of human nature seldom prevented students of the West generally or American politics specifically from attributing a genuine Reformed influence on at least one of the late eighteenth century's political revolutions responsible for modern estimates of the value of liberty. From

Alexis de Tocqueville and Max Weber to Ralph Barton Perry and David Gress, political and social theorists have regarded Calvinism as crucial to the modern construction of a free society and the economic engine that sustains it. Whether evidence came from the theory of political resistance that Reformed clergy and theologians used during the sixteenth and seventeenth centuries to create space for Protestant state churches or simply from counting the number of clergy who most vigorously supported America's war for independence, historians and social scientists have had no lack of support for a credible case linking Calvinism to the political, legal, and economic engines of modern Western society.[35]

The scholarly consensus in favor of a Calvinist leavening within the lump of modern liberal society has not done justice, however, to two other features of Reformed teaching that bear explicitly on the politics of freedom. The first is the subject of liberty itself. The Westminster Confession, to which libertarian and authoritarian American Presbyterians profess allegiance, has a chapter on the liberty of conscience, one of the only Reformed creeds to devote an entire section to this subject. Because of the Whiggish reading of Calvinism that has gained so wide a hearing in the church and academy, many readers would expect to see in this chapter some evidence that directly connects liberty of conscience to civil liberty. But the authors of the Westminster Confession clearly assert that the Christian idea of liberty of conscience may not be used for any kind of political liberty. On the one hand, Christian liberty pertains exclusively to the liberation from the bondage of sin and the penalty of death through the merits of Christ. On the other hand, the confession teaches that any who "upon pretense of Christian liberty, shall oppose any lawful power, or the lawful exercise of it, whether it be civil or ecclesiastical, resist the ordinance of God" and may be "proceeded against by the censures of the church, and by the power of the civil magistrate" (original Westminster Confession of Faith, 20.4). This clear differentiation between civil and spiritual liberty was unremarkable among sixteenth- and seventeenth-century Reformed theologians and creeds. Only after the Enlightenment and the American framers' idea of a "new science of politics" did Calvinists begin to blur that distinction.

The second subject is the actual teaching of the Reformed churches about the duties of the magistrate. Here, again, the creedal record is not even mixed but decidedly hostile toward a view that would use Calvinism to underwrite the sort of civil and religious liberties so highly valued by modern theories of politics. As the experience of American Presbyterianism shows, to rally behind the liberties promoted in the American founding, ministers and theologians in the mainstream denominations needed a version of the Westminster Confession that had been gutted of the idea that the state holds responsibility for the health of the church. Conversely, American Presbyterians who still clung to the politics that had informed the writing of the Westminster standards, namely, the Covenanters, took a different and non-Whiggish view of the American experiment. These Calvinists were law abiding and recognized the legitimacy of the United States, while they also refused to become involved in the affairs of the nation that would compromise the kingship of Christ over both the church and the state.

One possible way to resolve the tension among libertarian Presbyterians, their authoritarian counterparts, and the scholarship on Calvinism and modernity is the tactic employed by Philip Benedict in his valuable social history of Reformed Protestantism from 1500 to 1750. In response to the argument that Calvinism encouraged the rise of liberal democracy, Benedict makes two important points on the way to a wise conclusion. The first is that Calvinists had no monopoly on resistance theory since Lutherans and Roman Catholics also employed it during the political uncertainties of the early modern era. The second is that the Presbyterian polity was actually more aristocratic than democratic and that, if the roots of representative government can be found anywhere, they are in the common European experience of a feudal, decentralized society during the Middle Ages. For these reasons, Benedict is unpersuaded by efforts to connect Calvinism or the Protestant Reformation to metanarratives of modernization. Yet, this perspective does not prevent him from concluding that Calvinism was profoundly important for the rise of the West. It was a faith that deeply shaped the lives of individuals, families, and the communities and congregations to which they belonged. Calvinism was not a political or economic orientation but a religious sensibility that "became a vital component of [its adherents'] social identity." Reformed Protestantism had its own "style of devotion," its own "doctrinal and psychological points of friction."[36]

Benedict's disavowal of ties between Calvinism and modern political and economic life diminishes considerably the efforts to justify Reformed Protestantism in the way that both Presbyterian adherents and students of the West have. Obviously, his conclusion that Calvinism was (and is) first and foremost a religion with profound implications for personal and familial identity is a long way from Kuyper's distended remarks on behalf of Calvinism's genius. But the value of Benedict's perspective is that it makes sense of those parts of Calvinism (that is, the nature of Christian liberty and the responsibility of the magistrate) that do not fit a Whiggish interpretation, a worthwhile reminder to Presbyterian apologists for "the American way of life." The advantage is no less real for historians and social theorists. If ordinary and local aspects of human experience are as worthy of attention as public policy, legislation, or economic statistics, then Calvinism (along with its religious competitors) may still deserve attention simply as a faith—not because it created the West, but because it mattered to real people who were worried about a narrative with claims even grander than those of modernity.

NOTES

1. Abraham Kuyper, *Lectures on Calvinism* (1898; repr., Grand Rapids, Mich.: Eerdmans, 1931), 78.

2. Ibid., 108–9, 32, 34.

3. James Anthony Froude, *Calvinism: An Address Delivered at St. Andrews, March 17, 1871* (New York: Scribner, 1871), 7–8, 46.

4. The following paragraphs on Witherspoon are slightly adapted from D. G. Hart, "The Use and Abuse of Christian Liberty," in *The Faith Once Delivered: Essays in Honor of Dr. Wayne R. Spear*, ed. Anthony T. Selvaggio (Phillipsburg, N.J.: P&R Publishing, 2007), chap. 10. The best treatment of Witherspoon's politics is Mark A. Noll, *Princeton and the Republic, 1768–1822: The Search for a Christian Enlightenment in the Era of Samuel Stanhope Smith* (Princeton, N.J.: Princeton University Press, 1989), chaps. 3–4.

5. Witherspoon's sermon is reprinted in Ellis Sandoz, ed., *Political Sermons of the American Founding Era, 1730–1805*, 2 vols. (Indianapolis, Ind.: Liberty Fund, 1998), 2:549.

6. On the synthesis of Protestantism and republican politics in the era of the American founding, see Mark A. Noll, *America's God: From Jonathan Edwards to Abraham Lincoln* (New York: Oxford University Press, 2002); and Frank Lambert, *The Founding Fathers and the Place of Religion in America* (Princeton, N.J.: Princeton University Press, 2003).

7. Charles Hodge, *What Is Presbyterianism? An Address Delivered before the Presbyterian Historical Society . . .* (Philadelphia: Presbyterian Board of Publication, 1855), 14, 15, 16.

8. Ibid., 79, 78.

9. Albert Barnes, *Presbyterianism: Its Affinities* (New York: Sherwood, 1863), 10, 11.

10. Ibid., 21–22.

11. Ibid., 31, 30–31.

12. William Henry Roberts, *The Presbyterian System: Its Characteristics* (Philadelphia: Presbyterian Board of Publication and Sabbath School Work, 1895), 6, 7, 10, 11.

13. Ibid., 28, 36, 37.

14. Francis R. Beattie, *Calvinism and Modern Thought* (Philadelphia: Westminster, 1901), 46, 48.

15. Ibid., 10, 14.

16. On the effects of the fundamentalist controversy on the PCUSA, see D. G. Hart and John R. Muether, *Seeking a Better Country: 300 Years of American Presbyterianism* (Phillipsburg, N.J.: P&R Publishing, 2007), chaps. 9–10.

17. Hugh T. Kerr, *What the Presbyterian Church Stands For* (Philadelphia: Presbyterian Board of Publication and Sabbath School Work, 1919), 11, 12.

18. Leonard J. Trinterud, *The Forming of an American Tradition: A Re-examination of Colonial Presbyterianism* (Philadelphia: Westminster, 1949), 241, 252.

19. H. Gordon Harold, "Service in Founding and Preserving the Nation," in *They Seek a Country: The American Presbyterians, Some Aspects*, ed. Gaius Jackson Slosser (New York: Macmillan, 1955), 153, 162.

20. Garry Wills, *Under God: Religion and American Politics* (New York: Simon and Schuster, 1990), 321.

21. Francis A. Schaeffer, *How Should We Then Live? The Rise and Decline of Western Thought and Culture* (Old Tappan, N.J.: Revell, 1976), 109–10.

22. Quotations in this paragraph all come from Arthur C. Cochrane, ed., *Reformed Confessions of the Sixteenth Century* (1966; repr., Louisville, Ky.: Westminster John Knox, 2003), 158, 183, 217.

23. The original text of the Westminster Confession is understandably difficult to come by in American publishing. The version used here comes from the Publication Committee of the Free Presbyterian Church of Scotland, *The Confession of Faith and Larger and Shorter Catechisms . . .* (Inverness, Scotland: Eccles, 1976).

24. On the significance of the phrase "essential and necessary" to subscribing to the Westminster standards in American Presbyterianism, see John Murray, "Creed Subscription in the Presbyterian Church in the U.S.A.," in *The Practice of Confessional Subscription*, ed. David W. Hall (Lanham, Md.: University Press of America, 1995), chap. 12.

25. The following paragraphs on the American revisions of the Westminster Confession are adapted from D. G. Hart, "American Presbyterians: Exceptional," *Journal of Presbyterian History* 84, no. 1 (Spring–Summer 2006): 12–16.

26. See Publication Committee, *The Confession of Faith*.

27. For the American revisions, see *The Constitution of the Presbyterian Church (U.S.A.)*: part 1, 147, 151, 162–63, *Book of Confessions* (Louisville, Ky.: Office of the General Assembly, 1996). The American revision also includes additional material in the first paragraph of chapter 31 that describes in greater detail the value of convening synods and councils.

28. "The National Covenant; or, The Confession of Faith," reprinted in Publication Committee, *The Confession of Faith*, 351.

29. Useful articles on the King's Confession, the National Covenant, and the Solemn League and Covenant may be found in the *Dictionary of Scottish Church History and Theology*, ed. Nigel M. S. Cameron, David F. Wright, David C. Lachman, and Donald E. Meek (Downers Grove, Ill.: InterVarsity, 1993).

30. On theonomy and its critics, see Rousas John Rushdoony, *The Institutes of Biblical Law* (Nutley, N.J.: P&R Publishing, 1973); Greg L. Bahnsen, *Theonomy in Christian Ethics* (Nacogdoches, Tex.: Covenant Media, 1977); and William S. Barker and W. Robert Godfrey, eds., *Theonomy: A Reformed Critique* (Grand Rapids, Mich.: Zondervan, 1990).

31. For an overview of the Covenanter tradition before 1888, see W. Melanchthon Glasgow, *History of the Reformed Presbyterian Church in America* (Baltimore, Md.: Hill and Harvey, 1888); for the assimilation of the Reformed Presbyterians into the mainstream American Presbyterian tradition, see George P. Hutchinson, *The History*

behind the Reformed Presbyterian Church, Evangelical Synod (Cherry Hill, N.J.: Mack, 1974).

32. Reformed Presbyterian Church of North America, *The Constitution of the Reformed Presbyterian Church of North America* (Pittsburgh, Pa.: Synod of the RPCNA, 1949), 222.

33. Ibid., 208–9.

34. RPCNA, *The Constitution of the Reformed Presbyterian Church of North America*, available at http://reformedpresbyterian.org/assets/pdf/Constitution04.pdf, p. A77.

35. For a useful summary of older arguments about Calvinism's influence on modernity such as those advanced by Tocqueville and Weber, see Philip Benedict, *Christ's Churches Purely Reformed: A Social History of Calvinism* (New Haven, Conn.: Yale University Press, 2002), 533–46. For other assessments, see Ralph Barton Perry, *Puritanism and Democracy* (New York: Vanguard, 1944), chap. 5; and David Gress, *From Plato to NATO: The Idea of the West and Its Opponents* (New York: Free Press, 1998), 261.

36. Benedict, *Christ's Churches*, 544.

PART II

Theology

4

Practical Ecclesiology in John Calvin and Jonathan Edwards

Amy Plantinga Pauw

"Tho' his Principles were *Calvinistic*, yet he called no Man, Father. He thought and judged for himself, and was truly very much of an Original." This assessment of Jonathan Edwards by his protégé Samuel Hopkins has not encouraged interpretations of Edwards as a faithful bearer of John Calvin's legacy. The paucity of direct references to Calvin in Edwards's writings and the conspicuous absence of Calvin's name from Edwards's "catalogue" of books and his account book have likewise contributed to an impression that there is little direct theological connection between the two. Finally, we have Edwards's own disclaimer in the preface to *Freedom of the Will*, where he declared, "I should not take it at all amiss, to be called a Calvinist, for distinction's sake: though I utterly disclaim a dependence on Calvin, or believing the doctrines which I hold, because he believed and taught them; and cannot justly be charged with believing in everything just as he taught."[1] Particularly when it comes to Calvin's doctrine of the church, American historians have tended to take Edwards at his word. They have generally dismissed any strong theological connection with Calvin's "high" churchmanship and have read Edwards's ecclesiology as an anticipation of the populist Protestant evangelicalism that would later take center stage.

It is rare, however, for persons to be truly cognizant of their own intellectual debts. While Edwards "cannot justly be charged with believing in everything just as [Calvin] taught," Edwards's doctrine of the church displays deep commonalities with Calvin's, especially in its persistent tension between the ideals of inclusiveness and holiness. We know that Edwards did read Calvin, first of all the *Institutes of the Christian Religion*, which he quoted three times in his treatise on *Religious Affections*, and probably also some of Calvin's commentaries and other works. Moreover, the main themes of Calvin's theology were thoroughly transmitted to Edwards by the transatlantic Anglo-Puritan tradition and, to a lesser degree, by the continental Reformed scholasticism of the seventeenth and eighteenth centuries via such figures as Hermann Witsius, François Turretin, Peter Van Mastricht, and Johann Friedrich Stapfer. In his fine book on Nathaniel Taylor, Douglas Sweeney complains that "only those whose doctrinal articulations evinced a sufficient reverence for and a seemingly literal continuity with Edwards's own phraseology—or who proved so culturally conservative that they refused to adapt to the changing times—have been deemed authentically Edwardsian."[2] It would be unfortunate to replicate this false standard of authenticity in the case of John Calvin. Neither Edwards's breezy irreverence toward Calvin nor his willingness to adapt Calvin's ecclesiology to his own pastoral circumstances should disqualify him from being considered a rightful heir to Calvin's theological legacy.

Practical Theology

It has been common to trace Calvin's theological influence on Edwards with broad strokes, focusing on doctrines such as divine sovereignty, original sin, and election. But these aerial surveys of soteriology do not do justice to the practical, "on the ground" theological reflection that was at the center of their pastoral work. Both Calvin and Edwards understood theology as practical in a broad sense, as concerning knowledge about God's gracious relations with humankind, a knowledge that informed Christian life and led to the good of reconciliation and union with God. Theology is, according to Edwards, "the doctrine of living to God by Christ."[3] But their theology was also practical in the narrower sense of requiring continual pastoral discernment about the operations of grace in specific situations, and here, too, theological links between Calvin and Edwards can be discerned. Both devoted themselves to pastoral ministry; and pastoral ministry is never primarily a theological recital of God's saving deeds, a matter of standing above the fray of daily experience and witnessing to the timeless truths of the gospel. The lives of pastors revolve around the church's daily life in the world as it negotiates the material issues of community. Pastors testify to and embody divine grace through their attention to the ordinary tasks of nurtur and education, through concrete decisions about polity and budget, discovering in the process that the redeeming work of God regularly eludes human comprehension and control. In pastoral work, neither scorn for established Christian practice nor slavish adherence to it is appropriate; instead, what is required is careful and critical reflection on the difficulties and opportunities of the church's present context. Attention to this kind of practical theology reveals the theological convergences of Calvin and Edwards at a different level, one that has as much to do with the challenges of pastoral discernment as with doctrine.

Though their theological convictions about the centrality of divine grace in the salvation of sinners never wavered, their ability to discern this grace in particular pastoral situations was much less steady. Divine grace has many counterfeits, and, often, the pastoral discernment of grace is a retrospective exercise. All true grace leads to practice, but Christian practice is stuttering and ambiguous, and even God's best gifts are marred by human sin. The earthly progress of God's work of salvation seems agonizingly slow and indirect most of the time. Calvin's and Edwards's pastoral experiences yielded an unsentimental realism about the church and its wandering path toward holiness. After an overview of the theological elements that seem to make pastoral frustration endemic to Reformed views of the church, the remainder of this chapter will focus on two concrete examples of Calvin's and Edwards's practical ecclesiology: Calvin's arguments against requiring clerical celibacy and Edwards's arguments in support of the revivals. Both are cases of pastoral discernment that represented a break from established church practice and laid bare their ecclesiological commitments.

Reformed Ecclesiology

John Milton's poignant final portrait of Adam and Eve captures a central dynamic in Reformed ecclesiology. At the very end of *Paradise Lost*, the archangel Michael assures Adam and Eve that their grievous fall into sin will be remedied by Christ, who will come and restore all things. But as Adam and Eve leave Paradise, the mood is wistful: "They hand in hand with wandering steps and slow, / Through Eden took their solitary way."[4] Though they have received God's promise of salvation, they are keenly aware of the enormity of what they have lost, and they anticipate a long and difficult journey ahead. Likewise, the Reformed doctrine of the church declares that Christians live in the assurance that their salvation has been accomplished in Christ; but, as fallen creatures, their way back to Paradise is "wandering and slow." This characteristic Reformed theme is displayed in the ecclesiologies of both John Calvin and Jonathan Edwards.[5]

A Reformed narrative of the church has no Eden. Like Milton's Adam and Eve, the church on earth has always existed "after the fall," often in the midst of great religious and political turmoil. The perception of scandalous failings in the established church significantly shaped Reformed ecclesiology from the beginning. According to Calvin, God has entrusted the church with the "power of the keys" (Matthew 16:19), but Christian communities can so abuse this trust that, in them, "Christ lies hidden, half buried, the gospel overthrown, piety scattered, the worship of God nearly wiped out." Reformed ecclesiology emphatically affirms the church's peccability. It may seem unnecessary to affirm the empirically obvious, but theologies of the church have often stopped short of confessing the church's sinfulness. As George Lindbeck asserts, Christians have generally "either assumed with the Catholics that the church does not sin in itself but only [in] its members, or, with the Protestants, that it ceases to be the true church when it does." By contrast, Reformed theologians have generally been more candid about the church's failings. "We claim too much for ourselves," Calvin insisted, if we are tempted to withdraw "from the communion of the church just because the morals of all do not meet our standard or even square with the profession of Christian faith."[6]

Remaining in the fellowship of the earthly church is essential, not because the church is spiritually exemplary, but because God's promises can be trusted. Old Testament Israel is often referred to as "the Church" in early Reformed writings, and the ecclesiological significance of this should not be underestimated. The paradigm for the church's self-understanding on this model is not an idealized community of Christian disciples but the believing community of Israel, struggling and often failing to respond adequately to God's covenantal faithfulness. Like the prophets of Israel, Calvin and Edwards were capable of unstinting criticism of the moral and spiritual failings of God's people. Commenting on the Apostles' Creed, Calvin noted that the church is properly an article of belief, "because often no other distinction can be made between God's children and the ungodly, between his own flock and wild beasts." Jonathan Edwards extended this bestial metaphor even further, comparing the church to Noah's ark: just as the door of the ark "was open to receive all sorts of creatures—tigers, wolves, bears, lions, leopards, serpents, vipers, dragons— such as men would not by any means admit into the doors of their houses," so likewise "Christ stands ready to receive all, even the vilest and worst." Because of the dubious constitution of the earthly church, Calvin insisted that Christians do not properly believe in the church: "We testify that we believe in God because our mind reposes in him as truthful, and our trust rests in him."[7]

Both Calvin and Edwards found support for their vision of the church as a haven for sinners in the long Christian tradition of appealing to the church as the mother of believers. Christians are conceived in the womb of the church, fed at her breast, guided and instructed by her throughout life. As Calvin wrote in his commentary on Ephesians 4:12, "The Church is the common mother of all the godly, which bears, nourishes, and governs in the Lord both kings and commoners." Drawing, no doubt, on the experiences of his own household, Edwards declared that the church watches over and feeds her spiritual children in much the same way as "tender mothers are wont to do to their little children":

> When the mother wakes up in the night, she has her child to look after, and nourish at her breast; and it sleeps in her bosom, and it must be continually in the mother's bosom, or arms, there to be upheld and cherished. It needs its food and nourishment much oftener than adult persons; it must be fed both day and night. It must be very frequently cleansed, for 'tis very often defiled. It must in everything be gratified and pleased; the mother must bear the burden of it as she goes to and fro. This is also a lively image of the care that the church, especially the ministers of the gospel, should have of the interest of Christ committed to their care.

But both Calvin and Edwards were concerned to guard against any spiritual complacency that this tender maternal imagery might encourage. Commenting on Ephesians 4:14, Calvin insisted that there must be growth after birth. Christians are not to remain infants, eternally confined to a milk diet. In a daring analogy, Calvin declared that "the life of believers, longing constantly for their appointed state, is like adolescence."[8] In the midst of turbulent spiritual emotions and repeated moral failures, Christians are to strive by God's grace to grow into a mature life of gratitude and holiness. Portraying the earthly church as a mother not of a helpless infant but of a large band of unruly adolescents better reflects both Reformed ecclesiology and Calvin's and Edwards's pastoral experiences.

The eschatological dynamism of Reformed ecclesiology is captured in another feminine image: the church as the bride of Christ. At its best, the Reformed tradition has held these two ecclesial images of mother and bride not only in tension but also in paradoxical relation: the church as a gasping, panting mother is on her way to becoming the pristine bride of Christ.[9] The perfect holiness and faithfulness of the church as bride is an eschatological reality. While "the Lord is daily at work in smoothing out wrinkles and cleansing spots [Ephesians 5:27]," Calvin saw the earthly church as holy "in the sense that it is daily advancing and is not yet perfect."[10] He urged believers not to "toil slowly or listlessly, much less give up," but declared it "a devilish invention for our minds, while as yet we are in the earthly race, to be cocksure about our perfection." Even the lifelong process of sanctification does not yield the perfect holiness that characterizes Christ's bride. As Edwards insisted, "the time of Christ's last coming is the time of the consummation of the church's marriage with the Lamb, and the time of the complete and most perfect joy of the wedding."[11] The pastoral question for both Calvin and Edwards was the extent to which this eschatological reality could be anticipated in the visible church. As will become evident, Edwards as pastor was repeatedly tempted by an ecclesiology of glory that sought the eschatological perfection of Christ's bride within the frailties of the earthly community of saints.

The image of the church as bride must remain eschatological not only because of the imperfections of the saints, but also because the earthly church is a mixture of the regenerate and unregenerate. Some of the unregenerate will eventually experience the saving work of the Spirit, but others will be left in their lost state. Calvin and Edwards followed Augustine in positing, within and beyond the visible church, a church invisible to all but God, composed of the elect saints from every time and place. Forged in the fire of the Donatist debates, Augustine's understanding of the church rejected rigorist conceptions of the earthly Christian community that would confine its membership to the truly holy. It was a given for Augustine that the visible church is a mixed body, and he repudiated the violence and hypocrisy of premature human attempts to separate saints from the non-elect. Following Augustine, Calvin and Edwards identified the "true" church with the invisible church of the elect, its membership past and present determined by God's secret decree. It is this invisible church that will be wed to Christ. Together, they will rejoice "in consummate, uninterrupted, immutable, and everlasting glory, in the love and embraces of each other, and joint enjoyment of the love of the Father." Indeed, for Edwards, the marriage of the church with Christ is the culmination of God's magnificent work of redemption:

> The creation of the world seems to have been especially for this end,
> that the eternal Son of God might obtain a spouse, towards whom he
> might fully exercise the infinite benevolence of his nature, and to
> whom he might, as it were, open and pour forth all that immense
> fountain of condescension, love and grace that was in his heart, and
> that in this way God might be glorified.[12]

The shadow church of the truly elect stood in some tension with the Reformed insistence on the importance of the Israel-like visible church as the primary site of God's redemptive work. Appeal to an invisible church of the elect tends to diminish the significance of the comfort and spiritual nourishment provided by the visible church and encourages uneasy Christians to seek other grounds for spiritual assurance. The doctrine of the invisible church is also a tempting theological refuge for pastors tired of the stresses and disappointments of ministering to flesh-and-blood parishioners. If Calvin and Edwards regarded the invisible church as the true church in some respects, the visible church was the real context for their pastoral ministries. As pastors, they were not to speculate about the identities of the elect but, rather, to preach the good news to all and benevolently pray for the salvation of all members of the gathered community. "Christ has flung the door of mercy wide open, and stands in the door calling and crying with a loud voice to poor sinners," Edwards proclaimed in his famous sermon "Sinners in the Hands of an Angry God." But, in the end, as Brian Gerrish notes, it seems that preachers are called to be more benevolent than God, for not all who have been ardently preached to and prayed for were from eternity chosen by God as members of the invisible church.[13]

The tension between the ecclesial concepts represented by the images of mother and bride creates distinctive pastoral dilemmas in Reformed ecclesiology. Calvin, and Edwards after him, attempted to draw together the Catholic notion of the church as a sacrament of grace for all sinners and the radical Reformation image of the holy gathered church. In Calvin's Geneva and in the Puritan society Edwards longed to restore in New England, the church was to exist both as an established institution demanding the allegiance of everyone *and* as a community set apart by its disciplined life. The church strives for comprehensive membership *and* for visible holiness. The interplay of these aims can be seen in Reformed theologies of the Lord's Supper. The emphasis on church as mother led Calvin to call for frequent celebrations of communion to nurture and strengthen faith, while the stress on church as bride encouraged an ongoing concern, though variably enacted, to fence the table against all who would pollute it by their unworthiness. In Edwards's church in Northampton, the clash between views of the Lord's Supper as nourishment for the spiritually weak and as love feast for none but the truly faithful brought an acrimonious end to his pastorate.

In their doctrine of the church, Calvin and Edwards seemed to set themselves up for pastoral frustration. Their rigorous ecclesiology called for both breadth of membership and depth of spiritual transformation, and yet their theological anthropology reminded them that they had only mediocre human material with which to work. As Edwards's biographer George Marsden notes, "Edwards's ideal for the church and ultimately for the town was that everyone should follow a virtually monastic standard for all of life."[14] Given the fallenness of humanity in general, and the pragmatic, family-oriented religiosity of

Northampton in particular, this was clearly an unrealistic aim. Calvin and Edwards both strove for a high degree of spiritual self-discipline themselves, but they were continually disappointed by what they judged to be the spiritual and moral laxness of their parishioners. It is not surprising, then, that impatience and uncharitableness could get the best of them at times. What follows are two snapshots of their pastoral responses to this theological conundrum.

John Calvin on Clerical Celibacy

Calvin's arguments against requiring clerical celibacy were a part of his polemic against what he saw as the Roman Catholic corruption of church practices and theology. Celibacy, in Calvin's view, while a good in itself, had become an idol, a law that the clergy used to justify themselves, to proclaim their own righteousness, and to tyrannize others. "There was no law requiring celibacy in the early church," Calvin noted, "but an absurd admiration for it became so strong that marriage was condemned as shameful for bishops. Afterward, the severity of a law gradually crept in and has produced countless forms of evils for us." According to Calvin, the result of making celibacy mandatory for clergy was to introduce "a sink of iniquities" into the church and to "cast many souls into the abyss of despair."[15]

In his commentary on 1 Corinthians 7, Calvin was explicit about what he saw as the practical evils of enforced clerical celibacy. Because "pious and prudent men" refused to vow perpetual celibacy, "the church was robbed of very many good and faithful ministers." Meanwhile, those who imprudently vowed celibacy, without being "endowed with the power and gift" to keep that vow, were assailed by lust and, after a time, resorted to keeping concubines and to even more "monstrous enormities." From Calvin's perspective, these practical troubles grew from a mistaken theology of sin and grace. The church had promulgated a falsely exalted view of clergy as free from the weaknesses that assailed ordinary Christians. This led to regarding marriage "as a kind of life unbecoming the holiness of their order." Calvin agreed with the apostle Paul that the unmarried state is a good thing; in his view, sexual continency "lends not a little dignity to the ministry." But, in Calvin's experience, ministers of the gospel did not tower over other Christians in spiritual discipline and maturity. Of the gifts that God has given to "properly adorn" the ministry, it was clear to Calvin that "celibacy is not among them." By extravagantly honoring celibacy, "good men [are] frightened away from marriage, even when their need of it is urgent." It is no good for ministers to pretend that they have "made an agreement with God as to perpetual strength" from sexual temptation. Calvin thought that "the infirmity of our flesh" exposed all Christians, ministers included, to Satan's wiles, and they should not "aspire beyond their limits" by rashly vowing "what is not in their power and what they will not obtain as a gift."[16]

Furthermore, in Calvin's view, even if some church authorities found that clerical celibacy was not "an obstacle for [them] at present," that was not reason enough to continue this practice. "Austerity" about this matter, he insisted, "can be a great obstacle to future generations, for whom, as you know, we must take thought."[17] Augustinian that he was, Calvin foresaw no huge gains in the spiritual and moral discipline of ministers before the eschaton. Given the ongoing Christian struggle against sin, unduly austere practices that exerted pressure and tyranny on future generations of ministers would only lead to spiritual hypocrisy or despair.

While Calvin regarded celibacy as "an excellent gift," he mocked those who extolled it "as if it were the most excellent of all virtues," or even a form of the worship of God. "Celibacy has its own disadvantages," Calvin coolly noted, even apart from "the difficulty of sexual continence." Indeed, he found that "celibate men are distracted by no slighter and fewer distractions than married men." In an uncharacteristically autobiographical aside in a sermon on 1 Timothy, Calvin confided:

> For me, I would not want anyone to attribute my unmarried state to
> virtue; if I could best serve God in marriage, it would be a vice to stay
> as I am. Being unable to claim before God and others that I was
> unmarried would not worry me at all. But I know my weakness,
> so that perhaps a woman would not find herself well with me.
> However that may be, if I abstain, it is only to be freer to serve God.
> It is not that I think myself more virtuous than my brothers.

Even if every minister received the gift of celibacy—and, as it was, Calvin thought that this was true of "scarce a hundredth part of them"—this gift, too, has been marred by human sin and would not place clergy anywhere near the "angelical perfection" that some claimed for themselves.[18]

Like celibacy, marriage, too, is a good and holy gift from God, and Calvin vigorously denounced those who would "despise it as if it savoured of the pollution of the flesh." "Christ deems marriage worthy of such honor that he wills it to be an image of his sacred union with the church," Calvin declared in the *Institutes*. "What more splendid commendation could be spoken of the dignity of marriage?" Yet, in his sermons and commentaries, he was remarkably candid about its real-life difficulties. He did not respond to those who exalted the holiness of celibacy by exalting the holy joys of marriage. Calvin's pastoral experience, as indicated by the frequency with which marital problems surface in the *Registers of the Consistory of Geneva*, seems to have tempered his estimate of the benefits and pleasures of marriage. While God instituted marriage as "a good plan, sin afterwards came in to corrupt that institution of God." The result, according to Calvin's frank assessment, was that "in place of so great a blessing there has been substituted a grievous punishment, so that marriage is the source and occasion of many miseries." Marriage, Calvin conceded, is "attended by innumerable vexations" and afflicted by many "anxieties and distresses." The annoyances of marriage are indeed so great that "Satan has always endeavoured to make it an object of hatred and detestation, in order to withdraw men from it." Thus, though God ordained marriage for humankind's general advantage, it is attended by so much disagreeableness that many are prone to despise it. In humanity's sinful state, marriage is an effective but bitter medicine. "Let us therefore learn not to be delicate and saucy," Calvin counseled, "but to use with reverence the gifts of God, even if there be something in them that does not please us." In the eschaton, there will be no marriage nor giving in marriage (Matthew 22:30), for the church will be the bride of Christ. But, for the time being, considering ministers' urgent need of it, marriage is a gift to be accepted gratefully, despite its innumerable vexations.[19]

Jonathan Edwards on Revivals

Innumerable vexations also attended the eighteenth-century New England revivals. There are some broad parallels between Calvin's defense of married clergy and Jonathan Edwards's defense of the revivals. Like clerical marriage, the revivals were viewed by their opponents as an unwarranted break with established church tradition, a threat to the order and holiness of the church. Edwards, like Calvin, was in the difficult pastoral position of defending what he saw as a gift of God when there were legitimate reasons to despise it. In polemical contexts, Edwards could be as uncompromising in defense of the revivals as Calvin was in the case of marriage, yet there were also moments of candor, when Edwards was honest about the revivals' bitter fruit. But whereas Calvin's sober assessment of marriage remained quite consistent, Edwards's theological evaluations of the revivals were as volatile as the revivals themselves, revealing the strains that pastoral circumstances placed on his ecclesiology.

In the immediate wake of the Northampton area revivals of 1734–1735, Edwards was effusive about both their extent and their positive effects. In a May 1735 letter to Benjamin Colman, later expanded into *A Faithful Narrative of the Surprising Work of God*, Edwards described at length the "truly wonderful and astonishing manner of the Spirit's saving influences," reveling:

[How] many seem to have been suddenly taken from a loose way
of living, and to be so changed as to become truly holy, spiritual,
heavenly persons; 'tis extraordinary as to the degrees of gracious
communications, and the abundant measures in which the Spirit of
God has been poured out on many persons; 'tis extraordinary as to
the extent of it, God's Spirit being so remarkably poured out on so
many towns at once, and its making such swift progress from place
to place.[20]

This "surprising work of God" was understandably gratifying to Edwards, both
as a minister and as a writer who early on had ambitions to make a name for
himself beyond the colonial hinterlands. Moreover, the revivals relieved some
of the pastoral frustrations endemic to Edwards's Reformed ecclesiology: now
that nearly everyone in Northampton seemed to be exhibiting extraordinary
spiritual progress, a comprehensive community of converted and sanctified
believers did not seem completely out of reach.

But this relief from pastoral frustration proved disappointingly fleeting.
In 1737, as the first edition of A Faithful Narrative appeared, Edwards was
writing again to Colman, confessing that it was "a great damp to that joy to
consider how we decline, and what decays that lively spirit in religion suffers
amongst us, while others are rejoicing and praising God for us."[21] By the end
of the 1730s, the gap between Northampton's international reputation for
holiness and its spiritual declension had yawned even wider. It was clear to
Edwards that he had seriously overestimated the genuine spiritual gains of
the revivals. The way of redemption for his parishioners was to be wandering
and slow after all.

Despite their mixed results, these early revivals seem to have encouraged
Edwards to attribute glorious significance to the role of periodic awakenings in
God's work of redemption. This revivalist "theology of glory," to borrow Avihu
Zakai's characterization,[22] was a departure from Calvin's pragmatism about the
visible church and seems to have fostered in Edwards, at least intermittently, an
un-Calvinist optimism regarding the prospects for spiritual advancement in
his congregation and in Protestantism more generally. But pastoral realities in
Northampton repeatedly chastened Edwards's theology of glory, drawing him
back toward a Calvinist sobriety about the church's progress toward redemption. If revivals were indeed the appointed means of establishing Christ's kingdom, the spiritual gains they brought seemed disturbingly transitory. Edwards
lamented how the surprising outpourings of the Spirit in his congregation
could be closely followed by a deluge of party spirit, moral confusion, and spiritual arrogance. Even what Edwards judged to be the genuine work of the Spirit

was unsettling, threatening the institutional control of established ministers like himself and sowing agitation, innovation, and dissension.

In a December 1740 sermon on 1 Chronicles 15:12–13, Edwards expressed remorse about the untempered enthusiasm he had nurtured during Northampton's revivals:

> Let us strictly inquire whether or no we were not too much lifted up with our privilege. Was there too much of an appearance of a public pride, if I may so call it? Were we not lifted up with the honor that God had put upon us as a people, beyond most other people? Were we not foolishly taken with our comparative honor, and pleased to see ourselves lifted above others, too much forgetting what a stiff-necked unworthy people we were? . . . Did it not make us something self-sufficient in our way of talking to others, as though we thought we were the *people*, and we were confident that we ourselves were guides to the blind, and a light of them that are in darkness, and instructors of the foolish, and teachers of babes?

Rehearsing the central themes of Calvinist soteriology, Edwards reasserted the ambiguous, conflict-ridden nature of the earthly work of redemption, noting that, even after conversion, Christians will have "an exceeding disposition" to self-righteousness as long as they live and, in particular, will be tempted to "make a righteousness of spiritual experiences."[23] Edwards was still reeling from the blow to his own pastoral pride, and, in the spiritual trough following the revivals, Edwards found patient, generous dealings with his "stiff-necked unworthy" parishioners to be difficult.

So, perhaps, it is not surprising that, when the winds of revival blew through New England again in the larger colonial awakenings of the 1740s, Edwards was tempted once more by a theology of glory regarding the course of God's work of redemption. In *Some Thoughts on the Revival*, his fullest account of the ongoing revivals in New England, Edwards reached for biblical typology to portray the significance of the "new world," particularly New England, in God's overarching purposes. The New World is like Joseph, who "fed and saved the world when [it was] ready to perish with famine, and was a fruitful bough by a well, whose branches ran over the wall, and was blessed with all manner of blessings and precious things, of heaven and earth, through the good-will of him that dwelt in the bush." In the same way, Edwards predicted, America would feed and save the Old World spiritually, having been given "the honor of communicating religion in its most glorious state" to the rest of humanity.[24]

Unfortunately, even religion in its most glorious state was plagued by embarrassing disorders and bitter divisions. In his analysis of the colonial revivals, James West Davidson has described an "afflictive model of progress" that paradoxically made it possible for Edwards and his contemporaries to see the most troubling aspects of the revivals "as confirmation of their validity because 'the more Satan was chained, the more he raged.'" There would be, Edwards predicted, "many sore conflicts and terrible convulsions, and many changes, revivings, and intermissions, and returns of dark clouds, and threatening appearances, before this work shall have subdued the world, and Christ's kingdom shall be everywhere established and settled in peace." In the uncompromising apologetics of *Some Thoughts on the Revival*, Edwards saw satanic agency at work principally in those who criticized the revivals' alarming excesses and failed to recognize the seasons "when God manifests himself in such a great work for his church." Davidson notes, "That was the beauty of the afflictive model of progress. It promised redemption of a sort which the mixed temper of the Awakening could provide."[25]

Eager to avoid repeating the embarrassment of spiritual declension following the earlier revivals, Edwards drew up an elaborate church covenant in the spring of 1742 in an attempt to preserve the spiritual progress achieved during the revivals. As George Marsden remarks, Edwards was "like the disciple Peter on the mount of transfiguration, . . . proposing to build a permanent structure that would conserve so spectacular a spiritual outpouring." But Edwards's pastoral strategy proved futile, and, soon after the covenant ceremony, Northampton returned to its selfish and divisive ways. Across the New England region, spiritual fervor was also on the decline, and the shocking irregularities and virulent hostilities unleashed by New Light sympathizers made claims that the revivals were the work of the Holy Spirit increasingly implausible. As Edwards confessed in a letter to the Reverend William McCullogh, "Many high professors are fallen, some into gross immoralities; some into the opinions of sectaries; some into a rooted, spiritual pride, enthusiasm, and an incorrigible wildness of behavior; some into a cold, carnal frame of mind, showing a great indifference to things of religion."[26] Once again, Edwards's revivalist theology of glory was deflated by pastoral realities.

Edwards's theological response to the discouraging outcome of the revivals was to draw closer to Calvin's ecclesiological principles. Rather than an afflictive model of progress, Calvin could be said to have embraced an afflictive model of Christian existence, famously describing his pastorate in Geneva as "that cross, on which one had to perish daily a thousand times over." The church's comfort, in Calvin's view, is not trusting that its afflictions paradoxically indicate spiritual progress but simply the assurance that the church is finally in God's hands, come what may. Edwards's mature reflections on the revivals reflect a similar view. In words that could have come from Calvin's pen, Edwards wrote to a Scottish correspondent in November 1745:

> [E]vents have tended remarkably to show us our weakness, infirmity, insufficiency, and great and universal need of God's help; we have been many ways rebuked for our self-confidence and looking to instruments, and trusting in an arm of flesh; and God is now showing us that we are nothing, and letting us see that we can do nothing.[27]

Edwards's earlier self-confident attempts to explain and capitalize on the New England revivals now had given way to an admission of human ignorance and weakness. Only God could pierce through the obscurities and ambiguities of the wandering and slow path of human redemption.

Calvin's ecclesiological legacy in Edwards's reflections on the revivals is displayed most clearly in his 1746 treatise *Religious Affections*. The revivals had brought home to him the mystery "that so much good, and so much bad, should be mixed together in the church of God." But the revivals had also revealed the fallibility of his pastoral judgment in distinguishing the good from the bad. A humbled Edwards exclaimed, "How great therefore may the resemblance be, as to all outward expression and appearances, between an hypocrite and a true saint! . . . And what an indecent self-exaltation, and arrogance is it, in poor fallible dark mortals, to pretend that they can determine and know, who are really sincere and upright before God, and who are not!"[28] That this humility would not survive the end of Edwards's Northampton pastorate only underlines the Calvinist insistence that ministers are promised no "perpetual strength" in confronting spiritual temptations.

Unlike Edwards's earlier treatises on the revivals, *Religious Affections* was directed primarily at the misguided *supporters* of the revivals. Edwards's criticisms of those who claimed extraordinary gifts of the Spirit have striking parallels with Calvin's admonitions to the defenders of mandatory clerical celibacy. According to Edwards, the extreme New Lights were deluded about their degree of spiritual strength and were prone to an extravagant honoring of their particular spiritual gifts. Because they claimed a much higher degree of holiness than they actually had, they were driven to hypocrisy. They were also guilty of dangerous spiritual arrogance, wrongly assuming the prerogative to judge others as deficient in spiritual gifts. The misguided severity of their standards for genuine conversion plunged other Christians into despair and wounded the community of faith. Edwards, who had himself struggled with unduly austere understandings of the required steps in Christian conversion, was, like Calvin, not eager to burden future generations of believers with narrow understandings of the Spirit's work in individuals.

The remedy that Edwards proposed to misguided New Lights in *Religious Affections* is a reminder that the visible church was still for Edwards, as it was for Calvin, the center of God's redeeming work. Edwards's hope had been that revivals would strengthen the life of local congregations, including their traditional patterns of deference to established pastoral authority. The revivals were supposed to be a catalyst for the revitalization of traditional ecclesial structures, not a replacement for them. The populist, schismatic character of revivalist religion surprised and dismayed Edwards. "Christian practice," he concluded at the end of *Religious Affections*, "is the sign of signs, in this sense that it is the great evidence which confirms and crowns all other signs of godliness." Contrary to New Light claims, the presence of the Spirit was not primarily a matter of personal intuition or private experience. Instead, holy love visibly exercised in the Christian community was at the heart of the Spirit's work. Loving practice within the established community of faith is not only "one kind or part of Christian experience," but "both reason and Scripture represent it as the chief, and most important, and most distinguishing part of it."[29] The Holy Spirit's presence in the heart is most clearly displayed by outward acts of love within the community of the visible church.

Edwards would not live to see another large revival in the colonies. His fondest hopes for the New England revivals dashed, he became disillusioned about the breadth of the Spirit's work there. In the bitter communion controversy that spelled the end of his Northampton pastorate, Edwards abandoned the Reformed ecclesiological tension between comprehensive membership and visible holiness. Though acknowledging that "you can't keep out hypocrites, when all is said and done," his treatise *An Humble Inquiry* defended stringent membership requirements that attempted to do just that. Written in 1749, at the height of his pastoral disappointment and frustration, this treatise revealed Edwards's yearning for a realized eschatology in the life of the church. Not surprisingly, Edwards's "new" views on qualifications for communion were most popular among Separatists and "strict Congregationalists." Calvinist that he was, this was a source of dismay to him. Calvin's eucharistic theology had maintained an uneasy balance between open invitation and table fencing: the Lord's Supper was at once nourishment for the spiritually weak and "the sacred food that Our Saviour Jesus Christ gives to none but the faithful of his own household." Under the pressure of his pastoral circumstances, Edwards lost that precarious theological equilibrium and insisted that communion privileges in the earthly church belonged solely to those who could already declare themselves "by profession and in visibility a part of that heavenly and divine family." Tellingly, Edwards reverted to nuptial images to describe this required profession of faith: "In marriage the bride professes to yield to the bridegroom's suit, and to take him for her husband, renouncing all others, and to give up herself to him to be entirely and forever possessed by him as his wife. But he that professes this towards Christ, professes saving faith." In the ecclesiology of *An Humble Inquiry*, the earthly church was to be the faithful, pristine bride of Christ. The mother church, standing "ready to receive all, even the vilest and worst,"[30] was nowhere in view.

Eschatology and Providence

Calvin was an amillennialist who professed not to understand the book of Revelation. He rejected the idea, common in his time, that the world was just about to end and, along with it, the anxious preoccupation with eschatological signs. Calvin's pious agnosticism about eschatological details meant that the doctrine of providence served as the main backdrop for his ecclesiology. Providence, as Joe R. Jones notes, is "a grammar of a long and meaningful middle."[31] Pastoral faithfulness in this "long and meaningful middle" requires sustaining hope in God's redemptive presence without presuming to know its exact present contours, much less the day or the hour of the kingdom's arrival. The frailties of the church's past require that the central pastoral task not be the maintenance of a historic tradition but the prayerful discernment of the best *present* form of ecclesial life. Pastoral faithfulness may thus involve advocacy for genuine change. For Calvin, this included the discernment that pastors should be permitted to marry. But marriage was not a harbinger of the kingdom: it was God's gift to the church to sustain it for the long haul of earthly existence.

Edwards's intermittent departures from Calvin's ecclesiology were, in part, a function of his eschatology. Edwards spent much of his adult life making "notes on the apocalypse" and viewed his pastoral triumphs and frustrations through the eschatological lens of the saints' progress toward glory. He fit the particulars of his own ministry into a larger narrative in which "all the unhappy commotions, tumults, and calamities" attending the revivals eventually subside, "the whole heathen world" is converted, and the church enjoys "the happy state of the millennium." For Edwards, the colonial revivals were a harbinger of this glorious millennial future. What made his revivalism un-Calvinist was not his pastoral discernment that revivals could be a new gift of God to the church but his tendency, in the process, to lose sight of God's continuing redemptive presence in the church over the long haul. By defining the advance of God's work of redemption in terms of special seasons of revival and awakening, he was tempted to view ordinary life in the church, in Sidney Mead's words, as "a struggle across dull plateaus between peaks of spiritual refreshing," an ecclesiological perspective that fed Edwards's pastoral impatience and frustration.[32]

Yet, it has been the argument of this chapter that the ecclesiological contrast between Edwards and Calvin should not be too sharply drawn. If the grand narrative of Edwards's theology sometimes departed from Calvin in its confident eschatological prognostications, his concrete pastoral experience repeatedly threw him back on the doctrine of providence.[33] While, in the privacy of his study, Edwards continued to exult in what he took to be definitive signs of progress toward the last days, revivals and millennial expectations were not the totality of Edwards's pastoral experience. The world he encountered both in Northampton and on the Stockbridge frontier was a precarious place full of disappointments and unforeseen calamities; much of the affliction in Christian lives could not be neatly accommodated in a theological algorithm of redemptive progress. As Edwards preached at the funeral of a beloved minister, often the best that bewildered and disheartened Christians could do was to spread their sorrows before Jesus.[34] The sorrows and frustrations of Edwards's pastoral experience drew his practical ecclesiology closer to a Calvinist view of the peccable church existing in the long and meaningful middle of divine providence.

Ecclesiologies of glory continue to tempt North American Christians even in the twenty-first century. In the fragmented landscape of North American Protestantism, one trend is the resurgence of a Calvinist evangelicalism that claims Jonathan Edwards as one of its heroes. Ironically, it is marked by a glorification of heterosexual marriage and a confident appeal to individual religious experience. Calvin's frankness about the vexations that Christians experience in marriage and Edwards's admonitions against the opportunities for self-deception lurking in reliance on personal religious experience are nowhere in view. In its traditionalism, this contemporary ecclesiology of glory has abandoned Calvin's and Edwards's willingness to call established church practices into question and to improvise appropriate pastoral strategies. The church is seen as the emissary of truth and the exemplar of holiness for a dark and corrupt world, not the nurturer of the spiritually weak and immature. Edwards's dismayed recognition "that so much good, and so much bad, should be mixed together in the church of God" has been lost and, with it, the modesty of a practical ecclesiology that aims, in Karl Barth's words, at "doing the relatively better relatively well."[35]

Perhaps the twenty-first century, marking the 500th anniversary of Calvin's birth, will also give us another H. Richard Niebuhr, who lifted up both Calvin and Edwards as theologians who help us to face resolutely the hard and unpalatable facts about God and ourselves.[36] In the meantime, the ecclesiological legacy of Calvin and Edwards lives on in the unsentimental realism of count-less pastors who quietly fund the spiritual capital of North American churches with a combination of pastoral improvisation and trust in God's redemptive perseverance.

NOTES

1. Samuel Hopkins, *The Life and Character of the Late Reverend Mr. Jonathan Edwards* (Boston: Kneeland, 1765), 41; Jonathan Edwards, *The Works of Jonathan Edwards*, vol. 1, *Freedom of the Will*, ed. Paul Ramsey (New Haven, Conn.: Yale University Press, 1957), 131.

2. Douglas A. Sweeney, *Nathaniel Taylor, New Haven Theology, and the Legacy of Jonathan Edwards* (New York: Oxford University Press, 2003), 10.

3. Jonathan Edwards, "Thorough Knowledge of Divine Truth," in *The Works of Jonathan Edwards*, vol. 22, *Sermons and Discourses, 1739–1742*, ed. Harry S. Stout, Nathan O. Hatch, and Kyle P. Farley (New Haven, Conn.: Yale University Press, 2003), 86.

4. John Milton, *Paradise Lost*, 2nd ed., ed. Alastair Fowler (Harlow, England: Pearson Education, 2007), 678. Edwards listed *Paradise Lost* twice in his "catalogue" of books he wished to obtain or consult.

5. A fuller exposition of Reformed ecclesiology can be found in Amy Plantinga Pauw, "The Graced Infirmity of the Church," in *Feminist and Womanist Essays in Reformed Dogmatics*, ed. Amy Plantinga Pauw and Serene Jones (Louisville, Ky.: Westminster John Knox, 2006), 189–203.

6. John Calvin, *Institutes of the Christian Religion*, ed. John T. McNeill, trans. Ford Lewis Battles (Philadelphia: Westminster, 1960), 4.2.12; George Lindbeck, "The Gospel's Uniqueness: Election and Untranslatability," in *The Church in a Postliberal Age*, ed. James J. Buckley (Grand Rapids, Mich.: Eerdmans, 2002), 246; Calvin, *Institutes*, 4.1.18.

7. Calvin, *Institutes*, 4.1.2; Jonathan Edwards, *The Works of Jonathan Edwards*, vol. 15, *Notes on Scripture*, ed. Stephen J. Stein (New Haven, Conn.: Yale University Press, 1998), 271; Calvin, *Institutes*, 4.1.2.

8. John Calvin, *Calvin's New Testament Commentaries*, ed. David W. Torrance and Thomas F. Torrance, vol. 11, *The Epistles of Paul the Apostle to the Galatians, Ephesians, Philippians, and Colossians*, trans. T. H. L. Parker (Grand Rapids, Mich.: Eerdmans, 1965), 181; Edwards, *Notes on Scripture*, 289; Calvin, *Epistles of Paul the Apostle*, 182–83.

9. I explore the interplay of these images in Amy Plantinga Pauw, "The Church as Mother and Bride in the Reformed Tradition: Challenge and Promise," in *Many Voices, One God: Being Faithful in a Pluralistic World*, ed. Walter Brueggemann and George Stroup (Louisville, Ky.: Westminster John Knox, 1998), 122–38.

10. Calvin, *Institutes*, 4.1.17. Here, Calvin disagreed with his Anabaptist contemporaries, who found in nuptial imagery "a description or lifelike portrait of the Christian congregation," not only "in the perfection of heavenly existence," but also "how it goes on here," in the power of the Spirit. See Dietrich Philips, "The Church of

God," in *Spiritual and Anabaptist Writers*, ed. George H. Williams and Angel M. Mergal (Philadelphia: Westminster, 1970), 255.

11. Calvin, *Institutes*, 4.1.21; Jonathan Edwards, "Church's Marriage to Her Sons, and to Her God," in *The Works of Jonathan Edwards*, vol. 25, *Sermons and Discourses, 1743–1758*, ed. Wilson H. Kimnach (New Haven, Conn.: Yale University Press, 2006), 183.

12. Edwards, "Church's Marriage," 184, 187.

13. Jonathan Edwards, "Sinners in the Hands of an Angry God," in *Sermons and Discourses, 1739–1742*, 416; B. A. Gerrish, *Grace and Gratitude: The Eucharistic Theology of John Calvin* (Minneapolis, Minn.: Fortress, 1993), 171.

14. George Marsden, *Jonathan Edwards: A Life* (New Haven, Conn.: Yale University Press, 2003), 160.

15. John Calvin, *Calvin's Ecclesiastical Advice*, trans. Mary Beaty and Benjamin W. Farley (Louisville, Ky.: Westminster John Knox, 1991), 115; Calvin, *Institutes*, 4.12.23.

16. John Calvin, *Calvin's Commentaries*, vol. 20, *Commentary on the Epistles of Paul to the Corinthians*, vol. 1, trans. John Pringle (Grand Rapids, Mich.: Baker, 1993), 233; Calvin, *Calvin's Ecclesiastical Advice*, 115; Calvin, *Commentary on the Epistles of Paul*, 229, 232.

17. Calvin, *Calvin's Ecclesiastical Advice*, 115.

18. Calvin, *Commentary on the Epistles of Paul*, 232–33; Calvin, *Calvin's Ecclesiastical Advice*, 114; Calvin, "Vingtunième Sermon sur la Première à Timothée," in *Corpus Reformatorum*, vol. 81 (Braunschweig: Schwetschke, 1895; repr., New York: Johnson Reprint, 1964), 255 (my translation); Calvin, *Commentary on the Epistles of Paul*, 233.

19. Calvin, *Calvin's Commentaries*, vol. 21, *Commentaries on the Epistles to Timothy, Titus, and Philemon*, trans. William Pringle (Grand Rapids, Mich.: Baker Book House, 1993), 134; Calvin, *Institutes*, 4.12.24; Calvin, *Commentary on the Epistles of Paul*, 224; Calvin, *Commentaries on the Epistles to Timothy, Titus, and Philemon*, 134; Calvin, *Commentary on the Epistles of Paul*, 255; Calvin, *Calvin's Commentaries*, vol. 16, *Commentary on a Harmony of the Evangelists, Matthew, Mark, and Luke*, vol. 2, trans. William Pringle (Grand Rapids, Mich.: Baker Book House, 1993), 386, 385–86. A book that deals with marriage in the consistory records is John Witte Jr. and Robert Kingdon, *Sex, Marriage, and Family Life in John Calvin's Geneva: Courtship, Engagement, and Marriage* (Grand Rapids, Mich.: Eerdmans, 2005).

20. Jonathan Edwards, *The Works of Jonathan Edwards*, vol. 4, *The Great Awakening*, ed. C. C. Goen (New Haven, Conn.: Yale University Press, 1972), 101, 107.

21. Jonathan Edwards, *The Works of Jonathan Edwards*, vol. 16, *Letters and Personal Writings*, ed. George S. Claghorn (New Haven, Conn.: Yale University Press, 1998), 67.

22. Avihu Zakai, *Jonathan Edwards's Philosophy of History: The Reenchantment of the World in the Age of Enlightenment* (Princeton, N.J.: Princeton University Press, 2003), 56–58.

23. Jonathan Edwards, "Bringing the Ark to Zion a Second Time," in *Sermons and Discourses 1739–1742*, 255, 256.

24. Edwards, *The Great Awakening*, 354–55.

25. James West Davidson, *The Logic of Millennial Thought: Eighteenth-Century New England* (New Haven, Conn.: Yale University Press, 1977), 169; Edwards, *Letters and Personal Writings*, 136; Edwards, *The Great Awakening*, 349; Davidson, *The Logic of Millennial Thought*, 168.

26. Marsden, *Jonathan Edwards*, 262; Edwards, *Letters and Personal Writings*, 135.

27. John Calvin to Guillaume Farel, March 29, 1540, in *Letters of John Calvin*, vol. 1, ed. Jules Bonnet (Whitefish, Mont.: Kessinger, 2006), 151; Edwards, *Letters and Personal Writings*, 181.

28. Jonathan Edwards, *The Works of Jonathan Edwards*, vol. 2, *Religious Affections*, ed. John E. Smith (New Haven, Conn.: Yale University Press, 1959), 85, 183–84.

29. Ibid., 444, 451.

30. Jonathan Edwards, *The Works of Jonathan Edwards*, vol. 12, *Ecclesiastical Writings*, ed. David D. Hall (New Haven, Conn.: Yale University Press, 1994), 310; Kenneth P. Minkema, "Jonathan Edwards: A Theological Life," in *The Princeton Companion to Jonathan Edwards*, ed. Sang Hyun Lee (Princeton, N.J.: Princeton University Press, 2005), 11; John Calvin, "The Form of Prayers and Manner of Ministering the Sacrament according to the Use of the Ancient Church," quoted in John T. McNeill, *The History and Character of Calvinism* (Oxford: Oxford University Press, 1954), 151; Edwards, *Ecclesiastical Writings*, 321, 205; Edwards, *Notes on Scripture*, 271.

31. Joe R. Jones, *A Grammar of Christian Faith: Systematic Explorations in Christian Life and Doctrine*, 2 vols. (Lanham, Md.: Rowman and Littlefield, 2002), 1:259.

32. Edwards, "Notes on the Apocalypse," in *The Works of Jonathan Edwards*, vol. 5, *Apocalyptic Writings*, ed. Stephen J. Stein (New Haven, Conn.: Yale University Press, 1977), 411; Sidney E. Mead, *The Lively Experiment: The Shaping of Christianity in America* (New York: Harper and Row, 1963), 125.

33. I draw out this contrast between Edwards's theological grand narrative and his pastoral experience in Amy Plantinga Pauw, "Edwards as American Theologian: Grand Narratives and Pastoral Narratives," in *Jonathan Edwards at 300: Essays on the Tercentenary of His Birth*, ed. Harry S. Stout, Kenneth P. Minkema, and Caleb J. D. Maskell (Lanham, Md.: University Press of America, 2005), 14–24.

34. Edwards, "The Sorrows of the Bereaved Spread before Jesus," in *Sermons and Discourses 1739–1742*, 464–75.

35. Edwards, *Religious Affections*, 85; Karl Barth, *The Christian Life: Church Dogmatics IV, 4: Lecture Fragments*, trans. Geoffrey W. Bromiley (Grand Rapids, Mich.: Eerdmans, 1981), 271.

36. H. Richard Niebuhr, preface to Joseph Haroutunian, *Wisdom and Folly in Religion*, quoted in Stephen D. Crocco, "Edwards's Intellectual Legacy," in *The Cambridge Companion to Jonathan Edwards*, ed. Stephen J. Stein (Cambridge: Cambridge University Press, 2007), 312.

5

"Falling Away from the General Faith of the Reformation"? The Contest over Calvinism in Nineteenth-Century America

Douglas A. Sweeney

"From an early period in the history of the Church, there have been two great systems of doctrine in perpetual conflict." So wrote Princeton's Charles Hodge in April 1851 amidst a polemic against what he considered New England's modern heresies. "The one [system] begins with God, the other with man. The one has for its object the vindication of the Divine supremacy and sovereignty in the salvation of men; the other [contends for] the rights of human nature." Hodge went on to label these systems "Augustinian" and "Pelagian" (or "anti-Augustinian") but described the "Augustinian" system in largely Calvinist terms—terms that seemed to suggest that, in his opinion, Princeton's own Calvinism was nothing less than Christian orthodoxy at its best. "It is an undeniable historical fact," Hodge claimed of his system, "that [it] underlies the piety of the Church in all ages. It is the great granitic formation whose peaks tower toward heaven, and draw thence the waters of life. . . . It has withstood all changes, and it still stands. Heat and cold, snow and rain, gentle abrasion and violent convulsions leave it as it was. It cannot be moved." To those who objected to the "tone of confidence" with which he spoke, Hodge retorted, "How can we help it? A man behind the walls of Gibraltar, or of Ehrenbreitstein, cannot, if he would, tremble" before feeble assaults on their integrity. "His confidence is due to his position, not to a consciousness of personal strength. . . . We then, who are within these old walls which have stood for ages, even from the beginning, who can look around and see the names of all generations of saints inscribed on those walls, and who feel the solid rock of God's word under their feet, must be excused for a feeling of security."[1]

Hodge and his colleagues at old Princeton have earned a reputation for making brash pronouncements such as this, for assuming that they had been appointed as keepers of orthodoxy. Many have heard of Hodge's statement, made on numerous occasions, that "a new idea never originated" at Princeton Seminary, whose faculty simply taught the faith that God had "once delivered" (Jude 3).[2] Others have read the works of Hodge's colleagues at the school, noting the "tone of confidence" with which they, too, were wont to suggest that they possessed the one, true faith. As B. B. Warfield stated roughly a half century after Hodge defended his "great granitic formation," Princeton's Calvinism was nothing more than "religion in its purity." There is "no true religion in the world," Warfield boasted, "which is not Calvinistic—Calvinistic in its essence, Calvinistic in its implications." Calvinism "is not merely the hope of true religion in the world: it *is* true religion in the world—as far as true religion is in the world at all."[3]

Such bravado notwithstanding, Hodge and Warfield did turn out to be as dependable as anyone at defending Calvinist orthodoxy in nineteenth-century America. They held the fort, however, in a controversial way, a rather ahistorical way, a manner criticized by friends and foes alike. They defended what they often claimed was *the* Reformed system, or *the* Augustinian system, in a day and age when terms like these were being redefined, when Calvinist churches and their leaders differed sharply over questions of identity and mission, and when all of them were coming under fire from non-Calvinists for falling out of touch with modern Western cultural values.[4] Some historians interpret these stresses and strains as signs of Calvinism's decline in modern America. Still others assume, like Hodge, that Calvinism is a monolith that stands or falls as one. However, as I will argue here, there was a *contest* over Calvinism in the nineteenth-century United States—and this was a sign not of dissolution but of vitality.[5]

I focus in what follows on the three major theaters of Calvinist theology in the late 1840s and the early 1850s, a time that Darryl Hart has termed "the critical period for Protestant thought in America."[6] In the realm of school theology, no place in the United States outshone the constellations gleaming from Presbyterian Princeton, German Reformed Mercersburg, and Congregationalist New England (which will receive the least attention, as elucidated below). All three of these major theaters boasted world-class divines. All of them felt the intellectual ground shifting beneath them. All of them recognized that Calvinism was under siege. And all of them responded with defenses of their heritage. They disagreed severely over the nature of that heritage and the tactics now required if they were to hand it on to others. Yet, their disagreements yielded clear and abundant signs of life—signs that also abounded among the millions of other American Calvinists to survive the nineteenth century (in a host of Presbyterian and Reformed denominations, many Baptist congregations, some Episcopalian churches, and even a smattering of Calvinistic Methodists from Wales). Indeed, as I will contend below, the biggest question on their minds was not *whether* American Calvinism would live to see the future, but *who* would control that future—and on what terms.[7]

Princeton versus Mercersburg

The contest over Calvinism in Hart's critical period might be said to have begun in a rather out-of-the-way location. Deep in the woods of Pennsylvania lay the tiny town of Mercersburg, a hamlet that had lately become a haven of higher learning in the German Reformed Church. In 1836, Marshall College was founded there, a German Reformed institution named for the recently deceased John Marshall, chief justice of the U.S. Supreme Court. Then, in 1837, Mercersburg assumed control of the only seminary then serving the German Reformed Church in America. In the early 1840s, John Nevin (1840) and Philip Schaff (1844) joined its fledgling faculty, moving it quickly to the top tier of American divinity.[8] By 1842, Nevin, especially, began to stir the theological pot by thwarting the pending installation of a winsome Finneyite, William Ramsay, as the town's parish pastor. The following year, Nevin fired off a draft of what would become his best-known book, *The Anxious Bench*, aimed at the Finneyites' "new measures" and the havoc they were wreaking in the evangelical churches. Then, in 1846, he published another diatribe against his evangelical peers, *The Mystical Presence*, which ignited the struggle for Calvinism represented here and staked a lasting place for Mercersburg on the theological map (one that survived his school's removal to nearby Lancaster in 1871).[9]

Nevin asserted in this latter work that modern American Calvinists, indeed modern Protestants in much of the Western world, were "falling away from the general faith of the Reformation." They had "fallen away sadly from the theological earnestness and depth" of the reformers. And their churches had "receded . . . from the ground on which they stood" during the time of Luther and Calvin. "This falling away from the creed of the Reformation," Nevin underlined, "is not confined to any particular country or . . . confession." It was worst, in fact, in Europe, "in the form of . . . rampant rationalism." But Nevin worried most anxiously about its effects in America.[10]

The Mystical Presence focused on the doctrine of the Eucharist, which Nevin believed "is intimately connected with all that is most deep and central" in Christianity.[11] As the Lord's Supper fares, he thought, so fares the rest of the faith. And "it cannot be denied," he wrote, "that the view generally entertained of the Lord's Supper [today] . . . involves a . . . departure from the faith of the sixteenth century." More important, it represents a "defection from . . . orthodoxy." Homing in on his own tradition, Nevin specified this concern:

> The view of the Eucharist now generally predominant in the Reformed
> Church . . . involves a . . . departure . . . from its proper original creed,
> as exhibited in its symbolical books. An unchurchly, rationalistic
> tendency, has been allowed to carry the Church gradually more and
> more off from the ground it occupied in the beginning, till its position
> is found to be at length, to a large extent, a new one altogether.[12]

Nevin crystallized the differences between "the old Reformed view" of the nature of the Eucharist and what he often liked to call "the modern Puritan view" (taking a stab at Yankee youthfulness and prideful insularity) in a chapter at the heart of *The Mystical Presence*. His "contrast" between these views contained five points:

1. "In the old Reformed view," he said, "the communion of the believer with Christ in the Supper is taken to be *specific* in its nature, and *different* from all that has place in the common exercises of worship." In the modern Reformed or Puritan view, by contrast, it is not.
2. "In the old Reformed view, the sacramental transaction is a *mystery;* nay, in some sense an actual *miracle*." In the modern Reformed view, Nevin claimed, it is not.
3. "The old Reformed doctrine includes always the idea of an *objective force* in the sacraments. The sacramental union between the sign and the thing signified is real, and holds in virtue of the constitution of the ordinance itself, not in the faith simply or inward frame of the communicant." Again, not so in the modern Puritan view.
4. "According to the old Reformed doctrine the invisible grace of the sacrament, includes a real participation in [Christ's] *person*." But, according to the modern Puritan doctrine, it does not.
5. Finally, "in the old Reformed view . . . , the communion of the believer in the true person of Christ . . . is supposed to hold with him especially

as the Word made *flesh*. His humanity forms the medium of his union with the Church." In the modern, Puritan, rationalistic view, he said, it does not.[13]

Calvin stood, for Nevin, as the standard of the old view. "To obtain a proper view" of it, he said, "we must have recourse particularly to Calvin." Not that Calvin created the old Reformed doctrine by himself. Rather, "Calvin . . . was the theological organ, by which it first came to that clear expression, under which it continued to be uttered subsequently in the symbolical books. . . . He may be regarded then as the accredited interpreter and expounder of the article, for all later times. A better interpreter in the case," Nevin concluded, "we could not possibly possess."[14]

What did Calvin himself teach regarding the doctrine of the Eucharist? And how did his doctrine differ from those of other Protestant thinkers?

> Over and over again, in all forms of expression and explanation, [Calvin] tells us, that Christ's body is indeed locally in heaven only, and in no sense included in the elements; that he can be apprehended by faith only, and not at all by the hands or lips; that nothing is to be imagined like a transfusion or intromission of the particles of his body, materially considered, into our persons. And yet that our communion with him, notwithstanding, by the power of the Holy Ghost, involves a real participation—not in his doctrine merely—not in his promises merely—not in the sensible manifestations of his love merely—not in his righteousness and merit merely—not in the gifts and endowments of his Spirit merely; but in his own true substantial life itself; and this not as comprehended in his divine nature merely, but most immediately and peculiarly as embodied in his humanity itself, for us men and our salvation. The Word became flesh, according to this view, for the purpose not simply of effecting a salvation that might become available for men in an outward way, but to open a fountain of life in our nature itself, that might thenceforward continue to flow over to other men, as a vivific stream, to the end of time.

According to Nevin, Calvin held a *high* view of the Lord's Supper—not a Lutheran view, to be sure (for Calvin denied a bodily presence of the Lord among the elements), but one in which Christ is present by the power of his Spirit, feeding the faithful supernaturally, objectively, substantially, with his risen body and blood. Calvin promoted what Nevin often termed "a real communication with Christ's life in the Lord's Supper. . . . He held and taught the *fact* of a real presence of the Saviour's human life, for the soul of the believer, in the sacramental transaction."[15]

Nevin confessed that Calvin's doctrine "labours under serious difficulties." He harbored no hope to replicate it verbatim. Nevin believed, rather, that Calvin had a defective metaphysic, which obfuscated his doctrine with superfluous concerns. Calvin worried too much, he thought, about how Christ could be in the supper when his body sat at the right hand of God the Father in heaven. "Bound as he felt himself to be to resist everything like the idea of a local presence [of Christ in the eucharistic elements], he found it necessary to resolve the whole process into a special . . . agency of the Holy Ghost, as a sort of foreign medium introduced to meet the wants of the case." Calvin's conception of Jesus' risen human nature was "too abstract," he thought, too distant from the humanity that Jesus came to redeem. Indeed, his understanding of human nature itself was "too abstract." He tended to sunder "soul and body in the person of the believer." These abstractions harmed his effort to teach "a true organic connection" between the Savior's risen life and the daily lives of his earthly people. Calvin needed a more organic, less mechanical philosophy. And Nevin sought to provide him one in the light of modern psychology (which he understood as a broad, metaphysical field of study). "Christ's person is one," he said,

> and the person of the believer is one; and to secure a real
> communication of the whole human life of the first over into the
> personality of the second, it is only necessary that the communication
> should spring from the centre of Christ's life and pass over to the
> centre of ours. This can be [accomplished] only by the Holy Ghost.
> But the Holy Ghost in this case is not to be sundered from the Person
> of Christ. We must say rather that this, and no other, is the very form
> in which Christ's life is made present in the Church, for the purposes
> of the christian [*sic*] salvation.[16]

Though he sought to improve, however, upon the *metaphysics* of Calvin, Nevin insisted that he retained the *substance* of Calvin's view of the supper. In fact, he claimed to have a clearer view of Calvinism generally than did his major rivals mainly *because* he understood that doctrinal forms evolve inevitably. The Christian faith, he wrote, "in its substantial contents, has been always the same. The form of its apprehension however, on the part of the Church, has varied with the . . . progress of its history." The Eucharist served Nevin as a capital case in point. It had always pertained primarily to the presence of Christ in the Supper, the communion of the faithful with his risen human life. Our manner of understanding that presence, though, had changed from time to time. So it was possible to retain the substance of Calvin's view of the Eucharist, he thought, and also improve on its verbal form. As he would explain two decades later in the *Mercersburg Review:*

> For us now, the age of the Reformation is not really accessible or available for right theological use, except *through* the consequent progress of its life in the following period.
>
> There can be for us no such thing as a mechanical going back to the thinking of the Reformation period, . . . as though all right thought on every point began then, and became all at once complete then, in such sort as to admit no possible progress through all following time. . . . It is idle, to talk of honoring the Reformation fathers in this way. We never communicate with their actual life at all, by a simply outward echoing of its forms; but only by entering into its inward spirit. And this we can never do effectually except as it is brought near to us in forms answerable to the changed conditions of our own time.

No one ever simply repristinates a doctrine from the past. Whether we recognize it or not, all of us modify traditions by adapting them for use within our own cultural forms. Conservatives hold fast to the doctrinal substance of their forebears, but even they repackage it. "Here we stand divided," Nevin asserted disputatiously, from modern liberal Protestants and naïve modern Puritans. All appear to agree that Calvin's doctrine had its problems. "But, to get clear of these, *they* have thought good to cast away the whole doctrine, substance and form together. . . . *We* hold fast to the substance, while, for the very sake of doing so, we endeavour to place it in a better form."[17]

Charles Hodge proved to be Nevin's most important interlocutor on the doctrine of the Eucharist and the nature of genuine Calvinism. And Hodge, as we have seen, was not the kind of man to grant the force of Nevin's historical argument. Six years Nevin's senior and Nevin's former teacher at Princeton, he disdained his student's critique of what, in truth, were Hodge's views. Nevin had subbed for Hodge at Princeton when the latter traveled in Europe (1826–1828). He had won his ordination from the Presbyterian Church. So, when he turned against his teacher and the doctrines of his youth, he might have expected to be treated as a traitor. Hodge did not respond immediately to Nevin's criticism. He paused for a time to ponder how to engage his former pupil. Eventually, however, in April 1848, he retaliated against the younger, Teutonizing turncoat—as he had come by then to perceive him—in a fifty-page assault in the *Princeton Review.*[18]

"Dr. Nevin is tenfold further from the doctrines of our common fathers, than those whom he commiserates and condemns," Hodge declared. His eucharistic doctrine not only demonstrates his "radical rejection" of Calvinism, but a "rejection . . . of some of the leading principles" of Christian faith. Even "the lowest Puritan, ultra Protestant, or sectary . . . who truly believes in Christ" is closer to Calvin than Nevin is, Hodge insisted hyperbolically. It was hard for Hodge to see how Nevin himself could have fallen any further from the faith of the Reformation.[19]

As for Nevin's fivefold contrast of the "old Reformed" and "modern Puritan" doctrines of the Eucharist, Hodge contended that Nevin had grown confused and far too Catholic to present himself as an heir of classical Calvinism. The Reformed had always *denied* that the Lord's Supper functions as a singular, mysterious, objective means of grace. The sacraments, for them, presented Christ "in no other sense than he is present in the word." Indeed, "the question, whether eating the flesh of Christ, and drinking his blood is confined to the Lord's supper," or "whether there is any special benefit or communion with Christ to be had there, . . . the Romanists and Lutherans" had always answered yes, while the Calvinists "unanimously" retorted with a no. Calvinists affirmed a real presence of Christ in the supper but not a "local nearness. . . . The presence is to the mind," said Hodge. "The object is not presented to the sense" but to our faith. And, as for Calvin's strange notion of a "vivifying efficacy" of the body of Christ in the Eucharist, it had failed to find a stable home in Calvinist theology. It "died out of the church" almost as soon as it arose. "It had no root" in Reformed Protestantism and, therefore, "could not live." Hodge saw "nothing from the immediate successors of Calvin and Beza, of this mysterious, or as it was sometimes called, miraculous influence of Christ's heavenly body."[20]

Hodge admitted that the doctrine of the Eucharist was difficult, that even among the stalwarts there were subtle shades of difference. During the early Reformation, in fact, the Calvinists had labored to conciliate the Lutherans, compromising their doctrine for the sake of Christian unity. On the Lord's Supper itself, then, Calvin had not become as influential as the Zwinglians for later Reformed dogmatics.[21] This did not give Nevin the right, however, to claim the mantle of Calvin for his own, romantic conception of the Eucharist. Calvin had nothing to do with Nevin's obsession with the sacraments or penchant for organic modes of speaking theologically. These he had contracted from the "Romanists" and Germans. Of the Roman Catholic drift of Nevin's thought in *The Mystical Presence*, Hodge protested that "its whole spirit is churchy":

> It makes religion to be a church life, its manifestations a liturgical
> service, its support sacramental grace. It is the form, the spirit, the

predominance of these things, which give his book a character as different as can be from the healthful, evangelical free spirit of Luther or Calvin. The main question whether we come to Christ, and then to the church; whether we by a personal act of faith receive him, and by union with him become a member of his mystical body; or whether all our access to Christ is through a mediating church, Dr. Nevin decides against the evangelical system.

Regarding Nevin's view of the "mystical presence" of Christ within the church, moreover, Hodge detected modern, liberal, Germanizing tendencies. It "is in all its essential features Schleiermacher's," he repined. Not surprisingly, then, Nevin's doctrine of God was nearly "Sabellian," his Christology "Eutychian," and his general manner of speaking of God and the world "pantheistic" (Hodge's substitute for Nevin's word "organic"). Hodge had worried for several years that, since his move to Mercersburg, Nevin had started to allow the "German modes of thinking to get the mastery over him." Before he read *The Mystical Presence*, though, he never dared imagine that Nevin "had so far given himself up to their influence."[22]

These "German modes of thinking" were all the rage in the 1840s, especially among the American literati. Most Anglo-American elders found them threatening and subversive. Many patriots affirmed the racist stereotypes of Germans tendered by men like Edward Robinson—an Andover professor who had studied at length in Germany and married a German woman—who said that Germans were "a people of comparatively little practical energy, but of vast intellectual exertion."[23] Of course, in the United States, impractical abstraction was a nuisance. From the founding of the country, national leaders had railed against it. Even the worldly Thomas Jefferson had warned against the allure of the effete culture of Europe for young Americans.[24] In the early nineteenth century, the Napoleonic Wars had kept most young people at bay. During the 1820s and '30s, some Americans, like Hodge, had made it to Germany for study, but most imbibed Germanic thought through English-language channels such as Samuel Taylor Coleridge and Scotland's Thomas Carlyle.[25] In the next hundred years, however, 10,000 Americans would study in German schools. By the late 1840s, they were doing so with alacrity, as if released at last to compensate for lost time.[26] Noah Porter depicted their pilgrimages in 1857:

> The impulse to go has for the last ten years gathered strength in a geometrical ratio, and is becoming almost a *furore*. Pastors leave their pulpits, professors their chairs, graduates rush from their Alma-Mater[s], undergraduates separate themselves from their college classes, that they may study in Germany, as though in

Germany alone were the keys of knowledge; and as though from
the very atmosphere of that favored land, a man must inhale the
inspiration both of scholarship and genius.

Many would continue to bemoan this German influence, but others now
embraced it. Porter encouraged his audience to cross the sea to Germany, but
with their eyes wide open to the risks that were involved. "The theologians who
are infected with the tendency to Germanize in the worst sense of the term,"
he said, "are those whose German studies are prosecuted at second hand and
perhaps with little knowledge of the language":

> But let a student of a manly intellect and an honest faith go to
> Germany and hear for himself, and the charm if any with which error
> was invested at a distance will be likely to disappear on closer
> inspection. The heresy and falsehood which smelled like musk across
> the ocean emits the rank odor of putrefaction as he draws near. . . .
> The power to separate the truth from error is greatly enhanced, when
> the language is made familiar and unusual modes of thinking are
> mastered.[27]

Hodge was not so confident in Americans' critical faculties. He knew of
German cultural life himself, at firsthand.[28] He had studied German theology and
written about the effects of German thought on American minds.[29] He had several
German friends, fond memories of the piety of his former German teachers, and
great respect for the standards of the German universities. But he also had reason
to worry as he examined Nevin's work that Nevin was substituting the vagaries of
German metaphysics for a truly Protestant understanding of God's saving grace
imputed forensically to undeserving sinners. Calvinists like Hodge contended that
God saves sinners with their Savior's *alien* righteousness—not the risen life of
Christ conveyed *organically* by means of history, church, and sacraments.[30]

Nevin developed a dual response to Hodge's ethnic concerns. First, he
acknowledged his attraction to the Germans while insisting that he disavowed
their heresies. "I am a debtor . . . both to the English and the Germans," he
explained, "both to Princeton and Berlin." He admired Schleiermacher, but he
had no wish to ape him. The German thinker August Neander had changed his
life by helping him think historically about the nature and progress of the faith.
But even Neander, he knew, relied too heavily on Schleiermacher and failed to
guard sufficiently against romantic error. Still, Nevin could hardly understand
why thinkers such as Hodge wanted to throw the German baby out with the
bathwater. As he had expressed this frank bewilderment in the introduction to
Philip Schaff's *The Principle of Protestantism* (1845):

> Some . . . seem to have the idea that whatever is characteristically
> German must be theologically bad. . . . Now I would be sorry to
> appear as the apologist of either German philosophy or German
> theology as a whole. Few probably have been exercised with more
> solemn fears than myself, in this very direction. One thing however
> is most certain. The zeal affected by a large class of persons in this
> country against German thinking is not according to knowledge.

Nevin's colleague Frederick Gast verified his sound discernment when it came
to German views: "Certain thinkers," granted Gast, such as "Schleiermacher,
Neander and Rothe possessed a wonderful fascination for him; but he never
followed them blindly, or surrendered himself to them." So, in response to
Hodge's claim that he *had* surrendered to the Germans, Nevin balked and
begged for empathy from Presbyterian Princeton: "am I not a teacher in the
German church," he asked, "and as such bound, in common honesty, to cultivate a proper connection with the theological life of Germany, as well as with
that of Scotland and New England?" In Nevin's ecclesial world, Hodge's "great
granitic formation" proved too narrow and provincial.[31]

Second, Nevin averred that he had never sought to replace Reformed foren-
sics with German romanticism; he had only sought to ground the doctrines of
grace in real life. "The whole Gospel," he attested, "centres in the death of
Christ." But Christ's death on Calvary was not just ancient history or spiritual
pie in the sky. Its saving power, or spiritual efficacy, depended upon his risen
life today within the church. Although modern evangelicals were "ever inclined
to place Christ wholly in the clouds," ignoring the ongoing force of the incarnation in the church, their "Docetic or Gnostic" views were "incompatible . . . with
sound Christian orthodoxy." Calvin had contended that the benefits of Christ
(among his followers in the church) are gained in vital union with Christ: "I do
not see," he had testified, "how anyone can trust that he has redemption and
righteousness in the cross of Christ, and life in his death, unless he relies
chiefly upon a true participation in Christ himself. For those benefits would not
come to us unless Christ first made himself ours." Nevin could not have said it
any better.[32]

Nevin also answered Hodge's critique of the doctrine of the Eucharist laid
out in *The Mystical Presence*, first in a series of missives in his church's *Weekly
Messenger* and later in the *Mercersburg Review*.[33] He complained that Hodge had
treated their disagreement *ex cathedra*, in a magisterial way, refusing to stoop
to Nevin's argument and address it in detail. Consequently, his response to
Nevin "sets up a man of straw, and shows off a harmless sham battle in bringing him to the ground." Hodge seemed to think that the "only alternative" for

evangelical churches to a Lutheran view of Christ's corporeal presence in the supper was "a presence in the intelligence," or merely in the "mind," that "to deny a local presence is to affirm an actual absence." But this was not what Calvin said, so Hodge should quit dismissing Nevin's mediating view. "Right or wrong," wrote Nevin, Calvin taught throughout his ministry "that we have in the Lord's supper something far beyond a mere occasion for the exercise of our faith." Indeed, *most* of the "old Reformed" taught "a real presence" of Christ in the eucharistic meal,

> not simply as an object of thought or intelligence on the part of men, but in the way of actual communication on the part of Christ; a presence not conditioned by the relations of space, but transcending these altogether in a higher sphere of life; a presence, not material, but dynamic, like that of the root in its branches, and only the more intimate and deep by its distance from all that belongs to the experiment of sense.

Hodge had proven so impatient with any kind of "German" subtlety that he failed to recognize this fact of Calvinistic history and condemned all those who did. Nevin was happy to report, however, that Erlangen's Reformed theologian Johannes Ebrard—in a massive, two-volume history of the doctrine of the Eucharist—had recently confirmed his own perspective on the past.[34]

Nevin called Hodge to task for lifting the Zwinglians to the place of Calvin himself as standards of orthodoxy. Hodge had appealed in his essay to the *Consensus Tigurinus* (Zurich Consensus, 1549), penned by Heinrich Bullinger and Calvin, as the prime symbol of Calvinistic doctrine on the supper.[35] But, in Nevin's estimation, "it is arbitrary, in the extreme, to exalt the *Consensus Tigurinus* to the rank of a supreme law for the entire creed of the church." It was also rather "arbitrary" to "question the right of Calvin" to interpret the significance of the document. Calvin had made it clear that the *Consensus* was a compromise and did not express the fullness of his eucharistic faith. His prior statements on the supper had expressed his views more accurately. For example, at the Synod of Bern in 1537, he and his colleagues had declared that, in the eucharistic meal, Jesus "makes us to partake of his *life-giving flesh*, (carnis suae vivificae,) by which participation we are fed unto everlasting life. . . . When therefore we speak of the communion which believers have with Christ," they confessed, "we mean that they *communicate with his flesh and blood not less than with his Spirit.*" While in Strassburg (1538–1541), Calvin had formed a friendship with Philipp Melanchthon, identified with Lutherans, attended Lutheran synods, signed the Augsburg Confession (the *Confessio Augustana Variata* of 1540), and wrote a treatise on the Supper, "the great object of which was precisely to carry the whole question above the old Zuinglian [sic] and Lutheran antithesis."[36] When interpreting the *Consensus Tigurinus* later on, moreover, he did so in a manner very different from that of Hodge. Gnesio-Lutherans such as Joachim Westphal and Tilemann Hesshus had berated Calvin for compromising with Bullinger and Zurich. Calvin answered them, however, by interpreting the *Consensus* in relation to his other, higher statements on the supper. In his *Consensionis Capitum Expositio* (1553), for instance, Calvin assured his Lutheran colleagues that they would "find in this Consensus all that is contained in the . . . Augsburg Confession" (as revised in 1540). "In the holy supper," he added to assure them of his doctrine, "with the bread and wine are truly given Christ's body and blood."[37]

According to Nevin, Calvin had *always* held a high view of the supper, a view influenced by Melanchthon, who had long exerted a theological force upon the Reformed.[38] Throughout the whole of Calvin's corpus and the later Reformed confessions, Nevin found a clear profession of the Savior's real presence in the Eucharist itself. Indeed, the "Gallic, Scotch, Belgic, and Second Helvetic Confessions" taught this, as did the Heidelberg Catechism, so important to the creed of the German Reformed in every age. Most important of all, however, Calvin heralded this view in nearly everything he wrote upon the subject. Calvin's "sacramental doctrine," Nevin contended unequivocally, "is too plain for question or contradiction":

> It is no isolated or merely occasional utterance in his theological
> system. His writings are full of it, from the first edition of his
> *Institutes* to the last tract he ever published; and it is presented always
> as an article, not of secondary, but of primary and fundamental
> interest, which it lay near his heart to have rightly understood. . . . He
> comes upon it from all sides, and considers it under all imaginable
> aspects; sometimes in the form of direct positive statement and
> discussion; at other times polemically or apologetically.[39]

Brian Gerrish has described Calvin's eucharistic doctrine as elusive and confusing. The "clarity and consistency of his teaching," writes Gerrish, can be easily "exaggerated. . . . His language is complex; it could lead in more than one direction, and it is not easy to harmonize all his different assertions." Nevin disagreed: in all of Calvin's "multitudinous and diversified" pronouncements, he maintained, "the doctrine remains from first to last one and the same, always in harmony with itself, and true to its own original type."[40]

Mark Noll has noted that Nevin "never spoke for all, or even a majority of, the German Reformed." At first, he amassed a following of Mercersburg supporters eager to shore up the traditions of the German Reformed Church. He

always enjoyed a coterie of deeply devoted disciples. But eventually, he also suffered strident opposition—even among his fellow churchmen—especially after
Schaff employed the Mercersburg theology in a movement to reform their
worship services. Schaff chaired a committee that, in 1858, published *A Liturgy;
or, Order of Christian Worship* for the church. Based on early Christian sources,
full of historic Catholic forms, this worship manual piqued a rebellion in the
pews. Even erstwhile supporters now suspected Nevin and Schaff of seeking to
undermine their Reformation heritage. One such colleague, J. H. A. Bomberger,
would lead the opposition. Once a staunch defender of Nevin, he came soon
after the Civil War to agree with Hodge that Nevin had compromised historic
Calvinism, leading the German Reformed churches down the slippery slope to
Rome. He railed against Nevin in the Pennsylvania press. In 1868, he launched
the *Reformed Church Monthly* to oppose the harmful effects of Nevin's *Mercersburg
Review*. Then, in 1869, he opened Ursinus College in Collegeville (outside of
Philadelphia), named for the sixteenth-century leader who had done so much
to found Reformed churches in the Palatinate. A low-church, anti-Catholic,
German Reformed school, Ursinus soon became a rival to the older schools in
Lancaster. Some of the German Reformed left their native church completely,
seeking refuge with the Dutch, whose congregations shared their ardor for the
unadorned authority of the Heidelberg Catechism. Most who remained now
seemed to wish that Nevin had not been so contentious. From Lake Erie to
North Carolina, Cincinnati to Philadelphia, Nevin's doctrine had divided the
German Reformed like never before.[41]

To the end of their lives, Nevin and Hodge remained at odds regarding what
it meant to be a faithful Calvinist in nineteenth-century America. Hodge continued to label Nevin a pantheistic heretic. Nevin continued to shy away from
Hodge's accusations.[42] Several other Calvinists weighed in on their debate, usually leaning closer to Nevin on the history of the Eucharist while standing closer
to Hodge's general system of theology. The southern Presbyterian church historian John Adger, who had studied with Hodge at Princeton, told his students
that Nevin was right about the doctrine of the supper and that other southern
clergymen—like Robert J. Breckinridge and James Henley Thornwell—agreed
with him on the matter. The prominent New York Presbyterian pastor Henry
Van Dyke, who also studied with Hodge at Princeton, penned an essay on the
Eucharist that echoed Nevin's views—lamenting his church's fall from early
Calvinistic standards and its clergy's lack of competence in eucharistic ministry.
"In the Presbyterian Church," he wrote in 1887,

> there is a widespread defection from the doctrine of our standards in
> regard to the Lord's Supper. . . . This is the subject in which our

candidates for the ministry are most frequently deficient. They are
better prepared to tell what the Lord's Supper is not than to define
what it is. The instruction our people receive consists too largely
in warnings against expecting too much from the sacraments.
The human soul cannot live on negations. Faith may be defended,
but cannot be nourished by protesting against the belief of others.
The picket-fence may keep out wild beasts, but cannot make the
garden grow.

Most people who studied the matter concurred that Hodge was more conservative in doctrinal demeanor but that Nevin was closer to Calvin on the Eucharist.
Historians have just begun to understand this paradox. Few of them have
noticed it. And most of those who have are people who find Hodge's scholarship incredibly naïve (and have a hard time concealing their esteem for Nevin's
views). In the words of William DiPuccio, "Hodge's historical method . . . was
attended by a certain danger: for the most part Nevin was aware of his differences with the Reformed tradition; Hodge was not. Indeed, Hodge refused
to admit them even after they were . . . exposed." It "was not that he was dis-
honest," ruled James Hastings Nichols, "he just lacked understanding of what
history is."[43]

Princeton versus New England

No sooner had Hodge completed his early paper war with Nevin than he turned
around to face a new opponent in New England who was also problematizing
his conception of Calvinism. Andover's Edwards Amasa Park, known as the
last "consistent Calvinist" (that is, Edwardsean theologian) and the first to write
a history of his region's own theology (that is, the New England theology), had
recently given a lecture to a convention of the Congregational pastors of his
state, "The Theology of the Intellect and That of the Feelings," which aroused a
storm of controversy up and down the seaboard—vexing Princeton by suggesting that its quest for doctrinal stringency and loyalty to the past was
overwrought, misdirected, even sinful. "Many" of the differences dividing
evangelicals were "far less important, than they seem to be," said Park. In their
haste to battle heterodoxy, many theologians "treated the language of a sensitive heart," or language of the feelings—which was rarely framed precisely or
for doctrinal subscription—like "the guarded and wary" language "of the intellect." Heresy hunting harms the church, however, even when done by Calvinists concerned for biblical truth. (Since the end of the 1820s, Princetonians like

Hodge had hunted "heretics" in New England for revising the way they spoke of original sin and regeneration.) Although difficult to translate in analytic terms, godly feelings play a crucial role in daily Christian living. The Bible is replete with them. They constitute the heart and soul of genuine religion. We should break the habit of straightening them in propositional statements and then pouncing on the ones that stray from the herd. The "theology of the feelings" has an integrity of its own, he said. It complements our doctrines and reveals a basic unity of genuine believers whose polemics often make them ardent foes.[44]

Hodge decried what he interpreted as Park's flagrant attempt to minimize their crucial differences and whitewash the cracks and stains in modern Calvinism. Park's distinction between the theologies of intellect and feelings was misleading, he objected. It was a ruse, in fact, intended to conceal New England's heresies. "He has obviously adopted it as a convenient way of getting rid of . . . doctrines," Hodge proclaimed, "which [are] far too [clear] in scripture . . . to allow of their being denied." Everyone knew that Park's New England had abandoned tried and true Reformed views of sin and conversion. Now, Park was seeking to chalk these doctrines up to pious "feelings" never intended for subscription nor as boundaries for the church. Hodge believed that godly feelings should *conform* to Bible doctrine, that there ought to be what he called "a perfect consistency" between our understanding and our sentiment. The "theology of the feeling is the theology of the intellect," he said, "in all its accuracy of thought and expression." He would come much later in life to soften his view of Park's distinction. But for now, he clung doggedly to Princeton's propositions and employed them to measure the distance Park had fallen from the truth.[45]

I have written about this controversy numerous times before and so will not rehearse it now in great detail.[46] Suffice it to say that, here again, we see the leading theologians on the eve of the Civil War debating not whether to leave their vaunted Calvinism behind but the strategies and language used to hand it on to others. Park replied to Hodge's complaints about his ecumenical Calvinism in several later essays on New England's Protestant thought. The series culminated famously in *New England Theology* (1852), a lengthy history of the Calvinism shaped by Jonathan Edwards. Park confessed that recent New Englanders had moved a bit from Edwards, seeking to synthesize and further his important spiritual insights. Few of them had felt the need to parrot Edwards's teaching. The genius of their movement, rather, stemmed from Edwards's willingness to emend Reformed theology to meet the needs of the day.[47]

For years, Yankee Calvinists had championed the value of enhancing their inheritance—from Zwingli, Calvin, Westminster, and even from Edwards himself—for the sake of gospel progress. Like Nevin, they insisted that the *substance* of the Protestant faith had always been the same. Its frame of reference, though, had varied. It was impossible to improve upon the truth of revelation. But they felt an urgent need to keep reforming merely "human views and statements" of that truth. In so doing, they considered themselves the region's "true conservatives," the party most devoted to Edwards's own religious program. In the words of one of their essays, aired in 1838 in Yale's *Quarterly Christian Spectator*, "he who will not tolerate *new inquiries* . . . cannot be a conservative, or one who desires to keep alive the old New England spirit." The author of this essay, never named, went on to expound upon this controversial notion. "To judge and condemn the present for no other reason, except that it is not the past over again," he claimed, raising the stakes of disagreement with Hodge and other alleged "conservatives,"

> is not only to betray a stupid ignorance, but it is to contend directly
> against the providence of God, who never intended that it should be.
> To insist that every opinion in theological and metaphysical science,
> shall be stated in the unaltered phraseology of an ancient
> scholasticism, or if that phraseology is improved or explained, or
> anything thereto is added, to raise the cry of innovation or heresy,
> and only because it was not known in former days, is to possess a
> *spirit* which under the name of conservatism has, in every age . . .
> made void the law of God. . . . The True Conservative . . . , though he
> often retires into the past, does not there make his dwelling-place,
> but lives and acts in the present. From the past, he derives
> instructions that are most important, and catches nobler and brighter
> views of the truths which never die; but these permanent principles
> are made each to read its appropriate lesson under the varying
> circumstances of present scenes, to strengthen and guide him the
> more efficiently to act his part in his own generation.

Yale's George Park Fisher repeated this theme three decades later. "It is a grand merit of our New England theologians," he affirmed, "that while holding the past in due reverence, they have not bowed down before it, but have expected progress. To our mind," he continued, now confident that he was speaking for hundreds of his colleagues over the past several decades,

> there is something noble in this willing, hopeful spirit of progress
> and emancipation from slavish deference to human authority. . . .
> There is no contempt for the past; there is no rash and flighty
> desertion of received doctrine; but there is a readiness to learn, to

modify traditional tenets at the coming of new light, and a disposition to confront the errors of good men by dispassionate argument instead of church anathemas.[48]

In the debate with Hodge and Princeton, then, Park was representing a common refrain within New England. In the main, and at its best, his region's Calvinism had sought to be historic and progressive, orthodox and up-to-date. Though its substance never changed, its theologians ever sought for ways to make it more compelling.

Hodge and Park resembled two ships passing in the night. Both of them flew the Calvinist flag. Much of their cargo was the same. However, they moved in different directions and, at times, even communicated on vastly different frequencies. Park's ship was more agile. Hodge's had more ballast. Park traversed a wider range. Hodge steered a steadier course, believing that theology was not so much a voyage of discovery as a delivery of the deposit of faith entrusted to the saints. He granted that "every generation has . . . its own life to live," its own "battles" to engage. In response to Park's depiction of the nature of these battles, though, Hodge said that those who understood the scope of history knew they were seldom as momentous as their soldiers usually thought. They "are only a repetition of the conflicts" of the past, he said. "The same great questions are constantly recurring." To be sure, we must continue to engage them for ourselves. "But these are mostly personal struggles. The doctrines are fixed," he emphasized. "They have taken their place in the settled faith of the Church," once and for all, "and the real struggle is in the breast of each individual, to come to a comprehension, appreciation, and acknowledgment of the truth."[49]

Conclusion

Hodge was a brilliant man, a genuine polymath who used his gifts primarily in the service of the Presbyterian Church. He was intentionally conservative and tried his level best to be consistently conservative, which set him apart from many other leading Calvinist thinkers. Nevin sought to repackage Calvinist thought in modern terms, pursuing a newer, better, higher form of Christian faith and practice. Park thought that the best theologians in the church had always adapted Bible doctrine to the cultures of their day. But Hodge believed that his tradition got the Bible right, that God's truth was absolute, and that the job of Christian clergy was to understand, defend, and inculcate what they had received. It was easy for him to think, then, that he and his affiliates should function as officially sanctioned arbiters of orthodoxy, judges in the contest over Calvinism. Many modern American scholars have assumed the same thing—whether or not they held to Hodge's faith or to any faith at all. However, as I have tried to show, this shared assumption has misled us as to the status, scope, and strength of nineteenth-century American Calvinism. Hodge revised his heritage, too, even if inadvertently. He often oversimplified its history and traditions. He was not the last bastion in its battle for survival but one of many Calvinists competing for adherents. He was conservative, indeed, but neither kind nor always true as an interpreter of the history of Reformed Christianity. Earl Kennedy noticed in a long-forgotten article that "Hodge had a 'tin ear' with regard to historical development." James Turner explained this in relation to Hodge's bearing: his "habit of confident assertion," Turner wrote, "sometimes outran his erudition."[50]

Even Hodge's fellow nineteenth-century Protestant conservatives often noted that his magisterial manner led him astray. Of course, in Mercersburg and New England, this was noted all the time, but it was also pointed out in less predictable locales. In Philadelphia, the confessional Lutheran Charles Porterfield Krauth, a great admirer of Hodge, disagreed with his construal of Calvinist doctrine on the question of the destiny of those who die in infancy. His thorough response to Hodge's work on this most delicate concern purported that Hodge's "greatest weakness" as a theological scholar "is where it might least have been suspected—it is in Calvinistic theology." Presbyterians questioned Hodge's view of the past as well. Robert Landis, the conservative heir of Robert J. Breckinridge at Danville Seminary, wrote a massive book on Hodge's view of the imputation of sin, depicting him as a heretic and claiming the support of other Presbyterian worthies (such as Breckinridge himself and even James Henley Thornwell of Columbia Seminary). Hodge's doctrine, stated Landis, was "a radical departure from the recognized Augustinian theology, or Calvinism." The problem was that Hodge was not an ontological realist. He did not believe that the human race was present in the fall, and, thus, he failed to account persuasively for the imputation of Adam's guilt to those who would succeed him. Union's Henry Boynton Smith did not find Hodge's views heretical, but even he preferred a more robustly Augustinian frame of reference for theology. And William G. T. Shedd, who also taught at Union Seminary, disagreed with Hodge on Presbyterian metaphysics, advancing what he called "the Augustinian and Elder-Calvinistic" view of doctrine over Princeton's more empirical, ironically modern view.[51]

Some Reformed scholars today believe their movement has no center but has always been reforming and adapting to the changes in its multiple social contexts. Their critics view these scholars as aberrant and disloyal, as deserters who have willfully ignored their movement's history of stout, centripetal faith. The contest over Calvinism in nineteenth-century America, though, provides us ample reason to resist these two extremes. All my subjects were conservative to one degree or another. They thought it meant something definite to call oneself a Calvinist. They wanted to be faithful to the best of their traditions. They were even willing to bind themselves to Calvin's own theology (again, in different ways). Yet, most also wanted to contextualize their faith, rearticulate their views for the sake of reaching out within their own spheres of influence. They disagreed incessantly about how best to do so. Hodge proved to be the most important single voice. Hodge and Princeton also proved, however, to be the least persuasive on the history of their movement and its changes over time (seemingly tone-deaf to the modulations in their movement's song). In their great age of historicism—an age that saw the birth of the modern disciplines of history and historical theology—most of the best and brightest turned to Union, Yale, and Europe, often to German universities, for guidance on these matters. The churchmen most committed to conserving their tradition lost the power to shape the story told of their movement in the academy—and lost it to the people they most frequently opposed. This is an irony that scholars today, whatever their traditions, would do well to recognize.

NOTES

My thanks go to Oliver Crisp, Paul Gutjahr, David Kling, Hans Madueme, Scott Manetsch, Robert Yarbrough, and the Deerfield Dialogue Group for helpful comments on drafts of this chapter.

1. Charles Hodge, "Professor Park's Remarks on the *Princeton Review*," *Biblical Repertory and Princeton Review* 23 (April 1851): 308–9, 319.

2. The best-known version of this statement was made at the semicentennial anniversary celebration of Hodge's tenure at the school (April 24, 1872), at which he reminisced about its early history:

> Drs. Alexander and Miller were not speculative men. They were not given to new methods or new theories. They were content with the faith once delivered to the saints. I am not afraid to say that a new idea never originated in this Seminary. Their theological method was very simple. The Bible is the word of God. That is to be assumed or proved. If granted; then it follows, that what the Bible says, God says. That ends the matter.

See Alexander A. Hodge, *The Life of Charles Hodge, D.D., LL.D., Professor in the Theological Seminary, Princeton* (London: Nelson, 1881), 521.

3. B. B. Warfield, "What Is Calvinism?" (*Presbyterian*, March 2, 1904), in *Selected Shorter Writings of Benjamin B. Warfield*, vol. 1, ed. John E. Meeter (Nutley, N.J.: Presbyterian and Reformed Publishing, 1970), 389, 392.

4. On the increasing criticism (and spread of negative stereotypes) of Calvin and Calvinism in this period, see Thomas J. Davis, "Images of Intolerance: John Calvin in Nineteenth-Century History Textbooks," *Church History* 65 (Summer 1996): 234–48; and Davis, "Rhetorical War and Reflex: Calvin and Calvinism in Nineteenth-Century Fiction and Twentieth-Century Criticism," *Calvin Theological Journal* 33 (November 1998): 443–56.

5. Standard sources on the decline of Calvinism in this period include Joseph Haroutunian, *Piety versus Moralism: The Passing of the New England Theology* (New York: Holt, 1932); Donald Meyer, "The Dissolution of Calvinism," in *Paths of American Thought*, ed. Arthur M. Schlesinger Jr. and Morton White (Boston: Houghton Mifflin, 1963), 71–85; Timothy L. Smith, *Revivalism and Social Reform in Mid-Nineteenth-Century America* (New York: Abingdon, 1957), 88–94; William G. McLoughlin, *Modern Revivalism: Charles Grandison Finney to Billy Graham* (New York: Ronald, 1959), 3–64; McLoughlin, "Introduction: The American Evangelicals: 1800–1900," in *The American Evangelicals, 1800–1900: An Anthology*, ed. McLoughlin (New York: Harper and Row, 1968), 4–5; McLoughlin, *Revivals, Awakenings, and Reform: An Essay on Religion and Social Change in America, 1607–1977* (Chicago: University of Chicago Press, 1978), 98–140; and Ann Douglas, *The Feminization of American Culture* (New York: Knopf, 1977), 6–8, 12–13, 17–19. Many proponents of this declension thesis treat Calvinism as a monolithic system. Cf. Mark A. Noll, *America's God: From Jonathan Edwards to Abraham Lincoln* (New York: Oxford University Press, 2002), who tends to speak not so much of a sharp decline as of a gradual co-optation and marginalization, even a "self-immolation" (294), of Calvinism in the face of nineteenth-century cultural trends; and Nathan O. Hatch, *The Democratization of American Christianity* (New Haven, Conn.: Yale University Press, 1989), who contends that fiercely democratic and populist social trends after the revolution undermined Calvinist doctrinal priorities: "As people became more insistent on thinking theologically for themselves, the carefully wrought dogmas of Calvin, Edwards, and Hopkins were dismissed as 'the senseless jargon of election and reprobation'" (173).

6. D. G. Hart, "Divided between Heart and Mind: The Critical Period for Protestant Thought in America," *Journal of Ecclesiastical History* 38 (April 1987): 254–70. Hart focuses in this essay on the ways in which Horace Bushnell, Charles Hodge, Henry B. Smith, and Edwards A. Park reconciled traditional Protestantism with German romantic philosophy, adumbrating the bitter doctrinal controversies that rankled America's churches at the nineteenth century's end. See also James D. Bratt, "The Reorientation of American Protestantism, 1835–1845," *Church History* 67 (March 1998): 52–82, who suggests that we should move the critical period back a decade to the time when the nation's Anglo-evangelical theological frame of reference first began to come under fire.

7. Of course, some forms of Calvinism declined in modern America, and none of the modern Calvinists enjoyed the legally sanctioned cultural power of Calvinist clergy in colonial New England. Further, non-Calvinist churches gained ground in the nineteenth century, crowding the stage of the nation's Christian leadership. Still, none of this is to say that Calvinism itself declined. It is certainly not to say, as many previous scholars have put it, that Calvinism passed away or that it was drowned by a

wave of anti-Calvinist religion. Rather, as Calvinism declined in places like Harvard and greater New England, it increased in other places (among new immigrant populations and some evangelical groups). The nation's centers of high culture would be gradually secularized. All religious groups—and especially those with strong claims to special revelation—would be marginalized in the nation's halls of power. But Calvinism survived and thrived in other public venues. (How it did so is an important question for another occasion.) The public force of Calvinist subgroups has ebbed and flowed in modern America. But, according to the estimates of Gary Scott Smith, there were 2,112,000 Calvinists in America in 1870. Today, there are even more. Smith, *The Seeds of Secularization: Calvinism, Culture, and Pluralism in America, 1870–1915* (Grand Rapids, Mich.: Christian University Press/Eerdmans, 1985), 1–22 (statistical tables on 12–13).

8. For an excellent brief history of the German Reformed Church in early America, see Charles Hambrick-Stowe, "Colonial and National Beginnings," in *The Living Theological Heritage of the United Church of Christ*, vol. 3, *Colonial and National Beginnings*, ed. Hambrick-Stowe (Cleveland, Ohio: Pilgrim, 1998), 1–20. Cf. Paul K. Conkin, *The Uneasy Center: Reformed Christianity in Antebellum America* (Chapel Hill: University of North Carolina Press, 1995), 169–76. For more extensive, detailed institutional histories of the church, see James I. Good, *History of the Reformed Church in the U.S. in the Nineteenth Century* (New York: Board of Publication of the Reformed Church in America, 1911); H. M. J. Klein, *The History of the Eastern Synod of the Reformed Church in the United States* (Lancaster, Pa.: Eastern Synod, 1943); and Joseph Henry Dubbs, *Historic Manual of the Reformed Church in the United States* (Lancaster, Pa.: Inquirer Printing, 1885). On the history of Mercersburg Seminary, start with the comparatively nonpolemical work of George Warren Richard, *History of the Theological Seminary of the Reformed Church in the United States, 1825–1934, Evangelical and Reformed Church, 1934–1952* (Lancaster, Pa.: Rudisill, 1952); and Luther J. Binkley, *The Mercersburg Theology* (Manheim, Pa.: Sentinel, 1953). (More polemical and theological histories of the school will be cited below.) On Nevin's life and thought, see D. G. Hart, *John Williamson Nevin: High-Church Calvinist* (Phillipsburg, N.J.: P&R Publishing, 2005); William DiPuccio, *The Interior Sense of Scripture: The Sacred Hermeneutics of John W. Nevin* (Macon, Ga.: Mercer University Press, 1998); Richard E. Wentz, *John Williamson Nevin: American Theologian* (New York: Oxford University Press, 1997); Sam Hamstra Jr. and Arie J. Griffioen, eds., *Reformed Confessionalism in Nineteenth-Century America: Essays on the Thought of John Williamson Nevin* (Lanham, Md.: Scarecrow, 1995); James Hastings Nichols, *Romanticism in American Theology: Nevin and Schaff at Mercersburg* (Chicago: University of Chicago Press, 1961); Theodore Appel, *The Life and Work of John Williamson Nevin* (Philadelphia: Reformed Church Publication House, 1889); E. V. Gerhart, "John Williamson Nevin: His Godliness," *Reformed Quarterly Review* 34 (January 1887): 13–19; and especially John W. Nevin, *My Own Life: The Earliest Years* (Lancaster, Pa.: Papers of the Eastern Chapter, Historical Society of the Evangelical and Reformed Church, 1964).

9. John W. Nevin, *The Anxious Bench* (Chambersburg, Pa.: Printed at the office of the *Weekly Messenger*, 1843; rev. ed., 1844); and Nevin, *The Mystical Presence: A Vindication of the Reformed or Calvinistic Doctrine of the Holy Eucharist* (Philadelphia:

Lippincott, 1846). Marshall College moved to Lancaster in 1853, joining with Franklin College (founded in 1787) to form Franklin and Marshall College. After its own move to Lancaster, Mercersburg Seminary became Lancaster Seminary and held its classes at Franklin and Marshall until 1893. On the Finneyites and their measures, see Charles E. Hambrick-Stowe, *Charles G. Finney and the Spirit of American Evangelicalism* (Grand Rapids, Mich.: Eerdmans, 1996); Keith J. Hardman, *Charles Grandison Finney, 1792–1875: Revivalist and Reformer* (Syracuse, N.Y.: Syracuse University Press, 1987); and the helpful bibliography in Garth M. Rosell and Richard A. G. Dupuis, eds., *The Memoirs of Charles G. Finney: The Complete Restored Text* (Grand Rapids, Mich.: Zondervan, 1989), 671–701. For more on Nevin's opposition to them, see James D. Bratt, "Eternally True, Variably Useful: How Confessions Worked in Some American Reformed Churches," in *Holding on to the Faith: Confessional Traditions in American Christianity*, ed. Douglas A. Sweeney and Charles Hambrick-Stowe (Lanham, Md.: University Press of America, 2008), 71–90; and Bratt, *Antirevivalism in Antebellum America: A Collection of Religious Voices* (New Brunswick, N.J.: Rutgers University Press, 2006).

   10. Nevin, *Mystical Presence*, 139, 151–52, 105.

   11. Ibid., 52:

> The doctrine of the eucharist is intimately connected with all that is most
> deep and central in the Christian system as a whole; and it is not possible
> for it to undergo any material modification in any direction, without a
> corresponding modification at the same time of the theory and life of religion
> at other points. If it be true then, that such a falling away from the eucharistic
> view of the sixteenth century, as is now asserted, has taken place in the
> Reformed Church, it is very certain that the revolution is not confined to this
> point. It must affect necessarily the whole view, that is entertained of Christ's
> person, the idea of the Church, and the doctrine of salvation throughout. Not
> that the change in the theory of the Lord's Supper may be considered
> the origin and cause, properly speaking, of any such general theological
> revolution; but because it could not occur, except as accompanied by this
> general revolution, of which it may be taken as the most significant exponent
> and measure.

I should note that "Eucharist" and "eucharistic" are inconsistently capitalized in modern Christian history. In what follows, I will capitalize the noun and lowercase the adjective except when quoting primary sources (which are literally transcribed).

   12. Nevin, *Mystical Presence*, 52–53, 105.

   13. Ibid., 117–26. Nevin's notion of the "objective force" of sacramental grace had roots in his doctrine of the church. See J. W. Nevin, *The Church: A Sermon Preached at the Opening of the Synod of the German Reformed Church at Carlisle, October 15, 1846* (Chambersburg, Pa.: Publication Office of the German Reformed Church, 1847), esp. 3–4:

> The German Reformed Church is bound, by her history and constitution,
> to hold fast the Protestant faith of the Sixteenth Century in the objective

character of the Church; and to remain true in this way to the *Catholic* side of the Reformation, which has been well nigh wrecked in the reigning tendency to an extreme in the opposite quarter. Her whole importance in this country, depends on her being faithful to herself in this way. It will not do to boast of our faith in God, if we put no trust in his institutions. . . . For our own sake, and for the sake of our children, let us not cast away our confidence in the Church. . . . The only religion that can stand in the end is that which carries the subject out of himself, and enables him to rest on something beyond his own individual nature. The sense of the *objective* in the Church lies thus at the ground of all solid piety.

14. Ibid., 54. Nevin unpacked this notion at length: "If there be any point clear in the history of the time, it is that the doctrine exhibited by Calvin on this subject is to be regarded as the same, in all substantial points, that was recognized in the end as of general symbolical authority, throughout the whole Reformed Church, in the sixteenth century" (67).

15. Ibid., 68, 73.

16. Ibid., 62, 155–61. Nevin's mentor Frederick A. Rauch, a senior colleague at Mercersburg, informed his understanding of modern psychology. See Rauch, *Psychology; or, A View of the Human Soul: Including Anthropology, Being the Substance of a Course of Lectures, Delivered to the Junior Class, Marshall College, Penn.* (New York: Dodd, 1840).

17. Nevin, *Mystical Presence*, 13, 155, 161–62. Nevin concluded *The Mystical Presence* by presenting his own view of the Lord's Supper and union with Christ, answering objections to his modern form of the doctrine (164–256). As Nevin and Hodge knew well, Nevin's understanding of doctrinal evolution owed a great deal to his colleague Philip Schaff's work, *The Principle of Protestantism*, trans. John W. Nevin (1845; repr., Philadelphia: United Church Press, 1964), which Nevin himself had introduced to Anglo-American readers. As Nevin expressed their views in his introduction to that work, "The present state of Protestantism is only interimistic. It can save itself only by passing beyond itself. . . . Christianity, we say, is organic. This implies, in the nature of the case, development, evolution, progress" (42, 44). See Nevin's further defense of this book in "True and False Protestantism," *Mercersburg Review* 1 (January 1849): 83–104. For Hodge's critique of Nevin's and Schaff's views of doctrinal progress, see Charles Hodge, "Schaf's [sic] Protestantism," *Biblical Repertory and Princeton Review* 17 (October 1845): 626–36, in which he called the book "thoroughly German. The mode of thinking, and the forms of expression are so unenglish, that it is not easy for an American to enter into the views of the authors" (626; more on Hodge's opposition to "German" thinking below); and Hodge, "Dr. Schaff's Apostolic Church," *Biblical Repertory and Princeton Review* 26 (January 1854): 148–92, in which he declared Schaff guilty by association with Nevin, asserting that Nevin had "justly . . . forfeited entirely the confidence of the Protestant community" (151). Hodge seems to have sensed at an early stage the post-Calvinist implications of Schaff's conception of doctrinal progress. This sense was vindicated, moreover, when Schaff (much later) came out clearly in favor of breaking the allegiance of the

Presbyterian Church to Calvinism. See, for example, Schaff's *Creed Revision in the Presbyterian Churches* (New York: Scribner's, 1890), 40–42:

> Let us be honest, and confess that old Calvinism is fast dying out. It has done a great work, and has done it well, but cannot satisfy the demands of the present age. We live in the nineteenth, and not the seventeenth century. Every age must produce its own theology and has its own mission to fulfil. . . . We must look to the future, when God will raise another theological genius, like Augustin [*sic*] or Calvin, who will substitute something better, broader, and deeper than the narrow and intolerant system which bears their honored names.

Nevin would never become as theologically liberal as Schaff, but he would continue to wrestle with related historical issues. For his later understanding of our access and relationship to Reformation doctrine, see Nevin, "Dorner's *History of Protestant Theology*," *Mercersburg Review* 15 (April 1868): 260–90, and (July 1868): 325–66 (quotation above from 362–63), an extensive review of I. A. Dorner, *Geschichte der Protestantischen Theologie, besonders in Deutschland, nach ihrer principiellen Bewegung und im Zusammenhang mit dem religiösen, sittlichen und intellectuellen Leben betrachtet* (Munich: Literarisch-artistische Anstalt der J. G. Cotta'schen Buchhandlung, 1867). Dorner's *History* lent support to Nevin's notion that modern Protestantism had fallen away from the faith of the Reformation, for it suggested that scholasticism in seventeenth-century Europe and then Enlightenment rationalism had transmogrified Protestantism and weakened Christianity.

18. Charles Hodge, "Doctrine of the Reformed Church on the Lord's Supper," *Biblical Repertory and Princeton Review* 20 (April 1848): 227–78. Regarding his delay in reviewing the book, Hodge explained: "We have had Dr. Nevin's work on the 'Mystical Presence' on our table since its publication, some two years ago, but have never really read it, until within a fortnight. We do not suppose other people are quite as bad, in this respect, as ourselves. Our experience, however, has been that it requires the stimulus of a special necessity to carry us through such a book" (227).

19. Ibid., 227, 259, 264, 269–70.

20. Ibid., 275, 245–47, 249–54.

21. Ibid., 230. Insofar as Hodge used Calvin as a eucharistic standard, he preferred to use the Calvin of the *Consensus Tigurinus* (Zurich Consensus), published in 1549, for there Calvin had worked to compromise with Swiss Reformed compatriots (rather than with Lutherans). As Hodge would put this later in his *Systematic Theology*, the *Consensus Tigurinus* was "the most important" eucharistic symbol of the Reformed "because [it was] drawn up for the express purpose of settling the disputes between the [Zwinglians and Calvinists], and because it was adopted by both. . . . No document . . . can have a higher claim to represent the true doctrine of the Reformed Church than this 'Consensus.'" Charles Hodge, *Systematic Theology*, 3 vols. (1871–1872; repr., New York: Scribner's, 1883–1884), 3:631–32. For more of Hodge's notion that the Reformed view of the Eucharist was clarified as the Reformed grew independent of the Lutherans, see his lecture notes from Princeton on the "Lord's Supper: Reformed Doctrine" [late 1840s], box 2, folder 32, Charles Hodge Manuscript Collection,

Princeton Theological Seminary (PTS) Archives. There, again, Hodge admitted the "abstruse & mysterious nature" of the doctrine, the diversity of early Reformed opinion on the matter, and even the role of the Lord's Supper in aiding the Christian's union with Christ. However, he emphasized that early Calvinist statements on the doctrine were predominantly "irenical. They were drawn up with the express design of harmonizing conflicting views, & of preventing the impending schism of Lutherans & Reformed." Only later was the Reformed view distinguished from the Lutheran in a clear and consistent manner, and on largely Zwinglian terms.

22.   Hodge, "Doctrine of the Reformed Church," 264–66, 270–71, 273, 275–78.

23.   Edward Robinson, "Theological Education in Germany," *Biblical Repository* 1 (January 1831): 1. Robinson studied with Moses Stuart at Andover Seminary before he went to Germany in 1826 (and remained until 1830). In 1828, he married Therese Albertine Luise von Jakob, the daughter of Heinrich von Jakob (a professor of philosophy and political studies at Halle) and a scholar, writer, and poet in her own right. For more on Robinson's importance as a conduit of German academic thought to America, see Thomas Albert Howard, "German Academic Theology in America: The Case of Edward Robinson and Philip Schaff," *History of Universities* 18, no. 1 (2003): 102–23.

24.   Jefferson wrote from Paris regarding the training of his nephew:

Of all the errors which can possibly be committed in the education of youth, that of sending them to Europe is the most fatal. I see [clearly] that no American should come to Europe under 30 years of age: and [he who] does, will lose in science, in virtue, in health and in happiness, for which manners are a poor compensation, were we even to admit the hollow, unmeaning manners of Europe to be preferable to the simplicity and sincerity of our own country.

Thomas Jefferson to Walker Maury, August 19, 1785, in *The Papers of Thomas Jefferson*, vol. 8, *25 February to 31 October 1785*, ed. Julian P. Boyd (Princeton, N.J.: Princeton University Press, 1953), 409–10.

25.   On this phenomenon, see especially Noah Porter, "Coleridge and His American Disciples," *Bibliotheca Sacra* 4 (February 1847): 117–71; and Anson Phelps Stokes, *Memorials of Eminent Yale Men: A Biographical Study of Student Life and University Influences during the Eighteenth and Nineteenth Centuries*, vol. 1, *Religion and Letters* (New Haven, Conn.: Yale University Press, 1914), 329–30, who tells us that Porter himself was fascinated with Coleridge during his student years: "Among the special influences exerted upon him as an undergraduate none was greater than the reading of Coleridge, so often a factor in broadening and deepening the horizon. His *Aids to Reflection* soon became the text book of a little group of students, of whom Porter and Atwater, later Professor of Logic and Moral Philosophy at Princeton, were conspicuous for enthusiasm."

26.   For a brief, current account of this American migration, see Gary Dorrien, *The Making of American Liberal Theology: Imagining Progressive Religion, 1805–1900* (Louisville, Ky.: Westminster John Knox, 2001), 403–4.

27. Noah Porter, "The American Student in Germany," *New Englander* 15 (November 1857): 575, 588.

28. The PTS Archives contain a written record of Hodge's student years in Germany. See Charles Hodge, "Journal of European Travels," February 1827–April 1828, box 16, folder 4, Charles Hodge Manuscript Collection, in which he confesses to his chronic struggle to master the German language and admits to his suspicion of German heterodoxy. Cf. Hodge's German lecture notes, taken down in German, box 2, Charles Hodge Papers, Department of Special Collections, Princeton University Library (PUL).

29. See especially Charles Hodge, "The Latest Form of Infidelity," *Biblical Repertory and Princeton Review* 12 (January 1840): 31–71; and his later critique of modern German "pantheism" in Hodge, "What Is Christianity?" *Biblical Repertory and Princeton Review* 32 (January 1860): 118–61. For Hodge's take on Samuel Coleridge as a mediating figure, see the fascinating letter from James Marsh (of the University of Vermont) to Hodge, November 4, 1830, box 17, folder 33, Charles Hodge Papers, PUL, in which Marsh defends his recent edition of Coleridge's *Aids to Reflection*, as well as Coleridge's and Marsh's own theological orthodoxy; and Hodge's brief notice of Marsh's American edition of Samuel T. Coleridge, *The Friend: A Series of Essays, to Aid in the Formation of Fixed Principles in Politics, Morals, and Religion, with Literary Amusements Interspersed* (Burlington, Vt.: Chauncey Goodrich, 1831), in the *Biblical Repertory and Princeton Review* 4 (January 1832): 143–44, in which Hodge says this about the book: "It reminds us of the sounds produced by a noble organ, out of tune. Mr. Coleridge stands up for the defence of orthodoxy; but his orthodoxy does not strike us as genuine or safe" (143).

30. For more on the roles of German thought in nineteenth-century America, see "German Neology," *Quarterly Christian Spectator* 6 (September 1834): 509–12, which deplores "the defection from the faith of the gospel, which has been so universal for the last half century in Germany" (509); James W. Alexander, "Neander's History of the Planting of the Church," *Biblical Repertory and Princeton Review* 16 (April 1844): 155–83, who says that "the taste for German writers on dogmatic theology, is factitious, alien to the genius of the Anglo-American mind, and productive, wherever it exists, of debilitating and rhapsodical musing" (183); Charles H. Brigham, "On the Study of German in America," *Christian Examiner* 8 (July 1869): 1–20, who applauds German learning and notes a "marvelous change" (3) in the attitudes of Americans about it during the previous generation: "If a theological student ventured upon this forbidden ground [during the antebellum period], he was solemnly warned of the probable consequence, and his spiritual ruin was predicted. To study German was to take the first step in unbelief. . . . How completely now the tables are turned! . . . Now that the fright has passed, each denomination is eager to get all that it can out of this dreadful jungle of lions and tigers" (6–7); Roland H. Bainton, "Yale and German Theology in the Middle of the Nineteenth Century," in Bainton, *Christian Unity and Religion in New England* (Boston: Beacon, 1964), 252–64; Carl Diehl, *Americans and German Scholarship, 1770–1870* (New Haven, Conn.: Yale University Press, 1978); and, on the view of these matters from Germany, Thomas Albert Howard, *Protestant*

Theology and the Making of the Modern German University (Oxford: Oxford University Press, 2006), esp. 348–78 on "'The Age of German Footnotes': Visitors from Abroad, Admirers from Afar"; and Howard, "Philip Schaff: Religion, Politics, and the Transatlantic World," *Journal of Church and State* 49 (Spring 2007): 191–210, which uses Schaff insightfully as a mediating figure (between the mutual stereotyping of both Germans and Americans) and offers historic perspective on more recent anti-Americanism in Germany and in Europe more generally.

31. John W. Nevin, *Antichrist; or, The Spirit of Sect and Schism* (New York: Taylor, 1848), 3–4, 17; Nevin, "Introduction," in Schaff, *Principle of Protestantism*, 30–32; Frederick A. Gast (a German Reformed pastor and a professor at Franklin and Marshall), "Introduction," in Appel, *Life and Work of John Williamson Nevin*, vii; and Nevin, *My Own Life*, 96–127, and 139–49, on Nevin's encounter with Neander (a Jewish-Christian scholar who became Nevin's most important source of inspiration):

> What he was for Germany on a large scale, this he became for me also in a private way, an epoch (to use one of his own terms), a grand crisis or turning point followed by a whole era of new existence. . . . How much I owe to him in the way of excitement, impulse, suggestion, knowledge, both literary and religious, reaching onward into all my later life, is more than I can pretend to explain; for it is in truth more than I have power to understand. . . . I do not wish to be understood, of course, as bestowing on Neander unmeasured or unqualified praise. . . . His faults and defects are now generally admitted.

Still, he "[taught me to see] what history properly means. . . . Before my acquaintance with Neander, . . . this sense of the historical was something which I could hardly be said to have even begun to possess at all. Since then it has come to condition all my views of life" (139, 141–44).

For further testimony regarding Nevin's and Mercersburg's ambivalent admiration of the Germans, see J. W. Nevins [*sic*], "A Plea for Philosophy," *American Review: Devoted to Politics and Literature* 1 (February 1848): 143–55; and John Williamson Nevin, "Our Relations to Germany," *Mercersburg Review* 14 (October 1867): 627–33, in which he wrote this rather sarcastic, thinly veiled critique of Hodge (and other American evangelicals):

> We are not of that class who pique themselves on being good philosophers, because they have never read a line of Kant and have not the remotest conception of what was dreamed of by Fichte and Schelling; or who consider themselves good and safe theologians, because their dogmatic slumbers have never been for a moment disturbed by Schleiermacher or the dangerous school of Tübingen. We confess our obligations both to the philosophers and the theologians of Germany. They have done much to deepen our religious convictions, and to widen the range of our religious thought. . . . With all this high opinion, however, of the German mind and learning, we belong to no German school, and have never pretended to follow strictly any German system or scheme of thought. Neither have we been blind at all, or insensible, to the dangers of a too free and trustful communication with these foreign forms of thinking. (630–31)

Also see F. A. Rauch (Nevin's earliest mentor at Mercersburg), "Ecclesiastical Historiography in Germany," *American Biblical Repository* 10 (October 1837): 297–317; Philip Schaff, *Germany: Its Universities, Theology, and Religion* . . . (Philadelphia: Lindsay and Blakiston, 1857): "The German theology of the last thirty or forty years, whatever be its errors and defects, its extravagances and follies, which we would be among the last to deny, or to defend, is, upon the whole, the most learned, original, fertile, and progressive theology of the age, and no active branch of Protestantism can keep entirely aloof from its contact without injuring its own interests" (8); Schaff, "Neander as a Church Historian," *Mercersburg Review* 4 (November 1852): 564–77; and the brief section "German Theology in America" in Schaff, *Theological Propaedeutic: A General Introduction to the Study of Theology* . . . (New York: Scribner's, 1893), 402–4. Cf. Luther John Binkley, "The German Theological Antecedents of the Mercersburg Theology," *Bulletin: Theological Seminary of the Evangelical and Reformed Church in the United States* 21 (July 1950): 120–48; and Klaus Penzel, *The German Education of Christian Scholar Philip Schaff: The Formative Years, 1819–1844* (Lewiston, N.Y.: Mellen, 2004). Hodge had studied with Neander and held him in high esteem. See Hodge's entire book of notes on Neander's lectures on the epistles to the Corinthians and Ephesians (written in English but titled in German), "Neander über die Corinther und Ephesei Briefe," box 17, folder 1, Charles Hodge Manuscript Collection, PTS Archives; as well as his notes on Neander's lecture on the apostolic age, "Das Apostolische Zeitalter von Neander," Berlin, October 27, 1827, box 16, folder 3, Charles Hodge Manuscript Collection, PTS Archives. Cf. James W. Alexander, "Neander's History of the Planting of the Church," *Biblical Repertory and Princeton Review* 16 (April 1844): 155–83, which is typical of most American evangelical writers on the question of Neander's orthodoxy:

> It is impossible to name a writer of Germany, whose theological position it is more difficult to designate with precision. He must certainly be regarded as a friend of the gospel and an opposer of Neology. With the Deism of the cold, flat, sneering rationalists, he has no sympathy. Towards the other wing of the infidel army, that of the high-flying, transcendental, visionary, arrogant, pantheistic philosophists, he has expressed not only repugnance but horror. He is a supernaturalist, and a resolute defender of the doctrines of grace: but this expression must not be interpreted by English or American ideas. . . . Accustomed to refer theology more to the heart than the head, he is led to undervalue logical statements; and to express himself even on fundamental points with a vagueness which tantalizes the reader. . . . The forms into which his creed is thrown, are often so wide, that even a Sabellian might not scruple to adopt them. (156)

32. J. W. Nevin, "Once for All," *Mercersburg Review* 17 (January 1870): 100; Nevin, *Antichrist*, 46–47; and John Calvin, *Institutes of the Christian Religion*, ed. John T. McNeill, trans. Ford Lewis Battles (Philadelphia: Westminster, 1960), 4.17.11. (I have sought to track down Nevin's sources in Calvin's own corpus, citing accessible English translations when possible.) Cf. Nevin, *Mystical Presence*, 189–92; and Nevin, "Doctrine of the Reformed Church on the Lord's Supper," *Mercersburg Review* 2

(September 1850): 548, which he concluded by echoing the theme above from Calvin's *Institutes*:

> [I]n the age of the Reformation, it was felt on all sides unsafe to sunder the benefits and merits of Christ from his living person. How earnestly Calvin insisted on their connection, we have had ample opportunity to see. What Christ does or has done, must ever be conditioned certainly by what he is; and it is hard to see, how the force of his righteousness forensically taken can ever be impaired, by its being allowed to be in truth a part of himself and in union always with his own life.

Also see Nevin, "Bible Christianity," *Mercersburg Review* 2 (July 1850): 353–68; Nevin's organicist critique of Hodge's high predestinarianism in Nevin, "Hodge on the Ephesians," *Mercersburg Review* 9 (January 1857): 46–83, and (April 1857): 192–245; Nevin's suggestion that the Heidelberg Catechism excludes Hodge's type of abstract, sharply pointed Calvinism in Nevin, *History and Genius of the Heidelberg Catechism* (Chambersburg, Pa.: Publication Office of the German Reformed Church, 1847), esp. 125–39; and Appel, *Life and Work of John Williamson Nevin*, who offered insight into Nevin's critique of Hodge's work on Ephesians, which, to Nevin, was so abstract (and supralapsarian in its logic) that it rendered "the activity of man in fact into mere dumb show" (575). Nevin contrasted his "organic" Calvinist doctrine of election with Hodge's "mechanical" alternative in the light of his own commitment to the existential grounding of Christian doctrine. On the significance of union with Christ to Nevin's soteriology, see also William Borden Evans, "Imputation and Impartation: The Problem of Union with Christ in Nineteenth-Century American Reformed Theology" (Ph.D. diss., Vanderbilt University, 1996).

   33. As Nevin noted at the outset of the latter publication—a lengthy, critical synthesis of the conversation to date—it included key quotations from his earlier exchange with Hodge on eucharistic doctrine and a reply to Hodge's charges "taken mainly though not exclusively from the series of articles which appeared against Dr. Hodge in the Weekly Messenger, during the summer of 1848." Nevin, "Doctrine of the Reformed Church on the Lord's Supper," 422.

   34. Ibid., 433, 436–37, 448, 451, 455–57. Cf. Johannes Heinrich August Ebrard, *Das Dogma vom heiligen Abendmahl und seine Geschichte*, 2 vols. (Frankfurt: Heinrich Zimmer, 1845–1846). Formerly of Zurich, Ebrard during this time lectured in Erlangen and corresponded with Nevin.

   35. A brief but reliable English-language explication of this document may be found in Paul Robert Sanders, "Consensus Tigurinus," in *The Oxford Encyclopedia of the Reformation*, 4 vols., ed. Hans J. Hillerbrand et al. (New York: Oxford University Press, 1996), 1:414–15.

   36. Nevin, "Doctrine of the Reformed Church on the Lord's Supper," 458, 473–77. Cf. John Calvin (with G. Farel and P. Viret), *Confession of Faith concerning the Eucharist*, in *Calvin: Theological Treatises*, ed. J. K. S. Reid (Philadelphia: Westminster, 1954), 167–69; and Calvin, *Short Treatise on the Supper of Our Lord*, in *Selected Works of John Calvin: Tracts and Letters*, vol. 2, ed. and trans. Henry Beveridge (1849; repr., Grand Rapids, Mich.: Baker, 1983), in which he stated: "We all then confess with one

mouth, that on receiving the sacrament in faith, according to the ordinance of the Lord, we are truly made partakers of the proper substance of the body and blood of Jesus Christ" (197). The Latin and French originals of these short confessional statements may be found in Calvin, *Ioannis Calvini Opera Quae Supersunt Omnia*, ed. G. Baum et al. (Braunschweig: Schwetschke, 1863–1900), 9:711–12, and 5:429–60. (NB: Though Beveridge dates the latter treatise in 1540, it was actually published in 1541.) Nevin might have added here that, as Calvin said in a letter to a colleague written from Strassburg, he found Zwingli's view of the sacraments "false and pernicious" (*falsa et perniciosa*). John Calvin to André Zebedee, May 19, 1539, in *Thesaurus Epistolicus Calvinianus*, vol. 1, in *Calvini Opera*, 10:346. There is a slightly different English translation in Jules Bonnet, ed., *Letters of John Calvin*, vol. 4 (1858; repr., New York: Franklin, 1972), 402. On the broader Bernese context of the Confession of 1537, in which Martin Bucer proved immensely influential as a mediating figure on the doctrine of the Eucharist (charting a course between the Lutherans and Zwinglians), see Amy Nelson Burnett, "The Myth of the Swiss Lutherans: Martin Bucer and the Eucharistic Controversy in Bern," *Zwingliana: Beiträge zur Geschichte Zwinglis der Reformation und des Protestantismus in der Schweiz* 32 (2005): 45–70; and Cornelis Augustijn, "Bern and France: The Background to Calvin's Letter to Bucer Dated 12 January 1538," in *Ordenlich und Fruchtbar: Festschrift für Willem van't Spijker, Anlässlich seines Abschieds als Professor der Theologischen Universität Apeldoorn*, ed. Wilhelm H. Neuser and Herman J. Selderhuis (Leiden: Groen and Zoon, 1997), 155–69. Tellingly, even Karl Barth—who did not share Calvin's high view of the Lord's Supper—agreed with Nevin regarding the value of the *Consensus Tigurinus*. In the lectures he gave in Göttingen in 1923, he said, "I do not place too high an estimate upon the substantive value of the Consensus Tigurinus. . . . There is too much in it that was obvious to Calvin and that he only repeated to suit the Zurich group, while on the other hand much of that which is innovative in Calvinism is lacking here, so that it is not the work from which one should learn his doctrine of the Lord's Supper." Barth, *The Theology of the Reformed Confessions, 1923*, trans. Darrell L. Guder and Judith J. Guder (Louisville, Ky.: Westminster John Knox, 2002), 178.

    37. Nevin, "Doctrine of the Reformed Church on the Lord's Supper," 479–80, 485–86. For more on Calvin's controversy with Westphal and Hesshus, see Joseph N. Tylenda, "The Calvin-Westphal Exchange: The Genesis of Calvin's Treatises against Westphal," *Calvin Theological Journal* 9 (November 1974): 182–209; David C. Steinmetz, "Calvin and His Lutheran Critics," *Lutheran Quarterly* 4 (Summer 1990): 179–94; Joseph N. Tylenda, "Calvin and Westphal: Two Eucharistic Theologies in Conflict," in *Calvin's Books: Festschrift Dedicated to Peter De Klerk on the Occasion of His Seventieth Birthday*, ed. Wilhelm H. Neuser, Herman J. Selderhuis, and Willem van't Spijker (Heerenveen, Netherlands: Groen, 1997), 9–21; Wim Janse, "Calvin's Eucharistic Theology: Three Dogma-Historical Observations," in *Calvinus Sacrarum Literarum Interpres: Conference Proceedings of the Ninth Quadrennial International Congress on Calvin Research, Emden/Apeldoorn, August 22–26, 2006*, ed. Herman J. Selderhuis (Göttingen: Vandenhoeck and Ruprecht, 2008); and Janse, "Joachim Westphal's Sacramentology," *Lutheran Quarterly* 22 (Summer 2008): 137–60. These scholars disagree about whether or the extent to which the *Consensus Tigurinus*

represents a change in Calvin. For a helpful, English-language collection of Calvin's views on the issues and responses to the Lutherans, see Calvin, *Mutual Consent in Regard to the Sacraments . . .*; Calvin, *Second Defence of the Pious and Orthodox Faith concerning the Sacraments, in Answer to the Calumnies of Joachim Westphal*; Calvin, *Last Admonition of John Calvin to Joachim Westphal*; Calvin, *Clear Explanation of Sound Doctrine concerning the True Partaking of the Flesh and Blood of Christ in the Holy Supper, in Order to Dissipate the Mists of Tileman Heshusius*; and Calvin, *The Best Method of Obtaining Concord, Provided the Truth Be Sought without Contention*, all in *Selected Works of John Calvin: Tracts and Letters*, 2:199–579 (most in *Calvini Opera*, vol. 9). Throughout these works, Calvin appeals to Philipp Melanchthon and the Augsburg Confession, claiming that the *Variata* "does not contain a word contrary to our doctrine" (*Last Admonition*, 355). Further:

> I do not teach that there is only a bare and shadowy figure, but distinctly
> declare that the bread is a sure pledge of that communion with the flesh and
> blood of Christ which it figures. For Christ is neither a painter, nor a player,
> nor a kind of Archimedes, who presents an empty image to amuse the eye,
> but he truly and in reality performs what he promises by an external symbol.
> Hence I conclude that the bread which we break is truly the communion of
> the body of Christ. (*Clear Explanation*, 507–8)

38. The German Reformed Church historian Heinrich Heppe shaped Nevin's notion of the importance of Melanchthon to the reformed. In fact, in 1853, one of Heppe's German articles on the Melanchthonian origins of the German Reformed Church was translated and reprinted in the *Mercersburg Review*. See Heppe, "The Character of the German Reformed Church, and Its Relation to Lutheranism and Calvinism," *Mercersburg Review* 5 (April 1853): 181–207.

39. Nevin, "Doctrine of the Reformed Church on the Lord's Supper," 516, 508. Nevin ranged widely over Calvin's extant corpus, quoting Calvin's frequent assertions that "Christ feeds us with His flesh, which was sacrificed for us," "the eating is substantial," "we are truly united with" Christ during the eucharistic meal "so that he invigorates us by the proper substance of his body," Christ "transfuses the life-giving vigour of his flesh into us," etc. For confirmation of these statements (and many others like them) in Calvin's oeuvre, see especially John Calvin, *The First Epistle of Paul the Apostle to the Corinthians*, ed. David W. Torrance and Thomas F. Torrance, trans. John Fraser (Grand Rapids, Mich.: Eerdmans, 1960), 205 (*Calvini Opera*, 49:455–56); Calvin, *Confession of Faith in Name of the Reformed Churches of France* (1562), in *Selected Works of John Calvin: Tracts and Letters*, 2:159–60 (*Calvini Opera*, 9:769); and Calvin, *Second Defence of the Pious and Orthodox Faith concerning the Sacraments*, 245–345 (*Calvini Opera*, 9:41–120).

40. B. A. Gerrish, "Gospel and Eucharist: John Calvin on the Lord's Supper," in Gerrish, *The Old Protestantism and the New: Essays on the Reformation Heritage* (Chicago: University of Chicago Press, 1982), 106; Gerrish, *Grace and Gratitude: The Eucharistic Theology of John Calvin* (Minneapolis, Minn.: Fortress, 1993), 178–80; and Nevin, "Doctrine of the Reformed Church on the Lord's Supper," 508. For further English-language commentary on Calvin's view of the Eucharist, see Thomas J. Davis,

The Clearest Promises of God: The Development of Calvin's Eucharistic Teaching (New York: AMS, 1995); Christopher Elwood, *The Body Broken: The Calvinist Doctrine of the Eucharist and the Symbolization of Power in Sixteenth-Century France* (New York: Oxford University Press, 1999); and Thomas J. Davis, "'Not Hidden and Far Off': The Bodily Aspect of Salvation and Its Implications for Understanding the Body in Calvin's Theology," "Preaching and Presence: Constructing Calvin's Homiletic Legacy," and "'He Is Outwith the World . . . That He May Fill All Things': Calvin's Exegesis of the Ascension and Its Relation to the Eucharist," all in Davis, *This Is My Body: The Presence of Christ in Reformation Thought* (Grand Rapids, Mich.: Baker Academic, 2008), 79–90, 91–115, and 127–39. For a good general survey of eucharistic faith and practice during the Reformation era, see Lee Palmer Wandel, *The Eucharist in the Reformation: Incarnation and Liturgy* (Cambridge: Cambridge University Press, 2006). For more on Nevin's view, see Arie J. Griffioen, "Nevin on the Lord's Supper," in *Reformed Confessionalism in Nineteenth-Century America*, ed. Hamstra and Griffioen, 113–24; Linden J. de Bie, "Real Presence or Real Absence? The Spoils of War in Nineteenth-Century American Eucharistic Controversy," *Pro Ecclesia* 4 (Fall 1995): 431–41; B. A. Gerrish, "The Flesh of the Son of Man: John W. Nevin on the Church and the Eucharist," in Gerrish, *Tradition and the Modern World: Reformed Theology in the Nineteenth Century* (Chicago: University of Chicago Press, 1978), 49–70; and the books on Nevin cited above. (Significantly, Gerrish follows Nevin in placing the Eucharist at the heart of Calvin's doctrine and interpreting Calvin's eucharistic thought in Nevin's way. Like Nevin, Gerrish interprets Calvin mainly in relation to nineteenth-century German thought.) On the doctrine of the Eucharist in the major Reformed confessions, see B. A. Gerrish, "Sign and Reality: The Lord's Supper in the Reformed Confessions," in Gerrish, *The Old Protestantism and the New*, 118–30; and Jan Rohls, *Reformed Confessions: Theology from Zurich to Barmen*, trans. John Hoffmeyer (Louisville, Ky.: Westminster John Knox, 1998), 219–37.

41. Noll, *America's God*, 409; and *A Liturgy; or, Order of Christian Worship . . . of the German Reformed Church in the United States of America* (Philadelphia: Lindsay and Blakiston, 1858). For Bomberger's early defense of Nevin, see J. H. A. Bomberger, "Dr. Nevin and His Antagonists," *Mercersburg Review* 5 (January 1853): 89–123, and (April 1853): 145–81. In the end, Bomberger came to believe that Nevin emphasized the incarnation to the detriment of the doctrine of the atonement, depicting what Christ has done in such organic and imminent language that redemption seemed inevitable for those within the church—and conversion, regeneration, and justification paled in significance. Cf. Alan P. F. Sell, "J. H. A. Bomberger (1817–1890) versus J. W. Nevin: A Centenary Reappraisal," *New Mercersburg Review* 8 (Autumn 1990): 3–234. For the paper war between Nevin and Bomberger, see esp. Bomberger, *The Revised Liturgy: A History and Criticism of the Ritualistic Movement in the German Reformed Church* (Philadelphia: Rodgers, 1867); Nevin, *Vindication of the Revised Liturgy, Historical and Theological* (Philadelphia: Rodgers, 1867); and Bomberger, *Reformed, Not Ritualistic, Apostolic, Not Patristic: A Reply to Dr. Nevin's "Vindication" . . .* (Philadelphia: Rodgers, 1867). Cf. Bomberger's essays in the *Reformed Church Monthly*, such as "Mercersburg and Reformed Theology Contrasted," *Reformed Church Monthly* 4 (1871): 128–34, and "What They Mean by Development," *Reformed Church Monthly* 6 (1873): 521–25. Other

voices in the controversy included B. S. Schneck (a harsh critic of Nevin and Mercersburg), *Mercersburg Theology Inconsistent with Protestant and Reformed Doctrine* (Philadelphia: Lippincott, 1874); and Samuel Miller (a supporter in the German Reformed Church, not the Princetonian by that name), *A Treatise on Mercersburg Theology; or, Mercersburg and Modern Theology Compared* (Philadelphia: Fisher, 1866). For helpful summaries of the liturgical controversy sparked by Nevin, see esp. Jack Martin Maxwell, *Worship and Reformed Theology: The Liturgical Lessons of Mercersburg* (Pittsburgh, Pa.: Pickwick, 1976); and Hart, *John Williamson Nevin*, 197–223. On the founding of Ursinus, see Gerald Hahn Hinkle, "The Theology of the Ursinus Movement: Its Origins and Influence in the German Reformed Church" (Ph.D. diss., Yale University, 1964), including its dated but detailed bibliographical materials (288–307); and Calvin Daniel Yost, *Ursinus College: A History of Its First Hundred Years* (Collegeville, Pa.: Ursinus College, 1985).

42. See, for example, Hodge's *Systematic Theology*, 2:446–50, 3:204–12; and John Williamson Nevin to Charles Hodge, February 24, 1872, box 18, folder 3, Charles Hodge Papers, PUL, in which Nevin complained that, for years, both in print and in the classroom, Hodge had portrayed him as a harmful heretic. The occasion of Nevin's letter was a hatchet job by Hodge, in his *Systematic Theology*, 2:428–29, on a recent piece by Nevin on Karl Theodor Albert Liebner, "Liebner's Christology," *Mercersburg Review* 3 (January 1851): 55–73. Cf. George H. Shriver, "Passages in Friendship: John W. Nevin to Charles Hodge, 1872," *Journal of Presbyterian History* 58 (Summer 1980): 116–22. Apparently, this "friendship" was not as bad as it could have been, for as Appel reported, "Some years before his death Dr. Hodge made it convenient to visit Lancaster, and he was heartily received as a guest in Dr. Nevin's family. The meeting and intercourse were cordial in character, and tended very much to cement the friendship formed in their earlier years" (Appel, *Life and Work of John Williamson Nevin*, 298).

43. John B. Adger (a former missionary and Presbyterian minister who was teaching at Columbia Seminary in South Carolina), "Calvin Defended against Drs. Cunningham and Hodge," *Southern Presbyterian Review* 27 (January 1876): 133–66; Adger, "Calvin's Doctrine of the Lord's Supper," *Southern Presbyterian Review* 36 (October 1885): 785–800; Adger, *My Life and Times, 1810–1899* (Richmond, Va.: Presbyterian Committee on Publication, 1899), 310–26; Henry J. Van Dyke Sr., "The Lord's Supper," *Presbyterian Review* 8 (April 1887): 193–218 (quotation from 194); DiPuccio, *Interior Sense of Scripture*, 64–65; and Nichols, *Romanticism in American Theology*, 90. Cf. E. Brooks Holifield, "Mercersburg, Princeton, and the South: The Sacramental Controversy in the Nineteenth Century," *Journal of Presbyterian History* 54 (Summer 1976): 238–57; and Hart, *John Williamson Nevin*, in which he writes of Nevin and Schaff: "however good or bad their theology, their history was markedly superior to any of their contemporaries" (117).

44. Edwards Amasa Park, "The Theology of the Intellect and That of the Feelings," *Bibliotheca Sacra* 7 (July 1850): 533–69 (quotations from 558–61).

45. Charles Hodge, "Professor Park's Sermon," *Biblical Repertory and Princeton Review* 22 (October 1850): 646, 673, 660, 670. Hodge's dim view of Park was shaped

in part by the suspicions of his colleague Lyman Atwater, who had studied with Nathaniel W. Taylor at Yale Divinity School before becoming a teacher at Princeton College. Atwater believed Park to be a dangerous heretic. As he wrote in a letter to Hodge, Park's "invention of a theology of Intellect & a theology of feeling was a mere device for reconciling old fashioned Christians to his perversities." See Lyman Atwater to Charles Hodge, July 22, 1851, box 13, folder 32, Charles Hodge Papers, PUL. Ironically, twenty-one years later, Hodge's *Systematic Theology* included a distinction between "two theologies,—one of the intellect, and another of the heart. The one may find expression in creeds and systems of divinity, the other in their prayers and hymns. It would be safe for a man to resolve to admit into his theology nothing which is not sustained in the devotional writings of true Christians of every denomination." Hodge, *Systematic Theology*, 1:16–17. Despite his ecumenical sympathies and emphasis on feeling, Park was never the liberal thinker Princeton made him out to be. As the Unitarian minister and seminary president Rufus Stebbins noted of Park's convention sermon: "No one, orthodox or heterodox, dreamed that the eloquent speaker was scattering heresy in his glowing sentences. It required the sensitive olfactories of Princeton to scent, under the perfume of roses, the brimstone of heresy." Rufus P. Stebbins, "The Andover and Princeton Theologies," *Christian Examiner and Religious Miscellany* 52 (May 1852): 309–10.

46. See esp. Douglas A. Sweeney, "Edwards and His Mantle: The Historiography of the New England Theology," *New England Quarterly* 71 (March 1998): 97–119; Sweeney, *Nathaniel Taylor, New Haven Theology, and the Legacy of Jonathan Edwards* (New York: Oxford University Press, 2003); and Douglas A. Sweeney and Allen C. Guelzo, eds., *The New England Theology: From Jonathan Edwards to Edwards Amasa Park* (Grand Rapids, Mich.: Baker Academic, 2006).

47. Edwards A. Park, "New England Theology: With Comments on a Third Article in the *Biblical Repertory and Princeton Review*, Relating to a Convention Sermon," *Bibliotheca Sacra* 9 (January 1852): 170–220, reprinted in pamphlet form (Andover, Mass.: Draper, 1852).

48. "The Progress of Theological Science since the Reformation," *Quarterly Christian Spectator* 10 (August 1838): 477; "Who Are the True Conservatives?" *Quarterly Christian Spectator* 10 (November 1838): 617, 621, 624; George P. Fisher, "The System of Dr. N. W. Taylor in Its Connection with Prior New England Theology," reprinted in Fisher, *Discussions in History and Theology* (New York: Scribner's, 1880), 287–88.

49. Charles Hodge, "Professor Park and the *Princeton Review*," *Biblical Repertory and Princeton Review* 23 (October 1851): 676–77.

50. Earl William Kennedy, "From Pessimism to Optimism: Francis Turretin and Charles Hodge on 'The Last Things,'" in *Servant Gladly: Essays in Honor of John W. Beardslee III*, ed. Jack D. Klunder and Russell L. Gasero (Grand Rapids, Mich.: Eerdmans, 1989), 116; James Turner, "Charles Hodge in the Intellectual Weather of the Nineteenth Century," in *Charles Hodge Revisited: A Critical Appraisal of His Life and Work*, ed. John W. Stewart and James H. Moorhead (Grand Rapids, Mich.: Eerdmans, 2002), 43. Cf. Earl William Kennedy, "An Historical Analysis of Charles Hodge's Doctrines of Sin and Particular Grace" (Th.D. thesis, Princeton Theological Seminary, 1968).

51. C. P. Krauth, *Infant Baptism and Infant Salvation in the Calvinistic System: A Review of Dr. Hodge's Systematic Theology* (Philadelphia: Lutheran Book Store, 1874), 6; Robert W. Landis, *The Doctrine of Original Sin, as Received and Taught by the Churches of the Reformation, Stated and Defended, and the Error of Dr. Hodge in Claiming That This Doctrine Recognizes the Gratuitous Imputation of Sin, Pointed Out and Refuted* (Richmond, Va.: Whittet and Shepperson, 1884), xiii; and William G. T. Shedd, *Dogmatic Theology*, 3 vols. (1888–1894; repr., Grand Rapids, Mich.: Zondervan, 1953), esp. 2:3–94 and 3:iii. For further criticism (more or less explicit) of Hodge's and Princeton's understanding of Calvinism, see Robert J. Breckinridge, *The Knowledge of God, Objectively Considered: Being the First Part of Theology Considered as a Science of Positive Truth, Both Inductive and Deductive* (New York: Carter, 1858), 481–524; Breckinridge, *The Knowledge of God Subjectively Considered: Being the Second Part of Theology Considered as a Science of Positive Truth, Both Inductive and Deductive* (New York: Carter, 1860), which Landis claimed to be expounding in his critique of Hodge's doctrine; Henry B. Smith to Rev. Dr. J. F. Stearns, October 23, 1855, in *Henry Boynton Smith: His Life and Work*, ed. Elizabeth L. Smith (New York: Armstrong, 1881), 190–92, in which Smith defended his ontological realism against Hodge, claiming Calvin and Edwards for his side of the dispute; Smith, *The Reunion of the Presbyterian Churches, Called New School and Old School: A Reply to the "Princeton Review"* (New York: Sherwood, 1867); Smith, "Contemporary Literature: *Systematic Theology*, vol. 2, by Charles Hodge," *Presbyterian Quarterly and Princeton Review* 2 (April 1872): 395–400; William G. T. Shedd, "The Doctrine of Original Sin" (*Christian Review*, January 1852), in Shedd, *Theological Essays* (New York: Scribner, Armstrong, 1877), 211–64; and Shedd, *A History of Christian Doctrine*, 2 vols. (New York: Scribner's, 1889), 2:1–199. For more on Shedd's realistic Calvinism and differences with Hodge, see Oliver D. Crisp, *An American Augustinian: Sin and Salvation in the Dogmatic Theology of William G. T. Shedd* (Milton Keynes, England: Paternoster, 2007).

6

Calvin and Calvinism within Congregational and Unitarian Discourse in Nineteenth-Century America

David D. Hall

Let *Calvin* answer for me.
> —John Cotton in the midst of being questioned
> by his fellow ministers about his orthodoxy (1637)

It was Jonathan Edwards who went back to the doctrine from which the tradition had started; went back, not to what the first generation of New Englanders had held, but to Calvin, and who became, therefore, the first consistent and authentic Calvinist in New England.
> Perry Miller, "The Marrow of Puritan Divinity" (1935)[1]

In the sweep of American history, the year 1865 has a distinctive resonance, for, in April 1865, the surrender of the Confederate Army brought the U.S. Civil War to an end. Although the assassination of Abraham Lincoln that same month tempered the mood of celebration among the victorious, it was widely felt that the republic was on the verge of a deeper transition. The founders of a new weekly journal of political and cultural criticism called it the *Nation* for this reason, expecting that, at long last, their country had entered a promising phase of consolidation and maturity. The same mood arose within religious denominations. Thus, on June 14, 1865, the first-ever National Council of Congregational Churches met in Boston to consider how to participate in the postwar impulse for organization and coherence. Another ambition was to strengthen the denomination's capacity to grow outside of New England, where it had originated in the seventeenth century. Could it become fully national by expanding into the West and upper Midwest, where as yet only a few local churches existed?

As the council got under way, a subcommittee began to deliberate the shape of a Declaration of Faith. Everyone attending the event knew that a decision would have to be made about where the denomination stood doctrinally. Historically, Congregationalists in America had regarded themselves as in continuity with the Protestant Reformation and, more specifically, in continuity with Reformed orthodoxy as defined by the Westminster Confession of 1646 and John Calvin. The subcommittee took this allegiance for granted, declaring in a preliminary report that, despite "diversities of metaphysical theology" among the delegates attending the great event, a "singular unanimity" on doctrine and identity existed, a unanimity described as "the body of Christian doctrine known as Calvinistic; and hence such Confessions as those of the Westminster divines." Several days later, a new committee brought in a report that, like the first, recommended that the council "declare our acceptance of the system of truths which is commonly known among us as Calvinism." On the meeting's penultimate day (June 23), however, the council unanimously adopted what became known as the Burial Hill Declaration. From it, the words "Calvinistic" and "Calvinism" were strikingly absent, as was any reference to the Westminster Confession— even though the two initial committees had embraced them both.[2]

Why, at the close of their grand meeting, were these Congregationalists so reluctant to embrace either the figure of John Calvin or the words that descend from him? And what were the implications of this refusal for the future of Congregationalism and, a separate but related matter, the capacity of Congregationalists to understand their own origins in the seventeenth century? These are the questions that animate this chapter. My starting point is the Unitarian controversy of the 1820s and 1830s when newly self-identified "Unitarians" disputed the legitimacy of Calvinism with their orthodox (trinitarian) opponents. Thereafter, I turn to the debates at the National Council in 1865 and, at the end of the century, a New England Congregationalist's study of Calvin before concluding with the problem of Calvin and Calvinism within American Puritan studies of the mid-twentieth century as refracted through the writings of the most significant American student of Puritanism, Harvard professor Perry Miller. From one vantage, the story is utterly predictable to any reader of Karl Barth and H. Richard Niebuhr: the more that nineteenth-century liberal Protestants (especially *very* liberal Protestants) distanced themselves from the Reformation, the more they caricatured Calvin and Calvinism. I will add to this narrative some of the ironies and contradictions of that process.

Those ironies reappeared in someone who had no direct stake in liberal Protestantism, for Miller was a self-proclaimed atheist. Yet past is prologue, for, in wrestling with the relationship between Calvin (or Calvinism) and the theology of seventeenth-century New England Puritans, Miller could not free himself from the rhetoric of anti-Calvinism as it was voiced by nineteenth-century Americans. Indeed, the present-day confusion about "Calvin and Calvinism" in Puritan studies recapitulates the confusion of the reformers' nineteenth-century heirs within Congregationalism.[3]

Although I begin in the nineteenth century and end in the twentieth, a brief backward glance at theological debate in New England may help to set the stage. Given the purpose of this chapter, theological inquiry among eighteenth-century New England Congregationalists could be regarded as a version of the dog that didn't bark. The clergy who participated in the founding of New England in the seventeenth century rarely drew on Calvin and, to the best of my knowledge, never used the term "Calvinistic." No reference to any sixteenth-century Reformed theologian appears in the Westminster Confession, which was the product of Scottish and English Presbyterians in the mid-1640s. This creed was endorsed in New England by a clerical synod meeting in Cambridge, Massachusetts, in 1648, endorsed again in 1680, and again in the early eighteenth century. Jonathan Edwards, the great champion of orthodoxy against the liberalizing tendencies of the mid-eighteenth century—tendencies that, collectively, he named "Arminian"—never referred to himself as a Calvinist and, in the entirety of his published and unpublished writings, cited Calvin exactly three times in a single book, *A Treatise Concerning Religious Affections* (1746), each of these a reference to the *Institutes* (1.9.1 on there being no new revelations; 2.2.11 on humility; and 3.12.7 on the same).[4] According to the printed catalog of 1790, the Harvard College library contained nine volumes of Calvin in Latin, several commentaries and the *Institutes* in the same language, and a mid-seventeenth-century English translation of the *Institutes*, holdings that were surpassed by those of eighteenth-century English and New England ministers, virtually all of them in English.[5] No edition of any of Calvin's writings was printed in the colonies or early republic before 1800. Before 1840, the American book trade issued only three printings of the *Institutes* in translation (1815, 1819) and nothing else except his catechism, although local indifference must be juxtaposed with the practice of importing most "learned" books from Great Britain.[6] Incidental evidence of this kind suggests that a foreshortening of the past had occurred among the learned ministers of eighteenth-century New England. The sixteenth-century reformers had been replaced by seventeenth-century summaries of theology, including handbooks such as William Ames's *The Marrow of Theology* (1622 in Latin; 1638 in English), still in use at Yale College in the early eighteenth century and one of Jonathan Edwards's textbooks, and creeds such as the Westminster Confession. Perhaps it seemed that the basic questions had been settled, leaving "practical theology" as the terrain on which these ministers exercised their capacities as thinkers and debaters.[7]

This silence ended in the 1820s and 1830s when the terms Calvinism and Calvinistic were thrust into the foreground of interchurch debates in New England. What brought Calvinism and Calvin out of the shadows was the rupture between the liberal and evangelical wings of this tradition, which yielded a new denomination known as Unitarianism. Out of this rupture came as well a heightened emphasis on labels such as "Calvinist" and "orthodox" as useful markers for identifying what the liberal party was rejecting. "For the sake of convenience and brevity," a Unitarian minister-turned-historian declared in his retrospective narrative of the controversy,

> we shall freely use the terms *Unitarian* and *Orthodox* to designate the
> two parties. Our own sense of perfect justice to our predecessors
> would dispose us to use the word *Calvinist* instead of the word
> *Orthodox*, for it was Calvinism, the real concrete system of the
> Genevan Reformer, and not the vague and undefined abstraction
> entitled Orthodoxy, which our predecessors assailed.

"We have already said," the same writer added, "that the Unitarians understood and avowed that they were assailing . . . Calvinism which had expressed itself in positive formulas [i.e., creeds], and to which the Orthodox party professed an unqualified and unequivocal allegiance."[8]

What did Calvinism mean to these liberal Protestants? The term pervades the Boston minister William Ellery Channing's "The Moral Argument against Calvinism" (1823); the minister-turned-divinity-school-professor Henry Ware's attacks on the academic theologian Leonard Woods of Andover Seminary, who ventured to criticize Channing (1820–1823); and the polemics of Unitarian academic Andrews Norton. For Ware and Channing, the referents for their attacks were two: the Five Points associated with the Synod of Dort (for them, the very essence of Calvinism) and the Westminster Confession. Norton, a much more bookish man than either Ware or Channing, returned to the *Institutes* and other works by Calvin to make the liberal case. Theologically, the three agreed on what was wrong in Calvinism: a low estimation of human nature, given the imputation of Adam's sin to all humankind; the paralyzing consequences of divine sovereignty as embodied in the doctrine of election; the (to them) barbarous notion of sacrifice to satisfy an angry God; and the dismissal of human capacities for doing good. The alternative was as simple as imagining a benevolent God who wished humankind well, who respected powers of choice or free will, and who acknowledged those who performed the duties of the Christian life—in short, a God shorn of any markers of being "arbitrary," a master word in the vocabulary of the Unitarians' anti-Calvinism.[9]

Channing, in "The Moral Argument against Calvinism" and an earlier sermon, "Unitarian Christianity," laid down the main lines of criticism. Rehearsing the character of God, he insisted that "our best ideas of goodness and justice" deny the Calvinist emphasis on divine sovereignty. Rehearsing the relationship between human nature and morality, he described the "old and genuine" form of orthodoxy as holding that "under the innocent features of our childhood is hidden a nature averse to all good . . . a nature which exposes us to God's displeasure and wrath, even before we have acquired power to understand our duties." Free agency was a crucial premise of Channing's alternative. Without such agency, how can we be held responsible for our misdeeds? "We believe, that no dispositions infused into us without our own moral activity, are of the nature of virtue, and therefore, we reject the doctrine of irresistible divine influence on the human mind, moulding it into goodness, as marble is hewn into a statue." The darkest side of Calvinism was the denial of such agency, coupled with the unrelenting "cruelty" of its God: "were a human parent to form himself on the universal Father, as described by Calvinism, that is, were he to bring his children into life totally depraved, and then to pursue them with endless punishment, we should charge him with a cruelty not surpassed in the annals of the world."[10]

"The Moral Argument against Calvinism" brought the threads of anti-Calvinism together in a single accusation: no one who accepted the premises of Dortian Calvinism had any incentive to do good or, indeed, any real capacity to engage in acts of benevolence, for doing so made no difference in an economy of redemption so despotic. Even worse, people subjected to Calvinism were paralyzed by the emotion of terror. "Calvinism owes its perpetuity to the influence of fear in palsying the moral nature. Men's minds and consciences are subdued by terror, so that they dare not confess, even to themselves, the shrinking, which they feel, from the unworthy views which this system gives of God." The ultimate rebuke was a shudder or, as Channing put it, "the abhorrence with which every mind, uncorrupted by false theology, must look on Calvinism."[11]

In other Unitarian polemics as well as in Channing's, Calvinism acquired additional features. Treating "system" as a negative word and singling out the ambition to organize all of theology into a creed, the Unitarians celebrated their own biblicism, playing the card of biblical simplicity that, more than a century before them, John Locke had employed in *The Reasonableness of Christianity*. According to George Ellis, Unitarianism (and modernity) called for "the dethronement of dogmatism in religion,—that dogmatism which insists upon confining the power of the Gospel to a metaphysical system of doctrines set forth by men as the exponent of revealed truths." Persistently, therefore, the liberals spoke of "the dogmas of John Calvin" and, in writing about Jonathan Edwards, dismissed him as a "Calvinistic metaphysician," a double burden to bear, given the implication that to be "metaphysical" was to be detached from practical, living Christianity. When liberals described their own theological method, they boasted of relying on "reason" and insisted that "Unitarianism has no dogma, except in the quality of denying a dogma."[12]

Andrews Norton carried this vein of attack to an extreme: "false religion" manifested itself in "persecutors, zealots, and bigots," these being the inevitable consequence of a religious system stemming from "ages of ignorance" and wholly at odds with the modern temper. But his particular contribution to the onslaught on Calvinism was to return to the sources. Outraged when someone on the orthodox side insisted that "there never was a sect, or body of men" who espoused the ideas that Unitarians were attributing to the orthodox, Norton demonstrated otherwise in "Views of Calvinism" (meaning, the views offered by *soi-disant* Calvinists), an essay he published in 1822. His means of doing so was simple; he quoted from the sources: the Larger Catechism of Westminster and the confession itself; the acts of the Synod of Dort (from a 1620 edition in Latin); the Belgic Confession; passages from the seventeenth-century English theologian and high Calvinist William Twisse; Calvin's "Short Formula of a Confession of Faith," the *Institutes*, and other writings, all translated freshly from the Latin; and, most deliciously, passages from Jonathan Edwards's treatises and sermons, particularly "Sinners in the Hands of an Angry God." Using these texts, it was a simple matter to document the doctrine of original sin, its consequences for moral ability among humans, and the insistence that newborn children were immediately under sentence of reprobation or election. A long quotation from Calvin to this effect was followed by these words of Norton's: "*Decretum quidem horribile, fateor.* Calvin was not given to human relentings."[13]

Arbitrary, dogmatic, metaphysical, deterministic, antimodern, of a persecuting temper[14]—out of such terms and their many synonyms the Unitarian liberals wove their representation of Calvin and Calvinism. The warrant for lingering on Calvin, Edwards, and Westminster was simple: the official place of Westminster within New England Congregationalism and the high esteem in which Edwards was held. "Whoever will consult the famous Assembly's Catechisms and Confession," Channing declared in "The Moral Argument against Calvinism," "will see the peculiarities of the system in all their length and breadth of deformity."[15]

Yet, the liberals also sensed an uneasiness within the ranks of the orthodox, an uneasiness manifested in their opponents' reluctance to acclaim people, doctrines, and creeds that, by anyone's estimation, bore the label Calvinist. The liberals knew that, for several decades, one branch of the ministry in New England had referred to itself as "moderate" or "old" Calvinists in contrast to others, deemed "consistent" or "Hopkinsian" (after Samuel Hopkins, a minister in Newport, Rhode Island, who articulated a particularly stringent version of Edwardseanism). As Unitarians pointed out repeatedly, the more moderate Congregationalists hesitated to reiterate the formulas of Westminster and Dort. Hence the irony (as seen by the liberals) that "a large number, perhaps a majority of those, who surname themselves with the name of Calvin, have little more title to it than ourselves. They keep the name, and drop the principles which it signifies." In a rhetorical move that must have amused the liberals, Channing summoned the ghost of Calvin to rebuke his less-than-faithful heirs: "If the stern reformer of Geneva could lift up his head, and hear the mitigated tone, in which some of his professed followers dispense his fearful doctrines, we fear, that he could not lie down in peace, until he had poured out his displeasure on their cowardice and degeneracy."[16]

These Unitarians were on to something. By the 1830s, orthodox clergy were speaking in several voices, supporting rival seminaries, and frequently preaching the themes of free agency and divine benevolence. One strand within the tradition was doing so with a vengeance: the ministers collectively known as Old Calvinists (or, by the late 1820s, as advocates of the New Haven theology), who distanced themselves from another group, the ministers associated with the New Divinity. The ministers affiliated with the first of these strands were markedly reserved in their appreciation of Edwards and critical of Hopkins, who made himself notorious for advocating that "disinterested benevolence" (grounded in love of God) meant a willingness to accept damnation if this would advance the glory of God's kingdom. What warranted this attitude were several motifs of the New Divinity: its exaggerated emphasis on the natural depravity of humankind, its rejection of all means that sinners could employ to improve their situation, and its assertion that the more sin there was in the world, the more the glory of God was enhanced, a proposition that could be interpreted (or so critics complained) as saying that God wanted and therefore caused human sinfulness. Old Calvinists insisted to the contrary that humankind could gradually improve and indeed become visible saints under the nurturing care of the means of grace. In The Minister's Wooing (1859), a novel condemning the New Divinity, Harriet Beecher Stowe likened it to a ladder to heaven with all the rungs knocked out.[17] Old Calvinists also preferred "reasonableness" or common sense to the high-flying speculations they found in

Edwards. By the early nineteenth century, many were rejecting the Westminster position on original sin as transmitted by imputation.[18]

Some of these emphases emerged during debates between Congregationalists and Unitarians as the schism between the two was occurring. In the exchanges between Henry Ware and Leonard Woods of Andover Seminary, an institution that required its faculty to endorse Westminster, Woods insisted that the characteristics of benevolence and justice in God's nature were just as significant to his side as to the Unitarians. Denying that election was "arbitrary" (and complaining that the word "has acquired a bad sense; and is now understood to express the character of a master or ruler, who is tyrannical, or oppressive"), he struggled to introduce moral agency into the order of salvation, in part via a strained parsing of "efficacious."[19] Timothy Dwight, who ended his career as president of Yale, made moral agency a centerpiece of his efforts to construct a systematic theology. For Dwight, the telling aspect of the divine economy was God's ordaining of "means" that allowed humans "to become . . . agents in the great system, to coincide voluntarily with him in the furtherance of his perfect designs." Dwight avoided the topic of predestination, preferred "purpose" to "decree," and never used the word "imputation" in describing the connection between Adam and humankind, admitting, "I am unable to explain . . . the manner in which the state of things became such."[20]

These tokens of change have been thoroughly mapped in modern scholarship. In the context of my inquiry, however, two aspects of Old Calvinist/New Haven rhetoric are striking. One is a persisting ignorance of the Calvin of Geneva and the other major reformers of the sixteenth century. For that matter, these men had little firsthand knowledge of the "practical divinity" fashioned in Tudor-Stuart England and much reiterated by the seventeenth-century colonial ministry. As one modern historian has acerbically remarked, the Connecticut minister and Yale graduate Lyman Beecher "had no more knowledge of Calvin's *Institutes* than he did of the Hebrew testament" (Beecher could not read Hebrew). What animated Beecher was an anti-intellectualism that elevated piety over learning, the better to promote evangelism and moral reform. The second is the similarities in how the liberals who turned Unitarian and the moderates who remained within Congregationalism felt about the Calvin (or the Edwards) they thought they understood. Both fixated on the word "arbitrary," both complained of how the human will was disregarded, both opted for a kinder, gentler God as contrasted with the tyrant God whom they read back into the past.[21]

These decades in which Calvin and Calvinism became such problematic words form the background to what happened at the National Council of Congregational Churches at its initial meeting in Boston in 1865. Let us listen in on the delegates at that gathering as they discuss making a Declaration of Faith. In the second of the reports fashioned by the committee charged with preparing such a declaration, the opening paragraphs were resoundingly historical, citing the assent of the Cambridge Synod of 1648 to the Westminster Confession "for the substance thereof," the decision in 1680 of another synod to renew this assent, the decision in 1708 of a council of churches in Connecticut to make the same affirmation, and action of a similar kind taken by Congregationalists in England in 1692.[22] In keeping with this tradition, the committee called upon the delegates of 1865 to "profess" their "adherence to the above-named Westminster and Savoy Confessions for 'substance of doctrine.'"

Then, "Calvinism" made its first appearance in a sentence that specified two propositions of theology:

> We thus declare our acceptance of the system of truths which is
> commonly known among us as Calvinism, and which is
> distinguished from other systems by so exalting the sovereignty of
> God as to "establish" rather than take away the "liberty" or
> free-agency of man, and by so exhibiting the entire character of God
> as to show most clearly "the exceeding sinfulness of sin."

With this on the floor for discussion, the fat was in the fire. There were those who, although protesting that no authentic Congregationalist wanted a statement of faith "imposed" on him or her, welcomed the committee's report because it acknowledged "the great, strong, iron-ribbed doctrine which was the common faith in the Reformation; which has come down from Paul, through Augustine, and Calvin, and among us, through Edwards and Hopkins"—with the caveat that we do not "swallow the entire Westminster Catechism, in every angle of it." Sensing an uneasiness, a member of the committee rose to insist on the beneficial connections between Calvinism and "the reformation of men," adducing the ambitions and successes of "Puritans" in this regard. For him, it was entirely in order that the council profess "our faith as Calvinists, our faith as unsectarian, and our faith as reforming Puritans."[23]

Dissenters to the motion broached a range of objections. A person who declared himself a "Calvinist" argued that any "system" or, indeed, any evocation of "ancient, worn-out, obsolete confessions" would impair the progress of Congregationalism, the reason being that, in popular usage, the word Calvinist had acquired an "injurious" meaning. The same anxiety about being out of touch prompted someone else to imagine a statement of belief couched in "original, living words of our own," although his real objection may have been that "there is language in every one of those old standards which not a man on this floor receives." In the back-and-forth that followed, the evasive "substance of doctrine" was contrasted with being "honest"; the plea that we must "stand upon" the ground of Westminster was met with cries of "No, no"; and someone rose to point out that "the doctrine of the imputation of Adam's sin," a Westminster formula, "was not to be found in Calvin's writings," the implication being that "those who believed in imputation . . . were not Calvinists."[24]

Thus was put in play the tensions that, a day or so later, thwarted the attempt to claim the term Calvinist for Congregationalists in the United States. Some who wanted to dispense with creeds and labels were moved by a version of anti-intellectualism: the way to make people Christians (or religious), they argued, was to forgo abstractions and subtleties and to appeal directly to their hearts. Congregational ministers and missionaries working in the western regions of the United States—regions where, in 1865, few Congregational churches existed—were especially forceful in arguing against any creed. Many who wanted to dispense with creeds were surely hoping to escape the moral uneasiness they must have experienced at their ordinations when they professed their commitment to Westminster for "the substance thereof." But the deeper reality, though identified mainly in asides, was the shifting theological temper in seminaries and pulpits, a process that, some fifteen years later, would cause a dramatic transformation at Andover Seminary when its faculty espoused "progressive orthodoxy."[25]

It is tempting to end at a point where the taint associated with Calvin, Calvinism, and Edwards seemed inescapable. But the wheel does turn, and it did in part thanks to the scholarship of Williston Walker, a loyal son of Congregationalism and the most able American-born church historian at the beginning of the twentieth century. Born in 1860 in Portland, Maine, where his father ministered to a Congregational church, Walker studied at Hartford Theological Seminary and earned a doctorate at Leipzig in 1888. He returned to teach at Hartford Theological Seminary and, in 1901, was appointed Titus Street Professor of Ecclesiastical History at Yale. A major accomplishment of his years at Hartford was *The Creeds and Platforms of Congregationalism* (1893), which is still unsurpassed for the editorial apparatus of the documents it contains and the commentary on them that Walker provided. All but two of these documents trace the emergence of the polity that, in the seventeenth century, was usually known as the "Congregational Way" or, in England, "Independency," after its cardinal principle: that every congregation was subject to no higher ecclesiastical authority. The two exceptions were the Savoy Declaration of 1658, a slightly revised version of Westminster that English Congregationalists adopted, and the document with which this chapter began, the so-called Burial Hill Declaration of 1865. Attentive not to doctrine but to polity or church order, Walker framed his book as an unfolding of the Protestant Reformation, with Congregationalism in a starring role. Asserting in the second sentence of the book that "the fundamental religious thought of that movement [the Reformation] was the rejection of all authority save that of the Word of God," Walker suggested that the early reformers were unable to align "their systems of church polity" with this "standard." With a side glance at the Anabaptists ("positively fanatical" on some matters but "representing, however mistakenly, an attempt to apply the Word of God . . . to every feature of polity"), Walker found his heroes in the English Separatists of the late sixteenth century who, in organizing independent congregations in defiance of the civil state, passed beyond the first generation of English reformers in carrying "their principles to their logical or Scriptural result."[26]

This understanding of the Reformation was already current among New England Congregationalists and was all the more popular because it helped to counter the insistence of the Unitarians (who themselves practiced a congregational policy) that, historically, the "orthodox" were intolerant bigots and witch-hunters. Implicitly if not explicitly, therefore, Walker was aligning himself with a useful myth. He did so as well in an aside about the making of the Savoy Declaration, remarking on the addition of an entire chapter ("Of the Gospel, and of the extent of the Grace thereof") to Westminster that, in his estimation, "though intensely Calvinistic, . . . is nevertheless a pleasing token of that readiness, always characteristic of Congregationalism, to hold forth the more gracious aspects of the religion of Christ, in at least as clear a light as the sanctions of law."[27]

For the purposes of this chapter, Walker's biography of John Calvin is more pertinent; as its title immediately indicates, it foregrounds a particular Calvin: *John Calvin: The Organiser of Reformed Protestantism, 1509–1564* (1906). This is an impressive book, commanding as it does recent German and French scholarship[28] as well as sixteenth-century sources, and it is impressive, too, for his acknowledgment of Catholic scholarship[29] and the skill with which he works his way through competing interpretations of key episodes in Calvin's life, always grounding his judgments on the sixteenth-century sources. *John Calvin* stands at the other extreme from the uninformed or polemical evocations of Calvin and Calvinism that, with few exceptions, were pervasive in Unitarian and Congregationalist circles before the Civil War, a point Walker made indirectly via an extensive bibliographical note in which not a single work of American scholarship is cited.[30]

Who is Walker's Calvin? The short answer is that he is the central figure in the making of Reformed Protestantism, an answer based on Calvin's wide-ranging correspondence, the influence of the *Institutes*, and the many Reformed ministers who received their training in Geneva, but, above all, an answer based on Calvin's conviction regarding "the absolute and unique authority of the Word of God," an idea characteristic of the Reformation in general but to which he gave "classic expression."[31] But for any serious reader at the beginning of the twentieth century and especially for anyone familiar with German scholarship, the question Walker had to address was the place and significance of the doctrine of election (predestination) in Calvin's theology. As Richard Muller has shown, mid-nineteenth-century German scholar-theologians had elevated predestination to the rank of the "central idea" in Calvin's thinking, an argument with many consequences, including the role it would subsequently play in Max Weber's *The Protestant Ethic and the Spirit of Capitalism.*[32] Walker went in another direction. In the context of his times, the most striking pages of *John Calvin* are those in which he insists, first, that election was *not* the central idea, and, second, that Calvin always regarded the doctrine as pastorally significant in giving assurance of salvation to believers—precisely the opposite of what Weber would argue. In Walker's words, "election was a doctrine to strengthen practical Christian living far more than an abstract explanation of the divine government of the universe." Insisting that the German interpreters who made predestination the central doctrine of Calvinism were mistaken, Walker allowed that "it became so under his successors and interpreters." But, for Calvin himself, "its prime value . . . was always as comfort, as giving assurance of salvation to the Christian believer."[33] In keeping with this emphasis and, I surmise, as a means of diminishing the singularity of the doctrine, Walker associated Calvin on this point with Augustine.[34]

Here, we also encounter the voice of a conventional Protestant liberal, a voice made explicit in an allusion to "us": "Though to us Calvin's system gives the conviction of unendurable spiritual tyranny." This judgment was promptly qualified by the assertion that, in Calvin's own day, this was not how his contemporaries viewed the doctrine and by a quiet reversal of the adjective "arbitrary."[35] Elsewhere, Walker let his liberalism intrude in the assertion that "the modern sense of the extent of the divine compassion" works against the doctrine of a limited atonement and in an allusion to "cruelty." Liberalism may also account for the many references to Calvin as "logical" and, less commonly, to the "severe logic" of his thinking, expressions that seem associated with the Unitarian bugaboos of "system" and "dogma."[36] In the main, however, his was an act of sympathetic recovery. Walker was an unusual liberal, perhaps because he was an unusually thorough historian. Recognizing the impact of humanism on Calvin, he also celebrated the reformers' insistence on freeing the practice of church discipline from state control, a policy abandoned by other reformers for (in Walker's judgment) the short-term gain of the magistrates' support. Thus, the honor of taking a step in the direction of separating church and state belonged to Calvin, and this step, as the readers of *Creeds and Platforms* had already learned, was, for Walker, the most important legacy of Congregationalism. Like Congregationalism itself, Calvin and Calvinism pointed toward modernity.[37]

Walker's was an impressive act of recovery. Even more impressive to his contemporary readers—and impressive still—was Perry Miller's tour de force account of seventeenth-century Puritanism in New England. Arriving at Harvard in 1933 as an instructor of English and American literature, Miller published widely on this topic throughout the 1930s and, less frequently, in the 1940s and 1950s. In the earliest of his attempts to decipher the theology of the colonists, "The Marrow of Puritan Divinity" (1935), he employed Calvin and Calvinism as his starting point; did so again in another provocative essay, "'Preparation for Salvation' in Seventeenth-Century New England" (1943); and, in *The New England Mind: The Seventeenth Century* (1939), reiterated much of the argument of "Marrow of Puritan Divinity." What Miller said in these publications defined for decades the parameters of scholarship by others on theology in early New England and, more specifically, on the relationship between Geneva and the New World's Boston, Cambridge, and Hartford.

Miller would never have described himself as a scholar of John Calvin nor of the broader Reformed tradition. On whom or what he depended in writing about continental theology in the sixteenth and early seventeenth centuries is unclear (although he does cite Adolf Harnack's *History of Dogma*), and it can only be speculated that he read Walker's biography or much of Calvin.[38] One element of continuity is Walker's insistence on the Augustinian basis for election, a point Miller transposed into the opening chapter of *The New England Mind*, "The Augustinian Strain of Piety," meaning by this phrase "the doctrines of original sin, of the depravity of man, and of irresistible grace"; the sharp separation of nature and grace; and, above all, an "inner experience" of the truth of these ideas.[39] Akin to Walker, Miller wanted to convey the plausibility of divine sovereignty not as logic but as feeling to people in the sixteenth and seventeenth centuries. But Miller did not reiterate and may not have understood the older scholar's emphasis on the pastoral significance of predestination.

In this regard, the deeper affinity lay between Miller and the Unitarians I have cited, an affinity charged with paradox and tension since, most of the time in most places, Miller criticized their liberalism as inadequate and insufferable. The central connections are these: the references to Calvin/Calvinism are invariably linked with the adjectives "arbitrary," "rigid," and variations on the term "dogmatism"; and the references to election represent that doctrine as a species of "determinism." Repeatedly, it is suggested that, given the great distance between God and humans, being a Calvinist requires an extra measure of nerve.

Calvin himself seems virtually without nerves or fear. In a passage conflating Calvin and the Puritans that reveals Miller at his most rhetorical (or evocative), he attempts to capture the unbounded force of supernatural authority:

> The scheme of perfection became monotonous if restricted to
> flawless regularity; the human quest, the deep longings of the soul,
> went unsatisfied if the wheels of the world ground slowly, justly, and
> implacably. There must be room in the universe for a free and
> unpredictable power, for a lawless force that flashes through the
> night in unexpected brilliance.

Like Walker's radical Puritans, Calvin (or Calvin's God) never compromises. He is a thinker who thrives on "logic"—not just any old logic, but "inexorable logic." Such a God and such a system offers "little space for human needs and sympathies."[40]

Against this background, Miller told a story of change as, in the early seventeenth century, certain English minister-theologians deployed the motif of "covenant" as a means of warranting human responsiveness. As narrated in "Marrow of Puritan Divinity," covenant increasingly came to signify contract, or an instrument entered into voluntarily on both sides, with conditions attached. Hence, Miller could insist that the description of colonial theology as "absolute authoritarianism" was mistaken, for covenant theology rendered divine sovereignty more "comprehensible" to human reason and more responsive to human initiative.[41] Some years later, Miller seized upon the theme of "preparation for salvation" to complement this story of change, preparation being, in his view, the Trojan horse that inserted elements of works' righteousness into the colonists' ostensible Calvinism. Narrating these modifications and how the emphasis on them expanded over time, Miller claimed to be charting the origins of the softer, milder Calvinism of the eighteenth century and the Unitarian liberalism of the nineteenth.[42]

Given the ways in which Miller characterized Calvin and his theology, readers might well have expected that his own sympathies would be with the liberals. This was not the case. In asides, he suggested that the emergence of the covenant theology flowed from a failure of nerve on the part of Calvin's successors,[43] and he excoriated Cotton Mather, the third-generation minister, for promoting a simplified pietism more in common with American boosters and bourgeois values than with authentic religion. First in "Marrow of Puritan Divinity" and then in "'Preparation for Salvation,'" Miller singled out two men who resisted contract-covenant and preparationism. In the latter essay, he saluted the minister John Cotton as "the better Calvinist, and he knew it: not only would he plead the authority of federalists like Pemble in rejecting preparation, he would also cry out, 'Let *Calvin* answer for me.'"[44] In the earlier essay, Miller praised Edwards in the language quoted at the outset of this chapter. Two axes of rhetoric regarding Calvin and Calvinism thus figure in these essays and *The New England Mind*, the first closely resembling the Calvin of the Unitarians, the second an appreciation of the personal authenticity and mental toughness that Miller attributed to Edwards, Cotton, and, by implication, Calvin. That Miller thought of himself as having the same posture became more explicit in the work he published on nineteenth-century American figures. Initially, however, he tried out that posture via the figures of Calvin and Edwards.

Good stories are remarkably resilient, and the story of authentic religion betrayed by its supposed friends seems invulnerable to criticism. So does its obverse, however: the story of an embittered, angry God acting arbitrarily and ignoring the real needs of humans. In nineteenth-century New England, these stories crisscrossed in the ways I have outlined, and both have persisted into our own time, driven in Miller's case by a mixture of sympathies and goals too complex to be fully charted in this chapter. Paradigms—or, better, stereotypes—do indeed die hard.

NOTES

1. John Cotton, *A Conference Mr. John Cotton Held at Boston* (London, 1646), reprinted in David D. Hall, *The Antinomian Controversy, 1636–1638: A Documentary History* (Middletown, Conn.: Wesleyan University Press, 1968), 185; Perry Miller, "The Marrow of Puritan Divinity" (1935), reprinted in Miller, *Errand into the Wilderness* (Cambridge, Mass.: Harvard University Press, 1956), 98.

2. The story of the council is succinctly narrated in Williston Walker, *The Creeds and Platforms of Congregationalism* (New York, 1893), chap. 18 (quotations 556, 559), where the Burial Hill Declaration is also printed (562–64). The hill in question was the site in Plymouth, Massachusetts, where people who arrived on the *Mayflower* in 1620 were buried, a holy ground of sorts for these Congregationalists.

3. Too large a topic to pursue within the compass of this chapter, the Calvin-and-Calvinism question as it bears on early New England history is discussed in David D. Hall, "On Common Ground: The Coherence of American Puritan Studies," *William and Mary Quarterly*, 3rd ser., 44, no. 2 (1987): 193–229.

4. I have relied on Jonathan Edwards, *The Works of Jonathan Edwards*, vol. 26, *Catalogues of Books*, ed. Peter J. Thuesen (New Haven, Conn.: Yale University Press, 2008), which contains an index to every source cited in Edwards's printed books and private notebooks. Citations from Calvin's *Institutes* are given in standard form: book number, chapter number, section number.

5. W. H. Bond and Hugh Armory, eds., *The Printed Catalogues of the Harvard College Library 1723–1790* (Boston: Colonial Society of Massachusetts, 1996).

6. This assessment of the printings of Calvin's works is based on the holdings of the American Antiquarian Society.

7. Forerunners of the nineteenth-century liberals are described in C. Conrad Wright, *The Beginnings of Unitarianism 1740–1800* (Boston: Starr King, 1955), which notes occasional allusions to Calvin.

8. George E. Ellis, *A Half-Century of the Unitarian Controversy* (Boston, 1857), 4, 55.

9. The use of "arbitrary" as a master word can be seen, for example, in the rhetoric of the Unitarian minister and eventual transcendentalist George Ripley. See Charles Crowe, *George Ripley: Transcendentalist and Utopian Socialist* (Athens: University of Georgia Press, 1967), 52–53.

10. William E. Channing, "The Moral Argument against Calvinism," in *The Works of William E. Channing, D.D.*, 6 vols. (New York, 1848), 1:222, 238; Channing, "Unitarian Christianity," ibid., 3:93, 85.

11. Channing, "Moral Argument against Calvinism," in *Works of Channing*, 1:218.

12. Ellis, *Half-Century of the Unitarian Controversy*, 142, 130; Channing, "Unitarian Christianity," in *Works of Channing*, 3:64–66.

13. Andrews Norton, *Tracts concerning Christianity* (Cambridge, 1852), 113, 115, 168, 190.

14. A point documented by the liberals in the treatment of Roger Williams and Anne Hutchinson.

15. Channing, "Moral Argument against Calvinism," in *Works of Channing*, 1:223.

16. Ibid., 1:239, 222; see also Ellis, *Half-Century of the Unitarian Controversy*, 56–60.

17. Stowe was referring specifically to Samuel Hopkins. My all-too-brief account is largely based on Allen C. Guelzo, *Edwards on the Will: A Century of American Theological Debate* (Middletown, Conn.: Wesleyan University Press, 1989), where orthodox resistance to the liberals is also described, supplemented by Joseph A. Conforti, *Jonathan Edwards, Religious Tradition, and American Culture* (Chapel Hill: University of North Carolina Press, 1995), chap. 5 (dealing with another variant, the New England theology).

18. See Guelzo, *Edwards on the Will*, 160; and E. Brooks Holifield, *Theology in America: Christian Thought from the Age of the Puritans to the Civil War* (New Haven, Conn.: Yale University Press, 2003), 144, 145, 350.

> In their own conception the New England fathers [a reference to Samuel Hopkins, Jonathan Edwards, and others] were always defending the truth, not by giving it up, but rather by stating it better. Thus they remained in conscious sympathy with their Calvinistic fathers, and thus called themselves Calvinists, and quoted and taught the Westminster Catechism, though in fact they had substantially abandoned the philosophy and many of the minor doctrines of the Westminster scheme. For the arbitrary will of God they had substituted his character, love; for a sinful nature, a nature occasioning sin; for imputation, a strict personal responsibility; for a limited, a general atonement; for a bound, a free will.

Frank Hugh Foster, *A Genetic History of the New England Theology* (Chicago: University of Chicago Press, 1907), 282, a statement containing many half-truths.

19. Leonard Woods, *Letters to Unitarians Occasioned by the Sermon of the Reverend William E. Channing* (Andover, Mass., 1820), 85ff., 110ff., 63–64. Woods insisted as well that moral agency and natural depravity were not at odds with each other given that, as soon as humans act, they behave immorally (85ff.). A historian relatively sympathetic to him noted that "no theoretical explanation is attempted" of this last point. Foster, *Genetic History*, 305.

20. Quotations taken from Marie Caskey, *Chariot of Fire: Religion and the Beecher Family* (New Haven, Conn.: Yale University Press, 1978), 38, 39, 40.

21. Ibid., 46.

22. *Debates and Proceedings of the National Council of Congregational Churches Held at Boston, Mass., June 14–24, 1865* (Boston, 1866), 344.

23. Ibid., 345, 352, 353.

24. Ibid., 356, 357.

25. The story is told in Daniel D. Williams, *The Andover Liberals: A Study in American Theology* (New York: King's Crown, 1941).

26. Walker, *Creeds and Platforms*, 1, 2, 6, 16.

27. Ibid., 351.

28. For example, writing of Émile Doumergue's multivolume biography, Walker remarked that the French scholar was "a worshipper of his hero, but a very painstaking worshipper, who is undoubtedly led into occasional exaggeration by his enthusiasm. . . . For the student of Calvin the work is, nonetheless, of much value." Williston Walker, *John Calvin: The Organiser of Reformed Protestantism, 1509–1564* (New York: Putnam's, 1906), xvii–xviii.

29. Ibid., xiv–xv.

30. The exception is the German-trained Philip Schaff's *The Reformation*, possibly listed out of courtesy to the veritable founder of church history in the United States.

31. Walker, *John Calvin*, 411–12.

32. Richard A. Muller, *After Calvin: Studies in the Development of a Theological Tradition* (New York: Oxford University Press, 2003), 63, referencing in particular Alexander Schweizer. The two German scholars whom Walker cited in this regard (*John Calvin*, 416) were Schweizer and Reinhold Seeberg.

33. Walker, *John Calvin*, 416–17, 148–49, 316. Walker also cited Luther and Zwingli as Calvin's predecessors in this regard (416).

34. Ibid., 148.

35. Ibid., 377. Referring to the role of the Holy Spirit and faith in Calvin's account of how to understand the Word, Walker wrote: "The Bible is therefore no arbitrary body of truth to be accepted on the authority of the Church or of external miracles" (411).

36. Ibid., 427, 145, 424, 417.

37. Ibid., 190–91.

38. When it was published in 1939, Miller's *The New England Mind: The Seventeenth Century* (New York: Macmillan) was missing most references to secondary and primary sources. Miller deposited a typescript of the complete notes with the Harvard College Library. These were eventually published in Perry Miller, *Sources for*

"The New England Mind: The Seventeenth Century," ed. James Hoopes (Williamsburg, Va.: Institute of Early American History and Culture, 1981). The *Institutes* are cited four times in the truncated notes to the printed version of *The New England Mind*.

39. Miller, *New England Mind*, 22, 9.

40. Ibid., 17, 34; Miller, *Errand into the Wilderness*, 53, 69; Perry Miller, "'Preparation for Salvation' in Seventeenth-Century New England" (1943), reprinted in Miller, *Nature's Nation* (Cambridge, Mass.: Harvard University Press, 1967), 50, 53, 57. In an essay published in 1970, I pointed to the similarities between Miller's Calvin and the "stick-figure" that appears in the pages of Vernon L. Parrington, *Main Currents in American Thought*, vol. 1: *The Colonial Mind* (New York: Harcourt, Brace, 1927), my point being to expose the irony of Miller's debt to Parrington even though elsewhere he was disputing the latter's interpretation of the Puritans. In the context of this essay, Parrington's description of Calvinism as "a composite of oriental despotism and sixteenth-century monarchism" and his characterization of Calvin's God as exerting an "arbitrary and absolute will" (13) signal the persistence of the anti-Calvinism described in the earlier sections of this chapter. David D. Hall, "Understanding the Puritans," in *The State of American History*, ed. Herbert Bass (Chicago: Quadrangle, 1970), 330–49.

41. Miller, "Marrow of Puritan Divinity," 70 and passim.

42. Miller, "'Preparation for Salvation.'"

43. "Puritanism failed to hold later generations largely because the children were unable to face reality as unflinchingly as their forefathers." Miller, *New England Mind*, 37.

44. Miller, "'Preparation for Salvation,'" 61.

7

Whose Calvin, Which Calvinism? John Calvin and the Development of Twentieth-Century American Theology

Stephen D. Crocco

In *The Theology of John Calvin*, Charles Partee claims that Calvin's influence on the development of theology was "tremendous" in comparison with anybody else's.[1] If Partee is correct, it is not a stretch to say that Calvin's influence on the development of theology in the United States was also likely "tremendous" in comparison with anybody else's. But that remark does not bode well for a chapter that aspires to be more than a dense bibliographic essay or a lengthy encyclopedia article. There is simply no escaping the fact that, to one degree or another, Calvin "influenced" American Protestantism across virtually every theological spectrum imaginable, even traditions that were sustained in reaction against basic features of his thought. But questions of influence and development are notoriously complex and controversial. Put bluntly, one person's idea of influence and development is another person's plunge into apostasy or fundamentalism. And Calvin's legacy has been debated exactly along those lines. To complicate matters, regardless of how Calvin's contributions are measured, American theology rarely developed in discussions and arguments drawn directly from the pages of Calvin's own writings. And when they were, theologians did not draw on him alone. His contributions were usually from a distance, mediated by other theologians, creeds, catechisms, and traditions, as well as by the passing of time.

This chapter is divided into three uneven parts. The first part "talks about talking about" Calvin's legacy to American theology. The second part sets a highly selective, necessarily somewhat arbitrary (given the length of a book chapter) account of that legacy in the context of the United States as a nation of immigrants—both literally and theologically. The third part, the conclusion, offers some notes toward a typology of Calvin as a mountain dominating the theological landscape.

A second observation by Partee seems to work against his first: "To put the point briefly and sharply, Calvin was not a Calvinist."[2] Here, Partee points to the well-known distinction between Calvin and his followers a generation or so later, namely, the Calvinists. This distinction goes back long before R. T. Kendell's 1979 *Calvin and English Calvinism to 1694* and the response by Paul Helm in 1982, *Calvin and the Calvinists*. Because Calvin did not live to see the rise of Arminianism and the Counter-Reformation, his followers needed to address questions that he himself could not have addressed. The problem on which the distinction is based is whether or to what extent those responses were "consistent" with Calvin's own thought. Kendell argued that the majority of Calvinists departed from Calvin on the extent of the atonement, for example. Helm, in contrast, argued that there was consistent development and that the broad Reformed consensus in the seventeenth century stood squarely in line with Calvin. The issues behind this distinction have widened beyond the extent of the atonement to include other positions developed after Calvin's death and associated with his name—doctrines such as double predestination, the covenant of works, and the inerrancy of scripture. As a lifelong student of Calvin, Partee wants to give modern readers an opportunity to hear the voice of the reformer apart from the other voices in the Reformed choir. It is hard to underestimate the importance of this distinction, especially in interpreting Calvin. But to introduce it as an opening principle in a chapter on Calvin and American theology is to miss the ways that Calvin actually functioned in theological work. Moreover, it is to risk making Calvin a museum piece rather than the living resource for theological and ecumenical work that he surely was and is.

Many modern readers have been sensitized to the distinction between "Calvin" and the "Calvinists" and have preferred the more generic term "Reformed" over Calvinist. Fair enough. It should not be anachronistically imposed, however, on earlier generations, who often used "Calvin" and "Calvinist" almost interchangeably and had plausible reasons for doing so. Parenthetically, the dissimilarity between Calvin and the Calvinists need not be limited to the ossification of Calvin by the Protestant scholastics and Puritans.

The distinction applies just as readily to the dissolution of Calvin at the hands of his liberal interpreters, though the distinction is not often used that way. Any attempt to enlist Calvin into a modern theological program raises the questions: were additions to Calvin—the federalist view of the covenant or modern views of scripture—an extension or confirmation of what was important for Calvin, or were they parasitic accretions? Were the things that were subtracted from Calvin for the twentieth century—his views on civil government and double predestination and his anti-Romanist polemics—life-saving amputations, or did they drain the life blood of Calvin?

The form of the Calvin-Calvinist distinction applies to the legacy of any significant theologian: Augustine and the Augustinians, Edwards and the Edwardseans, Barth and the Barthians. In the narratives behind all of these relationships, there is considerable debate about what constitutes a tradition and, more particularly, what counts as progress or regression in it. Certainly Barth, for example, claimed to resist epigones and instead welcomed creative efforts to carry on his work. In these terms, if Calvin saw himself as an Augustinian—carrying on with the best insights of Augustine—surely he could have been accused of an Augustine-Augustinians error. Calvin would likely have argued that neither he nor Augustine were at the heads of the traditions associated with their names. Calvin's contention was that, rather than promulgating any new doctrines, his accomplishment was to uncover certain emphases in the Bible that had been obscured.

The simple fact is that Calvin played a variety of roles in the theological discussions in the twentieth century. The authority of Calvin was not an insignificant endorsement, and he was an important ally in a number of conflicting causes. Theologians who considered themselves to be Calvinists or Reformed wanted and needed to incorporate Calvin into their narratives, and they had arguments for doing so. It is almost as though Calvin had a wax nose—not in the sense that he himself was easily influenced or pliant, but thinkers and traditions needed particular "Calvins" as foundations for the narratives they developed long after his death. For some, the idea or symbol of Calvin was important, and what he actually taught was viewed as mostly time-bound and deemed largely irrelevant for the present day. Others were convinced that Calvin's thought as a whole held up well over the years because it was so clear and biblical. As a result, it was still useful for modern discussions. Many were able to incorporate Calvin into their narratives after improving him by removing or correcting some distasteful or unnecessary features. The picture of a dozen or so Calvins sporting different noses is humorous but accurate. Efforts to link Calvin to particular lines of interpretation prompted claims and counterclaims about who got Calvin right and who did not. These claims often led to assertions but not necessarily arguments about Calvin. Because there are a variety of Calvinisms out there, it is no surprise that there are a variety of Calvins. Determining how these Calvins contributed to the development of American theology is the task ahead.[3]

Calvin's exegetical and theological writings are a treasure trove for all Christian people. For these reasons, he is a great resource for ecumenical theology. But Calvin was also a champion of Reformed thinking—a part of the ecumenical church that is larger than Calvin. It is a tradition that can be described by its commitment to the struggle over a certain set of biblical ideas. Presbyterian theologian George H. Kehm's description of the predoctrinal biblical themes associated with the Reformed tradition provides a fresh way to look at Calvin's standing and contributions:

> All Christian traditions center upon the biblical message of God's gracious action in Jesus Christ for the salvation of the world. . . . [In] articulating that message the Reformed [including Calvin] have characteristically focused upon some of its most mysterious, wonderful and "awful" aspects: the utterly "unconditioned" but also "invincible" character of the divine "election" to salvation; the terrible "judgment" of God upon those who will not trust that gracious election; "sin" as not merely a misuse of a freedom still available but as a kind of hereditary defect, a "pre-volitional malady" of the will inclining it to evil incurable by any humanly devised therapy; the blood of the pure victim "appeasing" the holy anger of God, or juridically interpreted, the suffering of the just "penalty" by the substitute victim making it possible for God "legally" to acquit guilty sinners; the life of a Christian as one of utter "self-abandonment" grounded in overwhelming gratitude for God's forgiveness in Christ, striving to be "totally" at the disposal of God—these are among the most salient themes that have given Reformed theology, in all its varieties, its characteristic shape.[4]

For Kehm, a commitment to stick with these predoctrinal biblical themes is what Calvin shares with Edwards, Schleiermacher, and Barth, and, arguably, it is one of the things that distinguishes him from Aquinas, Luther, and Wesley.

Although the usefulness of the Westminster Confession or Schleiermacher for modern theological work has been debated, it is hard to imagine a Reformed theologian not wanting to honor Calvin as the great thinker of the Protestant Reformation. The challenge for American theology comes into focus when Calvin is invoked as an important predecessor in the theological programs articulated by people as diverse as Joseph Haroutunian, Wilhelm Pauck, Cornelius Van Til,

James M. Gustafson, and Serene Jones. Whose Calvin? Which Calvinism? The cynical answer to both questions is: whichever Calvin I need! The more reasoned answer acknowledges that Calvin can and does support a variety of seemingly contradictory claims based on the theories of doctrinal development associated with his thought. That Calvin wrote on nearly every biblical, theological, and ethical topic has given later scholars plenty of opportunities to link their agendas to the Great Reformer. In that sense, in addition to having a wax nose, Calvin also is a mirror that reflects the particular beliefs and agendas of those who claim him for their own. In the twentieth century, Calvin was claimed for and against the inerrancy of scripture, the doctrine of limited atonement, double predestination, the ecumenical movement, democracy, natural theology, women's ordination, abortion rights, freedom of conscience, and many other things. When "properly understood for our times," Calvin stood for just about anything.[5]

In the twentieth century, not all who used Calvin to advance theological arguments were Calvin scholars who wrote about him systematically or historically. People often used "Calvin," "Calvinist," or "Calvinism" as shorthand expressions for doctrinal, ethical, ecclesiastical, and political views that could be associated with the Reformation's leading theologian. For that reason, Calvin studies—the discipline devoted to Calvin's life, thought, and times—is only tangential to the story of the development of American theology. Theologians and ethicists have a different agenda than historians, though the best ones have made efforts to be sensitive to historical concerns. Their goal has been to find a usable Calvin for theological work, even if that means treating Calvin's writings like coal in a strip mine—taking what was needed and leaving the rest behind, regardless of the full range of his thought or the latest historical, sociological, and economic studies.

The question of Calvin and the development of American theology took on a new dimension at the end of the twentieth century, when hundreds of theologians, both professional and amateur, began to use the Internet for theological work. There are an amazing number of Web and blog sites devoted to Calvin and Calvinism, as well as polemics against them. Most of the sites, other than those that sprang up recently for the quincentenary celebrations, are oriented to doctrinal and historical debates. They seem to rehearse older, perennial questions: did Calvin teach double predestination? Did he teach limited atonement? (Not according to the so-called Four Point Calvinists.) Is Barth's Calvin more Barth than Calvin? Did Calvin teach the inerrancy of the scriptures? What is not clear is how this cyber-theology can be measured and assessed. As younger theologians who are avid bloggers come into their own, the amount of discourse on the Internet will undoubtedly increase. New models of theological work will surely emerge from all this activity. What sort of influence does it suggest? It may be worth asking whether blog and Web sites have any parallel with medieval notions of influence. In that period, one measure of influence was the number of times a name or idea appeared on extant manuscripts. What sort or degree of influence can be measured by the number of times a name appears in a Google search? In late 2008, a search for John Calvin produced over a million hits. Even if a few of those are misplaced results for Calvin Klein, the number is still impressive. A Google search comparison between Brian A. Gerrish, a liberal Calvin scholar, and Gary North, part of the Christian Reconstruction movement with strong debts to Calvin, shows North with nearly 100,000 hits—more than ten times the number of Gerrish. R. C. Sproul, a popularizer of Old Princeton Calvinism, has well over 200,000 hits—compared with 3,800 for Jane Dempsey Douglass, a notable Calvin scholar and author of *Women, Freedom, and Calvin*.

In 2009 (as this is being written), Calvin is being celebrated widely in Reformed circles, and it is important to remember that, for many people and for much of the twentieth century, he was persona non grata. He was viewed as the embodiment of severity, coldness, and a relentless logic that birthed a double predestinarian theology that elevated the arbitrariness of God and emphasized the worthlessness of human beings. For many, Calvin's harshness was epitomized by the Servetus episode, an event that continues to bludgeon Calvin's reputation and that of his defenders. In addition to being cold, rational, and autocratic, Calvin showed that he was intolerant to the extreme when he approved the death of Servetus. Some of Calvin's interpreters simply have chalked it up to the sixteenth century: everybody was killing opponents. Others have argued that Calvin's hand was forced by the eager martyr. Calvin's defenders have tried mightily to cast Calvin in a positive light by pointing out that, though he signed Servetus's death warrant, he preferred that Servetus die quickly by the sword rather than by conflagration. When people are ignorant of Calvin or predisposed against him, however, there is little chance of getting over this stumbling block.[6]

At the turn of the twentieth century, America's Protestant immigrants brought their ecclesiastical and theological traditions with them from Europe and gradually contextualized them in America. Just how gradually or willingly they contextualized them is one of the interesting stories in the development of American theology. As an illustration, in 1880, many of the European immigrant groups that had Reformed and Presbyterian histories participated in the Council of the Alliance of the Reformed Churches Holding the Presbyterian System in Philadelphia. The meeting space was decorated with large banners to welcome international visitors, who would recognize in the banners the signs of their churches and countries. Developing the image of "every man under his vine and under his fig tree," the conveners reasoned, "Certainly the

American church is a vineyard whose growth is but the product of transplantings from the fields of Europe." Europe was mentioned specifically to counter the widespread impression that "Presbyterianism is a type of Scotch and Scotch-Irish Protestantism—a local product of Great Britain or, at furthest, of Geneva."[7] Perhaps to stress the point that every Protestant in North America was a transplant, there were no banners from the United States or Canada. Two banners hung behind the podium: one acknowledged the Westminster standards and the other displayed the emblem of the alliance. The countries in the council with banners at the meeting were Bohemia and Moravia, England and Wales, France, Germany, Holland, Hungary, Ireland, Italy, Scotland, and Spain. Each banner was marked by several ecclesiastical symbols, seals, coats of arms, commemorative sentences, references to revivals and martyrdoms, and names of leaders. Hungary's banner, for example, had a seal from the Reformed Church of Debrecen and listed Matthias Dévay, István Szegedi Kis, and other theologians and church leaders. The banner from Holland featured the Dutch motto, "In Union There Is Strength," a coat of arms from the Reformed Church of America, and an inscription commemorating the Synod of Dort. England and Wales's banner featured the Puritans, the Westminster Assembly of Faith, and names such as William Twisse, Richard Baxter, and John Pym.

Switzerland's banner featured the seal of the Reformed Church of Geneva, Calvin and his seal, and church leaders and theologians such as Huldrych Zwingli, Guillaume Farel, Johannes Oecolampadius, and François Turretin. Not surprisingly, the Swiss banner described Calvin as "the great theologian of the Reformed Churches." (The French banner also listed Calvin, but only after Jacques LeFèvre d'Étaples and Louis de Berquin.) Those are the only two times Calvin was mentioned on a dozen banners. This is not to minimize Calvin. In fact, it does the opposite: Calvin was acknowledged as the great theologian behind these traditions. However, given the purpose of the conference—to lift up the individual identities and contributions of the churches of these nations— the banners reflected the historical picture more accurately than would simply claiming that Calvin was more influential than anybody else—even though he was. The banners showed that Calvin's influence was mediated or related to particular communities and churches by people who had special historical or ecclesiastical connections to those communities. The heroes of the faith of particular nations—figures such as Zacharias Ursinus and John Knox and creeds such as the Westminster Confession, the Synod of Dort, and the Heidelberg Confession—were the paths back to Calvin and the paths forward to the broader Reformed tradition. This pattern—where Calvin is acknowledged as the great theologian of the Reformed tradition whose teachings were mediated both by indigenous influences and by subsequent theological development—is at the heart of his role in the development of American theology in the twentieth century just as it was in the nineteenth, eighteenth, and seventeenth centuries.

Until the early nineteenth century, American Protestantism was most heavily influenced by the Reformed traditions coming out of England and Scotland, with some undercurrents from places such as Holland and France. Even though the English and Scottish were among the earliest settlers in the New World, their views need to be seen as the immigrant traditions they were. In 1939, Harvard literary historian Perry Miller observed that the American Puritans admired, emulated, and sometimes read John Calvin.[8] Like Jonathan Edwards, a generation or so later, Puritans were willing to be called followers of Calvin, but for the sake of distinction, not because they were particularly in debt to the Swiss reformer. As Miller argued, what the Puritans saw in Calvin was a bold and courageous statement of biblical truths for his time, the very calling to which each Puritan minister aspired in his time. There was no doubt that Calvin had advanced theological thinking in his day. The same task fell to the Puritans, and they believed that God had provided several generations of theologians since Calvin to develop and apply his central insights to their own circumstances. Still, in Calvin, they saw God's steady hand providing sound leadership and theology at a critical juncture in history. The Puritans appreciated Calvin as a thinker whose significance lay as much with his leadership role in the Reformation, an event to which Puritans attached millennial significance, as it did with his theological and biblical writings.

The development of the main lines in theology in colonial America came through the Puritans and the Protestant scholastics. As these theologians developed their programs, they continued to "improve" their understanding of the faith once delivered to them. William Ames's *Marrow of Theology*, François Turretin's *Institutes of Elenctic Theology*, and the Westminster Confession were more immediately influential than was Calvin himself. As an illustration, Charles Briggs's 1885 *American Presbyterianism: Its Origin and Early History* mentioned Calvin only four times.[9] (And one of those references is an argument for a sharp distinction between Calvin and Calvinism.) In contrast, Briggs mentioned the Westminster Assembly dozens of times. Many "Calvinist" pastors and teachers in the nineteenth century learned their Calvin and Calvinism from summaries of his thought by the Protestant scholastics, the Puritans, various confessions, and books such as W. G. T. Shedd's *Dogmatic Theology* and Charles Hodge's *Systematic Theology*.

To celebrate the 400th anniversary of Calvin's birth, faculty members at Union Theological Seminary in New York—William Walker Rockwell, William Adams Brown, and Thomas Cuming Hall—spoke on Calvin and his influence.[10] All three speakers resisted others' efforts to make him palatable to modern readers. Instead, they argued that Calvin was a product of his times. Sometimes, he was an enlightened product and, at other times, he was not so enlightened. In any case, he was not a man of the twentieth century, but he was a man whom people of the twentieth century could and should admire. Calvin's accomplishments were staggering and had a lasting impact on the church through the centuries. Arguments went something like this: because of Servetus, we now believe in tolerance. Because of Calvin's exacting dedication to the Bible, we can show our own dedication by bringing all of the insights of biblical criticism to bear on the Holy Scriptures.

The question for Hall and his colleagues was: what is valuable in Calvin for 1909 and what is not? Hall, for example, acknowledged that Calvin's views on the inspiration of scripture and his political philosophy were no longer viable and, thus, no longer valuable. Calvin's conception of the relationship between church and state, wherein the church's authority, aristocracy, and the "moral supervision of every detail of conduct" had a place in Calvin's day but not in the twentieth century. In this regard, Hall likened Calvin to the Jesuits. The Roman Catholic Church needed the Jesuits to firmly establish itself and to ward off enemies. But to get enough space to breathe and grow, the Roman hierarchy needed to throw them off. The same was true with the Swiss reformer. Hall also likened Calvin to John the Baptist, standing at the threshold of a new world. "But because he [Calvin] lived and died for his God, we through him have entered into the more splendid vision of the unfailing mercy and the everlasting kindness of the God and Father of our Lord Jesus Christ." There is gold in Calvin, the argument went, if modern people are willing to submit themselves to the kind of discipline he evokes. But to get at the gold, impurities need to be burned off and discarded. Separating the gold from the dross is the task of the theologian, pastor, and educated elder. That Calvin stood for things that Hall now repudiated did not stop Hall from saying, "While yet we render all honor to the old hero may each of us in his time and place render one tithe of his service in something like his loyalty and fidelity."[11]

On the 400th anniversary of Calvin, Princeton theologian and noted Calvin scholar B. B. Warfield gave addresses on the significance of Calvin. In "The Present-Day Attitude toward Calvinism: Its Causes and Significance," Warfield began with the bad news: major theological and intellectual currents, whether influenced by German Lutheranism, Anglicanism, or naturalism, are likely to find Calvinism stifling. The good news, according to Warfield, is that there "are very likely more Calvinists in the world to-day than ever before." "Even relatively, the professedly Calvinistic churches are, no doubt, holding their own." Here, he cited numerous denominations with direct links to Calvin and Calvinism—much along the lines of the pan-Presbyterian conference cited earlier. "Above all," Warfield continued, "there are to be found everywhere humble souls, who, in the quiet of retired lives, have caught a vision of God in His glory, and are cherishing in their hearts that vital flame of complete dependence on Him which is the very essence of Calvinism."[12] Warfield's use of the word "essence" should not be taken too far. With a few exceptions, Warfield believed that the full range of Calvin's doctrines stood up remarkably well over the years. That was because Calvin set up the *Institutes of the Christian Religion* as a "plan of a complete structure of Christian apologetics." For Warfield:

> The elements of Calvin's thought . . . reduce themselves to a few
> great fundamental principles. These embrace particularly the
> following doctrines: the doctrine of the innate knowledge of God; the
> doctrine of the general revelation of God in nature and history; the
> doctrine of the special revelation of God and its embodiment in
> Scriptures; the doctrine of the noetic effects of sin; and the doctrine
> of the testimony of the Holy Spirit.[13]

Ironically, it was on some of these topics that Calvin's legacy was most hotly debated in the decades following Warfield's death.[14] Although the estimations of Calvin at Union and Princeton overlapped at a number of points, where they differed provided fairly predictable trajectories of the kinds of influence Calvin would have in twentieth-century American theology.

Religious revivals, ecclesiastical and theological controversies, and new ideas traveled with the steady streams of immigrants eager to recreate the best of the old country in the United States. A robust Calvinism in the Netherlands found its way to America in the second half of the nineteenth century. Dutch immigrants in the Midwest set up religious and educational communities where Calvin and Calvinism were welcomed and institutionalized. What are today Calvin College and Seminary grew out of a junior college founded in Grand Rapids in 1876. College founders took Calvin for the name at a time when the Swiss reformer was hardly in favor in the broader culture. They did it precisely because they wanted to make a statement about their allegiance to the Reformed tradition in a free but spiritually suspect New World. In these circles, Calvin—not just Calvinism—was taught and read at the high school level in parochial schools well into the middle decades of the twentieth century. Why Calvin? Calvin was widely regarded as the father of the Reformed faith, and there was no Dutch thinker whose name was comparable. Today, Calvin College is home to the Meeter Center for Calvin Studies, arguably the most comprehensive center for the study of John Calvin in the world.

Eager to embrace Calvinism wherever he found it, B. B. Warfield was impressed with the Dutch version, even though it differed considerably from his own. Mainly, it did not share Princeton's interest in deductive forms of apologetics—something Warfield traced to Calvin himself. Instead, it favored a critique of the religious presuppositions of different worldviews as a prolegomena to doctrinal work—a direct extension, Abraham Kuyper argued, from Calvin's notion of the sovereignty of God. Dutch Calvinism—sometimes called Neo-Calvinism—took root in Princeton when Kuyper delivered the Stone Lectures there in 1898, and he was followed by Herman Bavinck in 1908. Kuyper's lectures were published as *Lectures on Calvinism*. There, he argued that God's redemptive will extended beyond the personal and ecclesiastical realms to include all spheres of life: education, politics, and art, as well as ecclesiastical life and theology. Viewed this way, Kuyper argued, Calvinism was the only sufficiently robust form of Christianity to withstand the assaults of modernity. Bavinck's lectures were published as *The Philosophy of Revelation*, and the importance of Bavinck's later *Reformed Dogmatics* can hardly be underestimated for Dutch Calvinism in North America. Many specialized theological studies were built on that foundation. To celebrate the 400th anniversary of Calvin's birth, Bavinck published "Calvin and Common Grace" to show the close connection between John Calvin and Neo-Calvinism.[15] The Dutch foothold in Princeton—with connections between Holland and Michigan—led to the eventual hiring of Dutch immigrants Geerhardus Vos in biblical theology and Cornelius Van Til in apologetics.

As the theological differences between the Union and Princeton theologians entered the realms of institutional life and ecclesiastical journalism, things came to a head in the 1920s. Calvinists of various stripes squared off over the place of theological diversity in the church. Questions about the meaning of subscription to the Westminster standards were the focal point of the debates. After a group of faculty members at Princeton—including Van Til but not Vos—concluded that the Calvinist cause at Princeton was lost, or at least on the way to being lost, they left in 1929 to form Westminster Theological Seminary. Their leader, J. Gresham Machen, reserved his harshest words not for the Arminians and Roman Catholics, whose differences with Calvinism were real and important. But those differences were minor compared with the ones between orthodox and liberal Calvinists. His famous 1923 tract, *Christianity and Liberalism*, would have been more accurately titled *Liberalism Is Not Christianity*, given how differently he viewed the two systems. Machen died in 1937, and, over time, Van Til emerged as the intellectual leader at Westminster Seminary. An immigrant from Holland who was educated at Calvin College and then returned to Europe for graduate work, Van Til was hired at Princeton in 1928 to teach apologetics. He shared Old Princeton's commitment to inerrancy but developed an approach to apologetics along different lines than Warfield, who relied on identifying common starting assumptions with unbelievers and then building arguments from there. In contrast, Van Til used Kuyper's rejection of neutrality for an apologetic approach that stressed the consistency of Christianity and the inconsistency of every other worldview. He made much of the opening words of Calvin's *Institutes* about the knowledge of God and human beings to stress the properly theological character of apologetics:

> Aquinas offers Christianity to the natural man as an hypothesis that, in his open-minded search for truth, he will find to be better than any other. Calvin challenges the natural man to relinquish his claim to be the rightful judge as to whether the claims of Christ to be *the* way, *the* truth, and *the* life are true or false and, with true repentance for following the god of this world, prostrate himself before *the* triune God of Scripture.[16]

Van Til's brand of Calvinism, a mix of Neo-Calvinist and Old Princeton influences, has had a narrow but persistent influence on the American theological landscape, even more so in the years since his death in 1987.

In the 1920s and 1930s, American theologians and pastors with an eye on Europe heard about "dialectical theology," "crisis theology," "belief-ful realism," "back to Luther" and "back to Calvin" movements, and "Barthianism." A decade earlier, World War I had stirred nationalist spirits among many immigrant groups. Sentiments favoring Germany largely disappeared or went underground when the United States entered the war. After the war, American immigrant communities shared the pain of devastation and poverty with relatives in postwar Europe. According to Paul T. Fuhrmann, in Europe and, by extension, in many communities in America with relatives in Europe who had suffered, cultural conditions demanded answers to questions such as: how could this happen? And how can we prevent this from happening again? The sobering conclusion for many was that human nature was congenitally diseased and corrupt, so there were no guarantees about the future. Swiss and French youth were drawn to Dostoevsky, Kierkegaard, Pascal, and Calvin for substantial theological responses to the chaos and destruction of World War I. According to Fuhrmann, Calvin received a fresh hearing among youths weary of war. His theology was an antidote to the "mediocre man-centered and man-pleasing theology" that offers nothing uplifting or challenging. "If we are conscious of this, if we suffer because of it, and long for a remedy, Calvin will help us . . . [and] he will make us realize the grandeur and loftiness from which our Protestant Christendom has fallen."[17] Not all American Calvinists fully embraced the Back to Calvin movement. For many, they had never left Calvin.

Beginning in the late 1920s, H. Richard Niebuhr was actively involved in efforts to broker theological insights from Germany to America. In this regard, he is best known for translating Paul Tillich's *The Religious Situation* and coming up with the term "belief-ful realism" to characterize Tillich's theological orientation. H. Richard and his brother, Reinhold, were part of the German Evangelical Synod of North America, an immigrant denomination that was active mostly in Illinois and Missouri. The Niebuhrs are sometimes associated with the Reformed tradition, but it is better to view them as products of a nineteenth-century political compromise called the Prussian Union of 1817, which brought Lutherans and Reformed together in a noncreedal community known as "evangelical." Not surprisingly, the irenic Philipp Melanchthon was the Evangelical Synod's house theologian from the Reformation period. Neither Niebuhr brother was interested in doctrine per se. That was consistent with the evangelical suspicion that doctrine divided more than it united, but it also spoke to the way they used Luther and Calvin. Reinhold often invoked Calvin as the premier representative of orthodox Christianity—a sturdy and persistent but antiquated theology. But he also found in Calvin a willingness to resist unjust authority—over and against a more socially conservative Luther—and he found strong links among Calvin, natural law, and democracy.[18]

Joseph Haroutunian (1904–1968) was an Armenian immigrant drawn first to Edwards and later to Calvin on his pilgrimage to understand the theological orientation of his new country. His 1932 *Piety versus Moralism: The Passing of the New England Theology* lifted up the theocentric character of Edwards's theology—an orientation he later discovered in Calvin. Haroutunian deliberately distinguished his own theological position from neo-orthodoxy because its obsession with human sin and salvation made it anthropocentric rather than theocentric. In his iconoclastic 1940 tract, *Wisdom and Folly in Religion,* Haroutunian noted that anthropocentrism—the doctrine that human beings are at the center of the world and the reason for it—was deeply suspect for intelligent modern people who knew suffering and meaninglessness. Religion of both the liberal and conservative kinds lost an audience with modern people because their theologians and church leaders maintained convictions that human beings were at the center of the universe's intentions—something modern people simply could not believe. Haroutunian found in Calvin and Reformed theology an emphasis on the honor of God that was not mitigated by the excessive attention Luther gave to human sin and justification. Haroutunian gloried in Protestantism's insistence that God's sovereignty pushed the conclusion that God decrees evil as well as good. Double predestination was, for him, the "last assertion of God's ultimate freedom as He creates the world, a last terrible tribute to the fact of reprobation as known in this world." For this

reason, the doctrine was one of "the iron badges of the Protestant's wisdom."[19]
These doctrines distinguished Calvinism from theological traditions that suffered a failure of nerve and let down a culture that was desperate for a theology
with iron in its blood. In his preface to *Wisdom and Folly in Religion*, H. Richard
Niebuhr wrote that Haroutunian set out two tasks: to interpret, in Christian
terms, the "implicit religious content of the modern mind," and to state

> afresh the faith of the Reformers which modern Protestantism sets
> forth in pale images when it does not pervert it. Luther, Calvin and
> Edwards—read with a humble desire to understand their meaning . . .
> have illuminated for the author the state of every man in need of God.
> In them he has found that resolute facing of the hard and unpalatable
> facts about man and God the twentieth-century mind demands. So he
> brings the sixteenth and twentieth centuries together.[20]

The debates about Calvin and his legacy that occupied theologians in 1909
were alive fifty and sixty years later, but the Back to Calvin movement and neo-
orthodoxy altered the landscape of those debates. Sydney Ahlstrom described
neo-orthodoxy as "a period when Augustine, Luther, and Calvin became nearly
contemporary theologians again."[21] What did it mean for Calvin to become
nearly contemporary? It meant different things to different people. In 1947,
three immigrants—Clarence Bouma, Joseph Haroutunian, and Wilhelm
Pauck—set a helpful benchmark for considering Calvin's role in the development of American theology.

An article by Bouma, published in the *Journal of Religion*, prompted the
exchange. In "Calvinism in American Theology Today," Bouma, who was born in
the Netherlands and became a professor at Calvin Theological Seminary, observed
that the God-centered faith of the early American settlers was reinforced by later
immigrants who came to America with great catechisms and confessions. He
listed "the Heidelberg Catechism, the Belgic or Netherland Confession, the Canons of Dort, the Westminster Confession, and the Westminster catechisms, of
which the 'Shorter' was by far the more valued and in use. . . . This faith was carried by thousands of immigrants to the shores of the New World and placed its
indelible stamp upon our American life."[22] Citing Haroutunian's *Piety versus
Moralism*, Bouma noted that Calvinism in the United States had been assaulted
by waves of humanism and rationalism until it suffered serious decline. The
ecclesiastical bodies that once supported Calvinism—the mainline Presbyterian
churches, for example—still had many adherents who welcomed the Westminster Shorter Catechism, but the leadership in these churches did not. In spite of
this decline, Bouma believed that the resurgence of interest in Calvin in Europe
and America would lead to a resurgence of interest in orthodox Calvinism.

Haroutunian, a professor at McCormick Theological Seminary, struggled to begin his response on a positive note. When Bouma "calls for a God-centered faith in the Pauline-Augustinian-Calvinistic tradition, there will be many who will respond with enthusiasm." In this sense, Bouma's commitments give expression to a "mood and a conviction which is becoming increasingly prevalent." However, Haroutunian was clearly irritated by Bouma's assumption that "in order to be a Calvinist one must be a fundamentalist of the Machen variety." He further questioned Bouma's facile identification of Calvinism with the theology of Calvin, his complete rejection of the contributions of liberalism to historical study, his rejection of the Social Gospel without taking seriously Calvin's own attempts to "bring our economic and political life under the will of God," and his "utter failure at self-criticism in view of the Bible and Calvinism or Calvinisms."[23]

Pauck, an immigrant from Germany and a historical theologian at the University of Chicago, also took Bouma to task for limiting Calvin's legitimate legacy to conservative denominational bodies. Pauck acknowledged the strengths of historic Calvinism in the Christian Reformed Church and the Orthodox Presbyterian Church—two examples cited by Bouma. He also acknowledged that Bouma was right in asserting that religious liberalism did not take the best insights of Calvin seriously. Like Bouma, Pauck welcomed a resurgence of interest in the reformers. But Pauck did not believe that a new interest in Calvin would lead to a resurgence of orthodox Protestantism or even orthodox Protestant doctrine. Although Calvin was interested in doctrine, Pauck argued, it was an interest secondary to his views on the church. In that light, "conformity with creedal and theological orthodoxy can hardly be regarded as the most important feature of Calvinism." To emphasize anything else would lead to factionalism. Pauck continued, there "is no good reason to suspect, as Dr. Bouma does, that Karl Barth and Emil Brunner do not stand firmly in the Calvinist theological tradition. Yet they have much to criticize in the thought of J. Gresham Machen, whom Dr. Bouma regards as a champion of Calvinist orthodoxy and, as such, as a true heir of the historic 'gospel of John Calvin.'" Pauck conceded the failures of liberalism to take Calvin seriously, but he saw neo-orthodox interpretations of the reformers as an instance of liberalism's ability to correct itself. Pauck took Bouma and the whole orthodox school of Calvin interpretation to task for killing the prophetic character of Reformed theology "by substituting doctrinal knowledge for it."[24] And he argued instead that Calvin's legacy is more fruitfully alive in liberal ecumenical bodies that promote the unity of the church than in conservative ones that do not. Pauck lamented that modern men and women, given a choice between orthodoxy and naturalism, were driven to the latter out of intellectual honesty. An honest liberalism would have been a viable alternative.

Meanwhile, Calvin scholarship continued apace. John T. McNeill's 1948 essay, "Thirty Years of Calvin Study," shows a large outpouring of attention to Calvin in the first half of the twentieth century, though very little was written by Americans. Despite the distractions of war and its accompanying evils, he observed that "a surprising number of competent and illuminating studies are to be reported"—studies of Calvin's life, writings, doctrines, ecclesiology, and ethics. He noted that the "clash of divergent Protestant theologies has stimulated historical inquiry . . . [and] there has been added an increasing circle of eager investigators who hold him in some sense as either an authority or an ally. Historical investigations generated in controversy sometimes emerge as works of sincere historical research, profitable to the open-minded inquirer"[25]—and sometimes not. What Fuhrmann called "classical Calvinism" joined with "Barthian Calvinism" in rejecting faith in human nature to embrace "a new appreciation of Calvin as the supreme representative of theocentric thought."[26] The impressions were new, not because Calvin had been neglected, as McNeill's essay pointed out; rather, Calvin had been rediscovered for current issues of faith and practice by Calvin scholars and followers of Barth. Even those who argued that they had never left Calvin were caught up in the newfound attention given to the reformer. It bears repeating that there were many students of Calvin in the United States who rejected Barth's Calvin as being too much Barth and too little Calvin.

In his magisterial 1954 *The History and Character of Calvinism*, McNeill staked out his own claim for Calvin's legacy. There, he described the revival of interest in Calvin and Calvinism in the Protestant world and what it meant for theological work. McNeill reminded his readers that the revival was not a replica of the Calvinism of Calvin's time. That would be both impossible and undesirable. Why? "Because of the fertility of the modern mind and the ceaseless interchange of ideas the survival or revival of any system of theology cannot be looked for." Since no one can reconstruct Calvin's Calvinism, McNeill argued, moderns must recover the "spirit of Calvinism." But that quest, he said, "does not require a restoration of the entire system. Any such reappropriation is bound to be selective with respect to specific doctrines and practices." Furthermore, "the revival is not a complete conversion to Calvinism but is marked by a willingness to learn from it and to appropriate its usable elements."[27] McNeill's comment, in a nutshell, points to basic questions about Calvin's legacy to North American theology in the twentieth and now the twenty-first century. What does the spirit of Calvin—or the spirit of Calvinism—have to say to the present day? What are the usable elements of Calvin's thought for today?

How did McNeill answer the question for himself? What we gain from Calvin for today, according to McNeill, is making a "faithful response to the

Scripture revelation of a sovereign and redeeming God."[28] Although it hardly sounds contentious, it was certainly not without prejudice. In making that statement—surely a summary of McNeill's position—he asserted rather gratuitously that the spirit of Calvinism for his day could no longer be tied to the doctrine of reprobation or to doctrines of scripture that approach modern conceptions of inerrancy. According to McNeill, these doctrines were part of Calvin's thought world, but they were better left in the sixteenth century. The trouble with simply following McNeill here, however, is that other theologians staked claims on the very things McNeill rejected as being close to the heart of Calvin's distinctive contributions to the twentieth century.[29]

Like many of his generation, H. Richard Niebuhr also turned to Luther, Calvin, and increasingly to Edwards as proponents of theocentric religion. Arguably unintentionally, Niebuhr presented an interpretation of Calvin that gained enormous popularity in the twentieth century, though not through his writings on Calvin, which are meager. Niebuhr's *Christ and Culture* was one of the most popular theological books of the century.[30] There, he identified Calvin with the position that "Christ [is] the transformer of culture," Niebuhr's preferred type of the five logical relationships between Christ and culture. When Niebuhr published the book in 1951, it still made sense to identify specific ecclesiastical traditions with particular types, though the link between traditions and types was never meant to be exhaustive or exclusive. It is probably possible to find the whole range of types in each ecclesiastical tradition. Popular reaction to *Christ and Culture*—apart from general admiration—sparked conversations about the adequacy or accuracy of associating types with traditions. This was particularly true of Anabaptists, who resisted being identified with the "Christ against culture" position. Peace was *for* culture, not against it! By the 1970s, all ecclesiastical traditions and the theologians associated with them wanted to be thought of as being involved in transforming culture rather than being in some sort of antagonistic or paradoxical relationship to it. Anabaptists, Lutherans, and Roman Catholics made arguments to show that, although their traditions had some historical resemblances to the descriptions of Niebuhr's types, the traditions themselves, when properly understood, were all about the transformation of culture. But, in spite of these discussions, Calvin was lifted up as transformationist and associated with positive social change—in spite of Servetus.

To contend, as this chapter has done, that Calvin's roles in American theology were largely mediated does not imply that they were entirely mediated. Calvin may not have been read as often as the Westminster Confession, but he was read, and increasingly so as the twentieth century progressed. Calvin was given four of the twenty-six volumes of the Library of Christian Classics published by Westminster Press in the 1950s and 1960s: *Calvin: Theological*

Treatises, edited by J. K. S. Reid; *Calvin: Commentaries*, edited by Joseph Haroutunian; and a two-volume edition of the *Institutes of the Christian Religion*, edited
by John T. McNeill and translated by Ford Lewis Battles. The Library of Christian Classics editions of Calvin reflected mainline scholarship and were
designed to reach audiences with ecumenical interests. Until the Westminster
Press edition, most American students of Calvin's *Institutes* relied on a translation by John Allen, published in 1909 and 1936 by the Presbyterian Board of
Education. These editions contained B. B. Warfield's 1909 essay, "An Introduction to the Literary History of the *Institutes*." Allen updated Henry Beveridge's
nineteenth-century translation, done under the auspices of the Calvin Translation Society, which also published Calvin's commentaries and occasional writings. For the previous thirty or forty years, publishers such as Banner of Truth
and Baker Books kept older editions of Calvin available while critical editions
were being prepared. However, the ridiculously low prices of the reprints often
kept frugal readers from purchasing the new editions. In 1939, Hugh Thompson
Kerr published a *Compend of the Institutes of the Christian Religion*. Kerr's lean
volume, much closer in spirit to the first edition of Calvin's *Institutes*, received
wide circulation in seminaries, colleges, and churches.[31]

The developments that came to be known as neo-orthodoxy mitigated
some of the theological differences between Union and Princeton seminaries
but exacerbated the differences between Union and Princeton, on the one
hand, and Westminster Seminary, on the other.[32] Van Til burst on the conservative theological scene in 1946 with his diatribe against neo-orthodoxy,
The New Modernism: An Appraisal of the Theology of Barth and Brunner (1946).
Westminster's antipathy to Princeton for what the orthodox lost there twenty
years earlier and for Princeton's adoption of a Barthian Calvin generated considerable polemics.[33] Van Til's later *Christianity and Barthianism* (1962)
invoked Machen's *Christianity and Liberalism* to make his point crystal clear.
Van Til had many disciples from his fifty-year tenure at Westminster Seminary and many others who knew him only by his writings. Those disciples
ranged from Michael Horton, the author of a multivolume dogmatic theology
with strong ecumenical overtones, to Gary North, a leader in the Christian
Reconstruction movement. North established an ethical program based on
Van Til's sharp distinction between autonomy and theonomy. Laws were
either human laws or God's laws, but the Bible is God's standard for individuals, families, the church, communities, and nations. In an enormous body of
literature, North and other theonomists, as they came to be called, argued that
Calvin was on the right track in Geneva when he sought to implement God's
laws as the laws of the land. These Christian reconstructionists made much of
their relation to Calvin and to the subsequent developments of Calvin's ideas

for society that were advanced by the Westminster Confession and American Puritans.[34]

At about the same time that Christian Reconstructionists were writing biblical blueprints for American society and influencing the Christian right, University of Chicago theologian and ethicist James M. Gustafson prepared a two-volume theological ethics that drew heavily on the Reformed tradition and John Calvin. Gustafson, earlier a student and colleague of H. Richard Niebuhr at Yale, proposed to develop his teacher's thought, reinforced with his own insights, to develop an ethics that was both plausible to modern men and women and theological. In *Ethics from a Theocentric Perspective*, Gustafson identified the work of John Calvin as the "one decisive generating source" for the identity of the Reformed theology while at the same time acknowledging a variety of expressions. He lifted up three aspects of the Reformed tradition as being viable for the present day: a sense of a powerful Other, the centrality of piety in the religious life, and an understanding of God that requires that human life lived in response to God be ordered in relation to what can be discerned about God's will. Gustafson found strong and direct precedent for his three strands in Calvin, though he acknowledged that these themes may also be found in other Reformed thinkers—Dutch Calvinists, the Puritans, Edwards, Schleiermacher, H. Richard Niebuhr, and Barth—and even in Augustine, whom he linked to the Reformed tradition. However, Gustafson also acknowledged that, "in the eyes of some," his ethics had "left out the heart of the matter [in Calvin's theology, namely], the redemptive work of Christ known in the Scriptures."[35]

Neo-orthodox versions of Calvin and Calvinism gained ascendancy in mainline Protestant denominations and theological seminaries in the middle decades of the twentieth century. Emil Brunner was probably more influential than Karl Barth until well into the 1970s. Brunner's three-volume *Dogmatics*, published in English in the 1940s, was a staple for generations of theological students. It appeared before Barth's *Church Dogmatics* and was far more accessible. With the exception of the 1936 translation of *Church Dogmatics* I/1, most of Barth's writings in English were occasional pieces until the mid-1950s, when T&T Clark issued the rest of *Church Dogmatics* in rapid succession, mostly from 1955 to 1962.[36] Barth's interpretation of Calvin—his effort to take Calvin where Calvin could not get himself, but where Barth thought the logic of his theology pointed—made a lasting impact on American theology. Barth's acceptance of biblical criticism gave his theology credibility in mainline circles. As a result, Calvin was disassociated from modern doctrines of inerrancy, much to the consternation of conservative interpreters. Barth's rejection of natural theology helped to move American theology away from being grounded in apologetics by using a Calvin who relied more on the testimony of the Holy Spirit than on deductive arguments. (Warfield certainly had affirmed the importance of the testimony of the Spirit in Calvin and in apologetics.) Barth's reworking of the doctrine of election removed the stumbling block of double predestination to the relief of mainline theologians and pastors. His notion that all are elect in Christ was eagerly embraced, while the scandal of Christ being the elected and reprobated was largely ignored. Predestination in Calvin was lifted up as a comfort to believers undergoing persecution rather than seen as the logical outcome of the divine decrees before the foundation of the world. In all of this, Barth's reworking of Calvin emerged as a major force for church unity and the ecumenical movement.

As this chapter draws to a close, it is important to consider two expressions that, for many, are the epitome of Calvin and Calvinism.[37] The acronym TULIP and the slogan "Reformed Ever Reforming" are shorthand formulations of the Reformed tradition associated with Calvin. Both continued to have much currency in twentieth-century American theology. Both were developed in the seventeenth century, generations after Calvin, and both are trotted out early and often—not infrequently as the essence of Calvin's contribution to the modern period. The acronym TULIP—*t*otal depravity, *u*nconditional election, *l*imited atonement, *i*rresistible grace, and *p*erseverance or *p*reservation of the saints— is a summary of Calvinistic doctrine that is still considered, by many, to be the fairest flower in God's garden. (In late 2008, there was a Web site hosted by a Calvinist-turned-Roman-Catholic called "Snipping Calvin's TULIP.") The slogan, probably also developed in the scholastic period, exists in two forms: "Reformed Ever Reforming" and "Reformed and Reforming according to the Word of God." In sorting out Calvin's roles in the development of American theology, these shorthand expressions have taken on a life of their own—sometimes quite apart from any reasonable resemblance to Calvin. Used alone, TULIP reduces Calvin to a set of doctrines that summarizes the life out of him. Used alone, "Reformed Ever Reforming" reduces Calvin to mean just about whatever a writer wants Calvin to mean, even if "according to the Word of God" is added to it. These distinctions are probably too facile or harsh. However, something needs to account for the empirical fact that ecclesiastical bodies and thinkers claiming deep debts to Calvin look and think so differently. Incidentally, when used with Kehm's predoctrinal biblical themes as a hermeneutical key, TULIP is broadened and "Reformed Ever Reforming" is focused.

Twentieth-century Protestant theologians inherited a landscape in which Calvin was in the air they breathed; he affected every horizon, and the bedrock of his thought was just below the surface of every step they took. To speak in terms of a landscape lends itself to a picture of Calvin as a mountain that dominates the geography. Images of Mount Hood (Calvin) looming above the city of

Portland (American theology) or Pikes Peak over Colorado Springs come to mind. The mountains are present, dominant, undeniable; they are unavoidable but not always consciously acknowledged. There are other mountains—some as high—but none that so dominate the horizon from the city. Some people are inspired by a mountain without ever setting a foot on it. Others are tourists who climb well-worn paths and take in the vistas. Then, there are those who decide to work the mountain. Some stake a claim, extract raw ore, and refine it to arrive at something valuable, and then they discard the dross. Still others use the mountain as a quarry from which they cut blocks and slabs, shape and polish them a bit, and use them pretty much intact. Others, such as civil engineers, grade and shape the mountain to meet some broader purpose, such as flood control, road building, or fire prevention. Then, there are environmental and geological factors at work quite apart from any human activity. Geothermal activity, gigantic plates that press against each other until the land is folded or cracks, and erosion all shape a mountain over the centuries.

Calvin-as-a-mountain suggests that his presence in twentieth-century American theology was undeniable. True enough. Practically speaking, however, he served very different functions for very different ends. For some, the idea of Calvin was what was important; there was very little that was useful for today about what he actually wrote. For others, various mining images seemed to be useful. Separating what was valuable from what was not was the dominant question concerning Calvin's role in the development of American theology. A common image in the literature is one of refining Calvin's thought for the present time. The interesting question, and one that is rarely answered is: what stokes the refiner's fire? In Calvin's case, modernity, orthodoxy, feminism, liberation theology, and ecumenism have all fueled various refining fires to get at what was valuable about Calvin. His thought was so biblical and clear that some theologians treated Calvin as a quarry, cutting slabs of thought and putting them to work in contemporary theological argumentation with just some basic shaping and sanding. Constructive or systematic theologians took a civil engineering approach to Calvin, shaping the mountain to fit larger pictures and discussions. Calvin's doctrines of the Trinity and the church have been particularly useful for ecumenical work. Theologians who glory in Calvin as an ecumenical resource need to be reminded that other theologians have found great wealth in Calvin's unwillingness to depart from the biblical themes that give the Reformed tradition its distinct identity. Similarly, those who glory in Calvin the Reformed theologian often miss natural opportunities he provides to connect to the wider church.[38]

In spite of all the theological work of the twentieth century, Calvin remains. He still dominates the horizon. He has patiently endured a variety of assaults

on his slopes, some friendly and some not. Although theologians and ecclesiastical movements have grown accustomed to the inspiring, hospitable, and
malleable character of his writings, history has shown that, 500 years after his
birth, Calvin is still capable of pointing to a God who resists all efforts to be
domesticated by the church or the academy. Perhaps Mount Hood's neighbor,
Mount St. Helens, provides an apt metaphor of the power that can be unleashed
when God decides to speak through his gifted and faithful servants.

NOTES

1. Charles Partee, *The Theology of John Calvin* (Louisville, Ky.: Westminster John
Knox, 2008), xi. The opening words of William J. Bouwsma's biography of Calvin set
the challenge for this chapter in a little more detail than does Partee:

> Calvinism has been widely credited—or blamed—for much that is thought to
> characterize the modern world: for capitalism and modern science, for
> the discipline and rationalization of the complex societies of the West, for
> the revolutionary spirit and democracy, for secularization and social
> activism, for individualism, utilitarianism, and empiricism. What John
> Calvin thought is by no means necessarily identical with what is meant
> by the "Calvinism" to which these large consequences have been attributed.
> He is, nevertheless, implicated in the supposed achievements of the
> movement that bears his name, if only because of the propensity of many
> "Calvinists" to invoke the authority of Calvin to legitimate their own ways of
> life and thought.

William J. Bouwsma, *John Calvin: A Sixteenth-Century Portrait* (New York: Oxford
University Press, 1988), 1.

2. Partee, *Theology of John Calvin*, 27.

3. The title of this chapter is an allusion to Alasdair McIntyre's *Whose Justice,
Which Rationality?* (South Bend, Ind.: University of Notre Dame Press, 1988).

4. George H. Kehm, "What Is Reformed Theology?" *Panorama* [Pittsburgh
Theological Seminary] 22, no. 1 (Fall 1981): 22, 7.

5. According to a booklet published by the World Alliance of Reformed Churches
for the 2009 Calvin anniversary, the three great contributions of Calvin to the modern
world are his commitments to the unity of the church, justice, and ending war and
violence. One might make the same remark about any number of theologians. Lukas
Vischer and Setri Nyomi, *The Legacy of John Calvin: Some Actions for the Church in the
21st Century* (Geneva: World Alliance of Reformed Churches and the John Knox
International Reformed Center, 2009).

6. Incidentally, the Servetus episode has functioned very similarly to the way
"Sinners in the Hands of an Angry God" continues to plague Jonathan Edwards and
his sympathetic interpreters.

7. Henry Christopher McCook, *Historic Decorations of the Pan-Presbyterian
Council* (Philadelphia: Presbyterian Publishing, 1880), 6.

8. Perry Miller, *The New England Mind: The Seventeenth Century* (New York: Macmillan, 1939), 92ff.

9. Charles Augustus Briggs, *American Presbyterianism: Its Origin and Early History* (New York: Scribner's, 1885).

10. William Walker Rockwell, William Adams Brown, and Thomas Cuming Hall, *Three Addresses Delivered by Professors in Union Theological Seminary: At a Service in Commemoration of the Four-Hundredth Anniversary of the Birth of John Calvin, in the Adams Chapel, on Monday Evening, the Third of May, Nineteen Hundred and Nine* (New York: Union Theological Seminary, 1909).

11. Ibid., 47.

12. B. B. Warfield, "The Present-Day Attitude toward Calvinism: Its Causes and Significance," in B. B. Warfield, *Calvin as a Theologian and Calvinism To-Day* (Edinburgh: Hope Trust, 1909), 21.

13. Warfield, "Calvin's Doctrine of the Knowledge of God," in *Calvin and Augustine* (Philadelphia: Presbyterian and Reformed Publishing, 1956), 30, 33.

14. Old Princeton Calvinism lived in the second half of the twentieth century in John H. Gerstner and R. C. Sproul, two apologists who invoked Calvin as a proponent of the inerrancy of scripture. Princeton's Edward A. Dowey's most important work, *The Knowledge of God in Calvin's Theology* (New York: Columbia University Press, 1952), marked his long debate with Old Princeton. In the 1960s, Dowey and Gerstner traveled around to local congregations of the Presbyterian Church, debating the Confession of 1967, Dowey defending it, and Gerstner criticizing it.

15. Herman Bavinck, "Calvin and Common Grace" (1909), trans. Geerhardus Vos, available at www.contra-mundum.org/books/Calvin.pdf (accessed October 15, 2008).

16. Cornelius Van Til, "Calvin as a Controversialist," available at www.the-highway.com/articleAug00.html (accessed October 15, 2008). This article was taken from R. C. Sproul, ed., *Soli Deo Gloria: Essays in Reformed Theology* (Nutley, N.J.: Presbyterian and Reformed Publishing, 1976). It originally appeared as chapter 1.

17. Paul Fuhrmann, *God-Centered Religion: An Essay Inspired by Some French and Swiss Protestant Writers* (Grand Rapids, Mich.: Zondervan, 1942), 17.

18. See, for example, Reinhold Niebuhr, *An Interpretation of Christian Ethics* (New York: Harper, 1935), 159ff. H. Richard Niebuhr's contributions will be discussed later in the chapter.

19. Joseph Haroutunian, *Wisdom and Folly in Religion* (New York: Scribner's, 1940), 89, 110.

20. H. Richard Niebuhr, preface, ibid., viii–ix.

21. Sydney E. Ahlstrom, *Theology in America: The Major Protestant Voices from Puritanism to Neo-Orthodoxy* (Indianapolis, Ind.: Bobbs-Merrill, 1967), 83.

22. Clarence Bouma, "Calvinism in American Theology Today," *Journal of Religion* 27 (January 1947): 34, 36.

23. Joseph Haroutunian, "Reply to Dr. Bouma: Calvinism Is Not Fundamentalism," *Journal of Religion* 27 (January 1947): 46.

24. Wilhelm Pauck, "The Prospects of Orthodoxy," *Journal of Religion* 27 (January 1947): 50–51.

25. John T. McNeill, "Thirty Years of Calvin Study," *Church History* 17, no. 3 (1948): 208.

26. Fuhrmann, *God-Centered Religion*, 23.

27. John T. McNeill, *The History and Character of Calvinism* (New York: Oxford University Press, 1954), 433.

28. Ibid.

29. See J. I. Packer, "Calvin's View of Scripture," in *God's Inerrant Word*, ed. John W. Montgomery (Minneapolis, Minn.: Bethany Fellowship, 1974), 95–114.

30. H. Richard Niebuhr, *Christ and Culture* (New York: Harper, 1951).

31. Donald K. McKim released a new edition of a compend with *Calvin's Institutes: Abridged Edition* (Louisville, Ky.: Westminster John Knox, 2001).

32. An informative though partisan guide through the complexities of orthodox American Calvinism is found in Curt Daniel, *The History and Theology of Calvinism* (Springfield, Ill.: Good Books, 2003).

33. A good modern example of this kind of polemics is Gary North's work of more than a thousand pages, *Crossed Fingers: How the Liberals Captured the Presbyterian Church* (Tyler, Tex.: Institute for Christian Economics, 1996).

34. See Greg L. Bahnsen, *Theonomy in Christian Ethics*, expanded ed. (Phillipsburg, N.J.: Presbyterian and Reformed Publishing, 1984); and Gary North, *Westminster's Confession: The Abandonment of Van Til's Legacy* (Tyler, Tex.: Institute for Christian Economics, 1991). Interestingly, North's argument is that Westminster Seminary's fatal turn came when it embraced Calvin's natural law over Van Til's apologetic starting point.

35. James M. Gustafson, *Ethics from a Theocentric Perspective*, 2 vols. (Chicago: University of Chicago Press, 1980), 1:163, 167. In the 1980s, Brian A. Gerrish, then Gustafson's colleague at Chicago, went to great lengths to establish and document theological development from Calvin to Schleiermacher to Troeltsch as the foundation for a liberal theological program true to Calvin. See, for example, B. A. Gerrish, *The Old Protestantism and the New: Essays on the Reformation Heritage* (Chicago: University of Chicago Press, 1982).

36. The fragment on baptism was published in 1969 and the section on the Lord's Prayer in 1981. Volume I/1 was retranslated and appeared in 1975.

37. See Donald K. McKim, *Introducing the Reformed Faith* (Louisville, Ky.: Westminster John Knox, 2001), for a helpful guide to the Reformed tradition in a modern American context.

38. For any future attempts at a typology, it is worth noting that the dust jacket to Van Til's *Christianity and Barthianism* (Philadelphia: Presbyterian and Reformed Publishing, 1962) depicts a castle on a piece of mountain hovering in mid-air. This is a visual reference to Van Til's contention that there is no foundation for Barth's theology in spite of its orthodox appearance. The missing epistemological foundation is the doctrine of the inerrancy of scripture, something Van Til found in Calvin.

PART III

Letters

8

"Strange Providence": Indigenist Calvinism in the Writings of Mohegan Minister Samson Occom (1723–1792)

Denise T. Askin

In December 1766, while waiting in Boston to board the ship that would carry him across the "great Water" for a long preaching tour in England, the Mohegan Samson Occom wrote to his mentor, the Reverend Eleazar Wheelock:

> I have a Struggle in my Mind At times, knowing not where I am going, I don't know but I am looking for a Spot of Ground where my Bones must be Buried, and never to See my Poor Family again, but I verily believe I am Call'd of god by Strange Providence and that is Enough, he will take Care of me if I do but put my Whole trust in him and he will Provide for mine, I want nothing but the Will of God, to be Wholly Swallowed up in it. (*CW*, 74)[1]

Occom, a tribal councilor and an ordained Presbyterian minister, was setting out on a mission to advance the cause of education for Indians. Invited to England by George Whitefield, Occom was raising funds for a school for Indians run by Wheelock, his teacher and a Congregational New Light. Occom's mission depended for its success on his being at once fully Indian and fully Christian—and a recognizably Calvinist Christian at that.

The "struggle" Occom describes in his letter was not solely the anxiety of a provincial subject embarking on a dangerous sea voyage to

Europe for the first time. As a member of the Algonquian-speaking Mohegan tribe, whose thought world was centered in communal lands and for whose members the highest obligation was to family and the larger tribal community, this journey threatened Occom's sense of identity and duty. He acknowledges his very real concern about providing for a family that had been rendered dependent, like most eastern indigenous people, by colonial encroachment. He imagines himself dying homeless and seeking a grave in unwelcoming ground. What propels him on this unknown path, however, is his sense of spiritual vocation, a providential calling that he finds both "strange" and empowering.

Strange, indeed, that an Indian Calvinist was reversing the sea voyage that first brought Calvin to New England on the *Mayflower* over a century earlier. Empowering, in that Occom trusted wholeheartedly in the Christian God, even in the face of the historic betrayals and predations that had accompanied Christian colonialism. In an expression of faith as impassioned as those of his close contemporary, Jonathan Edwards—"I want nothing but . . . to be wholly swallowed up in [the will of God]"—Occom places his people and himself in God's care and casts his—and their—fate with God's will.

Occom spent his entire life on journeys, traveling endlessly to fulfill his duties as an itinerant preacher, a Presbyterian missionary, and a tribal leader and diplomat. He traveled throughout southern New England, New York, and New Jersey, crossing and recrossing the borders of colonies, crossing and recrossing the Long Island Sound, weaving and reweaving strands of connection among Indian communities and among Christian communities. He reinforced ties between the Mohegan tribe and both the natives of coastal New England/New York and the Oneida in "the wilderness." He preached in native languages and in English; in the sophisticated pulpits of New York, Boston, and London; to rural and frontier gatherings in New England and New York; to audiences of all denominations, races, and social classes, from English nobility to American slaves. His primary mission, however, was to his "brethren according to the flesh," his fellow Indians, and he concluded his lifelong journey by joining with and leading Christian members of several eastern tribes to move away from their homelands and found a new settlement in upstate New York named Brotherton.

In the course of his fifty years serving both kin and Christ, in advancing both tribal rights and the Word of God, Occom evolved a worldview that adapted Calvinism in such a way that it became not only his mode of serving God but also both the basis of his indictment of colonial Christianity and the very foundation for his continued native communal vision—a phenomenon that can be termed "indigenist Calvinism."

Calvinism in Native America

John Calvin's journey into the world of the Native American was begun in the 1640s by English ministers like John Eliot and the Mayhews and rekindled in the 1740s during the more ecumenical and spirit-driven Great Awakening. The Mohegan tribe was "heathen" (Occom's term) until 1739, when land controversies had begun to erode their sachemship and their self-sufficiency and the evangelical fervor of the awakening erupted in their very backyard. Ironically, among the reasons native leaders had given for resisting conversion was the scandalous behavior of the Christians themselves. As William Simmons notes, to native eyes, "Christianity had not made better people of the English and the English themselves disagreed over which denomination was best."[2] Christians had usurped Indian lands and had introduced blasphemy, alcohol, whoring, and disease. In one sermon, Occom accused the white society of corrupting Indians: "you have learnt them many of the Sins they are Guilty of" (CW, 227). Additionally, unlike the practice of the French Jesuits, whose belief in "inculturation" led them to at least attempt a more culturally embedded missionary practice,[3] English missionary methodology required first that Native Americans be "civilized" (that is, become like the English) in order to be "Christianized." This meant not only cultivating literacy for the study of scripture but also adopting English dress, habits, and customs. Converts were expected to reject their own cultures and traditions in seeking salvation.

By the nineteenth century, as Drew Lopenzina argues, "the discourse of white civilization offered only two possibilities for Native Americans: they must either assimilate or face extinction."[4] Conjuring a mortal opposition between Indianness and regenerate humanity, the English colonial missionary agenda required not only that Indians turn from sin to grace but also that they turn from native life to "civilized" customs. Wheelock's dream of training Indian missionaries to "reduce" natives to religion necessitated strict lifelong monitoring and control by mentors such as himself. When his promising Indian scholars reverted (as he saw it) to their Indian ways and broke their ties to him, Wheelock could interpret this only as their falling away from God as well.

Although Samson Occom famously seemed to repudiate his traditional ways by distantly referring to his early life and that of his family as "heathen" in his 1768 autobiographical sketch (CW, 52), new scholarship continues to find evidence of his successful merging of his Calvinist faith with his primary responsibilities, as a Native American, to tribe and kin.

What did that native tradition look like? In *That the People Might Live*, Jace Weaver (Cherokee) explains that, unlike the Pauline and Calvinist disjunctive thinking that opposes carnal and spiritual, mundane and sacred, nature and grace, the native worldview reveals "no such dualistic thinking." Because there is "no split between sacred and secular spheres," the native worldview is "essentially religious." In fact, there is no such entity as "religion" because native lifeways embody the continuum—not the separation—of spirit, cosmos, and humankind. The native worldview is spatial, based on the relationship to land and place, something Weaver calls "geomythology." Just as native religion is spatial, native morality is relational. It depends on right relationships to the community (kinship) and to the cosmos. The Calvinist sense of sin as total depravity, therefore, has no place in the native worldview. Its only equivalent would be a "failure to live up to one's responsibilities to the community," and the only equivalent to Christian salvation would be "the continuance of the People."[5] The state of Indian "grace" is to be in harmony with one's people and with the cosmos.

Ethnographic and literary analysis in recent scholarship sheds light on how Occom managed his two cultural inheritances, Native American and Calvinist. Native scholars Robert Allen Warrior, Lisa Brooks, and Jace Weaver have established Occom as a key figure in "Native intellectual history,"[6] redirecting the discussion about native writers. Occom's enduring Indianness, camouflaged in eighteenth-century prose, is now emerging from studies of his letters, diaries, and tribal documents. Similarly, scholars Joanna Brooks, Hilary Wyss, Kristina Bross, Eileen Elrod, and others are exploring Occom's Christianity as an integral and enduring element of his identity.[7]

With regard to the neglect of Indian converts in earlier scholarship, Wyss suggests that natives who accepted Christianity "have been largely overlooked or downplayed because they do not have appropriately 'authentic' pedigrees." Their Indianness, in other words, seemed to be compromised by their accept-ance of Christianity. Joanna Brooks, however, finds in Occom's later, more politicized preaching a "Christian indigenist worldview." Native converts' appropriation of Christianity, these scholars argue, need not be viewed as a pas-sive submission to a dominant culture. It can be seen, in fact, as a sign of their agency. Indian converts, according to Philip H. Round, adapted both their lit-eracy and their command of Christianity to construct "new personal and com-munal identities that would function well in the new colonial context." For example, Brooks shows the importance of hymn singing to the continuance of Native American communal rituals and, therefore, the significance of Occom's own hymns and nondenominational hymnal in forging the new community of Christian Indians gathered from numerous tribes in Brotherton. "Occom's Christianity . . . defies simple characterization as 'assimilative,' or 'accommo-dationist,'" she argues, and knowing this "helps us to see him more accurately as a native intellectual taking part in the broader pan-tribal revitalization movements of the late eighteenth century."[8]

Native American as Calvinist

If Occom's identity as an Indian was based on tribe, clan, and kin, his Christian identity shows an affinity with John Calvin. Occom was grounded in the doctrines of God's sovereignty, human depravity, *sola fides*, and *sola scriptura*. He squared off against papists, universalists, and deists in his defense of "the right kind of religion" (*CW*, 104). His sermons address conversion, regeneration, "unbelief" as the root of all sin (*CW*, 216), and justification by faith. Above all, however, Occom shows himself to be Calvin's descendant in his understanding of his role as a preacher of the Word.

Like the Puritans of seventeenth-century New England, Occom believed that scripture, the Word of God, not only had meaning but also that it was efficacious. As Thomas J. Davis observes, Calvin believed that "one has access to Christ through means appointed by God, and the primary means is through preaching." The preacher, as instrument, could provide an occasion for the action of the Holy Spirit in the hearts of the hearers. This was his highest obligation. The sermon, further, had a sacramental role in opening scripture and in opening hearts to the movement of the Spirit. Like the Lord's Supper, "the function of the preached word for Calvin is to make Christ present."[9]

Hundreds of entries in Occom's spare and accountant-like journals make clear his dedication to preaching whenever and wherever the occasion permitted. His meticulous notations record three things about his preaching: the scripture text he chose, evidence of the Spirit's presence among the people, and whether he experienced a sense of "freedom" and "divine things" while he preached. There are scores of passages such as "there was a flow of Tears, I believe the Lord was present with his word" (*CW*, 355); "I believe they felt the Power of the Truth of the Word of God" (*CW*, 298); "the Lord was present with us, the Christians were much movd" (*CW*, 299); "I had Some freedom in Speaking this Night" (*CW*, 282); or "I had but little Sense of Divine things, however, the People attended with great attention" (*CW*, 282).

Readers have registered disappointment that so much of Occom's journal writing is impersonal. One can see, however, that the entries reflect a mindset close to Calvin's view of the preacher as instrument. We may surmise that Occom consciously disciplined himself as a preacher. In one sermon, he told of a minister who accused himself of "pride" if he took pleasure from people's approval of his preaching, or if he was ashamed if he preached badly (*CW*, 212).

Occom's journal passages chronicle the movement of the Spirit, which alone is efficacious; they omit blame or credit for himself. Regarding himself as solely instrumental, Occom focuses instead on discerning signs of grace in his hearers. While those signs often were affective (tears, rising emotion), he does draw a distinction between the Spirit and human spirits: "many were affected, but I believe there was more Natural affection than Gracious" (*CW*, 347).

Centered, therefore, on the Word of scripture and on the role of the sermon in the plan of salvation as Calvin defined it, Samson Occom's encounter with Christianity occasioned an intensive encounter with language. An illiterate "heathen" by his own account until the age of seventeen, Occom was propelled by his religious "awakening" to learn to speak and read English first and then, within the space of four years, to learn Hebrew, Greek, and Latin. He mastered the "dominant voice"[10] with a vengeance, surpassing many an itinerant preacher in his ability to read scripture, at least to some extent, in the original languages. As a missionary to the Indians, he preached in his native Algonquian to tribes in New England and on Long Island, and he learned the language of the Oneida of upstate New York. One might say that Occom's dedication to the Word led him to a lifetime of wordcraft.

In effect, language became the context of Occom's long career. His *voice*, therefore, was key to his vocation. Occom clearly enjoyed a more diverse range of audiences than virtually any other preacher of his day. His encounter with languages, far from compromising his identity, gave him the versatility that his intercultural position required, enabling him to cultivate a range of voices for a variety of audiences. In 1761, Samuel Buell made the tantalizing remark that Occom's preaching to Indians was "vastly more natural and free; clear and eloquent, quick and powerful, than 'tis wont to be, when he preaches to others." Unfortunately, we have no way of reconstructing his preaching in his native tongue, but, by exploring the written texts of his sermons from a rhetorical perspective, we discover both Occom's versatility as a "spiritual intermediary"[11] and the undeniably Calvinist scaffolding of his spiritual life.

Until the 2006 publication of Joanna Brooks's groundbreaking edition of *The Collected Writings of Samson Occom*, discussion of Occom was limited typically to the two works available in anthologies: a 1768 autobiographical sketch, unpublished in his lifetime, and his one published sermon, the 1772 execution sermon for the Indian Moses Paul. To discover a fuller sense of Occom's world, we must look beyond the published and polished execution sermon to the unpublished notes for his regular sermons.

Just as Harry Stout, in his monumental work on the unpublished sermons of early New England, *The New England Soul* (1986), argues for the importance of unpublished sermons in understanding New England culture ("not everyone in New England read sermons, . . . but nearly everyone heard them"), the critic Bernd Peyer writes that "the authentic voice of early Northern American Indian writers is . . . often discernible only if published material can be compared with unpublished sources." A precondition for publication, he argues, is control by the dominant cultural voice. For this reason, Peyer believes that Samson Occom's "authentic voice . . . breaks through much more frequently in his unpublished manuscripts, or 'undisguised transcripts.'"[12] In addition to the letters and autobiographical pieces, Peyer points scholars to Occom's sermons, which are notably absent from Stout's extensive study of the unpublished sermons of New England.

In the unpublished sermons, we can trace Occom's Calvinist theology, his mastery of the major literary form of colonial New England, and his appropriation of the dominant voice and genre for the salvation—temporal and spiritual—of his Indian brothers and sisters. Occom's ministerial persona, his use of literary and rhetorical devices, his style, strategies, and cultural messages in the unpublished sermons reveal a man whose Calvinist piety was served by a complex use of irony and the unfolding of a powerful central narrative that bridged the temporal and spiritual realities of his world, his indigenist Calvinism.

Occom came to Christianity at the height of the Great Awakening (1739–1740). It was a watershed moment for preaching styles.[13] The New Lights overthrew scholastic theology and style for a direct appeal to conversion of the heart, and many New Light itinerants moved outside the traditional church venue to bring their charismatic message to the masses and to the marginal. In his mastery of the sermon, Samson Occom appropriated a powerful medium. His role as preacher gave him an unprecedented entrée into the white world, and, at the same time, it was compatible with the native cultural tradition of respect for the oratorical powers of the individual. Finally, it reflected how the legacy from Calvin, the belief that "the preached Word not only conveys Christ, but also continues Christ's living presence in the world,"[14] informed the life of this Native American.

Occom's Calvinist formation took place at the epicenter of the Great Awakening. He moved in powerful Calvinist circles for the early part of his life, and, although he gradually separated himself from the dominance of the white ministerial culture later in life, he maintained his confession of Calvinist faith until his death. Converted in 1741 by the notorious James Davenport, educated by the New Light Yale-educated Eleazar Wheelock, mentored by Jonathan Edwards's protégé Samuel Buell, and admitted to the New England entourage of the English Methodist itinerant George Whitefield and then to the Calvinist network that included Selina, Countess of Huntington, Lord Dartmouth, and

Susannah Wheatley, Occom found in his acquaintances a who's who of the Great Awakening.

Regarding doctrine, Occom passed, not one, but two examinations for ordination (first by Connecticut Congregational ministers and then by New York Presbyterians) and was ordained by the Long Island Presbytery in 1759. Until the end of his life, Occom maintained his ties with Buell and the Long Island Presbytery. In a letter he wrote in 1791, the year before his death, he claimed that his New Stockbridge Indian church "willingly and Cheerfully adopted the Confession of Faith of the Presbyterian Church of the United States in America. They joyfully put themselves under the care and inspection of Albany Presbytery—and thankfully receive the gospel fellowship open'd for them. . . . Our Professors keep on Steady in Religion" (CW, 136).

For all of this circumstantial evidence of Occom's Calvinism, however, readers have noted the absence in his writings of the traditional conversion narrative associated with New England Calvinism.[15] Significantly, when it came to Occom's ordination, his experience of conversion was at the center of the proceedings. Aftershocks of the threat posed by itinerant New Light preachers to the authority of the ministry could still be felt in New York. "Inthusiastical exhorters" visiting Montauk, for instance, had led the natives to reject more established ministers until Occom's moderation brought them around (CW, 56). In August 1759, the Reverend Samuel Buell, the New Light pastor at East Hampton, preached the ordination sermon. Buell, whose own ordination sermon had been preached by none other than Jonathan Edwards, passed the institutional mantle to Occom, so to speak, and validated the ministry of the Mohegan Indian.

The title of Buell's sermon, "The Excellence and Importance of the Saving Knowledge of the Lord Jesus Christ in the Gospel-Preacher, Plainly and Seriously Represented and Enforced: And Christ Preached to the Gentiles in Obedience to the Call of GOD," reveals his rhetorical strategy: to affirm the New Light insistence on a converted ministry, to validate Occom's own conversion, and to portray Occom's mission to his fellow Indians as a divine vocation. To distinguish him from the "Inthusiastical exhorters," it seems that Buell was at pains to demonstrate Occom's ministerial lineage.

Buell published this sermon in 1761, prefaced by his letter to David Bostwick in which he details Occom's personal conversion narrative, apparently as told to him by his friend Occom. He writes that Occom had a "clear, powerful, and practical Conviction of the moral Pollution of his Nature, and of the great Defilement of his life, by actual Sin." Buell thus provides the familiar (and obligatory) conversion morphology that scholars have sought in vain among Occom's papers.[16] It is impossible to know whether Buell's account reflects

Occom's own wording or whether this is a formulaic composition grafted onto his friend's experience. Regardless, the result is that Buell validated Occom for the reading and religious public in the powerfully recognizable language of the conversion narrative.

In the ordination sermon itself, Buell sanctions the lifting of Occom's voice to preach the Word of God. Dwelling almost exclusively on the need for ministers to know the Lord "savingly," Buell uses the occasion of Occom's ordination to reiterate the New Light position in the controversy about an unconverted ministry. Only by the assistance of the Spirit can a minister's voice be efficacious. We can trace here a linguistic ritual by which Buell validates Occom's "saving knowledge of Christ." Buell declares Occom to be called by God and associates him with two biblical figures: Paul, the apostle to the Gentiles, and the Old Testament prophet Samuel.

In addition to such conventional claims, however, Buell situates Occom's mission to his fellow Indians within the concentric narratives of Judeo-Christian salvation history and contemporary American history. Viewed teleologically, the recent decisive victory over the Catholic Marquis de Montcalm in the French and Indian War and the ordination of a Calvinist Mohegan missionary merged rhetorically as signs of providential design:

> And this too, in a Day in which we have Reason to believe from
> Scripture Prophecy, and the present Aspect of Divine Providence,
> that the Latter-Day Glory is dawning; a Day also, in which, by the
> Smiles of Heaven upon our Forces, and the Success of our Armies in
> America, a joyous Prospect opens to View far beyond all that ever
> appear'd before, for evangelizing the Heathen in these Ends of the
> Earth. At this very Day of growing Wonder and refreshing Hope, the
> Lord calls you to preach the Gospel to those, who from Time
> immemorial, have been wandering out of the Way of Salvation.[17]

Buell here employs the well-known Calvinist and Puritan traditions of typology and the millennial interpretation of current events. As Harry Stout points out, the audiences of New England ministers had been trained "to view Scripture on multiple levels of significance and so to become rudimentary literary critics . . . and to insert themselves directly into the world of biblical promise and prophecy."[18] Buell simultaneously invests Occom's ministry with theological significance and inscribes it within the Euro-American narrative.

Buell's rhetorical "laying on of hands" admitted Occom to a powerful venue in colonial America, enabling him to lift his "voice" in a world where authorized preachers held a near-monopoly on the privilege of speaking, and "preaching was virtually the only form of public communication."[19]

Style

Granted that most of Occom's manuscript sermons are aimed at effecting personal regeneration in his hearers, an examination of the texts shows that Occom
had a more diverse set of rhetorical devices than is commonly assumed. He
consciously manipulated the level of discourse according to the situation at
hand. We know from his letters that Occom mastered a wide range of tones in
written English. He adopted the conventional posture of obsequiousness in
letters to his benefactors, a biting sarcasm toward his detractor the Reverend
Robert Clelland, righteous indignation toward Wheelock, tenderness toward
his wife, and even witty playfulness toward his children. In one memorable passage in a letter to Wheelock condemning the transformation of his Indian school
into a college for English students (Dartmouth), Occom fires his linguistic salvo
in the very Latin that Wheelock had taught him, substituting *alba* (white) for *alma*
mater (*CW*, 98). And, when he saw fit, he used such technical terms as *regenera-*
tion, omniscience, condescension, and *omnipresence* as needed in his sermons. It is
reasonable to conclude, then, that Occom was sufficiently a master of tone and
rhetorical techniques to make stylistic choices in composing his sermons. By
turns, he modulated his voice to emphasize pastoral care, Pauline paradox and
native irony, ministerial authority, and prophetic social conscience.

Although several of the manuscripts contain rather wooden collections of
prefabricated biblical and doctrinal phrases (showing Occom's apprentice work of
memorizing and imitating the Christian language and conventions he had
learned), the corpus of sermons manifests a range of styles, rhetorical devices, and
voices. Given his lifelong role as a minister to Indians and rural communities,
Occom's most frequent rhetorical choice was simplicity, but the choice was by no
means simplistic. It suited his missionary function. Nor was Occom's mode of
simplicity purchased at the expense of literary and rhetorical devices. Calvin had
argued that sermons needed to move beyond imparting knowledge to moving the
heart. This crucial function, he said, was best accomplished by figurative language.
Metaphors "by their lively similitude better penetrate the soul."[20] Occom clearly
valued the power of figurative expression. We know, for instance, that he wrote to
Dr. Andrew Gifford in London (1772) requesting a copy of Benjamin Keach's book
on metaphor, because it was "the best book for the Instruction of the Indians of
Humane composure I ever saw" (*CW*, 101). The book itself, *Tropologia: A Key to*
Open Scripture Metaphors,[21] was a guide to figurative expressions in scripture.

In one sermon fragment, "Fight the Good Fight of Faith," Occom refers to
God's "Infinite Condesention," that is, God's use of a figurative mode in order

to communicate with humans. Occom explicitly models his own use of analogy on the style God uses in scripture: "And Since the Holy Ghost has Compared his Works to our Worldly Concerns, we will Endeavour to follow his Teachings, by Comparing the Spiritual Warfare with Carnal Warfare" (*CW*, 171). If God's own words were metaphorical, then the minister's best use of language was to make God manifest through figurative language in preaching. In various sermons, Occom developed lengthy sustained "similitudes," comparing temporal warfare or sleep or shadows, point for point, to spiritual states. Occom also shows that he was well schooled in the biblical literary device of typology. He writes, in more than one sermon, that Christ "was Represented by various Name[s], Titles, and Shadows and Figures" (*CW*, 176) in the Old Testament. Christ was foreshadowed as "the Seed of the Woman, . . . the Morning Star, . . . the Prince of Peace" (*CW*, 176).

The most common early claim about Occom's sermons is that they abounded in metaphors and narratives and that his preaching was effective because of his distinctive use of analogy. In 1761, Samuel Buell praised Occom's use of analogy, a trait he ascribes to Indian oratorical technique. The implication is that there was a transfer of Native American speech patterns and narrative into his sermons. In the sermon notes, however, Occom's analogies appear no more frequently than those of other Calvinist preachers of the day, nor are they examples of linguistic syncretism. The sustained similitudes that Occom uses invoke Euro-American culture and biblical imagery, such as crowns and thrones, rather than Native American culture. In light of the discrepancy between the manuscript evidence and the eyewitness accounts, it is reasonable to conclude that Occom used improvisation to develop the points in his written notes. These *ex tempore* passages were probably animated and memorable elements of his delivery, and they were most likely where the stories and analogies appeared. This is especially likely because so much of Occom's ministry consisted of itinerant preaching, which typically relied on a repertoire of illustrative material.

Biblical phrases, cadences, tropes, and narrative designs are so deeply embedded in Occom's use of English that, in the manuscript sermons, he moves from paraphrase to analysis to quotation seamlessly. His word hoard was quarried from the Bible. At times, Occom's own expression blends into biblical paraphrase, making the two almost indistinguishable. The language of the Bible, and of St. Paul in particular, permeates Occom's writing. In his letters and diaries, biblical quotations and allusions arise seemingly unbidden (Paul: "We have become a spectacle to the world"; Occom: "I have been a spectacle and a gazing stock"; Paul: "I am speaking as a fool"; Occom: "I speak like a fool").

It was, of course, typical for the letters of ministers to be peppered with biblical quotations and references, but, in Occom's case, we see that his personal narrative becomes inscribed within the Pauline and prophetic paradigm. Just as Paul's mission was to the Gentiles, so Occom's mission was to the "Gentiles" of North America—the Indians. As Paul had to justify himself to those who challenged his authority, so Occom was constrained to defend himself against detractors who spread rumors discrediting the authenticity of his Christianity or his Indianness and to decry his unequal treatment as a minister. Like St. Paul, Occom adjusted his style to the needs of his audience. Paul was capable of profound theological subtlety, but he wrote to the Corinthians, whom he calls "infants in Christ": "I fed you with milk, not solid food" (1 Corinthians 3). While Paul's sufferings resulted from society's rejection of his faith in Christ, however, most of Occom's sufferings were caused by society's marginalization of his race. In fact, he came to believe that white ministers "saw him more as a useful 'Gazing Stocke' than as a fully competent brother in Christ."[22] This made it even more important that Occom, like Paul, exercise discretion in choosing his level of discourse. He adapted his style to his audience.

Calvin spoke of God's accommodation, through the accessible language of scripture and of preachers, to the needs of finite humans. In words that recall Calvin, Occom addresses the topic of style. In a sermon written in 1766, Occom makes a particularly telling comment about God as a stylist: he expresses gratitude that "God levels his language [in the Bible] to weak capacities" (CW, 172). Only six years later, Occom would publish an apologia for his own style of language—a style that was accessible to all by virtue of its simplicity. In his preface to the execution sermon, Occom is highly aware of style—his own and that of the dominant culture. Modestly, he says that his words are simple enough to be understood by Indians, "little children . . . and poor Negroes." What he offers is "common, plain, every day talk."

His very modesty, however, becomes a vehicle for Occom to reveal the limitations of the language employed by the churches of the dominant culture: books are written in "very high and refined language," and "the sermons that are delivered every Sabbath in general, are in a very high and lofty stile, so that the common people understand but little of them" (CW, 177). Occom thus directs our attention to his own "simple" style of language, revealing its efficacy with "the common people" and, thereby, implying its greater usefulness as an instrument for "God's great work," particularly among the marginal. Occom again echoes Paul's letter to the Corinthians: "I did not come proclaiming the mystery of God to you in lofty words" (1 Corinthians 3). As Calvin argues, the humble preacher, "although he excels us in nothing,"[23] can be God's strategic choice.

Occom's pastoral voice rises in service of the unlearned souls whom he tended. He cultivates rhetorical simplicity, lyricism, homely analogy, repetition, and narrative. Samson Occom's simplicity of style served his primary role as preacher to the Indians ("infants in Christ"), and it was accessible to those marginalized by the Christian society in which he moved. It stood in stark contrast to the complex and degraded language of the civilized world. Occom repeatedly identifies in his sermons and other writings the abuse of language, the blasphemy, and the "genteel lies" (*CW*, 203) of so-called civilized society. There is implicit irony, then, in his plain talk. In contrast to the corrupt language of society, Occom offers the purity of Indian speech: "I am glad there is no Such Language among the Indians. . . . they have a Very great Veneration for the Name of the great God, in their perfect Heathenism they Calld God, Cauhtuntooct," and, to them, the Christian practice of swearing is "Horred" (*CW*, 227). Employing the Bible as the criterion for language use, Occom finds that "civilized" society has failed by this measure. By contrast, the Indians—whether by defect or virtue—come closer even in their language to the biblical standard than do members of the white society.

Like so many preachers of his day who shared a common quarry for tropes in the Bible, Occom constructs his sermons with well-known biblical terms and rhythms, typically intermeshing scripture passages with his own words. In a 1760 sermon on the text "Awake Thou That Sleepest" (Ephesians 5:14), composed at Montauk only months after his ordination, Occom addresses a tribe converted for less than a generation, not all of whose members spoke English. The sermon opens with a rather mechanical recitation of Calvinist doctrine, sustaining the predictable analogy between sleeping and waking, drawing an extended similitude between the two states of the human soul, sin and grace. He likens the state of sin to a state of "dead sleep," rendering the abstract concept of sin concrete: a person in a "dead" sleep can enjoy no pleasures and is not useful to others.

The second half of the sermon, however, moves into a lyrical improvisation on the tropes of sleeping and awakening. Here, Occom's pastoral voice emerges, shepherding his hearers through a gentle and even mystical repetition of phrases toward an encounter with grace. For example, he imagines the moment of the incarnation in language disarmingly simple and accessible to people whose culture stressed familial bonds: "The Dear Lamb of God Leaves the Bosom of his Dear Father As it were bids farewell to all" (*CW*, 169). After two passages of nearly metaphysical play with imagery (son/child/father; life/death; sleep/wake; alive/awake), Occom launches into a multitude of voices: the sound of the bridegroom, with his "melting invitation," the voice of Christ, the voice of the gospel, all presumably mediated by the pastoral voice of the minister. Occom ends with a lyrical and poetic flight, intensifying the musical devices of alliteration and assonance: "the glorious light of life, and light at last to the heavenly Jerusalem" (*CW*, 170). This alternation between a repetition of well-worn phrases, on the one hand, and original, lyrical outpourings, on the other, often appears in Occom's sermons.

Irony and the Pauline Paradox

Sherman Alexie suggests, in *The Toughest Indian in the World*, that irony is the "hallmark of the contemporary indigenous American." In the eighteenth century, however, Samson Occom developed a particular form of irony that reflected both his adherence to Christian scripture and his clear-sighted judgment of the Christian society. According to Kelly McCarthy, "there is a blind spot in much post colonial criticism: the assertion that Occom's interests are essentially in conflict with 'the process that produced him' does not leave space for Occom's agency for critique; it does not allow Occom to be within the missionary culture and also a critic of it."[24] It is, in fact, Occom's very fidelity to the Christian message and, specifically, his appropriation of the Pauline model that provide the material basis for his ironic expression, a form that might be described as *earnest irony*.

Emphasis on St. Paul, of course, was not unique to Occom. Calvin directed preachers to St. Paul, and, for over a century, the homiletic and doctrinal tradition of American ministers had given priority to Paul.[25] For Occom, the parallels, personal as well as formal, are pervasive. Rhetorically, Paul's use of paradox provided Occom with an effective model for the radical transvaluation that came with Christ. The foolishness of Christ confounds the wisdom of the world; weakness trades places with strength. Lowly clay vessels become the instruments of God's salvific work.

This leads to the question of "ethos" in the sermons. Occom's sermon notes typically subordinate the personal voice in favor of a transparent and authoritative mediation of the Word. An important exception is his address to his "brethren according to the flesh," when he gains power from his identity with them—"I am an Indian, too, your brother"—and calls them to attention (*CW*, 196). When he addresses a predominantly white audience, however, Occom employs a voice that exploits the dubious position he occupies in the Euro-American society. In a sermon in London in 1766, Occom foregrounds the ethos of a "poor Indian," drawing on the rhetoric of his biblical model, St. Paul, apostle to the Gentiles ("For I am the least of the apostles, unfit to be called an apostle" [1 Corinthians 15:9]). Occom structures his own paradoxical role on the Pauline model, positioning himself to invert the very social order that consigns the Indians to inferior status.

In this sermon, Occom constructs a complex rhetorical ethos. St. Paul forged his own ethos from paradox: he claims to be "unfit to be called an apostle," yet he also claims the highest authority to speak: "by the grace of God I am what I am" (1 Corinthians 15:10). His competence is "from God." Paul's "weakness" stands in ironic contrast to worldly strength. Similarly, Occom's sermon is a deft rhetorical performance. Occom calls attention to the lowly status assigned to him in Euro-American society. It is "dareing presumption" for him to stand before "this great congregation" whose members are "very refined and educated," learned in literature and the sciences. He is "but a Babe in Religion," profoundly ignorant, not gifted with "the Wisdom of the Wise nor . . . the Eloquence of the Orator" (CW, 174).

But his opening gesture of subordination, derived from Paul (1 Corinthians 1:18–29), is wound tight with ironic implications. His seemingly obsequious "I have not the Wisdom of the Wise nor Knowledg of the Learned" (CW, 174) points to the Pauline chapter that utterly explodes the values of the world. In that chapter, Paul invokes God's warning: "I will destroy the wisdom of the wise, and the learning of the learned I will set aside" (1 Corinthians 1:19). Occom steps into this Pauline persona: "God chose the weak of the world to shame the strong" (1 Corinthians 1:27). The alert listener, attuned to Paul and 1 Corinthians, is prepared for the reversal of roles Occom is about to perform.

Occom first builds the paradox by introducing the figure of St. Peter, the unlearned and flawed individual upon whom Christ founded his church. He has Peter declare his poverty—"silver and gold have I none"—and then counter it with his priceless treasure of the preached Word. Peter's power is a sign of divine approbation. Occom then presents himself in an almost parodic stereotype of the Indian: "from the dunghill of Heathenish Darkness [I] stand before you . . . if it is only as a spectacle and gazing stock" (CW, 175). By devoting over four pages of closely written manuscript to this trickster-like apology, Occom suggests that his self-abasing rhetorical posture will please the audience, the very group that has essentially made such self-abasement necessary. Ironically, it is precisely his identity as a lowly Indian that gives him membership in the divinely endorsed tradition of Peter and Paul. He flatters the "great congregation," preparing them for the reversal.

Moving at last to the "inexhaustible" text from Matthew, "Saying What Think Ye of Christ?" Occom abruptly shifts voices. He now assumes his authoritative role as mediator of the Word, shifting his ethos from Indian to minister. With confidence, he asserts that this is "the greatest Question in the Christian religion" (CW, 175). The right answer brings life, he says; the wrong one, death. The minister is no longer hat-in-hand; he holds instead the keys to spiritual life and death.

In a masterful move, Occom next reveals the context for his biblical text: Christ's confounding of the Pharisees, his overturning of the power of the learned. Occom now has transformed himself from self-abasing outsider to heir of Peter and emissary of Christ. The stereotype of the Indian explodes as Occom holds a rhetorical mirror to the arbitrary hierarchy of "civilization." This reversal is *earnest* because it glorifies divine providence for elevating the lowly and for humbling self-congratulation. The reversal is also *ironic* because a "poor ignorant Indian" is its agent. Society's judgment has been trumped by the kingdom of God. Paradoxically, he has confounded the learned in their own temple.

Prophetic Voice

In a compelling description of the preacher's prophetic role, Calvin wrote that he "may instruct and exhort the teachable; may accuse, rebuke, and subdue the rebellious and stubborn; . . . if need be, may launch thunderbolts and lightnings, but do all things in God's Word." Davis argues that, "for Calvin, all ministers stood in the line of prophets."[26] Occom's own ministry of the Word was shaped by his view of the minister's role as a prophetic one. In two lengthy sermons based on the same text from Isaiah 58:1, "Cry Aloud, Spare Not," Occom portrays the "Awful Charge layd upon [preachers] by the eternal God" (*CW*, 211). God authorizes the preacher ("go with my Authority and with my Power") to speak truth to power ("Shew my People their Transgression, and the House of Jacob their Sins" [*CW*, 211]). As Occom moved toward independence from the colonial ministerial model toward an integration of his native identity with his ministerial authority, Joanna Brooks argues, his later sermons document "his awareness of his unique situation as a person of color with significant public authority, and his willingness to use this authority to condemn the inhumanity and evil of empire."[27]

Native traditions value dreams as sources of spiritual direction, and two passages in Occom's writings suggest his blending of native and biblical dreams. In a 1786 diary entry, Occom recounts a dream he had of George Whitefield. Bernd Peyer has explicated the passage in light of Native American shamanism to show that it represented "a form of visionary power legitimizing Occom's . . . choice to initiate a revival among his people."[28] An equally striking passage occurs at the beginning of one of Occom's sermons (on Daniel 5:25). He tells of a recurring dream in which he sees the divine words ("Mene, Mene, Tekel, Upharsin") written on a wall:

> These Words I dreamt of and Preach'd from in my Dream Some time
> ago, and they have followed me a great deal by turn ever Since, and

last Spring I deliverd a Short Discourse from them, but I can not get
rid of them yet, they Will follow Some Times Night and Day, and I
am at last drove to write a Discourse from them. (*CW*, 198)

Here, we see a parallel to the biblical prophetic call. Occom, like Daniel or
Jeremiah, has no choice but to preach what he has been given to see. And what
he sees, as he expresses in a number of prophetic sermons, is a nominally
Christian (dominant) society in danger of being "weighed in the balance and
found wanting." Like Daniel, the interpreter of dreams, Occom decodes his
own dream. Belshazzar, the proud king, died because he ruled for himself, not
for God. In his prophetic sermons, Occom warns the Christian society that (1)
it fails when measured by the standard of its own gospel, and (2) this gives
scandal to the "poor Indians" who have been converted.

Just as Occom blended dream images, so he adapted the grand tradition of
the New England jeremiad—a sermon based on the perceived spiritual declension of the community. The offenses are magnified on two counts: the decline
from the standard of rectitude established by the first generation of settlers;
and the failure to fulfill the divine covenant upon which the founding of New
England, Samuel Danforth's "errand into the wilderness," was predicated.
Occom adapted the jeremiad form to suit his status as a voice of authority
speaking from the "wilderness" of his Indian culture against the vices of the
dominant culture. In contrast to the indirect and oblique criticism of white
society we find in the published execution sermon, we see prophetic denunciations of the hypocrisy and vice of the white society that are anything but oblique
in some of the unpublished sermons.

Occom's prophetic sermons usually open with a simple and detailed statement of the gospel mandate (for example, "love thy neighbour as thyself").
Next, he applies the doctrine directly to the behaviors he observes. In doing so,
he adjusts the New England jeremiad form to his own cultural history. In place
of the exodus-covenant-providence-errand-into-the-wilderness motif, he estab-
lishes an alternative model by which to measure the current spiritual declension: the natural virtuousness of Indian culture. The white Christian culture
practices slavery, whoring, "usury" (my term), and cursing. Indians, he posits,
although unenlightened by divine grace or the gospel, do not blaspheme (*CW*,
227), they abominate whoring (*CW*, 213), and they are edifyingly generous to
strangers even in times of want (*CW*, 203–4).

Unlike Montaigne and Swift, who held up idealized portraits of the innocent "savage" in order to satirize or criticize their own societies, Occom's portrayals of Indian language, religion, and cultural practices gain power because
they come from within the culture. He presents native culture as inherently

more congruent with Christianity than the nominally Christian culture. By holding up the "ignorant, naked, perishing, children of darkness" in order to admonish the Christians on the basis of their own scripture, Occom inscribes the Native American story within salvation history, thereby challenging the Euro-American monopoly on divine providence. Reversing the savage-civil dichotomy,[29] he presents the Indians as the more likely heirs to the kingdom.

Occom enjoys the prophetic power of one who takes the gospel message and mandate literally. He believes in the universal brotherhood of humanity deriving from common parents (Adam and Eve) and in spiritual equality deriving from Christ's salvific act. With inexorable logic, he proceeds from the mandate itself to denounce those who violate it. Occom employs three distinct devices to develop his transparent logic. First, he uses a simple either-or dichotomy that requires an active judgment on the part of the hearer. "Either I am right or I am wrong" (*CW*, 203), "it is either a false doctrine or it is a true one" (*CW*, 200). A variant of this is the rhetorical question he often poses: "Is it so as we have heard that . . . ?" (*CW*, 208). This technique reduces his argument to a stark Ramean disjunction. It forces an encounter with uncompromised truth. Second, proceeding from the either-or proposition, is the two-part "if-then" syllogism. "If these things be true, then what manner of Person ought we to be . . . ?" (*CW*, 209). Again, the logic is simple; it moves in a linear path toward an inevitable and inescapable conclusion. Finally, Occom develops a more complex, three-part syllogistic movement in his longer sermon notes. It is this pattern that he uses in his prophetic indictment of slaveholding ministers in his most highly rhetorical sermon, "Thou Shalt Love Thy Neighbour as Thyself."

This sermon uses logic and rhetoric to drive a rational audience inevitably to indict Christian slaveholding as contrary to Christ's mandate to love one's neighbor. Occom uses amplification, repetition, explication, *divisio* (classifying types of love), definitions of terms (neighbor, love), rhetorical questions, invented dialogue, and his entire arsenal of logical strategies. Appealing to reason more than to faith, however, he develops a simple and unassailable syllogism buttressed by careful definitions of terms.

The sermon follows a syllogistic movement: (1) Christ tells us that we must love our neighbor; (2) African slaves, like all humans, are our neighbors; (3) ergo, we must love, and not enslave, these neighbors. In this remarkable sermon, Occom privileges reason, harnessing the power of logic to serve faith: it is a "most Reasonable Command . . . most Rational and just" (*CW*, 201). The dispassionate rationality of Occom's march through linguistic analysis, philosophical definition, and logical syllogism provides a strong platform for his impassioned outcry at the end of the sermon: "if Ministers are True Liberty men, let them preach Liberty for the poor Negroes, fervently with great Zeal, and [the]

Ministers Who have [enslaved] Negroes set an Example before their People, by Freeing their Negroes, let them show their Faith by their Works" (*CW*, 207).

In the same sermon, Occom employs an exemplum that is a strikingly subtle and damning allusion to the parable of the vineyard. By rhetorically echoing the well-known biblical passage (Matthew 20:1–16), Occom intensifies his primary message. He is denouncing hoarding and price gouging by merchants, and he describes their mode of doing business:

> Extortioners[,] with holders of Corn and other Necessaries that they
> have to sell, from their Necessitous fellow men . . . especially in the
> Time of great Want and Distress, and When they have Horded up
> What they can then they will set an Extravagant Price upon Their
> Commodities at once; They will sell you their goods today, Yea this
> Morning, for Some of their goods for So much, and if another Comes
> at Noon or before, he must give a Little more for the Same
> Commodity, and if another Comes toward Night, he must give more
> Still, and so they go on and that which did not cost them more than a
> Shilling, Yesterday, they will Sell for twenty Shillings today, and are
> not ashamed of it. (*CW*, 202)

His straightforward indictment of predatory business practices, coming as it does after a lengthy development of the Good Samaritan theme, is clear enough. It gains force, however, by allusion. The triple reference to the times of the day would readily activate the parable of the vineyard for a Christian audience of the time. In that parable, a vineyard owner goes to the marketplace three times—at morning, at noon, and again late in the day—to hire workers for his vineyard. At the end of the day, he pays all of the workers the same amount, thereby confounding the logic of the marketplace and illustrating the gratuitous generosity of God. Occom's monopolizers, however, follow the logic of the marketplace, thereby inverting the echoed Christian paradigm and falling into Occom's trap. The imbedded irony doubles the effect of the judgment—an "economical" handling of biblical allusion.

Most forcefully of all, however, Occom offers a ringing and apocalyptic denunciation of the dominant society in the sermon "When He Drowned His Reason." He warns the learned and knowledgeable Christians that the "ignorant heathens . . . will rise up against you at the last Day for sins. . . . Don't they testify against you now in this Life?" (*CW*, 227). He also retells the history of contact from the native perspective, attributing to Europeans, and *not* to sin or to Satan, the cause of all the sufferings that Indians have endured. In such sermons, Occom speaks not as an aggrieved victim but, rather, with the spiritual authority of a minister of God's Word.

What is striking in such passages is that Occom presents the Indians as examples of natural virtue rather than as mere victims. He does not succumb in his sermons to complaining about the whites' treatment of Indians per se. This is a marked departure from his letters and diary entries. His prophetic claim is not that Christianity is an oppressor but that the oppressive practices of the dominant culture are not Christian. The failures of society are violations of God's Word, and it is Occom's prophetic function to "cry aloud" their transgressions. In one of the two sermons he composed on Isaiah 58:1, "Cry Aloud, Spare Not," he gathers global momentum and cries that "thousands and tens of thousands are groaning and crying under oppressions," sounding the thunderous voice of the prophet (*CW*, 213). Measuring Christian society by its own standard—the gospel—Occom finds it wanting.

The Covenant Narrative

Having looked at Occom's sermon style, themes, strategies, and voices, we turn now to tracing the scripture-based narrative that Occom evolved over a lifetime to unify his responsibilities and his identity as both Native American and Christian and to provide providential vigor to the Brotherton and New Stockbridge communities. Grounding his pan-tribal movement in typological language similar to that of the seventeenth-century Calvinists, Occom replicates the Puritan "errand" for his own people.

Stout argues that *the* unifying element in 200 years of New England Calvinist preaching was the narrative of God's covenant with a chosen people, exemplified by Exodus and recast for the American adventure in John Winthrop's "city on the hill" sermon and Danforth's "errand into the wilderness." For obvious reasons, Occom could not draw on this historical-covenantal tradition for his own sermons. The founding fathers were not the Indians' forefathers, and the "promised land" for these chosen people belonged, in fact, to the forefathers of the natives. It was the reverse side of the tapestry that the Native Americans read. Instead of using the covenant story, then, Occom develops a parallel narrative suited to his time, place, and race. His central story, derived from both Genesis and Isaiah's prophecy of the regeneration of Israel, serves as a new covenant for his own people as they leave their homelands to found the new settlements of Brotherton and New Stockbridge. It is in this narrative, finally, that we can see most clearly how Occom's indigenist Calvinism serves a typological purpose as significant for the continuance of his people as Exodus was for the Jews and the errand into the wilderness was for the earliest Calvinists of New England.

Occom places the Genesis narrative of the creation and fall of Adam and Eve in a pivotal position in four of the twenty extant sermon texts. Why this story? There are several plausible reasons. First, Charles Cohen notes the prominent place held by Genesis in early Indian conversion narratives, reminding us that the white conversion narrative hardly ever referred to the creation story because it was taken for granted. But the creation story held special power for "recent polytheists."[30] Second, it provided some congruence with their own religion, especially the supreme god, Cautantowwit,[31] mentioned by Occom on more than one occasion. The creation narrative, then, is a natural starting point for missionary discourse, especially useful because Calvinist doctrine locates in the fall of Adam the key to the doctrine of universal human depravity (Romans 5). Third, the genre of narrative itself is particularly appropriate for Native American audiences. Theirs is a literary tradition based on story, and mythological explanations of the origins of life and of human beings are central to Native American traditions. To the extent that Indians conceived of punishment for wrongdoing, or "sin," it involved immediate physical consequences, such as sickness, death, and drought.[32] The Genesis narrative pinpoints Adam's action as the cause of physical suffering and death for his descendants. From these perspectives, therefore, it made sense for Occom to concentrate on this narrative. Yet, I would like to offer another view, one that most clearly demonstrates his indigenist Calvinism.

Occom's use of the Genesis narrative in the mid-eighteenth century had the added power of congruence with the post-contact history of eastern Native Americans. In his retelling of the fall, he repeatedly writes that Adam "lost all." The biblical motifs of eviction from the garden and the introduction of sickness and death can be read as having a dual significance. The Genesis story is, of course, a mythic explanation of the universal sinful human condition, regardless of nation or race. But it can also support a typological reading as an analogy to the post-contact experience of Native Americans. In a sermon manuscript he wrote at the age of sixty-one, addressed "to all the Indians of this Boundless Continent," Occom retells the Genesis narrative, using the refrain "they have lost all . . . they have lost all . . . they have lost the garden that god made for them" (CW, 197). Adam and Eve and their descendants are "broke, and have become bankrupts, Fugitives and vagabonds," living in misery and sickness. It is a parable of loss—loss of communion with God, loss of Eden, loss of "all"—that resonates closely with the Indian post-contact narrative. That, too, is a parable of loss: loss of homeland, loss of independence (hunting), loss of life (sickness), and loss of dignity (alcohol). This fall, however, is not the work of Satan so much as a parable of predation by fellow human beings.

Christian faith is not the predator here, but rather those who call themselves "Christian nations" (*CW*, 206). In one of his sermons based on Isaiah 58:1, "Cry Aloud, Spare Not," Occom directly challenges first the Jews and then the "English" for breaking their covenants with God. He applies Isaiah's challenge to the Christians of his own time: "the English People are the Covenant People of god, they have enjoyd the Gospel Privileges for a long Time, an[d] they are now greatly Degenerated from the Purity and Simplicity of the Gospel and therefore they are the Very People that the Eternal Jehovah is Speaking of . . . in [this] Text" (*CW*, 215).

Occom accomplishes two important things in this sermon: he situates himself in the long line of declension preachers indicting New Englanders for their betrayal of the covenant, and he opens the possibility for others—even Native Americans—to fill the void left by the dispersed Jews and the degenerate "English." He asks, "Has God no Covenant People then in the World?" He responds hopefully, "Yet Blessed by God, where ever the Gospel of Jesus Christ is received by any People, they are the People of God" (*CW*, 215). He hereby prepares the way for his vision of a newly gathered native and Christian people from many tribes to become "the People of God," preserving both a pure Christianity and, equally important, a pan-tribal native identity.

In Occom's eyes, Christianity offered two kinds of salvation for his people: eternal and temporal. While he consistently sought the first for his audiences, he began to envision a temporal salvation that would foreshadow the dimensions of eternal salvation: a life of harmony, community, peace, unity, generosity, justice, fraternal love—the kingdom of God. In his artful sermon "Thou Shalt Love Thy Neighbour as Thyself," Occom conflates the ideal Christian community with the ideal tribal community: "They are Excellent in the Earth in Whom is all your Delight; their life is y[ou]r life, their Happiness, your Happiness, their Joy, your Joy, their Burden your Burden, their Sorrow your Sorrow, their Work your Work, their Kingdom your Kingdom, their People, your People, and their God, your God" (*CW*, 202).

The letters and journal entries of Occom's later years reveal a pattern of biblical references that give shape to the narrative of temporal salvation for his people. He envisions a future in which they will emerge as covenanted both with God and with each other, free to practice true Christianity away from the corrupting influences of the white society. In a letter from 1774, Occom wrote to the officers of the English Trust for Moor's Indian Charity School that the most efficacious way to bring the Oneida to Christ was for Christian Indians from various tribes to form a new settlement among them, a "Civil and Religious State," with the hope of introducing "the Religion of Jesus Christ *by their example*" (*CW*, 198; emphasis mine). Occom's "by their example" draws a sharp contrast to the bad example of quarreling Christians in the Revolutionary War, whom Occom called, in 1784, "a great Stumbling to the Heathen Indians" (*CW*, 123).

As Occom records the Brotherton story in letters and journal entries, we find deep emotion combined with powerful biblical associations. As Lopenzina puts it, Occom and his fellows were "employing the written word to imagine their community into being."[33] Occom's vision of the future for Brotherton, "the hopeful Prospect of the Indians future Happiness" (*CW*, 277), is a vision of Indian salvation—the continuance of the people. When he carries out the first baptism ceremony in the new settlement, it is for his son-in-law and four of his grandchildren—the next generation of his people. The moment brings into perfect harmony the deepest elements of his being—the future of his people and their salvation in Christ—and it yields the most heartfelt outpouring in a lifetime of journal entries: "These were the first that were Baptized in this New Settlement, and I hope and Pray that it may be only the bigining of multitudes in this Wilderness, till the whole Wilderness Shall Blossom as the Rose" (*CW*, 376). Here, Occom merges the future of his people with Isaiah's prophecy of Israel's deliverance and regeneration (Isaiah 35:1). The curse will be recalled, and the earth will be renewed: there will be a regenerated people in a regenerated land.

Like the Calvinist Winthrop investing the journey to New England with providential design and promise, Occom invests the new settlement with typological and providential significance. But while Winthrop employed the Exodus narrative for his purpose, Occom turned to the creation narrative and brought it full circle. The garden that was lost would be restored if the people kept the covenant. In a journal entry from 1787, he writes that the new land will be the new Eden:

> It is a fine Spot of Land, and a very large Spot too, and the People has
> made a rapped Progress in Cultivating the Land, if the People were as
> ingagd in Religion as they are in their Temporal Concerns this
> Settlement would be very much like the garden of Eden, which was
> the garden of god. The Lord be with them and Bless them that they
> may indeed be a Peculiar People unto god, and that they may be
> Lights in this Wilderness. (*CW*, 380)

Rooted in scriptural images, Occom's reflection offers a striking parallel to John Winthrop's sermon. Occom's prayer is that God be with the people and covenant with them and that the people keep that covenant so that Eden may be restored. By bringing the story of Eden full circle from God's garden to the new garden, Occom draws the story of salvation into a recognizably native circle. He is fulfilling his responsibility to his people and kin, and he is fulfilling his calling by God, weaving the two strands of his life into a single braid.

Through the vehicle of the sermon, furthermore, Occom explicitly applies the covenant typology to include his people when they finally gather in "the wilderness." As Joanna Brooks points out, "at the founding of Brotherton, on November 6, 1785, Occom preached in the morning from Joshua 24:22, in which the people affirm their covenant with God, declaring 'We are witnesses, after their arrival in the land of Canaan.'"[34]

The Mahican Stockbridge Indians also sounded the providential note when, in 1787, they called Occom to join them as their minister.

> We believe that this god has raised you up, and have kept you alive
> until this Time, and that he has Sent You up as an Ambassador into
> this Wilderness upon this purpose, that you might be the first
> Instrument or means to stir up Your own Nation, to try to embrace
> the Whole Religion. (*CW*, 154)

Clearly, this corporate political, religious, and pan-tribal venture of Christian natives had appropriated the unifying, hopeful, and vindicating narrative of covenant that had been the privilege of the "English" for nearly two centuries. A year before his death, despite the discouraging trials experienced by the Brotherton and New Stockbridge communities, Occom still had hope for the future of his people: "we may be Visited with great Light and yet become a People unto God. . . . I believe we are included in the Promises of the Bible, that all Nations shall be Blessd" (*CW*, 130–31).

Of course, the story did not end there, as the sad outcome of the Brotherton and New Stockbridge communities shows. Internal strife, division over land agreements, conflicts with white preachers, and the encroachment of "civilization" and subsequent removal of the natives to the Midwest caused the loss of this Eden, too. Ironically, the man who feared that he would find no place to lay his bones if he died abroad is buried somewhere without a marker in the Eden of his vision. From one historical perspective, Brotherton and New Stockbridge went the way of many of the other "Indian places" where Samson Occom had ministered throughout his life. The case can be made, however, even in the face of the harshness of history, that the cultural myth underlying a people's identity is housed in words and images. In his writings, Occom gave life to a vision modeled on Isaiah's peaceable kingdom and recognizable to the Native American worldview, where the inhabitants live in harmony with each other, with the cosmos, and with their God.

The well-known prophetic view of U.S. history, America's sense of ordained mission, and the metaphors of errand and wilderness, of calling and election, are distinctive to New England Calvinism. They are not found in the words of explorers in Canada or Mexico or even in the American South. The language of

"English" Calvinists, interpreted over and over again in sermon upon sermon, speech upon speech, created this foundational myth for the dominant culture that underlies the literature of westward expansion and even America's vision of its role on the world stage.

In like manner, as a "tawny" descendant of Calvin, Occom's writings reveal that he, like the Puritans, also looked through the lens of scripture and saw human events as eloquent both of God's will and of God's interaction with the community. He forged for his people a narrative that paralleled that of the founders of the New England colonies. And, like his native forebears, Occom looked for salvation in securing the future of his people. Occom's indigenist Calvinist imagination saw in the flat surface of life many layers of meaning that connected his present moment to the biblical past and projected it forward toward an apocalyptic future. In writing to the New Stockbridge community near the end of his life, he was writing his vision into being: "[I] pray, We may grow in Gospel Love and Peace—in Unity, Harmony and Gospel Fellowship. . . . May we be found to build up one another both in our Temporal and in our Religious Life, and let us try to do all the good that we are Capable of unto all men, and if it be possible let us Live in Peace with all men" (CW, 135). The words of Occom—in sermons, letters, and diaries—reveal the complex nature of his "strange providence" as a Native American and a Calvinist in a fragile and changing world.

NOTES

1. Quotations from Samson Occom's works will be cited from the following source (with the abbreviation CW): The Collected Writings of Samson Occom, Mohegan, ed. Joanna Brooks (New York: Oxford University Press, 2006).

2. William Simmons, Spirit of the New England Tribes: Indian History and Folklore, 1620–1984 (Hanover, N.H.: University Press of New England, 1986), 74.

3. James Axtell argues that the Jesuits "practiced a brand of cultural relativism." While they "sought to replace the Indians' cosmology with their own, they were more willing than their Christian counterparts [Dominicans and Franciscans, Puritans and Anglicans] to adopt the external lifestyle of the Indians until their goal could be realized." Axtell, Natives and Newcomers: The Cultural Origins of North America (New York: Oxford University Press, 2001), 163.

4. Drew Lopenzina, "'The Whole Wilderness Shall Blossom as the Rose': Samson Occom, Joseph Johnson, and the Question of Native Settlement on Cooper's Frontier," American Quarterly 58, no. 4 (2006): 1123.

5. Jace Weaver, That the People Might Live: Native American Literatures and Native American Community (New York: Oxford University Press, 1997), 40, 28, 182.

6. Robert Allen Warrior, Tribal Secrets: Recovering American Indian Intellectual Traditions (Minneapolis: University of Minnesota Press, 1995), 44; Lisa Brooks, The

Common Pot: The Recovery of Native Space in the Northeast (Minneapolis: University of Minnesota Press, 2008); Weaver, *That the People Might Live.*

7. Joanna Brooks, *American Lazarus: Religion and the Rise of African-American and Native American Literatures* (New York: Oxford University Press, 2003); Hilary Wyss, *Writing Indians: Literacy, Christianity, and Native Community in Early America* (Amherst: University of Massachusetts Press, 2000); Kristina Bross, *Dry Bones and Indian Sermons: Praying Indians in Colonial America* (Ithaca, N.Y.: Cornell University Press, 2004); Eileen Elrod, *Piety and Dissent: Race, Gender, and Biblical Rhetoric in Early American Autobiography* (Amherst: University of Massachusetts Press, 2008).

8. Wyss, *Writing Indians,* 3; Joanna Brooks, introduction to sermons, in *CW,* 164; Philip H. Round, "The Return of the Native: Recent Scholarship in the Literature of Christianization and Contact," *Early American Literature* 40, no. 2 (2005): 369. On Occom's hymns and hymnal, see Brooks, *American Lazarus;* Joanna Brooks, "'This Indian World': An Introduction to the Writings of Samson Occom," in *CW,* 36.

9. Thomas J. Davis, *This Is My Body: The Presence of Christ in Reformation Thought* (Grand Rapids, Mich.: Baker Academic, 2008), 100, 105.

10. Bernd Peyer, *The Tutor'd Mind: Indian Missionary-Writers in Antebellum America* (Amherst: University of Massachusetts Press, 1997), 101.

11. Samuel Buell, "A Letter to Mr. David Bostwick," in Buell, *The Excellence and Importance of the Saving Knowledge of the Lord Jesus Christ in the Gospel-Preacher . . . Preached . . . at the Ordination of Mr. Samson Occum* (New York: James Parker, 1761), ix; on Occom as spirited intermediary, see Margaret Connell Szasz, *Between Indian and White Worlds: The Cultural Broker* (Norman: University of Oklahoma Press, 1994), 61.

12. Harry Stout, *The New England Soul: Preaching and Religious Culture in Colonial New England* (New York: Oxford University Press, 1986), 5; Peyer, *Tutor'd Mind,* 90, 100.

13. Stout, *New England Soul,* 185–212.

14. Dawn DeVries, *Jesus Christ in the Preaching of Calvin and Schleiermacher* (Louisville, Ky.: Westminster John Knox, 1996), 19.

15. Occom provides only a sparse account in the autobiographical sketch: "I continued under Trouble of Mind about 6 months. . . . And When I was 17 years of age, I had, as I trust, a Discovery of the way of Salvation through Jesus, and was enabld to put my trust in him alone for Life and Salvation. From this Time the Distress and Burden of my mind was removd, and I found Serenity and Pleasure of Soul, in Serving god" (*CW,* 54). The passage includes no mention of sin or repentance, and the ellipses indicate passages that refer to his efforts to acquire the English language, structurally intertwining literacy with religion.

16. Buell, "Letter to Mr. David Bostwick," iv. We do know that Occom was thoroughly familiar with the genre of the conversion narrative and with its importance in gaining church membership. In 1754, he transcribed the testimony of a Montaukett woman, Temperance Hannabal, whose story is a truncated version of conversion morphology: self-reliance, followed by conviction of sin ("I saw my Self a great Sinner and an undone Creature before god, yea Saw myself fit for nothing but Hell and everlasting Distruction"), followed by experience of grace ("I heard a voice before me,

Saying follow me") (*CW*, 44). In his hymn "Wak'd by the Gospel's Joyful Sound" (*CW*, 237), Occom actually provides a textbook presentation of the stages in the Calvinist conversion experience. Employing a conversion refrain, "The sinner must be born again," at each step in the process, Occom's speaker proceeds through conviction of guilt, loss of direction, a failed attempt to save himself by "the law," the turning at last to Christ, the experience of "free grace and pardon," and, finally, the rapture of saving knowledge. Most significantly, the speaker is aided in his journey by two pivotal experiences that can be seen as the dual pillars of reformed theology: *sola scriptura* ("I read my bible" [*CW*, 237, line 22]) and *sola fides* ("My soul did mount on faith, its wing" [*CW*, 237, line 40]). Clearly, Occom both knew and instructed others in the Calvinist conversion experience.

17. Buell, *Excellence and Importance of the Saving Knowledge*, 31.

18. Stout, *New England Soul*, 45.

19. George M. Marsden, *Religion and American Culture* (New York: Harcourt Brace Jovanovich, 1990), 26.

20. Quoted in Davis, *This Is My Body*, 98n17.

21. *CW*, 101n72.

22. Thomas S. Kidd, *The Great Awakening: The Roots of Evangelical Christianity in Colonial America* (New Haven, Conn.: Yale University Press, 2007), 211.

23. Quoted in DeVries, *Jesus Christ in the Preaching of Calvin*, 19.

24. Sherman Alexie, *The Toughest Indian in the World* (New York: Grove Press, 2000), 190; Kelly McCarthy, "Conversion, Identity, and the Indian Missionary," *Early American Literature* 36, no. 3 (2001): 363.

25. Phyllis Jones, "Biblical Rhetoric and the Pulpit Literature of Early New England," *Early American Literature* 11 (1976–1977): 251.

26. Quoted in Karin Maag, "Preaching Practice: Reformed Students' Sermons," *Dutch Review of Church History* 85, no.1 (2006): 133; Davis, *This Is My Body*, 123.

27. Brooks, introduction to sermons, in *CW*, 165.

28. Peyer, *Tutor'd Mind*, 98.

29. McCarthy, "Conversion, Identity, and the Indian Missionary," 365.

30. Charles Cohen, "Conversion among Puritans and Amerindians: A Theological and Cultural Perspective," in *Puritanism: Transatlantic Perspectives on a Seventeenth-Century Anglo-American Faith*, ed. Francis J. Bremer (Boston: Massachusetts Historical Society, 1993), 246.

31. Simmons, *Spirit of the New England Tribes*, 49.

32. Clara Sue Kidwell, Homer Noley, and George E. "Tink" Tinker, *A Native American Theology* (Maryknoll, N.Y.: Orbis, 2001), 109.

33. Lopenzina, "The Whole Wilderness Shall Blossom as the Rose," 1121.

34. Brooks, introduction to journals, in *CW*, 246.

9

Geneva's Crystalline Clarity: Harriet Beecher Stowe and Max Weber on Calvinism and the American Character

Peter J. Thuesen

In June 1853, Harriet Beecher Stowe, exhausted from a triumphant publicity tour in England for her antislavery novel, *Uncle Tom's Cabin*, crossed the English Channel for a few weeks of leisure travel on the Continent. One of her first stops was Geneva, which afforded her the chance to reflect on John Calvin and his legacy in Western culture. Gazing at the view of Mont Blanc from the city, she wrote: "Calvinism, in its essential features, will never cease from the earth, because the great fundamental facts of nature are Calvinistic, and men with strong minds and wills always discover it."[1] It was a surprising statement, given her otherwise tortured relationship to her New England Puritan heritage, yet it signaled a recurring theme of her writings and anticipated in striking ways the arguments of the sociologist Max Weber a half century later in *The Protestant Ethic and the Spirit of Capitalism* (1905).

Both Stowe and Weber were reared in similarly anti-Catholic cultural contexts and regarded Calvinism as the most intellectually and morally vigorous form of Protestantism. Though Weber is usually credited with creating the ideal-type Calvinist—the sober-minded individual who constantly strives to prove her election through diligent labor in her calling—Stowe expressed the type earlier and in more popular idiom. Repeatedly in her fiction and prose, she lauded the industriousness of the New England Puritans and their heirs even while critiquing the harsher aspects of their theology. She also anticipated Weber in annexing the notion of the "Protestant ethic" to nationalism, in her case by identifying Calvinism as the source of the Yankee propensity for hard work and moral clarity. In idealizing the Calvinist spirit, she stood apart from her nineteenth-century literary peers, who more often portrayed Calvinism in purely negative terms as a system that was obscurantist, gloomy, and fatalistic. While Calvinism in popular liberal fiction drove its adherents to ethical paralysis and even insanity, Calvinism in Stowe's (and Weber's) imagination offered the best foundation for a virtuous society.

Anti-Calvinism in American Literature

The birth of the American republic brought with it a backlash against Calvinism, whose emphasis on original sin and absolute predestination seemed to violate the new nation's spirit of self-determination. America was the land of boundless possibilities, the endless frontier where people could remake themselves by shedding, as historian Bernard Bailyn put it, "the heavy crust of custom that was weighing down the spirit of man."[2] The quarrel with Calvinism in American literature began with works such as Charles Brockden Brown's gothic novel *Wieland* (1798), which, though evincing a Calvinist-like appreciation for the depths of human psychology, indicted what Brown regarded as the illusions perpetuated by religion. A Quaker turned skeptical deist, Brown spun a tale in which the melancholy male protagonist, Theodore Wieland, believing himself under the irresistible power of God's will, kills his wife and children, only to learn that, in reality, he was the victim of his own delusions and the suggestive powers of a traveling ventriloquist, Carwin. In revealing his voice-throwing technique, Carwin declares that he is imparting "a lesson to mankind on the evils of credulity on the one hand, and of imposture on the other."[3]

In the generation after Brown, liberal New Englanders, such as the Unitarian theologian Henry Ware Jr., penned further indictments of Calvinism's alleged morbidity. The protagonist of Ware's *Recollections of Jotham Anderson* (1824) is oppressed by the seemingly irreconcilable teachings of humans' total depravity and of their accountability for sin. The doctrine of predestination only adds to the torment: "My blood chilled when I heard the arbitrary decree of election announced, and, connected with it, the joy of the righteous in the sufferings of the wicked." All of it "was a wilderness to me. I turned on every side, and could find no relief."[4] Similarly, one of the most popular authors of domestic fiction, Catharine Maria Sedgwick, skewered the Calvinism of Jonathan Edwards and his New Divinity heirs in novels such as *A New England Tale* (1822).

Sedgwick later recalled in her autobiography how her sister and mother-figure, Eliza, suffered from the "horrors of Calvinism" until "her faith softened into a true comprehension of the filial relation to God" and she gained "redemption from the cruel doctrines of Geneva." Sedgwick joined a chorus of popular fiction writers bent on discrediting the old Calvinist establishment, including Lydia Maria Child in *Hobomok* (1824) and Sylvester Judd in *Margaret* (1845).[5]

Other New Englanders preferred the genres of poetic satire and prose criticism for castigating Calvinism, particularly in its Edwardsean form. In his poem "The Deacon's Masterpiece" (1858), Oliver Wendell Holmes imagined the logical system of Edwards's predestinarian *Freedom of the Will* (1754) as a "one-hoss shay" that lasted for a century until one day it self-destructed: "All at once, and nothing first, / Just as bubbles do when they burst."[6] Mark Twain began reading *Freedom of the Will* in 1902 after a visit with his best friend, the Congregational minister Joseph Hopkins Twichell, who gave the book to him to read on the train back to New York from Hartford. "Continuously until near midnight I wallowed and reeked with Jonathan in his insane debauch," Twain wrote in a letter to Twichell. "All through the book is the glare of a resplendent intellect gone mad—a marvelous spectacle." Edwards was at his most drunk near the end of the treatise, Twain observed, "where what I take to be Calvinism and its God" show up and "shine red and hideous in the glow from the fires of hell."[7]

Even as late as the mid-twentieth century, the New England preoccupation with Edwardseanism was evident in the career of the poet Robert Lowell, who had planned to write a biography of Edwards but abandoned the plan after growing "more and more numb" from perusing *Freedom of the Will*.[8] Instead, Lowell wrote four poems on Edwards, including "Mr. Edwards and the Spider" (1946), which begins by paraphrasing the young Edwards's "spider letter" in which he commented on the beauty and intricacy of spider webs. The poem's tone quickly turns ominous as Lowell borrows the lurid imagery of Edwards's "Sinners in the Hands of an Angry God" in portraying the dreadful omnipotence of the Calvinist sovereign: "What are we in the hands of the great God? / It was in vain you set up thorn and briar / In battle array against the fire." Edwards's spider becomes an "hourglass-blazoned" black widow, which, though venomous enough to kill a tiger, is powerless before the great God who dangles it by a thread over the pit of hell. Fiery annihilation is the "sinner's last retreat"— an inferno in which no human strength is sufficient to uphold the "abolished will."[9] In another poem, "After the Surprising Conversions" (1946), Lowell recreated the suicide of Edwards's uncle Joseph Hawley, who fatally slit his own throat, casting a pall over the revivals ignited by Edwards's preaching. The poem paraphrases Edwards's own words from his revival account, *A Faithful Narrative* (1737), describing Hawley as one who "durst not entertain much hope of his estate in heaven" and comparing the devil to a peddler who urges, "My friend, Cut your own throat. Cut your own throat. Now! Now!"[10]

Lowell's chilling poems bespeak the widespread assumption, by then firmly entrenched, that Calvinism was America's (particularly New England's) endemic religious pathology, a hairsplitting system that drove people to melancholic insanity. To be sure, two important writers in the American literary canon—Nathaniel Hawthorne and Herman Melville—found in Calvinism's dark side precisely its compelling power. Hawthorne, in *The Scarlet Letter* (1850), revealed himself to be what one critic has called an "unchurched Calvinist." Chillingworth, one of the novel's main characters, pronounces that his "old faith" (Calvinism) "explains all that we do, and all that we suffer." Similarly, Melville, in narrating *Pierre* (1852), comments that all "mature men" eventually know that we are not ultimately "our own factors." Nobody better illustrates this than Captain Ahab from Melville's *Moby-Dick* (1851), who represents a will inexorably bent on its own destruction.[11] Subtle as Hawthorne's or Melville's appreciation of Calvinistic determinism was, however, their novels inadvertently contributed to the popular use of Calvinism as an ideogram for doom and gloom.

Stowe's Complicated Affair with Calvinism

To Hawthorne and Melville, Calvinism's unflinching gaze at the depravity and determinism of human existence was a necessary corrective to the sentimentality purveyed by what Hawthorne famously derided as the "scribbling women" of his era.[12] One of these women was Stowe, whose own relationship to Calvinism was far from simple and who, ironically, shared some of Hawthorne's views about the inescapability of Calvinist conclusions. That her religious novels bear a strong Calvinist influence is no surprise: her father, the Congregational minister Lyman Beecher, traced his ancestry to the original Puritan settlement of the New Haven Colony. Harriet and her ten siblings grew up in Litchfield, Connecticut, in a deeply evangelical household where intense doctrinal discussions were everyday fare. All seven sons went on to become clergymen, but it was two of the daughters, Harriet and Catharine, who would produce the most intriguing religious reflections.[13]

After Lyman's first wife, Roxana Foote, died when Harriet was five, the sixteen-year-old Catharine became her surrogate mother and remained so even after Lyman remarried. Catharine, like all of Lyman's children, had felt heavy pressure from her father to yield to the Holy Spirit's workings and to give a public profession of conversion, which New England Calvinists had long required for full church participation. Yet, she was thrown into a spiritual crisis when her fiancé, Alexander Metcalf Fisher, a young Yale professor who had not experienced conversion himself, died in a shipwreck. According to the inherited New England theology, Fisher was in serious danger of spending eternity in hell, and Catharine tortured herself over this possibility while also entertaining increasing doubts about the logic of Calvinism. Later in life, she would reject Calvinism altogether and embrace a version of Common Sense philosophy that posited the intuitive nature of basic religious truths.[14] In the meantime, the young Harriet was absorbing Catharine's growing interest in metaphysics and was developing a precocious ability to engage in theological disputation. In what Lyman called the proudest moment of his life, Harriet was chosen at age twelve to read at a school assembly her composition "Can the Immortality of the Soul Be Proved by the Light of Nature?"[15] Soon thereafter, she experienced conversion, and, in 1824, she entered the Hartford Female Seminary, recently founded by Catharine, where she continued to hone her skills as a writer and, eventually, served for several years as a teacher.

In 1834, after Lyman became president of Lane Theological Seminary in Cincinnati, Harriet married his junior colleague Calvin Ellis Stowe, a Congregational minister and biblical studies professor. Though later in their marriage she would refer affectionately to her white-bearded husband as "my old rabbi," the couple's temperamental differences often strained domestic life. A number of family losses, including the suicide of Harriet's brother George and the death of the couple's eighteen-month-old son in a cholera epidemic, compounded their hardship even as Harriet was gaining fame as a writer for popular periodicals. Her big break finally came in 1852 with the publication of *Uncle Tom's Cabin*, which brought her international fame and the opportunity to tour Europe as the honored guest of antislavery societies.

Yet, in 1857, she suffered another wrenching loss that soon emerged as a turning point in her own religious quest. In an uncanny parallel to Alexander Fisher's death, her son Henry, a freshman at Dartmouth College, accidentally drowned while swimming in the Connecticut River. Like Fisher, Henry had not experienced the requisite conversion, and his mother's anguish over the state of his soul led her to a profound grappling with her Calvinist heritage. Stowe's religious reflections would appear most vividly in two novels, *The Minister's Wooing* (1859), first serialized in the *Atlantic Monthly*, and *Oldtown Folks* (1869). Her quarrel with the strict standard of conversion in the New England churches also led her to abandon Congregationalism for Anglicanism. Though she remained an Episcopalian until her death in 1896, her innermost theological views always defied easy denominational classification. Indeed, as Charles H. Foster has astutely argued, Stowe "said both yes and no to Calvinism."[16]

Stowe's no to Calvinism is obvious enough. Like other New England think-ers, she was haunted as much by Edwards as by Calvin. The male protagonist in *The Minister's Wooing* is based on Edwards's disciple Samuel Hopkins. The novel recreates the loss of Catharine Beecher's fiancé in the tale of a pious young woman, Mary Scudder, whose fiancé, James Marvyn, is presumed lost at sea while still in an unconverted state. Prodded by her mother, Mary accepts a marriage proposal from Dr. Hopkins, whom Stowe at once satirizes for his rigid Edwardseanism and lauds for his antislavery activism. At the end of the story, however, in an unlikely plot twist derided by some critics, James Marvyn miraculously returns. He promptly experiences conversion and is wed to Mary by the self-denying Hopkins, who weeps tears of joy over James's saved soul.[17]

The novel's plot line, however, often becomes mere scaffolding for long theological excurses in which Stowe sharply criticizes the New England Calvin-ist obsession with the "evidences" of conversion. The root of this pathology, as she saw it, was Edwards, whose revival sermons were "so terrific in their refined poetry of torture, that very few persons of quick sensibility could read them through without agony." Not only did Edwards and his disciples oppress the New England psyche with the notion that only an "infinitesimal" portion of humanity constituted the elect, but they also set an unrealistically high standard of regeneration, which Stowe likened to trying to reach heaven by a rungless ladder. To make matters worse, anxiety-wracked parishioners received scant comfort from religious services, which were devoid of the "softening poetries and tender draperies" of pre-Reformation ritual. Religion in New England was reduced to the logic of a system, and Stowe felt the "very chill of death in the analysis." When James Marvyn is presumed lost at sea, his grieving mother denounces the Calvinist God who would create humans as vessels of wrath fit-ted for destruction: "I can never love God! I can never praise Him! I am lost! lost! lost!" Significantly, the only character who is able to rescue Mrs. Marvyn from this abyss is the black servant Candace, who implores her to take her sor-rows to Jesus. As Joan Hedrick has argued, women and African Americans become, for Stowe, instruments of salvation. Stowe also employs the image of women as weavers who build webs of relations between humans, unlike the male systematicians who construct theological systems separating elect from damned. The motif of the feminine weaver radically recasts the image of a spider dangling over the pit of hell in Edwards's infamous sermon.[18]

Stowe continued her polemic against Edwards in *Oldtown Folks*, a lengthy local-color novel. In diagnosing the religious condition of New England families, she singled out their "constitutional melancholy," which Edwards exacerbated by departing from the "tender and paternal" confessionalism of some of his Puritan forebears. Edwards subjected the process of conversion to unremitting rational analysis, which many later New Englanders ironically carried to its logi-cal conclusion by abandoning orthodox religion altogether. Edwards further hastened this rebellion by imposing strict expectations of conversion before par-ents could bring their children for baptism. Stowe's own solution, hinted at in *Oldtown Folks*, was to take refuge in the sacraments, particularly baptism, as suf-ficient for salvation. This led her to embrace that "nice old motherly" institution, the Episcopal Church, which, in its high church wing, at least, retained a greater emphasis on sacramental efficacy.[19]

Yet, for all of the echoes of liberal anti-Calvinism in Stowe's work, her nov-els are more intriguing for their simultaneous affirmation of Calvinism as the refining fire that purified and strengthened the Yankee soul. Repeatedly in her writings, she commends the intellectual acuity of New England, where farmers debated theology "in intervals of plough and hoe" and where the "great unan-swerable questions which must perplex every thinking soul" were "posed with the severest and most appalling distinctness." This "intense clearness" was both the weakness and the strength of the New England mind: weakness, because it often had the effect of "lacerating the nerves of the soul"; strength, because it fostered a mental prowess that set New Englanders apart from most other peoples of the world.[20] In *Oldtown Folks*, Stowe lapsed into anti-Catholicism by comparing the intellectually agile yeomen of New England to the Spanish peasantry. The former were driven by "active-minded Calvinism," while the latter were awash in "pictures, statues, incense, architecture, and all the sentimental paraphernalia of ritualism."[21] Elsewhere, she even praised the predestinarian angst that had afflicted many a New Englander, including herself: "It is a mark of a shallow mind to scorn these theological wrestlings and surgings; they have in them something even sublime."[22] Indeed, though Stowe rejected Calvinism's negative psychological consequences, she embraced its unshrinking engagement with the fundamental problems of the human condition to the end of her career.

Even Hopkins's notion of disinterested benevolence, with his contro-versial suggestion that regenerate persons ought to be willing to be damned for the glory of God, was, for Stowe, "both noble and appalling," according to Lawrence Buell: appalling, because of its seemingly impossible demands on human nature; noble, because it encouraged self-sacrifice for the common good.[23] The antislavery preaching of Hopkins and his followers drew heavily on Edwardsean concepts of benevolence, a fact not lost on Stowe in her own crusade against human bondage. She regarded New England's indigenous Calvinism as the best resource for combating not only slavery but also the many lesser evils that slaveholding had overshadowed. In contrast to many of her literary and intellectual contemporaries, she saw Calvinism as essentially humanitarian in character—a system of thought that fueled the forces of social reform.[24]

This emphasis on the progressive aspect of Calvinism was especially apparent in her recollections of her 1853 visit to Geneva. One evening, she stopped at the spot just outside the city where the Spanish physician Michael Servetus was burned at the stake for denying the Trinity (a capital offense under civil law in Geneva's holy commonwealth). Calvin's complicity in the execution was a stock feature of textbook portrayals of the reformer, in which Calvinism emerged as the foil of intellectual freedom and human rights.[25] But Stowe took a different tack as she meditated at the site of the burning. "The world is always unjust to its progressive men," she wrote, referring not to Servetus but to Calvin. Inevitably, "one fragment of past absurdity cleaves to them," tarnishing their reputations. "Hence we hear so much of Luther's controversial harshness, of Calvin's burning Servetus, and of the witch persecutions of New England." Yet, the contributions of Luther and Calvin to civilization were profound, Stowe suggested, and she left little doubt about her greater admiration for the Geneva reformer: "Luther was the poet of the reformation, and Calvin its philosopher. Luther fused the mass, Calvin crystallized. He who fuses makes the most sensation in his day; he who crystallizes has a longer and wider power."[26]

Experience, she added, proves that the facts of nature are Calvinistic: "The predestination of a sovereign will is written over all things. The old Greek tragedians read it, and expressed it. So did Mahomet, Napoleon, Cromwell." They tried the forces of nature and discovered the limits of their own strength. Indeed, to all people who strive "in vain with the giant forces of evil," there is great serenity to be gained from the thought of an overpowering, yet ultimately benevolent, divine will. "However grim, to the distrusting, looks this fortress of sovereignty in times of flowery ease," in times of trouble it has always been the refuge of God's people. "All this I say," Stowe added, "while I fully sympathize with the causes which incline many fine and beautiful minds against the system."[27]

What emerges in Stowe's travelogue and in her novels is an alternative to the negative ideogram of Calvinism that so often prevailed in American culture and even, at times, in her own writings. On Stowe's reading, the term Calvinist was synonymous with the sober, virtuous Yankee yeoman—the sort of citizen whose industry built the American republic and whose clear moral thinking, Stowe assumed, would ultimately (with God's providential assistance) eradicate the evil of slavery. Thus, the United States would live out its destiny as a beacon of hope and freedom for the world. Calvin's native France might have gone in the same direction had Louis XIV—the "Jezebel de Medici"—not driven out the Protestants by revoking the Edict of Nantes. But France's loss was America's gain. "Some of the best blood in America," Stowe remarked, "is of the old Huguenot stock." The Huguenots, along with the Puritans, bequeathed to the United States the treasure of Calvinism, with its dual emphasis on divine sovereignty and human freedom and accountability. "Wherever John Calvin's system of theology has gone," she added, "civil liberty has gone with it."[28]

The Weber Thesis—and Parallels to Stowe

Though it is unclear that Max Weber ever read anything by Stowe, his remarkably similar view of Calvinism's moral superiority was shaped, as in her case, by biography and even by travel.[29] Weber (1864–1920) was born in Prussian Saxony in the town of Erfurt, where Luther had attended university. Precociously interested in history and ideas, the thirteen-year-old Weber, in an incident reminiscent of Stowe's essay-contest triumph at age twelve, presented two papers to his parents as a belated Christmas present: "About the Course of German History, with Special Regard to the Positions of the Emperor and the Pope" and "About the Roman Imperial Period from Constantine to the Migration of Nations."[30] Weber's father, Max Sr., was a cultural Lutheran who accepted religion's utility but was not personally pious. His mother, Helene Fallenstein, was descended from Huguenot immigrants and was far more introspective and driven by a strong social conscience. When the young Weber, having imitated his father's pleasure seeking, came home from university with a beer belly and a facial scar from a bar fight, his mother was horrified and reflexively slapped him across the face. Yet, Weber grew fonder of his mother over time and came to admire her ethical seriousness. Her ancestral Calvinism, secularized and liberalized in her own piety, seemed, to Weber, to offer a moral paradigm for the Germany of his day.[31]

Indeed, like Stowe, who believed that the United States had become ethically lax, Weber sensed a creeping quietism among the German bourgeoisie and feared it had become morally and politically complacent under the strong rule of Bismarck. Despite his own German nationalism, Weber was something of an Anglophile who resembled British Whig historians in regarding Puritanism as a major source of England's achievements.[32] In his inaugural lecture at the University of Freiburg in May 1895, Weber seemed to have in mind this imagined ideal of Puritan rectitude when he declared that Germany's future greatness depended on whether its "leading strata are able to raise themselves into the hard and clear atmosphere in which the sober activity of German politics flourishes."[33]

Weber also found examples of sober activity in the United States, to which he and his wife, Marianne, traveled in August 1904 to attend a scholarly congress in St. Louis. After the meeting, he toured other regions of the country, including rural locales in Oklahoma and North Carolina, where he witnessed the "inner-worldly asceticism" later made famous by his *Protestant Ethic*, which he was then writing. In contrast to medieval mystics who engaged in a contemplative flight from the world, inner-worldly ascetic Protestants sought to master the world and themselves through self-scrutiny and productive activity.[34] Weber regarded this inner-worldly asceticism as most characteristic of what he called the "sect" type of religious association rooted in the Calvinist-Puritan tradition. Its exemplars included Baptists, Quakers, Pietists, and Methodists, among others—all groups that thrived in rural and small-town America. A common denominator among these groups was their sectarian worldview: their self-selecting membership and enforced moralism, which contrasted with the all-inclusive, saints-and-sinners character of Europe's state churches. Like the Puritans of old, latter-day American Puritans organized societies of the godly, where acceptance by one's peers carried greater value than any sacramental rite administered by an umbrella-like state church.[35]

Everywhere he visited in the United States, Weber marveled at the level of religious participation. "This in a country," he wrote, "where there is a constitutional ban on official recognition of any church." He admitted that, from the standpoint of secularized Europeans such as himself, the ubiquity of churches and their centrality in Americans' lives seemed, at first, "grotesque and frequently repellent." Yet, he argued that the "exclusiveness of these circles"—their sectarian, faithful-remnant mentality—accounted for their "superiority in the struggle for existence." Membership in a church community "of good repute" was, for Americans, a sign of an individual's trustworthiness. In Oklahoma, Weber met a traveling salesman of iron tombstone lettering, who commented: "As far as I am concerned, everyone can believe what he likes, but if I discover that a client doesn't go to church, then I wouldn't trust him to pay me fifty cents: Why pay me, if he doesn't believe in anything?"[36]

Weber observed the Calvinist, sect-type church most vividly in Mount Airy, North Carolina (later the inspiration for Andy Griffith's Mayberry), where he and his wife visited several cousins on his mother's side. (Part of the family had changed its name from Fallenstein to Miller when the father immigrated to the United States.) With Frank Fallenstein, a more recent immigrant, serving as translator, the Webers attended what Marianne called a "Baptist christening"— a service of believers' baptism in which a number of people were baptized by immersion in an ice-cold mountain stream.[37] One of the persons being baptized was a businessman who was planning to open a bank in Mount Airy. Recounting the incident in a later essay, Weber cited the man's baptism as evidence of ascetic Protestantism's legitimating function in the community. The thorough scrutiny required for admission to the Baptist sect certified the businessman's probity in the eyes of prospective clients. This "ruthlessly rigorous control over the conduct of their members," in Weber's view, was the hallmark of the inner-worldly asceticism practiced by Protestants in the Calvinist-Puritan lineage. He conceded that the sects were starting to lose some of their hold over society as secular service clubs grew in popularity. "There is hardly a small businessman with ambitions who does not wear some badge in his buttonhole," he observed. Yet, the original model of such civic organizations, he added, was the church, particularly the gathered communities of the faithful in the ascetic Protestant sects. In such austere conventicles, in which members maintain "a check on each other through mutual confession," the real strength of Protestantism was apparent, in contrast to the decadence of Europe's established churches. "One only has to look at the Berlin Cathedral to know that it is certainly not in this grandiose Caesaro-Papist showpiece but rather in the small meeting halls of the Quakers and Baptists, where there is no such mystical adornment, that the 'spirit' of Protestantism is most truly manifested."[38]

Weber's romanticized ascetic Protestantism found its most enduring expression in his *Protestant Ethic*, in which he famously described anxiety-ridden Puritans determined to prove their elect status through hard work. Predestinarian uncertainty—the haunting question of elect or reprobate—was the wellspring of Puritan productivity even as it was redolent of tragedy. The doctrine of predestination, "with all the pathos of its inhumanity, had one principal consequence for the mood of a generation which yielded to its magnificent logic: it engendered, for each individual, a feeling of tremendous inner loneliness." A man, Weber explained, "was obliged to tread his path alone, toward a destiny which had been decreed from all eternity." None of the traditional persons, mechanisms, or institutions could help the individual facing this stark uncertainty: not the preacher (for Puritans ultimately afforded him little actual priestly status over an elect layperson), not the sacraments (because Puritans rejected the view that these conveyed grace in any substantial or automatic way), not the church (since, despite the self-policing of the community, nobody could be absolutely sure which visible saints corresponded to the invisible saints in the Lamb's Book of Life), and not even, in a sense, God (because Christ died for the elect alone, as the doctrine of limited atonement taught). Puritanism, like Protestantism generally, deprived the individual of the traditional way of relieving predestinarian anxiety: a "gradual storing up of meritorious achievements" through hearing masses, undertaking pilgrimages, and performing other works of satisfaction.[39]

Stowe had described the Puritan's inner isolation in strikingly similar terms in *The Minister's Wooing*: "No rite, no form, no paternal relation, no faith or prayer of church, earthly or heavenly, interposed the slightest shield between the trembling spirit and Eternal Justice. The individual entered eternity alone, as if he had no interceding relation in the universe." Likewise, in *Oldtown Folks*, she noted that, in New England society, "all the draperies and accessories of religious ritual" were "rigidly and unsparingly retrenched." There was "nothing between the soul and these austere and terrible problems; it was constantly and severely brought face to face with their infinite mystery." The idea that New Englanders had somehow gotten to the heart of the matter was still being echoed a century later by Robert Lowell, who once commented that the Calvinism of his Massachusetts Bay forebears focused on religion's "attenuated ideal."[40]

Both Weber and Stowe compared the Calvinist-Puritan lineage with traditions they regarded as less intellectually refined. For Weber, the "hand to mouth" existence perpetuated by Catholicism's sacramental system provided the most obvious contrast, though he detected significant holdovers from a Catholic subsistence economy in Lutheranism. Lutherans were "passive in character," unlike Calvinists, and were more interested in obtaining forgiveness of sins through repeated penitence than in doing the hard work of sanctification demanded by ascetic Protestants. Calvinism—not Lutheranism, with its relative "moral feebleness"—was the source of the "tough, upstanding, and active mind of the middle-class capitalist entrepreneur." Stowe lacked Weber's familial preoccupation with the comparative merits of Calvinism and Lutheranism, but, as her observation about the Spanish peasantry (quoted earlier) reveals, she shared Weber's view that a *merely* sacramental religion would never produce adherents of superior mental agility. However comforting Stowe may have found churchly ritual after her Anglican conversion, only the New England Calvinism of her ancestors had the "sharp-cut crystalline edges and needles of thought" necessary to yield a supremely active and virtuous citizenry.[41]

The razor-like quality of the Calvinist mind, according to Weber and Stowe, was honed especially on the Sabbath, which Puritan commonwealths on both sides of the Atlantic treated with special seriousness. Weber pointed to the controversy in early seventeenth-century England over the "Book of Sports" (issued by James I in 1618 and reissued by Charles I in 1633), which riled Puritans by allowing a number of recreations on Sundays. (Cromwell's protectorate subsequently enforced a strict sabbatarianism.) Puritans, Weber noted, were not opposed to sports in principle but were hostile toward any amusements that devolved into the "purely uninhibited expression of uncontrolled instincts" or encouraged pleasure for its own sake. Wasting time was the Puritans' cardinal sin. Time "is infinitely valuable, because every lost hour means one less hour devoted to labor in the service of God's glory." This did not mean, Weber hastened to add, that Puritanism "embodied a gloomy philistinism that despised culture." The Sabbath was meant, instead, as a day to cultivate learning for divine ends. Puritan laypeople in England and even more in New England heard sermons that were "deeply imbued with Renaissance learning" and that brimmed with "erudition in theological controversy." The Sunday sermon became, in effect, the equivalent of university training for the laity. "Probably no country has been so rich in 'graduates,'" Weber opined, "as New England in the first generation of its existence."[42]

Similarly, in her memoir of her European tour, Stowe praised the Puritan model of the Sabbath and its influence on Protestants in Switzerland, England, Scotland, and the United States. Significantly, she posited a direct link between the liberty in these societies and the self-discipline required for Sabbath keeping. "There must be enough intensity of individual self-control to make up for the lack of an extraneous pressure from the government." The Lutheran branch of the Reformation lacked Calvinism's tendency toward sabbatarian rigor, and, consequently, Lutheran principalities had been less successful in "sustaining popular rights." Stowe also anticipated Weber's argument about the intellectualizing function of Puritan Sunday sermons. "Ride through France, you see the laborer in his wooden shoes, with scarce a thought beyond his daily toil. His Sunday is a *fête* for dancing and recreation," she wrote. "Go through New England, and you will find the laborer, as he lays his stone fence, discussing the consistency of foreordination with free will." The average layperson in New England gains "more elements of mental discipline" in a single Sunday sermon than "a French peasant gets in a whole lifetime."[43]

This vigorous life of the mind, regulated by the rhythm of Sabbath discipline, translated into such productivity in the economic sphere that persons content to live merely hand-to-mouth existences stood out from the crowd. Every New England village, Stowe wrote in *Oldtown Folks*, had a "do-nothing" whose sloth made everybody else's diligence all the clearer: "Work, thrift, and industry are such an incessant steampower in Yankee life, that society would burn itself out with intense friction were there not interposed here and there the lubricating power of a decided do-nothing." Even so, the virtuous majority needed to be on guard constantly lest the temptation to laziness spread to other citizens. One of the characters in *Oldtown* remarks that the village do-nothing, Sam Lawson, "is enough to make the saints in Heaven fall from grace." Stowe's words anticipated the logic of Weber's *Protestant Ethic*: diligent labor is the best evidence of divine election since a lazy person cannot get into heaven. "Unwillingness to work," as Weber put it, "is a symptom of the absence of the state of grace."[44]

Conclusion: The Stowe-Weber Thesis

The Weber thesis, which deserves as much to be called the Stowe thesis, has never ceased to provoke debate among scholars, for, as historian Alastair Hamilton has observed, the theory is just as difficult to demolish as it is to substantiate.[45] Clearly, both Stowe and Weber were affected by their inbred anti-Catholicism, which partly blinded them to the disciplinary rigor and moral striving that are present in certain strains of Catholic devotionalism. The self-scrutiny so typical of Puritans was equally characteristic of Catholic rigorists in both the medieval and Counter-Reformation periods.[46] To his credit, Weber had some inkling of this. In *The Protestant Ethic*, he cited the parallel tendency in Reformed and Jesuit pieties to monitor one's state of grace. He also spoke of Calvinism's "affinity (as well as its specific antithesis) to Catholicism." Similarly, Stowe was not as hostile to all things Catholic as might first appear. In *The Minister's Wooing*, she hinted that the Catholic practice of prayers for the dead—rejected along with purgatory by the Protestant reformers—might have some redeeming value. She pointed to Augustine, who, in offering up fervent petitions for his departed mother, Monica, "solaced the dread anxieties of trembling love by prayers offered for the dead." In such practices, "the Church above and on earth presented itself to the eye of the mourner as a great assembly with one accord lifting interceding hands for the parted soul." Both Stowe and Weber were complex thinkers whose deepest religious sympathies were clearly mixed. They also appreciated the ambiguity of historical explanation, or what Weber called "the inexhaustible complexity of all historical phenomena." Indeed, Weber anticipated the scholarly firestorm that his *Protestant Ethic* would ignite. It was not his intention, he bristled, to defend "any foolishly doctrinaire thesis as that the 'capitalist spirit' . . . *could only* arise as a result of certain influences of the Reformation."[47]

Yet, in coining the concept of the Protestant ethic, Stowe and Weber reified an old confessional stereotype that equated Protestantism with dynamism and progress and Catholicism with passivity and retrogression. Historian Paul Münch has shown that such stereotypes first proliferated in the eighteenth century as Europeans, coming head-to-head with foreigners in the colonial arena, became more interested in cultural differences among peoples. The rise of pseudoscientific theories of race in the nineteenth century only reinforced the old confessional tendency to generalize about the "nature" of certain cultures.[48] Both Stowe and Weber were steeped in a Protestant triumphalism that equated popery with intellectual and political slavery. For New Englanders such as Stowe, this rhetoric had been perfected in the Glorious Revolution of 1688, when English Protestants on both sides of the Atlantic, in a burst of nationalistic propaganda, hailed the overthrow of England's last Catholic king. For German Protestants such as Weber, the *Kulturkampf* under Bismarck and Emperor Wilhelm I popularized notions of Catholicism's cultural inferiority. Stowe and Weber internalized this generalized Protestant chauvinism but also modified it in claiming the superiority of Calvinism as a basis for social progress. In so doing, they partly rehabilitated the image of Calvinism from the disfavor it had incurred among liberal critics.

Stowe's memoir of Geneva provides an apt concluding illustration of Calvinism's special place in the Stowe-Weber thesis. Switzerland's Protestant and Catholic cantons, she observed, "are as different as our slave and free states, and in the same ways." Geneva, in particular, "seems like New England—the country around is well cultivated, and speaks of thrift."[49] Such fertility and economy were the inevitable result, she believed, wherever Calvinism had taken root.

NOTES

1. Harriet Beecher Stowe, *Sunny Memories of Foreign Lands*, 2 vols. (Boston: Phillips, Sampson, 1854), 2:277. On Stowe's trip to the Continent, see Joan D. Hedrick, *Harriet Beecher Stowe: A Life* (New York: Oxford University Press, 1994), 250.

2. Bernard Bailyn, *The Ideological Origins of the American Revolution* (Cambridge, Mass.: Belknap Press of Harvard University Press, 1967), 34. On the anti-Calvinist backlash in the new republic, see Peter J. Thuesen, *Predestination: The American Career of a Contentious Doctrine* (New York: Oxford University Press, 2009), 100–135. On republican ideology as an acid corrosive of Calvinist and other forms of traditional confessionalism, see Mark A. Noll, *America's God: From Jonathan Edwards to Abraham Lincoln* (New York: Oxford University Press, 2002), esp. 53–92.

3. Charles Brockden Brown, *Wieland; or, The Transformation and Memoirs of Carwin the Biloquist*, ed. Emory Elliott (Oxford: Oxford University Press, 1998), 194. See also Leigh Eric Schmidt, *Hearing Things: Religion, Illusion, and the American Enlightenment* (Cambridge, Mass.: Harvard University Press, 2000), 149–50; and Perry D. Westbrook, *Free Will and Determinism in American Literature* (Rutherford, N.J.: Fairleigh Dickinson University Press, 1979), 62–64.

4. Henry Ware Jr., *The Recollections of Jotham Anderson* (1824; repr., Liverpool, England: Wright, 1830), 26. See also David S. Reynolds, *Faith in Fiction: The Emergence of Religious Literature in America* (Cambridge, Mass.: Harvard University Press, 1981), 115–16.

5. Mary Kelley, ed., *The Power of Her Sympathy: The Autobiography and Journal of Catharine Maria Sedgwick* (Boston: Massachusetts Historical Society, Northeastern University Press, 1993), 86. On anti-Calvinism in Sedgwick, Child, and Judd, see Thomas J. Davis, "Rhetorical War and Reflex: Calvinism in Nineteenth-Century Popular Fiction and Twentieth-Century Criticism," *Calvin Theological Journal* 33 (1998): 443–56.

6. Oliver Wendell Holmes, "The Deacon's Masterpiece; or, The Wonderful 'One-Hoss Shay': A Logical Story," in *The Poetical Works of Oliver Wendell Holmes* (Boston: Houghton, Mifflin, 1892), 1:421. See also the comments in Allen C. Guelzo, *Edwards on the Will: A Century of American Theological Debate* (Middletown, Conn.: Wesleyan University Press, 1989), 2; and in M. X. Lesser, "Edwards in 'American Culture,'" in *The Cambridge Companion to Jonathan Edwards*, ed. Stephen J. Stein (Cambridge: Cambridge University Press, 2007), 280.

7. Mark Twain to Joseph Hopkins Twichell, February 1902, in *Mark Twain's Letters*, 2 vols., ed. Albert Bigelow Paine (New York: Harper, 1917), 2:719. On Twain's friendship with Twichell, see Steve Courtney, *Joseph Hopkins Twichell: The Life and Times of Mark Twain's Closest Friend* (Athens: University of Georgia Press, 2008), 254 and passim.

8. Robert Lowell, *Collected Prose*, ed. Robert Giroux (New York: Farrar, Straus and Giroux, 1987), 240.

9. Robert Lowell, "Mr. Edwards and the Spider" (1946), in Lowell, *Collected Poems*, ed. Frank Bidart and David Gewanter (New York: Farrar, Straus and Giroux, 2003), 59–60. Edwards, in his sermon, quoted Isaiah 33:12–14: "as thorns cut up shall they be burnt in the fire." Jonathan Edwards, "Sinners in the Hands of an Angry God," in *The Works of Jonathan Edwards*, vol. 22, *Sermons and Discourses, 1739–1742*, ed. Harry S. Stout and Nathan O. Hatch, with Kyle P. Farley (New Haven, Conn.: Yale University Press, 2003), 415.

10. Lowell, "After the Surprising Conversions" (1946), in Lowell, *Collected Poems*, 61–62; Jonathan Edwards, *A Faithful Narrative of the Surprising Work of God*, in *The Works of Jonathan Edwards*, vol. 4, *The Great Awakening*, ed. C. C. Goen (New Haven, Conn.: Yale University Press, 1972), 206–7.

11. "Unchurched Calvinist" and quotations from Hawthorne's *Scarlet Letter* in Westbrook, *Free Will and Determinism*, 29. Agnes McNeill Donohue, *Hawthorne: Calvin's Ironic Stepchild* (Kent, Ohio: Kent State University Press, 1985), 62, makes a similar observation about Chillingworth's Calvinism. Quotations from *Pierre* and observations on *Moby-Dick* from Westbrook, *Free Will and Determinism*, 38–39.

12. Much has been written on the "scribbling women," including John T. Frederick, "Hawthorne's 'Scribbling Women,'" *New England Quarterly* 48, no. 2 (1975): 231–40; James D. Wallace, "Hawthorne and the Scribbling Women Reconsidered," *American Literature* 62, no. 2 (1990): 201–22; and Michael Winship, "Hawthorne and the 'Scribbling Women': Publishing *The Scarlet Letter* in the Nineteenth-Century United States," *Studies in American Fiction* 29, no. 1 (2001): 3–11. On the struggle against sentimentality, especially by Melville, see Ann Douglas, *The Feminization of American Culture* (New York: Anchor, 1977), esp. 294–96.

13. The best modern biography of Harriet is Hedrick, *Harriet Beecher Stowe*. On her upbringing, see also Marie Caskey, *Chariot of Fire: Religion and the Beecher Family* (New Haven, Conn.: Yale University Press, 1978), 3–33, 169–207. On Catharine, see Kathryn Kish Sklar, *Catharine Beecher: A Study in American Domesticity* (New York: Norton, 1973).

14. On the influence of Common Sense philosophy in Catharine's work, see Sklar, *Catharine Beecher*, 80–84.

15. Her essay (which argued that the soul's immortality is revealed not by the light of nature but by scripture) is printed in Charles Edward Stowe, *Life of Harriet Beecher Stowe, Compiled from Her Letters and Journals* (Boston: Houghton, Mifflin, 1889), 15–21.

16. Charles H. Foster, *The Rungless Ladder: Harriet Beecher Stowe and New England Puritanism* (Durham, N.C.: Duke University Press, 1954), 111. Similarly, Lawrence Buell notes, "Her New England Arcadia is finally a world of Romantic tragicomedy, in which, after a suitable amount of tribulation, even the apparent incompatibilities of Calvinism and sentimentalism can be reconciled." See Lawrence Buell, "Calvinism Romanticized: Harriet Beecher Stowe, Samuel Hopkins, and *The Minister's Wooing*," in *Critical Essays on Harriet Beecher Stowe*, ed. Elizabeth Ammons (Boston: Hall, 1980), 270.

17. Harriet Beecher Stowe, *The Minister's Wooing*, ed. Susan K. Harris (New York: Penguin, 1999), esp. 325 on James Marvyn's conversion. For an extended analysis of religious themes in *The Minister's Wooing*, see Foster, *Rungless Ladder*, 86–128.

18. Stowe, *Minister's Wooing*, 194, 195, 197, 200; Hedrick, *Harriet Beecher Stowe*, 279–80. On Harriet Beecher Stowe and Catharine Beecher in the larger American theological context, see Noll, *America's God*, 293–329.

19. Harriet Beecher Stowe, *Oldtown Folks*, ed. Dorothy Berkson (New Brunswick, N.J.: Rutgers University Press, 1987), 194–95, 385, 265. As one of the novel's characters, Deborah Kittery, tells her cousin: "If you'd try to come into the Church and believe, grace would be given to you. You've been baptized, and the Church admits your baptism. Now just assume your position" (265).

20. Stowe, *Minister's Wooing*, 50, 193–94; Stowe, *Oldtown Folks*, 29.

21. Stowe, *Oldtown Folks*, 373.

22. Stowe quoted in Foster, *Rungless Ladder*, 102. Ann Douglas has argued that, for Stowe, "sin itself is the sublime, and that only its enormity puts men on speaking terms with God." Douglas, *Feminization of American Culture*, 244–45.

23. Buell, "Calvinism Romanticized," 265. Hopkins's idea about being damned for the glory of God is mentioned in Joseph A. Conforti, *Jonathan Edwards, Religious Tradition, and American Culture* (Chapel Hill: University of North Carolina Press, 1995), 126.

24. On disinterested benevolence as a basis for antislavery thought, see Kenneth P. Minkema and Harry S. Stout, "The Edwardsean Tradition and the Antislavery Debate, 1740–1865," *Journal of American History* 92, no. 1 (2005): 47–74. On Stowe and the essential humanitarianism of the Edwardsean tradition, see Lawrence Buell, *New England Literary Culture: From Revolution through Renaissance* (Cambridge: Cambridge University Press, 1986), 267.

25. Thomas J. Davis, "Images of Intolerance: John Calvin in Nineteenth-Century History Textbooks," *Church History* 65, no. 2 (1996): 234–48, esp. 237–38 on the Servetus affair.

26. Stowe, *Sunny Memories*, 2:276–77.

27. Ibid.

28. Ibid., 2:408–9.

29. The similarity between Stowe's and Weber's views has been noticed by at least one other observer. In a brief thought piece, the sociologist Werner Stark

(1909–1985) noted that Stowe's *Oldtown Folks* contained "Max Weber's argument in a nutshell," though Stark did not explore the biographical or other factors behind the affinity. See Stark, "Harriet Beecher Stowe versus Max Weber," *Sociological Analysis* 42, no. 2 (1981): 173–75.

30. Marianne Weber, *Max Weber: A Biography*, trans. Harry Zohn (New York: Wiley, 1975), 46.

31. Martin Riesebrodt, "Dimensions of the Protestant Ethic," in *The Protestant Ethic Turns 100: Essays on the Centenary of the Weber Thesis*, ed. William H. Swatos Jr. and Lutz Kaelber (Boulder, Colo.: Paradigm, 2005), 23–51; on Weber's parents, 42–48. The slapping incident is told by Weber's wife in Weber, *Max Weber*, 69.

32. Guenther Roth, "Weber the Would-Be Englishman: Anglophilia and Family History," in *Weber's* Protestant Ethic*: Origins, Evidence, Contexts*, ed. Hartmut Lehmann and Guenther Roth (Cambridge: Cambridge University Press, 1993), 83–84. See also the discussion of Roth's thesis in Lutz Kaelber, "How Well Do We Know Max Weber after All? A New Look at Max Weber and His Anglo-German Family Connections," *International Journal of Politics, Culture, and Society* 17, no. 2 (2003): 307–27.

33. Max Weber, "The National State and Economic Policy," trans. Ben Fowkes, in *Reading Weber*, ed. Keith Tribe (London: Routledge, 1989), 208. On the ways in which this lecture anticipated the argument of Weber's *Protestant Ethic*, see J. M. Barbalet, "Weber's Inaugural Lecture and Its Place in His Sociology," *Journal of Classical Sociology* 1, no. 2 (2001): 147–70.

34. Fritz Ringer, *Max Weber: An Intellectual Biography* (Chicago: University of Chicago Press, 2004), 152–53.

35. On ascetic Protestantism, see ibid., 117–18. See also the editor's introduction to Max Weber, *The Protestant Ethic and the "Spirit" of Capitalism and Other Writings*, ed. and trans. Peter Baehr and Gordon C. Wells (New York: Penguin, 2002), xx–xxi; and Weber, *Economy and Society: An Outline of Interpretive Sociology*, 2 vols., ed. Guenther Roth and Claus Wittich, trans. Ephraim Fischoff et al. (New York: Bedminster, 1968), 2:479.

36. Weber, "'Churches' and 'Sects' in North America: An Ecclesiastical and Sociopolitical Sketch," in Weber, *Protestant Ethic*, 204–5.

37. Details of the Mount Airy visit are reconstructed in Larry G. Keeter, "Max Weber's Visit to North Carolina," *Journal of the History of Sociology* 3, no. 2 (1981): 108–14. On the "Baptist christening," see Weber, *Max Weber*, 298.

38. Weber, "'Churches' and 'Sects,'" 207, 208, 209.

39. Weber, *Protestant Ethic*, 73–74, 79.

40. Stowe, *Minister's Wooing*, 198; Stowe, *Oldtown Folks*, 29; Lowell, *Collected Prose*, 287.

41. Weber, *Protestant Ethic*, 78, 80, 86, 94, 95; Stowe, *Oldtown Folks*, 29.

42. Weber, *Protestant Ethic*, 107, 113, 114.

43. Stowe, *Sunny Memories*, 2:411–13.

44. Stowe, *Oldtown Folks*, 31, 33; Weber, *Protestant Ethic*, 107.

45. Alastair Hamilton, "Max Weber's *Protestant Ethic and the Spirit of Capitalism*," in *The Cambridge Companion to Weber*, ed. Stephen Turner (Cambridge: Cambridge University Press, 2000), 169.

46. See, for example, Theodore Dwight Bozeman, *The Precisianist Strain: Disciplinary Religion and Antinomian Backlash in Puritanism to 1638* (Chapel Hill: University of North Carolina Press, 2004), 74–83; and Charles E. Hambrick-Stowe, *The Practice of Piety: Puritan Devotional Disciplines in Seventeenth-Century New England* (Chapel Hill: University of North Carolina Press, 1982), 25–39.

47. Weber, *Protestant Ethic*, 81, 84; Stowe, *Minister's Wooing*, 197 (see Augustine's prayer for his mother at the conclusion of book IX of his *Confessions*, trans. R. S. Pine-Coffin [London: Penguin, 1961], 203–5); Weber, *Protestant Ethic*, 8, 36 (emphasis in original).

48. Paul Münch, "The Thesis before Weber: An Archaeology," in Lehmann and Roth, ed., *Weber's* Protestant Ethic, 66–71.

49. Stowe, *Sunny Memories*, 2:281.

10

"Jonathan Edwards, Calvin, Baxter & Co.": Mark Twain and the Comedy of Calvinism

Joe B. Fulton

I wallowed & reeked with Jonathan in his insane debauch; rose immensely refreshed & fine at ten this morning, but with a strange & haunting sense of having been on a three days' tear with a drunken lunatic.

—Mark Twain, Letter to the Reverend Joe Twichell[1]

To Mark Twain, Jonathan Edwards "had no more sense of humor than a tombstone." While Edwards "scoffed" at the theological arguments of his rivals, those Arminian divines who privileged the free will of the individual believer, "he did not laugh" while doing so, Twain asserted in a manuscript portion of his dialogue *What Is Man?* (1906). According to one 1882 account, Twain even used Edwards's sermons on "eternal punishment" as a "barometer" of a person's sense of humor. Twain read the sermon as if he had written it to see if his audience was responding to the writing or to his own reputation. To his dismay, Twain found that, "for the first time in history, the gloomy periods provoked peals of laughter." Twain could obviously provide the humor when he found Edwards, or any other Calvinist, deficient in that regard. In one of many comments he made about eminent Calvinists, for example, he noted contemporary improvements in hell's accommodations: "In modern times the halls of heaven are warmed by registers connected with hell—& it is greatly applauded by Jonathan Edwards, Calvin, Baxter & Co.

because it adds a new pang to the sinner's sufferings to know that the very fire which tortures him is the means of making the righteous comfortable."[2] Twain often targeted this trinity of Calvinist divines: Jonathan Edwards (1703–1758), the inspiring preacher best known for "Sinners in the Hands of an Angry God"; John Calvin (1509–1564), the great Reformation leader whose Christian system continues to influence American and world culture; and Richard Baxter (1615–1691), the prominent English Puritan and author of *The Saints' Everlasting Rest* (1650).

Each of the directors of this "company" had an impact on Twain's thinking. Twain mentions Baxter frequently, generally to lampoon *The Saints' Everlasting Rest*. In the "God" section of the *What Is Man?* manuscript, Twain's Young Man says that parents looking down from heaven will react positively when seeing their children burn in hell: "It will increase the joys of heaven for them—as Baxter of the 'Saint's [sic] Rest' has pointed out." Twain marked a similar passage in a copy of the agnostic Robert Ingersoll's lectures, a copy inscribed to "Samuel Clemens Esq. From his Friend R. G. Ingersoll Dec 11, 74." On page 129, Twain printed a marginal line alongside this quotation from Edwards: "'Can the believing husband in heaven be happy with his unbelieving wife in hell? Can the loving wife in heaven be happy with her unbelieving husband in hell?' And he replies: 'I tell you, yea. Such will be their sense of justice, that it will increase rather than diminish their bliss.'"[3]

The Calvin division of the "company" provided Twain with a vocabulary for some of his most memorable comedic scenes. One thinks of the "prosy" Calvinist sermon in *The Adventures of Tom Sawyer* (1876), a discourse that lulls the parishioners to sleep despite the fact that it "was an argument that dealt in limitless fire and brimstone and thinned the predestined elect down to a company so small as to be hardly worth the saving." Or of the yet more satirical sermon from *Adventures of Huckleberry Finn* (1885), which is replete with dramatic and situational irony. As Huck settles into a pew, the Grangerfords and Shepherdsons, who are feuding, carefully lean their rifles against the church walls and listen appreciatively to a sermon on brotherly love:

> It was pretty ornery preaching—all about brotherly love and such-like
> tiresomeness, but everybody said it was a good sermon, and they all
> talked it over, going home, and had such a powerful lot to say about
> faith, and good works, and free grace, and preforeordestination, and I
> don't know what all, that it did seem to me to be one of the roughest
> Sundays I had run across yet.

Huck puzzles over "free grace," "predestination," "foreordained," and other elements of Calvinist theology. Readers chuckle, but the serious point is that an unexamined acceptance of a deterministic universe may free people from trying to reform themselves—hardly the point of Calvinist theology. No, the "Perseverance of the Saints" has no home in this church, and, for the feuding families who enjoy theological disputation but do not take the message of brotherly love to heart, the temporal wages of Calvinist theology just might be death. In a myriad of works, too, Twain employs Calvin's understanding of providence to create humor with a serious bite. In *Roughing It* (1872), for example, a drunken miner expatiates on the Calvinist definition: "Prov'dence don't fire no blank ca'tridges, boys." Throughout the passage, Jim Blaine explains the mystery of "Prov'dence," arguing that "there ain't no such thing as an accident" and "ain't anything ever reely lost." Twain burlesqued the theological concept of providence in *Roughing It* near the start of his career and in "Letters from the Earth" (1909) at the tail end of it when Satan discusses why the fly had been allowed to survive on earth: "Providentially. That is the word. For the fly had not been left behind by accident. No, the hand of Providence was in it. There are no accidents. All things that happen, happen for a purpose." With Jim Blaine in *Roughing It*, Satan in "Letters from the Earth," and numerous characters in between those works, Twain restates in parody the definition of providence asserted in chapter 5 of Presbyterianism's foundational text, the Westminster Confession of Faith (1647): "God, the great Creator of all things, doth uphold, direct, dispose, and govern all creatures, actions, and things, from the greatest even to the least." Calvin, in *The Institutes of the Christian Religion* (1559), similarly asserts that "all events are governed by God's secret plan." Twain delights in putting Calvinist definitions in the mouths of characters such as drunken miners and Satan.[4]

Owing, perhaps, to his position as America's foremost Calvinist, Jonathan Edwards, more than Baxter and even than Calvin himself, receives the most explicit attention from Twain. For Edwards, the clash between Calvinism and the creeping Arminianism of the eighteenth century was deadly serious, for it touched on issues central to a proper understanding of the relationship between God and humanity. The contest moved Edwards to pen many sermons, essays, and books, the greatest of which was his closely reasoned tome, *Freedom of the Will* (1754). Tellingly, the full title of that work is *A Careful and Strict Enquiry into the Modern Prevailing Notions of That Freedom of the Will, Which Is Supposed to Be Essential to Moral Agency, Vertue and Vice, Reward and Punishment, Praise and Blame.* For his epigraph, Edwards chose a fitting verse from Romans, "It is not of him that willeth" (9:16). In the work, Edwards provides a sound defense of Calvinist doctrine, praising the "first Reformers" and the doctrines "commonly called Calvinistic." In his conclusion, Edwards sums up the issue of salvation and free will, ascribing the "conversion of a sinner . . . to God's determination, and eternal election, which is absolute, and depending on the sovereign will of God, and not on the free will of man."[5]

Certainly, one cannot label Edwards's literary and theological endeavors "comic." Yet, for America's premier comic writer, Mark Twain, they offered a powerful catalyst for some of the most humorous—and greatest—works of the nineteenth century. The contribution of Calvinism to American literature has long been understood, but, not infrequently, its influence is tracked inversely: American literature germinates, thrives, then flowers precisely as it sheds the dead husk of Calvinism in which it had been entombed. Literary histories written in the early twentieth century were particularly prone to claiming such a relationship. Vernon Louis Parrington's *The Romantic Revolution in America: Main Currents in American Thought* (1930) argued that, for American culture to do its work of creating a literature "in the optative mood," as Emerson phrased it in "The Transcendentalist" (1842), some preliminary spadework had to take place first. Parrington believed that the last sources of Calvinism had to be rooted out, for "it conceived of human nature as evil, and accounting men incurably wicked, it opened no doors to Utopian dreams of a golden future." One easily summons contradicting examples, such as John Winthrop's utopian "A Model of Christian Charity" (1630), in which he envisions the biblical "city on a hill" arising from a reinstituting of the primitive church: "We must delight in each other, make other's conditions our own, rejoice together, mourn together, labor and suffer together, always having before our eyes our Commission and Community in the work, our Community as members of the same body." Winthrop's exhortation remains the laudable goal of church communities everywhere, but anyone familiar with church life must acknowledge its utopianism. Be that as may be, for many critics of American literature, the term Calvinism serves as convenient shorthand for all that has been repressive in U.S. history. Most notable are the comments of Van Wyck Brooks in *The Flowering of New England* (1936):

> In later years, when people spoke of the "renaissance" in New
> England, they spoke with a measure of reason; for in Boston, as in
> Florence, four hundred years before, there was a morning freshness
> and a thrill of conscious activity. The New England imagination had
> been roused by the tales of travelers and the gains of commerce, the
> revival of ancient learning, the introduction of modern learning, the
> excitements of religious controversy. After a long winter of Puritanism,
> spring had come at last, and the earth reappeared in its beauty.

However inaccurate the claims, Calvinism has often been depicted as an impediment to America's literary development rather than one of its primary sources.[6]

If the Calvinist bequest to the United States has frequently been viewed by modern critics as an unwanted inheritance, stunting free thought and quashing humor alike, nineteenth-century authors viewed it as a powerful cultural touchstone. Figures like Calvin, Edwards, and Baxter, along with Edwards's friend Samuel Hopkins (1721–1803), provided a *point d'appui* for personal belief as well as an interpretive vocabulary in which to discuss it. One sees the relationship in Hawthorne, Melville, and Stowe, among many others. One sees in these writers the truth of William Shurr's claim about Calvin's influence on American literature:

> From his generalized stimulus come the powerful controlling myths,
> the stories of our gods, the symbolic tales that express cultural values.
> It becomes immediately obvious, then, that his influence has not
> been a totally baneful one. Some of our best productions are given
> frameworks of steel by his harsh presence.[7]

Grappling with issues of predestination, free will, and the sovereignty of God, American writers have used theological ideas and a theological vocabulary drawn from Calvin. However wavering and various were the trends of their personal belief, American writers of the nineteenth century honored Calvin as the *point d'appui* for their questionings.

Criticism of Mark Twain has tended to be even more dismissive of the Calvinist influence. Raised in a frontier Presbyterian church in Hannibal, Missouri, Twain grew up memorizing the responses to the Shorter Catechism and remained a Presbyterian his entire life. When he died, his funeral service was held at New York City's Brick Presbyterian Church. Recalling his baptism in "Reflections on the Sabbath," Twain labeled himself a "brevet Presbyterian," having been "sprinkled in infancy." Throughout his life, Twain insistently defined himself as a Presbyterian, so much so that one must conclude that religion played an important formative role in his literary persona. In a speech entitled "Consistency," delivered on December 2, 1887, to the Hartford Monday Evening Club, Twain stated:

> No man *remains* the same sort of Presbyterian he was at *first*—the
> thing is *impossible;* time and various *influences modify* his
> Presbyterianism; it *narrows* or it *broadens*, grows *deeper* or *shallower*,
> but does not stand *still*. In some cases it grows so far beyond itself,
> upward *or* downward, that nothing is really *left of it* but the *name*, and
> perhaps an inconsequential *rag* of the original substance, the *bulk*
> being now Baptist or Buddhist or something.

It bears pointing out that Twain never became anything so foreign, so esoteric, so irredeemably exotic to American culture as a "Baptist or Buddhist or something." His literary work charts the ongoing dialogue among different denominations and different faiths, but, in his work, Twain draws on his Calvinist upbringing. Calvinist orthodoxy is the fountainhead from which springs Mark Twain's responses to other denominations and religions, so much so that he would even think to link "Baptist" in a line with "Buddhist or something" when discussing how far afield one might travel spiritually. Certainly, Twain questions his theological inheritance, but he often reinforces it and sometimes even invokes it in reactionary and chauvinistic ways. Twain's work engages in dialogue with "Baptist or Buddhist or something," that is, with the whole panoply of religious faiths, but even his way of expressing the conversation reinforces the Calvinist orthodoxy at the center of the dialogue. In a notebook entry near the turn of the twentieth century, Twain mordantly commented, "What God lacks is convictions—stability of character. He ought to be a Presbyterian or a Catholic or *something*—not try to be everything." Twain was *something*, and that something was a Presbyterian Calvinist.[8]

Despite the many creative uses to which Twain put Calvinism in his literature, that heritage has been, in the eyes of most scholars, something Twain had to overcome in order to convert Samuel Langhorne Clemens into the writer Mark Twain. Van Wyck Brooks, in *The Ordeal of Mark Twain*, first published in 1920, chastised Twain as never having reached his potential precisely because of "these morbid feelings of sin" imposed upon him by Calvinist theology. More recently, Sherwood Cummings identified the importance of Twain's reading of Thomas Paine's *The Age of Reason*, which "helped Clemens submerge his dreadful Calvinism." John Frederick similarly derided Twain's Calvinism as "religious baggage" that he lost on his journey. Such comments are apropos only in that Presbyterianism continued to influence Twain, not in the view that Twain "wishes to take vengeance upon the Jehovah of the Presbyterians," as Brooks says, a view that has blinded far too many critics to the role Calvinism plays as a creative force in Twain's work. Consider Jeffrey Steinbrink's comment in *Getting to Be Mark Twain*: "Clemens's imagination, for all its whimsy and iconoclasm, was chastened by the ambient Calvinism of his day and upbringing." How, one wonders, does one express iconoclasm without an icon? An iconoclast must have icons, if only to smash.[9]

Calvin was one such icon for Twain. According to a contemporary account, one of Twain's fellow passengers on the *Quaker City* tour of Europe and the Holy Land—a preacher—presented him with a bust of Calvin as a wedding present. Twain dutifully placed Calvin on his writing table, plopped a top hat on his head, and inked "a pair of spiral moustaches and a fanciful goatee" on his face, making him look "like a French barber." Later, Twain reportedly snatched a pair of iron fireplace tongs and "smashed the eminent theologian into a thousand little pieces."[10]

Calvin remained figuratively on Twain's writing table even after he smashed the bust, for each of those "thousand little pieces" worked their way into the literary classics he produced over the next four decades. For Twain, and for other American writers, Calvinism created the proper circumstances, mindset, and cosmic outlook for comedy. Brooks and others have made the extent to which Twain rejected Calvinism the mark of his aesthetic success. They have been far too ready to hiss "Calvinist!" when stumbling across the terms "providence" or "predestination" in the writer's works. Twain's grappling with Calvinism is earnest, and it is not enough to say, as Richard Calisch does of Twain's depictions of Calvinist characters, that "Twain has revealed to us in a few descriptive strokes the decay of Puritanism or at least its final rotten fragrance." Twain was not burlesquing something already dead. In an 1889 letter to Andrew Lang, Twain complained about the "cultivated class standard" that convinces people that what they like is no good and what they do not like is great:

> [T]he critic has actually imposed upon the world the superstition that
> a painting by Raphael is more valuable to the civilizations of the earth
> than is a chromo; and the august opera than the hurdy-gurdy and the
> villagers' singing society; and Homer than the little everybody's-poet
> whose rhymes are in all mouths to-day and will be in nobody's
> mouth next generation; and the Latin classics than Kipling's far-
> reaching bugle note; and Jonathan Edwards than the Salvation Army.

Edwards was revered in the late 1800s, but, like so many ministers today, the "Reverend" Mark Twain, as he sometimes called himself, thought religion ought to be more liberal, more relevant.[11]

There were limits, however. When he went west, Twain contrasted his own Presbyterianism to spiritualism in the article "The New Wildcat Religion" (1866):

> I do not take any credit to my better-balanced head because I never
> went crazy on Presbyterianism. We go too slow for that. You never
> see us ranting and shouting and tearing up the ground. You never
> heard of a Presbyterian going crazy on religion. . . . No frenzy—no
> fanaticism—no skirmishing; everything perfectly serene. You
> never see any of us Presbyterians getting in a sweat about
> religion and trying to massacre the neighbors. Let us all be
> content with the tried and safe old regular religions, and take no
> chances on wildcat.[12]

He burlesques spiritualism, but he also uses the occasion to poke fun at his own background and at society in general. Twain asserts that it is a good thing not to "massacre the neighbors," and, most of the time, readers have to agree.

At the same time, Twain depicts Presbyterianism as a bit too "serene," as the "frozen chosen." The "tried and safe old regular religions" have much to recommend them, but translate his words: old, boring, uninspiring. Twain describes Presbyterian services this way:

> Notice us, and you will see how we do. We get up of a Sunday
> morning and put on the best harness we have got and trip cheerfully
> down town; we subside into solemnity and enter the church; we
> stand up and duck our heads and bear down on a hymn book
> propped on the pew in front when the minister prays; we stand up
> again while our hired choir are singing, and look into the hymn book
> and check off the verses to see that they don't shirk any of the
> stanzas; we sit silent and grave while the minister is preaching, and
> count the waterfalls and bonnets furtively, and catch flies; we grab
> our hats and bonnets when the benediction is begun; when it is
> finished, we shove, so to speak.[13]

Twain could be describing churches today. In most churches, a subdued surreptitious rustling occurs as parishioners prepare to depart. They put away their hymn books, gather belongings and bulletins; even as the pastor is giving the charge to "go out into the world in peace," people are preparing to "shove." Here, Twain's criticism cuts both ways. Wildcat religions *are* dangerous, but shouldn't there be more in choosing a religion than searching for something "tried," "safe," and "regular"?

During his years in San Francisco, Twain wrote a number of burlesques of Asian religions, and his several pieces about the Chinese temple built by the Ning-Yong Company are good examples of his use of Calvinist conceptions of God's sovereignty and predestination for comic purposes. In these pieces, he criticizes both his own religious heritage and exotic Asian belief. The first of these, written August 19, 1864, "The New Chinese Temple," introduces the "Josh house, or place of worship," built by the Chinese for "their unchristian devotions." Twain's description of the statue of Josh is both a realistic depiction and a xenophobic rejection of the formal aspects of the worship, for, after lavishing much attention on the details of "gold leaf" and "glaring red" face, Twain concludes that "the general expression of this fat and happy god is as if he had eaten too much rice and rats for dinner, and would like his belt loosened if he only had the energy to do it."[14]

Twain put the Chinese temple to more sophisticated use in the next install-
ment, "The Chinese Temple" (August 23, 1864), using the figure of Josh to
comment on his own Calvinist God and the concept of predestination. The
Presbyterian document the Westminster Confession of Faith defines predestination this way: "By the decree of God, for the manifestation of his glory, some
men and angels are predestinated unto everlasting life, and others fore-ordained
to everlasting death." One can hear in the background Huck's mangling of
this definition when he discusses "preforeordestination" in the Grangerford-
Shepherdson episode of *Adventures of Huckleberry Finn*. In the sketch about the
Chinese temple, Twain explains that this "old original Josh" can "bless Chinamen or damn them, according to the best of his judgment." Twain ends the
passage by subjecting his own denomination to the treatment: "As far as we are
concerned, we don't believe it, for all it sounds so plausible." Twain uses the
exotic figure of Josh (his twisting of the proper term "Joss" to refer to the Western "josh" or "joke") to burlesque the Calvinist God so familiar to his contemporaries. Consider Calvin's definition of predestation in *The Institutes of the
Christian Religion*:

> We call predestination God's eternal decree, by which he compacted
> with himself what he willed to become of each man. For all are not
> created in equal condition; rather eternal life is foreordained for
> some, eternal damnation for others. Therefore, as any man has been
> created to one or the other of these ends, we speak of him as
> predestinated to life or to death.

Just as the Calvinist God "compacted with himself" whom to bless or damn, the
god "Josh" can "bless Chinamen or damn them." Twain casts the traditional
Calvinist doctrines into the den of a rat-eating God whose celebrations include
the "beating of drums, clanging of gongs and burning of yellow paper." By
doing so, he comically draws his readers' attention to the "log in their own eye,"
so to speak, causing a reconsideration of the doctrine. Surrounding the familiar
doctrine with new, exotic associations allows Twain to create a perspective that
looks at the old doctrines again, with a fresh perspective; perhaps the received
Calvinist doctrines appear unusual to others, just as "Josh" seems strange
to us.[15]

Decades later, in May 1902, Twain read Meredith Townsend's book *Asia
and Europe* (1901). Twain underlined some phrases, as indicated by italics
below:

> The truth is, the contempt is chiefly born of neglect and ignorance.
> A Scotch Calvinist, who believes very nearly the same thing, is

annoyed by belief in Kismet, though the greatest thinkers of all ages
have *failed to separate the foreknowledge of absolute power from absolute
destiny*. Englishmen cannot get rid of something to them ludicrous in
the notion of reincarnation, or as they usually call it transmigration,
and entirely fail to perceive that the reason it attracts the Asiatic is
because it solves the endless puzzle which the European has given up
in despair, viz, *the apparently unjust government of the world by a just
God*. . . . In the same way the Mahommedan moollah, tormented by
the same problem, explains it by his theory that God acts because He
wills, and not because He is bound by His own nature. "These to hell
and I care not, these to heaven and I reck not."

Next to the last sentence, Twain printed a double line in the margin and wrote
"Jonathan Edwards." Here, admittedly in a marginal comment not intended for
publication, Twain again points out the absurdity, as it seems to him, of Calvinist ideas of God's sovereignty and predestination, so much so that he observes
a similarity in Islam, just as he had earlier linked the concept to the rat-eating
god "Josh."[16]

"Jonathan Edwards, Calvin, Baxter & Co." influenced Twain's later work in
significant ways. This is particularly obvious in his late dialogue *What Is Man?*
One of the most significant theological issues discussed in the work is the idea
of free will. One portion of the dialogue, later excised, bears the title "Further
about Training." This portion relies heavily on Twain's reading of Jonathan
Edwards's *Freedom of the Will*. Twain's Old Man mentions Edwards's volume by
name, citing it as an example of poor reasoning and its author as a person with
"no more sense of humor than a tombstone." In passing, one has to scoff,
along with Edwards, if not laugh outright at some of the statements made about
Twain's work of this period. "It must be insisted," asserts John Frederick in his
much-cited work *The Darkened Sky*, "that there is no Calvinism in any accurate
sense in Twain's determinism, as has been sometimes suggested." Frederick
goes on to marvel that "in 1902 Twichell loaned Mark his copy of Jonathan
Edwards' *On the Freedom of the Will*, for reasons I can only guess at." Phillip
Gura expresses similar surprise: "it boggles the mind to figure out why he had
ever picked it up." Neither Frederick nor Gura need guess or be boggled; Twain
borrowed the book to consult as he wrote *What Is Man?* Twain tells us plainly,
in a letter to the Reverend Joseph Twichell, that reading *Freedom of the Will* gave
him "a strange & haunting sense of having been on a three days' tear with a
drunken lunatic," yet he still recognized that Edwards "could have written
Chapters III & IV of my suppressed Gospel." The "Gospel" was the dialogue
What Is Man? As he did with his other works, Twain engaged in research while

writing *What Is Man?* He borrowed Twichell's copy of *Freedom of the Will* for research, and the "Further about Training" section proves this. Any determinism in Twain's thinking has deep roots in his Calvinist inheritance and did not crop up with Darwin, Marx, and Freud.[17]

Twain's dialogue features two characters, the Old Man and the Young Man. Interestingly, in the excised passage, the Old Man accepts several fundamental premises of Calvinism: the absolute sovereignty of God, election, damnation, and predestination. What he rejects, however, is as important as what he accepts: free will. In all of this, both in what he accepts and in what he rejects, Twain's thinking closely follows Jonathan Edwards. The theologian's rejection of "Man as a Machine" in the culminating chapters of *Freedom of the Will* doubtless contributed to Twain's proposing just such an idea. It was not that Twain was rejecting Edwards. Actually, he accepts nearly all of Edwards's most important assumptions. Twain agrees that God is sovereign. Twain does not dispute the points in debate; however, he does disagree with several conclusions. In his letter to Joseph Twichell, Twain thanked the minister for loaning him his copy of *Freedom of the Will*, referring to the reading of it as "an insane debauch" and Edwards as a "drunken lunatic":

> All through the book is the glare of a resplendent intellect gone
> mad—a marvelous spectacle. No, not *all* through the book—the
> drunk does not come on till the last third, where what I take to be
> Calvinism and its God begins to show up and shine red and
> hideous in the glow from the fires of hell, their only right and
> proper adornment. By God I was ashamed to be in such company.
>
> Jonathan seems to hold (as against the Arminian position) that
> the Man (or his Soul or his Will) never *creates* an impulse itself, but is
> moved to action by an impulse *back* of it. That's sound![18]

Twain accepts Edwards's general argument that exogenous forces determine one's decisions and hence the course of one's life. Edwards approaches "that grand inquiry, what determines the will" by opposing what some designate the "sovereignty in the will, whereby it has the power to determine its own volitions."[19] Both Edwards and Twain agree on this fundamental Calvinist tenet: no such individual sovereignty exists. The question about how the Calvinist concepts of predestination and free will work together remains a thorny one. Twain, with his free will versus free choice discussion in *What Is Man?* follows his reading of Edwards:

Y. M. What is your opinion regarding Free Will?
O. M. That there is no such thing.

The Old Man's rejection of free will is crucially a part of the man-as-machine philosophy he propounds. Essentially, the Old Man rejects not the idea that people make no decisions but that they have any real say in the matter. The external conditions cause them inevitably to wrestle with moral decisions rather than arriving easily at an assessment. The true machine would be a person programmed inevitably to do right and who could do no wrong. Quite the contrary, Twain's Old Man asserts: "The fact that man knows right from wrong proves his *intellectual* superiority to the other creatures, but the fact that he can *do* wrong proves his *moral* inferiority to any creature that *cannot*."[20]

In response to his dilemma, the Old Man dispenses with the term free will entirely, substituting the term free choice, which he defines as "nothing beyond a mere *mental* process." With free choice, one enjoys no "untrammeled power to act as you please," but, rather, one has only the ability to observe the differences among various choices. For the Old Man, the *point d'appui* is a person's "born disposition and the character which has been built around it by training and environment."[21] One should note the passive construction of the Old Man's statement. Edwards, too, argues that no act arises on its own, so that, when considering a long line of acts, "none of them are free acts." Edwards uses the telling metaphor of "a chain of many links," each determining the next, so that "the motion of one link is before that of another in the order of nature; the last is moved by the next, and that by the next."[22]

So completely does Twain agree with Edwards that he adopts the metaphor of the chain of causality in an essay written in 1910, the year of his death. In this essay, Twain disputes the very idea of a single "turning point" in a life:

> It is only the last link in a very long chain of turning points commissioned to produce the weighty result; it is not any more important than the humblest of its ten thousand predecessors. Each of the ten thousand did its appointed share, on its appointed date, in forwarding the scheme, and they were all necessary; to have left out any one of them would have defeated the scheme and brought about some other result.

Twain proceeds to discuss the idea of "Necessity," a philosophical term used by Edwards throughout *Freedom of the Will*. For Twain, "Necessity is a *Circumstance*," that is, the situation in which one finds oneself. Coupling circumstance with temperament, Twain proceeds to discuss how those two forces have forged all of the links in the chain of his life. It is quite telling that Twain, as Edwards does, returns to the first link in the chain as he sums up his philosophy: "Necessarily the scene of the real turning point of my life (and of yours) was the Garden of Eden. It was there that the first link was forged of the chain that was ultimately to lead to the emptying of me into the literary guild."[23] Twain extracts quite a bit of comedy out of the idea that the fall of man was the turning point of his life, but, in this, he certainly agrees with "Jonathan Edwards, Calvin, Baxter & Co."

In fact, Twain agrees with the Calvinist triumvirate on every major assumption about the nature of God and humanity. So, why does he describe Edwards as "a drunken lunatic"? The answer has to do with Edwards's traditional Calvinist understanding of judgment. Consider again the full title of Edwards's book: *A Careful and Strict Enquiry into the Modern Prevailing Notions of That Freedom of the Will, Which Is Supposed to Be Essential to Moral Agency, Vertue and Vice, Reward and Punishment, Praise and Blame.* With his title, Edwards scoffs at the "Modern Prevailing Notions" that incorrectly assign "Punishment" and "Blame" only if actions are completely free. Edwards argues that, however strenuously necessity tugs and pulls, human beings are not "mere machines." Thus, because each person "has reason and understanding, and has a faculty of will, and so is capable of volition and choice," a person is likewise liable to judgment. Whatever the necessity of a person's life, judgment will come, Edwards assures his readers. Each person "is capable of moral habits and moral acts, such inclinations and actions as according to the common sense of mankind, are worthy of praise, esteem, love and reward; or on the contrary, of disesteem, detestation, indignation and punishment."[24]

Twain views this point in Edwards's argument as the moment where "we seem to separate." In "The Chronicle of Young Satan" (1897), one of the unfinished segments of what are collectively termed the Mysterious Stranger Manuscripts, Satan refers to a child's game to explain reality:

> Among you boys you have a game: you stand a row of bricks on end a few inches apart; you push a brick, it knocks its neighbor over, the neighbor knocks over the next brick—and so on till all the row is prostrate. That is human life. . . . If you could see into the future, as I can, you would see everything that was ever going to happen to that creature; for nothing can change the order of its life after the first event has determined it. That is, nothing *will* change it, because each act unfailingly begets *an* act, that act begets another, and so on to the end, and the seer can look forward down the line and see just when each act is to have birth, from cradle to grave.

When asked by the character Theodor if God foreordains the "chain of acts," Satan denies it. "Foreordain it? No. The man's circumstances and environment order it." This is indeed where Twain and Edwards part company. Twain disagrees with Edwards's conclusion that—whatever the determinism of their situations—people are liable to judgment. Twain's character Theodor concludes from Satan's insight that "it shows how foolish people are when they blame themselves for anything they have done."[25]

In section 5 of *Freedom of the Will*, Edwards derides those who object to Calvinism because it "makes men no more than mere machines in affairs of morality and religion." "I would say," Edwards insists, "that notwithstanding this doctrine, man is entirely, perfectly and unspeakably different from a mere machine, in that he has reason and understanding, and has a faculty of will, and so is capable of volition and choice." In his letter to Twichell, Twain labels this statement "frank insanity" and ascribes it to a kind of panicked reaction on Edwards's part at the direction his own argument was taking. Once Edwards concedes "the autocratic dominion of Motive and Necessity," Twain argues, "he grants a *third* position of mine—that a man's mind is a mere machine—an *automatic* machine—which is handled entirely from the *outside*." Arriving at such a conclusion, "it was time for him to get alarmed and *shirk*—for he was pointing straight for the only rational and possible next-station on *that* piece of road: the irresponsibility of man to God."[26]

Twain's criticism of Edwards and Calvinism is so compelling because it is a disagreement among writers who share most of the same fundamental theological conceptions. Both reject the Arminian view of unfettered free will. Both view God as sovereign. Both believe that individuals are driven by philosophical necessity. But where Edwards concludes that "necessity is not inconsistent with liberty" and so individuals are liable for judgment, Twain counters with a twisted version of Calvinist theology. Twain asserts that, because humans are depraved and cannot avoid sinning, they are excused from judgment. God, however, is not excused. To Twain, that was the logical conclusion to Edwards's argument. If Edwards, Twain asserts, "had been reared in an atmosphere where 2 and 2 made 4 instead of 75, he would have scoffed at such 'reasonings' as he puts on the market in his sermon called 'The Freedom of the Will.'" Even as Twain makes this comment, he seems to be responding to the "strange mathematical paradoxes" that Edwards discusses near the end of *Freedom of the Will*, where he contends that those who blame God for the fall of man make themselves as ridiculous as someone who contends that "a hundred multiplied by ten, makes but a single unit."[27]

It is not possible to know for sure when Twain first read Edwards's *Freedom of the Will*, but the comment in *Roughing It* (1872) that "Prov'dence don't fire no blank ca'tridges, boys. . . . There ain't no such a thing as an accident" seems quite close in both meaning and style to Edwards's statement "God don't do what he does, nor order what he orders, accidentally and unawares; either *without*, or *beside* his intention." Doubtless, with their firm Calvinist upbringings, neither author would ascribe the similarity to chance. While Twain read the works of many divines, from the obscure to the famous, from the outlandish to the eminent, he grappled most seriously with the works of Calvinist theologians. While many of his comments seem dismissive, one has to point out that he engaged with these works seriously, though with humor, and they charged his writing with what one might call an insistent humorousness of purpose. What other popular American writer of the Gilded Age was seriously reading Edwards's *Freedom of the Will?* In his outline for a speech at Princeton in 1902, Twain planned to speak of the university's first president: "The revered—late— Jona[than] Edwards being dead—I will attack him."[28] Twain frequently did, but he approached Edwards as a figure not just of fun, but as one with whom he had much in common. Edwards provided Twain with a worthy adversary, and like all worthy adversaries, the two were more alike than different. "Jonathan Edwards, Calvin, Baxter & Co." provided more than whipping boys for Twain's philosophical comedy. They shared a theological vocabulary, metaphysical assumptions, and a view of God as sovereign. Their disagreements were substantial, but Mark Twain and the Calvinists were partners in the same enterprise.

NOTES

1. Mark Twain's letter to the Reverend Joe Twichell of February 1902 is reprinted in Twain, *Mark Twain's Letters,* 2 vols., ed. Albert Bigelow Paine (New York: Harper, 1917), 2:719–21.

2. See the "Textual Notes" section in Mark Twain, *What Is Man? and Other Philosophical Writings,* ed. Paul Baender (Berkeley: University of California Press, 1973), 625. Twain's use of Jonathan Edwards as a "barometer" is described in "Mark Twain's Barometer," *New York Times,* November 21, 1882. The notebook entry on the three Calvinists dates from sometime in September 1883. See Twain, *Mark Twain's Notebooks and Journals,* vol. 3, *1883–1891,* ed. Robert Pack Browning, Michael Frank, and Lin Salamo (Berkeley: University of California Press, 1979), 32.

3. For Twain's comment on Baxter, see "Supplement A" in Twain, *What Is Man? and Other Philosophical Writings,* 482. The marginalia are in Twain's personal copy of Robert Ingersoll's *The Ghosts and Other Lectures* (Washington, D.C.: Farrell, 1879), held in the Mark Twain Project at the University of California at Berkeley.

4. Twain, *The Adventures of Tom Sawyer; Tom Sawyer Abroad; Tom Sawyer, Detective,* ed. John Gerber, Paul Baender, and Terry Firkins (Berkeley: University of California Press, 1980), 68; Twain, *Adventures of Huckleberry Finn,* ed. Victor Fischer and Lin Salamo, with Walter Blair (Berkeley: University of California Press, 2003), 147; Twain, *Roughing It,* ed. Harriet Elinor Smith and Edgar Marquess Branch (Berkeley: University of California Press, 1993), 366; Twain, "Letters from the Earth," in *What Is Man? and Other Philosophical Writings,* 424; Westminster Confession of Faith, in *The Constitution of the Presbyterian Church (U.S.A.),* part 1, *The Book of Confessions* (Louisville, Ky.: Geneva Press for the Office of the General Assembly, 1996), 126

(section 6.024); John Calvin, *The Institutes of the Christian Religion*, ed. John T. McNeill, trans. Ford Lewis Battles (Philadelphia: Westminster, 1960), 1.16.2 (citation to *Institutes* given in the standard form of book, chapter, section).

5. Edwards, *The Works of Jonathan Edwards*, vol. 1, *Freedom of the Will*, ed. Paul Ramsey (New Haven, Conn.: Yale University Press, 1957), 437, 436.

6. Vernon Louis Parrington, *The Romantic Revolution in America: Main Currents in American Thought*, 3 vols. in one (New York: Harcourt, Brace, 1930), 2:342; Ralph Waldo Emerson, "The Transcendentalist," in *The Complete Works of Ralph Waldo Emerson*, 12 vols., ed. Edward W. Emerson (Boston: Riverside, 1904), 1:329–59; Parrington, *Romantic Revolution in America*, 2:iv; John Winthrop, "A Model of Christian Charity," in *The American Tradition in Literature*, 8th ed., 2 vols. in one, ed. George Perkins and Barbara Perkins (New York: McGraw-Hill, 1994), 1:71; Van Wyck Brooks, *The Flowering of New England, 1815–1865* (New York: Dutton, 1936), 111.

7. William H. Shurr, *Rappaccini's Children: American Writers in a Calvinist World* (Lexington: University Press of Kentucky, 1981), 18. See also Elisa New, *The Regenerate Lyric: Theology and Innovation in American Poetry* (New York: Cambridge University Press, 1993; repr., New York: Cambridge University Press, 2009).

8. Twain, "Reflections on the Sabbath," in *What Is Man? and Other Philosophical Writings*, 40; Twain, "Consistency," in *Mark Twain: Collected Tales, Sketches, Speeches, & Essays, 1852–1890*, ed. Louis J. Budd (New York: Library of America, 1992), 910; Twain's comment is from his Unpublished Notebook 42 (old 32B), June 1897–March 1900, Mark Twain Papers, typescript, University of California at Berkeley, p. 63.

9. Van Wyck Brooks, *The Ordeal of Mark Twain* (1920; repr., New York: Meridian, 1965), 25; Sherwood Cummings, *Mark Twain and Science: Adventures of a Mind* (Baton Rouge: Louisiana State University Press, 1988), 21; John T. Frederick, *The Darkened Sky: Nineteenth-Century American Novelists and Religion* (Notre Dame, Ind.: University of Notre Dame Press, 1969), 150; Brooks, *Ordeal of Mark Twain*, 233; Jeffrey Steinbrink, *Getting to Be Mark Twain* (Berkeley: University of California Press, 1991), 183.

10. Jim McWilliams, *Mark Twain in the St. Louis Post-Dispatch, 1874–1891* (Troy, N.Y.: Whitson, 1997), 68, 69.

11. Richard Calisch, "Mark Twain and the American Myth," *English Journal* 75, no. 5 (1986): 61; Twain, *Mark Twain's Letters*, 2:526.

12. Twain, "The New Wildcat Religion," in Twain, *The Washoe Giant in San Francisco*, ed. Franklin Walker (San Francisco, Calif.: Fields, 1938), 134.

13. Ibid.

14. Twain, "The New Chinese Temple" (August 19, 1864), in *Early Tales and Sketches*, vol. 2, *1864–1865*, ed. Edgar M. Branch and Robert H. Hirst (Berkeley: University of California Press, 1981), 41.

15. Westminster Confession of Faith, 125 (section 6.016); "preforeordestination" is from Twain, *Adventures of Huckleberry Finn*, 147; Twain, "The Chinese Temple" (August 23, 1864), in *Early Tales and Sketches*, 2:44; Calvin, *Institutes*, 3.21.5; Twain, "The Chinese Temple," 2:44.

16. The underlining and marginalia are in Twain's personal copy of Townsend's book, now held in the collection at the Mark Twain Project at the University of California at Berkeley, pp. 13–14.

17. This was by no means Twain's first acquaintance with Edwards. He had likely heard many references to him from the pulpit at an early age, he read his work quoted in Ingersoll's volume in the 1870s, and, around June 1882, he made a note to purchase the "Life of Jon. Edwards about 1820 Northampton Mass." in his writing notebook. See Twain, *Mark Twain's Notebooks and Journals*, vol. 2, *1877–1883*, ed. Frederick Anderson, Lin Salamo, and Bernard L. Stein (Berkeley: University of California Press, 1975), 484. The note referred to an anthology of Edwards's sermons edited by the Calvinist minister Dr. Samuel Hopkins, the same satirized by Harriet Beecher Stowe in *The Minister's Wooing* (1859). Twain compared Edwards to a tombstone in a deleted portion of the manuscript, recorded in the "Textual Notes" section of Twain, *What Is Man? and Other Philosophical Writings*, 626. John T. Frederick, *The Darkened Sky: Nineteenth-Century American Novelists and Religion* (Notre Dame, Ind.: University of Notre Dame Press, 1969), 170; Phillip Gura, "Jonathan Edwards in American Literature," *Early American Literature* 39, no. 1 (2004): 153. The reference to the "suppressed gospel" is from Twain, *Mark Twain's Letters*, 2:720.

18. Twain, *Mark Twain's Letters*, 2:719–20.

19. Edwards, *Freedom of the Will*, 141, 176.

20. Twain, *What Is Man? and Other Philosophical Writings*, 199, 198–99.

21. Ibid., 200.

22. Edwards, *Freedom of the Will*, 177.

23. Twain, "The Turning Point of My Life," in *Mark Twain: Collected Tales, Sketches, Speeches, & Essays, 1891–1910*, ed. Louis J. Budd (New York: Library of America, 1992), 929, 932, 937.

24. Edwards, *Freedom of the Will*, 370.

25. Twain, *Mark Twain's Letters*, 2:720; Twain, "The Chronicle of Young Satan," in *Mark Twain's Mysterious Stranger Manuscripts*, ed. William M. Gibson (Berkeley: University of California Press, 1969), 114, 114–15, 115.

26. Edwards, *Freedom of the Will*, 365, 370; Twain, *Mark Twain's Letters*, 2:720.

27. Edwards, *Freedom of the Will*, 152; Twain's comment is from a deleted portion of the manuscript, recorded in the "Textual Notes" section of Twain, *What Is Man? and Other Philosophical Writings*, 625; Edwards, *Freedom of the Will*, 414.

28. Twain, *Roughing It*, 373–74; Edwards, *Freedom of the Will*, 434 (emphases in original); Mark Twain, Unpublished Notebook 45 (old 35), 1902, Mark Twain Papers, typescript, University of California at Berkeley, p. 31.

II

Cold Comforts: John Updike, Protestant Thought, and the Semantics of Paradox

Kyle A. Pasewark

Americans are not a people whose palates are sensitive to the taste of paradox. The strong and unambiguous flavors of progressivism, optimism, pessimism—all, in their way, opposites of paradox—are more our style, and we prefer them laid on a plate, or at the buffet stand, clearly distinguished from one another so that we can have one flavor at a time rather than components stacked upon each other or flavors melded to confront us with first salty, then sweet, then both together. This American preference is a little unexpected, since the United States is often portrayed—and portrays itself—as a "Christian nation," and one would think that the key Christian and, even more, the central Protestant category of "paradox" would fare a little better in American culture, that "paradox" would be a word that one hears more frequently.

Nowhere is the American preference for the directness of the nonparadoxical more in evidence than in the American understanding of freedom. Though "freedom" can mean many things, they are all good, and, though it can also mean contradictory things—frequently to the same person—we do not approach these contradictions *as* contradictions but as modalities of the same thing. Or, we play off the highest good against a presumed opposite, responsibility, for example (but usually when another's freedom is being asserted, not our own), and shrink from the actualization of the highest good, which remains always and everywhere freedom. In so doing, however, we throw ourselves into irresolvable contradiction (perhaps the purest opposite of paradox if only because the two appear so tightly linked), with consequences for our personal, political, and cultural lives.

That freedom was, at least until the 2008–2009 economic collapse, which threw most of our cultural deck of cards in the air, our "civil religion," in the classic sense of Robert Bellah, is hard to demonstrate precisely because of the ubiquity of references to it and its siblings and close relatives: opinion, rights, choice, and so on. Still, if it is difficult to remember the last time you heard the *political* content of the Declaration of Independence invoked, as opposed to personalist interpretations of "liberty" and the "pursuit of happiness," that is because the declaration is no longer a political document in the life of American culture but one that, judging by its current use, could as easily have been authored by a spiritualist, businessperson, skydiver, or actor. It is not, in other words, taken to refer irreducibly or necessarily to the polis, which means, if we take "politics" in the strong sense meant by Hannah Arendt, it does not refer to the polis at all.

A 1989 poll asked American teenagers what, if anything, "made America special." A whopping 63 percent answered "freedom."[1] As adults, those teens became scarcely less devoted. The linkage of political freedom and free markets as the inseparable twins of modern society has persisted despite the absence of conceptual or empirical evidence of their inseparability and has made us utterly unable to understand China (among others). And if the market tidal waves that have rammed our shores since 2007 have convinced us that maybe a little less freedom for the markets might have been in order, still, regulation is equated with "socialism" (the jingoistic opposite of freedom), and even those who advocate stronger government oversight seem to feel a twinge of guilt at removing a few sacrifices from the altar of freedom.

Although we are not a paradoxical people, it is not controversial to say that paradox is the fabric of John Updike's fiction. Can we describe in another way Roger, a conservative divinity school professor who, in *Roger's Version*, has lost his faith but is the strongest supporter of the doctoral project of an evangelical who wants to prove the existence of the unchangeable, primitive God by means of the most recent and advanced computer technology? Roger supports the project because he believes, correctly, that it will cause the student to lose his faith. Or what about Clarence Wilmot's final sermon in *In the Beauty of the Lilies*? Clarence has also lost his faith but believes more strongly than ever in the rigid Princeton interpretation of divine election. What he knows is that he is not elect. But, in contrast to what he knows, indubitably, to be true, Clarence tells his congregation that we can choose our own election. Nor does his congregation take a straighter path. It affirms against Clarence the classic doctrine but advises Clarence that he should, he must, recover his faith.[2]

Clarence Wilmot receives, for his part, a "revelation . . . of God's non-existence."[3] What else but paradox explains Clark, Clarence's great-grandson, who recovers faith and is accounted a hero, although it is he who ignites the murderous confrontation between the authorities and Clark's Temple of True and Actual Faith?

Nor, for that matter, is it controversial to say that the classic doctrine of election is paradoxical, although it is instructive that generations of mainline Protestants have been defensive about the doctrine when they have not simply abandoned it or "cast odium" upon it.[4] But there is no question that Calvin, and before him Luther, meant what they said (else it is difficult to understand why Protestantism was Protestantism rather than, as other movements were, an effort to reform the Roman Catholic Church). Generations of Protestants, from the radicalized movements of the sixteenth and seventeenth centuries, to the newer denominations of the nineteenth and twentieth, through those who refuse denominational affiliations in favor of the simple appellation "Christian," and ending with most of my former students (who carried with them the concept of freedom honed in analytic philosophy in the middle of the twentieth century), have asserted that the doctrine is either inhumane or anti-nomian and, perhaps, above all, a scourge to human freedom.

Any more than a superficial reading of Calvin's *Institutes* will show that this was hardly the intent of the doctrine of election. Rather, one's election was the *condition* for freedom, not its eradication. Of course, the argument presupposes the substantial accuracy of the Calvinist notion of human depravity, but that is really an empirical question, the answer to which is difficult, in the end, to doubt. If one accepts that premise, the argument is tight, if severe. Prior to God's justifying act (and its communication to the recipient by faith), there is no freedom; each action, thought, and intention is constrained by a host of distasteful motives and intentions, the most unsavory of which, the desire for salvation, however conceived, is often thought to be the highest. Instead, it is only after one *knows*, by the gift of faith, that one is saved that one can begin to act for the glory of God and, we might add, the betterment of the world. As a theological doctrine, the doctrine of election is not fundamentally about salvation; as a decided fact, salvific status is either true or not, and there is no particular reason for God to tell us about it. As a fact, it will be a happy surprise for the just at the end and an inevitable disappointment for others. The lucky (and they are really just that, the lucky) are told not for the sake of their salvation but for the sake of their freedom, indeed, for the sake of the world. The knowledge of salvation is the condition for the beginning of the good work, as one assist among others to the corrupt, to help us act rightly—or, at least, better.

Let's say that you have a tendency to the impolitic and sometimes the downright boorish. You have met a partner who forgives such things and you are to meet your prospective in-laws for the first time. Do you (a) set out to be at your worst, knowing that it doesn't matter that much (and it might be more fun), and all will be forgiven; (b) say what is in your heart, only "being honest," and let the chips fall where they may; or (c) monitor yourself, the clues of others, and the context as a whole in an attempt to be on your best behavior so that, irrespective of the forgiveness your partner might offer, he or she will not look the fool, a person of questionable judgment and taste? The antinomian interpretation of the reformers suggests that you will generally choose (a); the American penchant for self-expression suggests you will and should choose (b) (and this is irrespective of any theology); and Calvin believes that Christian freedom, to the extent present, will choose (c). You do not embarrass or dishonor those who love you and whom you love, not because you will be punished if you do but, in the end, because you don't want to, preferring instead to honor your friends and lovers rather than shame them.

And how do we know what is boorish and what is not? How do we train ourselves to give credit to those who love us? That is, what are the tools of faith? Chief among them is government, spiritual and civil, the latter being designed to keep us from malefactors—including our own impulses in that direction—but surely not only for that purpose. We cannot trust our impulses, whether we are justified or not, and so require institutions to guide and nurture us, to produce the worldly *content* of freedom, the ultimate and worldly *form* of which is made known to us in faith. That is a conception shot through from the beginning with paradox: the capacity to float untethered in form leads the just, in the life of Christian freedom, to *want* to fill that empty form with the content of thanksgiving.

What this is not is Updike's heroes'—or recent-vintage America's—conception of freedom. And what Updike's central characters have, especially in the *Rabbit* novels and *In the Beauty of the Lilies*—more consistently than the rest us, who chafe against the presumed opposite of freedom, responsibility—is a religious commitment to freedom. They answer our fantasy question: what would happen if one really did uncompromisingly and ruthlessly worship freedom? What would happen is precisely what does happen in Updike's work: as seekers of freedom, his major characters ask for nothing more than to be alone, but they still require others, and though they begin by demanding freedom, they become ugly dominators of others and, ultimately, self-destructive as well.

Late twentieth and early twenty-first-century American culture has been supported by the myth of individual autonomy, which is both an end and a means. On the one hand, as a means, autonomy is directed toward achievement:

we are to act to improve ourselves, and no dream is beyond our grasp. On the other hand, freedom is also the goal of the process: the myth of freedom refers to personal freedom, unhindered by others.

That is one paradox: the dream of achievement is social in character. In order to be aware that one has accomplished what one should, one must be recognized by others. Precisely the desired recognition depends, however, on those others from whom the dream of freedom needs to escape in order to be free. This paradox explains Rabbit's series of escapes and returns. He must run to escape the clutches of the "net" of responsibilities that holds him,[5] but he must return because he requires recognition, a place he is known. Anonymity is terror for Essie, Clark, Bech, Rabbit, and the Buchanan biographer in *Memories of the Ford Administration*. There are unmistakable echoes of Thoreau and, in a more violent version, the Unabomber: each could not give up his need for recognition. Each required simultaneously that he be free of others but also that the others admire and honor his freedom. Freedom bites its own tail.

We might look at this another way. Max Weber suggested that the social founding of a religion often arises from attachment to a charismatic figure.[6] And so it is in *S.* and *In the Beauty of the Lilies*. We might expect that these charismatic sects would not long survive in a culture of freedom, for, ultimately, the charismatic leader either cannot impose structure or imposes a structure that— as it must be—his followers understand as antithetical to their own freedom. We might say that Updike's characters have not left behind Weber's notion of charisma but localized it—in themselves, above and aloof from the net, which nevertheless they cannot do without. But we should note an important difference. In Weber's conception, a person is "charismatic" because of the vision that person proffers; charisma is not an ineffable, individual characteristic, a steroid-enhanced charm, but is inextricably tied to the content of the vision; nor is it the "vision thing" that makes one charismatic but the vision itself. Jesus was not a charismatic founder because *he* was mesmerizing but because what he *communicated* was.

Freedom's conflict with itself, its inability and simultaneous need to be free of content and yet be about something, to be untethered yet admired, is one problem. Another is that, in order that we and others know that we have maximized our freedom, our culture of achievement requires that each of us reach for the top. The proof of having reached for the top can be none other than being there. The American form of elevated accomplishment requires that others remain below one, that they become those whom one can influence but not be influenced by. The measure of redemption in our religion of freedom is the distance between ourselves and the crowd, the degree and frequency of our elevation above others and our own everyday lives. The ecstatic form of freedom *is* our religion. This is one reason that sex is such an obsession for Updike's men. Updike presents intercourse as elation and escape from lives that are uninteresting and deadening to those living them. To have achieved what we are promised we can achieve demands conquest of others and of one's own monotony. It demands the achievement of purity, but that achievement— because it is the distance between the isolated religious moment and profane time—renders ordinary time meaningless. Our meaning and religious fulfill-ment come in and during the extraordinary, exceptional event. Updike's main characters lack a meaningful relation to ordinary life. His ministers, for their part, generally either reemphasize the insistence on achievements and activity that we cannot fulfill (Jack Eccles of *Rabbit, Run*) or separate heaven and earth so that religion refers only to a realm above us from which we are infinitely separated except in rare moments of clarity (Fritz Kruppenbach, also of *Rabbit, Run*). What Updike's central characters lack is a religious relation (other than a negative one) to ordinary life. Consequently, their attempts to achieve grace, to be found worthy by God and others, rely on deception and manipulation, on falsifying and distorting love. Rabbit cannot tolerate women having affections that are not directed at him, while, at the same time, he must steal women's affections from others.

We should expect that, in the deepest possible sense, such freedom is aso-cial and apolitical. Indeed, in Updike's fiction, it is. Society and politics alike require institutional embodiments, but no devotee of freedom in the American sense will have the fortitude to build or maintain those structures. The reach for the top will be an undisciplined one. What, for Rabbit, appears to border on clinical attention deficit disorder really is less that than his revulsion, moral and religious to its core, at attachment. Even where we might expect political con-tent to Updike's novels, there is none. Political life is a mere backdrop to what the novels' figures think is really important. Ben Turnbull spends an extraordi-narily small amount of his time thinking about the politics of the Sino-American nuclear exchange in *Toward the End of Time*. Even as Ben and Gloria partici-pate in building a new order under the new national government developed out of the necessity to forestall anarchy and headed by Federal Express, there is no political discussion in the Turnbull household. In *Rabbit Redux*, Skeeter's claim to be the "black Jesus" has surprisingly little to do with American racial turmoil, while Rabbit's casual patriotism backgrounds Rabbit's rediscovered religious intensity but no more. Of all the tumults of the 1960s, Rabbit and Janice participate in only the most personal: sexual adventurism and drugs. The faint scent of apartheid just touches the Angstroms' bedroom romp with fifteen Krugerrands, the gold coins used for intimate purposes; the Iranian hostage crisis is only reflected in Rabbit's conversion of some of his assets into silver.[7] Nelson, the son, arrives at Kent State a decade after the National Guard departed and the blood had been washed away. This lack of political conscious-ness is not a weakness in Updike's work but an expression of his characters' deepest American contemporaneousness. For them, too, life, liberty, and the pursuit of happiness are personal, not social.

This, too, is a reversal and cancellation of Calvinist Protestantism from Geneva through the Puritans. It was always clear to those Protestants that the just remain wicked, that our own vision is through a darkened glass, and that the actualization of social and political life is not ecstatic but effortful. Protes-tantism requires of its adherents, as Weber argued, labor, which, in the social and political realm as it developed in industrial society, needed institutionalized and regularized bureaucracy. Even Weber rebelled against that conclusion in the famed description of the "iron cage." But that was only one part of his argu-ment; Weber did not dispute the functional necessity of such structures, and it is instructive that, if one remembers one phrase from *The Protestant Ethic and the Spirit of Capitalism*, it is generally the fearsome metaphor of the iron cage.

To say that the American vision of freedom is fundamentally asocial and apolitical is correct but incomplete. To the extent that Updike's main characters are embedded in social structure—as occasionally they must be in order to be recognized—the social and political consequences are demonic. Jesse of the Temple of True and Actual Faith, the leader of the commune in *S.*, and, in the end, S. herself are charismatic because they are able to make their adherents *feel* import and meaning despite the emptiness of their vision. Moreover, these charismatic figures grow in stature just because they are unaffected by what happens to others. Jesse's very aloofness from all others is what secures his status. When fulfillment comes only in the negation of the ordinary, it hardly matters what causes the break; nor, in the end, does it matter that feeling free is often the product of authoritarian control. Freedom devours not only itself but also the others whom it touches. Updike correctly notes that "a cultural emphasis on individual freedom makes choosing evil a lively option."[8] When charisma becomes power over others' feelings and only that, the vision of free-dom has reached its true demonic height and depth. Thus, the sociopolitical content (defined largely by its absence) of the religious devotion to freedom's purity—in Rabbit's conception, being "clean," having "nothing touching you that is not yourself"[9]—is a kind of feckless authoritarianism. What happens when that vision is inserted into social relations is precisely what happens to Clark, Essie, and Rabbit, or, rather, to those around them.

It is hardly necessary to speculate on what would happen if Harry Angstrom were an elected official. Inevitably, it is only a matter of time before a society's highest good finds more or less actualized expression in its political system. Approximately forty years after the publication of *Rabbit, Run*, "freedom" became the incessant mantra of the highest official in the land. Just a few years later, we saw, in all its glory, where it had brought us, and then it ended.

A prominent Republican strategist said of his first meeting with George W. Bush in an airport in the early 1990s that Bush was a man who had more charisma than any man should have. He did not mean that in the Weberian sense, we may assume, but in the sense of the Temple of True and Actual Faith. He had the vision thing but not vision, a lacuna itself exploited to marvelous effect in his campaigns. We saw, over the course of eight years, both of the elements we would expect to see—authoritarianism and fecklessness. And, while Puritans and Calvinists have sometimes been accused of authoritarianism, although on a quite different basis than the contemporary authoritarianism of freedom, never were they accused of fecklessness.

It is no accident that the chant of "freedom" was delivered in virtually every press conference (the few there were), campaign commercial (many), and public pronouncement of the president who viewed himself as "the decider." That is pure Harry. The ability to decide, unencumbered by others (and the corresponding need to impose that decision), is the very essence of freedom's self-consumption. This paradoxical but predictable self-consumption led a president who pronounced that terrorists want to destroy American freedoms (which ones were never clear but this, too, is simply the result of the formalism of freedom and, to be fair, the terrorists themselves were never lucid about what they hoped to accomplish) to vastly and often secretly circumscribe civil liberties and, as it shortly became clear, to perpetrate intentional misinformation about the reach of those circumscriptions for U.S. citizens. It led the party of national security to out a CIA agent and to commute the sentence of the offender. It led the Republican Party against government, that bureaucratic infringer of freedoms (a conception of government far from Calvin and his descendants), to produce the largest and most intrusive government in the history of the land. It made acceptable the practice of simply denying that the facts were the facts, and it permitted the alteration of consensual scientific judgments by sub-"deciders," since, after all, facts and arguments can be construed as simply a net in which to catch the unwary. And, of course, the market should be "free," although what that meant was never clear: it did not apply to labor organization, scientific research, nor the subsidy of the more conservative states by the more progressive ones.

None of that should surprise us, however, since freedom in this sense is ultimately singular; the very content of freedom is within the discretion of the person who, necessarily the lone decider, floats above us. In this sense, the American notion of freedom shows itself to be a postmodern concept of the most vicious sort, a concept that flails wildly into irresolvable opposites, a whip swirling this way and that, subject only to its holder.

What is not characteristic of all authoritarianisms, though it is assuredly true of many, is incompetence. Incompetence is, however, a necessary feature of freedom's authoritarianism. The ideological certainty of the universal desire for freedom, which stood in sharp contrast to the need to fight wars on its behalf, produced one and a half or two botched wars. It would have taken discipline, a channeling of our impure impulses, to plan differently or to plan at all, but, when there is no impurity, when all is clean, there is no need to think about contingencies. There is no need to have a functioning government that, well, actually governs, to respond to Hurricane Katrina. There is no need for bureaucrats to stay awake and attend to distortions in the "free" market, and the ownership society quickly collides with itself.

As a coda, it is no accident that references to freedom are decidedly less pronounced in the Barack Obama administration. A pragmatic temperament is less interested in ideology generally, in an ideology that will turn against itself in particular, and even less in a self-consuming ideology that is empty of content. "Change" is honestly formalistic and obviously in need of content; "freedom" deceives us and its adherents, making us believe that there is an object behind the mask. The pragmatist will have to channel what change means; to the ideologue, freedom means whatever he thinks it does.

It would have been perhaps too weird for Updike to write political novels and stories. The background whispers of political and cultural life are, in Updike's work, not the locus of meaning, and, indeed, the meanings that his characters draw from it are decidedly nonpolitical. Skeeter's self-assessment as the black Jesus simply reflects his self-conception as personally charismatic. There is no content. It would have been, perhaps, a little too weird and likely not artistically interesting to have asked, "What if S. were president?" It was politically interesting, of course, and we received our answer robustly, when W. was. The answer given showed, among other things, just how far from Calvin's view of freedom and government "this great roughly rectangular country severed from Christ by the breadth of the sea"[10] has come. We can hope, however, that the full glory of the ultimate destructiveness of the nonparadoxical understanding of freedom is now clear to us, and perhaps the way is clear for a conception of freedom that is both paradoxical and political.

NOTES

1. People for the American Way, *Democracy's Next Generation: A Study of Youth and Teachers* (Washington, D.C.: People for the American Way, 1989), 14, 67–75.

2. John Updike, *In the Beauty of the Lilies* (New York: Knopf, 1996), 49ff.

3. Ibid., 104.

4. Quote taken from a chapter heading in John Calvin, *Institutes of the Christian Religion*, ed. John T. McNeill, trans. Ford Lewis Battles (Philadelphia: Westminster, 1960), 3.16.

5. John Updike, *Rabbit, Run* (New York: Knopf, 1960), 25.

6. Max Weber, *The Sociology of Religion*, trans. Ephraim Fischoff (Boston: Beacon, 1963).

7. John Updike, *Rabbit Is Rich* (New York: Knopf, 1981), 200–203, 341–51.

8. John Updike, "The Persistence of Evil," *New Yorker*, July 22, 1996, 65.

9. Updike, *Rabbit, Run*, 134.

10. John Updike, *Self-Consciousness: Memoirs* (New York: Random House, 1989), 106.

Conclusion: John Calvin at "Home" in American Culture

Thomas J. Davis

The chapters of this book have indicated the breadth (and depth) of John Calvin's influence on American culture, in terms of his own ministry, writings, and thought and as those have been conveyed, modified, or adapted by the legatees of the tradition associated with his name. I will close the volume with a few remarks about Marilynne Robinson and her work.[1]

Robinson teaches at the University of Iowa's Writers' Workshop as the F. Wendell Miller Professor. In addition to numerous essays, she has published two works of nonfiction and three novels. Her first novel, *Housekeeping*, quickly earned her a national audience. This 1980 work became a book club favorite while also wowing critics and winning the Pen/Hemingway Award for fiction in 1981. Some years later, the work was included on lists of the best books of the twentieth century.[2]

In 1989, Robinson published a work of nonfiction, *Mother Country*, which was a finalist for the National Book Award for nonfiction. Therein, Robinson explores the problem of toxic dumping in England; more than that, she delves into the question of humanity's inhumanity, of how people are treated by their governments and by each other. Her scorn is especially reserved for those who would think of other people as "redundant." As she says, it is a word that "has a long and savage history, denoting an excess population, one whose sufferings prove it should not exist. . . . To conceive of others' lives in such terms is chilling, expressing a hostility to their hopes and interest[s] deeper and more intractable than ordinary hatred."[3]

The concern for the individual life, made clear in her first novel and in *Mother Country*, became a clarion call in her next book, a rather surprising tome entitled *The Death of Adam*. In this work, Robinson takes on many of the assumptions of modern thought and details how, in the end, they are destructive of the individual and the individual's worth. Surprisingly (at least, to many), John Calvin sits square in the middle of the book. He is hidden, however. She titled her chapter on Calvin "Marguerite de Navarre" because she thought no one would really want to read a chapter on Calvin. Indeed, even when writing on Calvin in that chapter, she uses his French name, Jean Cauvin, in order to "free the discussion of the almost comically negative associations of 'John Calvin.' . . . [The name] is so burdened that I choose to depart from [it]."[4] Calvin appears frequently in other places, however, as do the Calvinists.

Robinson understands herself to be engaged in a task of historical reclamation. As she says:

> In several of the essays in this book I talk about John Calvin, a figure of the greatest historical consequence, especially for our culture, who is more or less entirely unread. Learned-looking books on subjects to which he is entirely germane typically do not include a single work of his immense corpus in their bibliographies, nor indicate in the allusions to him a better knowledge than folklore can provide of what he thought and said. I have encountered an odd sort of social pressure as often as I have mentioned him. One does not read Calvin. One does not think of reading him. The prohibition is more absolute than it ever was against Marx, who always had the glamour of the subversive or the forbidden about him. Calvin seems to be neglected *on principle*. This is interesting. It is such a good example of the oddness of our approach to history, and to knowledge more generally. . . . Calvin somehow vanished.[5]

In her chapter on Calvin, and in various places throughout the book, Robinson strives to reinsert Calvin into the cultural conversation, hoping to show that there is a concern for the dignity and well-being of the human creature in Calvin's thought—and the thoughts of his heirs—that could well serve as a bulwark against the dehumanizing and depersonalizing forces of the modern world. I will not rehearse her arguments here; they deserve to be read in their entirety, and the very language Robinson uses serves her reasoning so well that detaching her points from that context and placing them in a bulleted list will not convey the richness of her thought.

While I applaud Robinson's efforts at reclaiming Calvin as a historical actor in *Death of Adam*, I am also aware that the nuanced understanding of Calvin that she exhibits can be found in some scholarly works on Calvin and the Calvinist tradition. Though it may seem to Robinson that hers is a voice in the wilderness—especially given much of the historiography in this regard, to which she refers—there are other laborers in the vineyard. The problem is that no one seems to listen. No one, that is, other than perhaps a handful of specialists who read *Death of Adam*, recognize all the valid points, and then still experience, both in the classroom and in more general scholarly works, much of the same old stereotyping that has come to stand in the place of examination. To have an effect, more complex understandings of Calvin and Calvinism must work their way into the broader currents of knowledge. Perhaps books such as this one can contribute to correcting the most egregious errors of textbook writers. I wonder, however, if Robinson's contribution to a more fully realized historical understanding of Calvin and Calvinism by the larger American body might not come about in the same manner that the negative stereotypes, I believe, gained their surest foothold: through fiction and its exposure to a large reading public.

It at least appears as if she is engaged in this very task. Her second novel and fourth book, *Gilead*, was very much anticipated, coming as it did more than twenty years after the publication of *Housekeeping*. Why so long? Robinson explained that the novel "had a long genesis because of my interest in theology." Specifically, it is clear that Robinson had developed a strong interest in the theology of John Calvin. Through the narrative of the story, she explores themes obviously dear to her heart: the beauty of creation, the place of grace in the world, the worth of the individual before God. And she weaves into her story the reflections of the main character, John Ames, a Congregationalist minister living in Gilead, Iowa, in mid-twentieth-century America, on these themes, often in explicit reference to Calvin's theology (although sometimes it remains at the level of the implicit). There even appears a serious consideration of predestination, humanized by the context of its discussion and a recognition of the complexity of the doctrine and its problems while still engaging the issue as a legitimate one for discussion. It is set within the broader context of the book's emphasis on the notion of grace—divine and human—in this world.[6] The novel won the Pulitzer Prize for fiction and the National Book Critics Circle Award. Its praise by reviewers was overwhelmingly positive. This is quite an achievement for a book about a Calvinist minister who takes John Calvin seriously. And it presents American readers with a way to think about Calvin and the Calvinist tradition that does not have to be bound up in critical clichés.

A third novel has since appeared: *Home*. Published in the fall of 2008 (a much shorter period of time between novels this time around), it also is set in Gilead, Iowa, in the same period as *Gilead*. The story follows the family trials of John Ames's best friend, Robert Boughton, who served until his retirement as the Presbyterian minister in town. Near the end of Boughton's life, his long-gone son comes home to see his now-widowed father and the sister, Glory, who has come to care for their father. Jack Boughton was the son who never felt he fit in; he was seen as a ne'er-do-well and caused the family considerable embarrassment and pain when he fathered a child out of wedlock but did not shoulder the responsibilities that come with that act. He did not attend his mother's funeral, though money was sent to help him come home. Yet, he finally does return to Gilead, bearing the burden of his past life, a burden that has become a barrier between him and the love of his life.

Again, here is a novel filled with the complexities of Calvinist theology. Though Calvin's name is mentioned somewhat less in *Home*, in many ways it is even more explicitly theological than *Gilead*. In the confines of this home, one sees a family trying to overcome the hurts of the past. In this book, guilt is real, but so is love. Forgiveness is held to be the highest virtue, but arms held out in forgiveness at times weaken and fail to embrace, despite especially the father's best efforts. And the language of grace permeates the book—grace not as an easy pick-me-up for what ails you, but as the mysterious and awe-inspiring grace that recognizes life and its meaning as gifts of the divine, shared with humans, which humans try and yet sometimes fail to embrace. *Home* shows the imperfections of good people trying to do the right thing, and the narrative brings home the point that even in good intentions and good actions there can lie unintended consequences of hurt and pain. The book's meditation on these things—on Jack and his place in the world, on his relations to his father, family, and friends—culminates, in some ways, in a heartbreakingly honest conversation about grace and predestination. Not long after the conversation, Glory is talking to her brother Jack, trying to console him. "Nobody deserves anything, good or bad. It's all grace."[7] Here is a Calvinist conversation taking place in the home, in the context of care and love. And, even if one, even within the context of the story, does not accept the Calvinist theology of the family (and I can imagine most would not), it is at least portrayed in such a way that one can see it in a nonstereotypical manner, upon which one can reflect without feeling a need to condemn. Calvinism wrapped up in family rather than abstraction appears more genuinely human and, thus, acceptable.

Perhaps through the work of Robinson, it will be easier to think of John Calvin and Calvinism as being at home in the American consciousness—as one of many influences that should have a recognized seat at the family table of American traditions.

NOTES

1. I have written on Marilynne Robinson's fiction and nonfiction as it relates to Calvin at greater length in Thomas J. Davis, "The Death of Adam, the Resurrection of Calvin: Marilynne Robinson's Alternative to an American Ideograph," in *Sober, Strict, and Scriptural: Collective Memories of John Calvin, 1800–2000*, ed. Johan de Niet, Herman Paul, and Bart Wallet (Leiden: Brill, 2009), 357–84.

2. Typical of reviews is this one from the *New York Times*: "It's as if, in writing it, she broke through the ordinary human condition with all its dissatisfactions, and achieved a kind of transfiguration. You can feel in the book a gathering voluptuous release of confidence, a delighted surprise at the unexpected capacities of language, a close, careful fondness for people that we thought only saints felt." Anatole Broyard, Review of *Housekeeping* by Marilynne Robinson, *New York Times*, January 7, 1981. For "best book" status, see New York Times Book Review, *Books of the Century: A Hundred Years of Authors, Ideas, and Literature* (New York: New York Times Book Review, 1998), 538; and Robert McCrum, "The 100 Greatest Novels of All Time: The List," *Guardian*, October 12, 2003.

3. Robinson, *Mother Country: The Truth about the Secret Toxic Dumping That Is Destroying the Environment* (New York: Farrar, Straus and Giroux, 1989), 51.

4. Robinson, *The Death of Adam: Essays on Modern Thought*, paperback ed. (New York: Picador, 2005), 175 (originally published in 1998).

5. Ibid., 6–7.

6. Jill Owens, "The Epistolary Marilynne Robinson," in *Exclusive to Powell's Author Interviews*, available at http://www.powells.com/authors/robinson.html (accessed April 15, 2009). For explicit references to Calvin, see Robinson, *Gilead* (New York: Farrar, Straus and Giroux, 2004), 115, 124, 166, 189, 208; for the explicit conversation on predestination, see 149–52.

7. For the extended discussion on predestination, see Robinson, *Home* (New York: Farrar, Straus and Giroux, 2009), 219–28, for the quote, 271. Though the book is saturated with the theology of Calvinism, and it is, so to speak, in the religious and intellectual air that the characters breathe, the book is about more: it is about home and family and the definitions of those things, both at the individual level and at a bigger, societal level; it is about who is included in the traditional family and in the societal family (indeed, the human family, a concern across all of Robinson's works). The woman who has made Jack want to be (and, sometimes, actually be) a better man, the love of his life, is an African American woman whose minister-father has found out about Jack's troubling past and has intervened to protect his daughter. While in Gilead, watching the police treatment of African Americans on TV, Jack tries to engage his father—and others, at times—in questions of racial justice.

Index

Adam and Eve, 48, 93–94, 129. *See also* original sin
 and Congregational-Unitarian discourse, 150, 154, 156
 and indigenous Calvinism, 208, 211, 213
Adams, John, 69
Adger, John B., 124, 144n43
Adventures of Huckleberry Finn, The (Twain), 240–41, 247
Adventures of Tom Sawyer, The (Twain), 240
afflictive model of Christian existence, 103–4, 107
"After the Surprising Conversions" (Lowell), 221–22
agency, moral, 151, 153–55, 163n19
Age of Reason, The (Paine), 244
Aids to Reflection (Coleridge), 137n29
Alexie, Sherman, 204
Allen, John, 182
almsgiving, 23, 26, 32
American creed. *See* constitutionalism, American
American Presbyterianism: Its Origin and Early History (Briggs), 172

American Revolution, 68–69, 71, 74, 84
Ames, William, 29, 149–50, 172
Anabaptists, 79, 108–9n10, 157, 181
Andover Seminary, 119, 125, 136n23, 144–45n45, 150, 154, 156
Anglican church, 26, 32, 34, 45, 52, 74–75, 173, 223, 230
anti-Calvinism, 149–52, 164n40
 in American literature, 220–22, 225
anti-Catholicism, 219, 225, 230, 232–33
anti-intellectualism, 154, 156
antislavery activism, 219, 223–25
Anxious Bench, The (Nevin), 113
Apostles' Creed, 94
Aquinas, 168, 176
Arbella (ship), 10
Arendt, Hannah, 258
Arminianism, 74, 149, 166, 175, 239, 241, 249, 252
asceticism, inner-worldly, 228–30
Asia and Europe (Townsend), 247–48
Askin, Denise T., 12, *191–217*
atheism, 44–45, 55, 58–59, 82, 149
Atlantic Monthly, 223

atonement, 143n41, 158, 162n18, 166, 169, 229

Atwater, Lyman, 144–45n45

Augsburg Confession (1540), 122–23, 141–42n37

Augustine/Augustinians, 6
    and Congregational-Unitarian discourse, 155, 159, 163n33
    and practical ecclesiology, 96, 99
    and Protestant ethic, 232, 237n47
    and twentieth-century American theology, 167, 178, 183
    and vitality of Calvinist theology in nineteenth century, 111–12, 129, 134–35n17

Axtell, James, 215n3

Back to Calvin movement, 176, 178

Bailyn, Bernard, 19–20, 220

Bancroft, George, 65, 74

Banner of Truth, 182

Baptists, 113, 228–29

Barnes, Albert, 70–72

Barth, Karl, 107, 140–41n36, 148, 167–69, 176, 179–80, 182–84, 187n36, 188n38

Barthian Calvinism, 167, 176, 180, 182

Battles, Ford Lewis, 182

Bavinck, Herman, 175

Baxter, Richard, 171, 240–41, 243, 248, 251, 253

Beattie, Francis R., 73

Beecher, Catharine, 222–23

Beecher, Lyman, 154, 222–23

Belgic Confession (1561), 77, 152, 178

Bellah, Robert, 258

Benedict, Philip, 85

Bern, Synod of (1537), 122, 140–41n36

Berquin, Louis de, 171

Beveridge, Henry, 140–41n36, 182

biblical law/scriptures, 4
    and American national identity, 49–52, 54–59

and American politics, 76, 81–82
    and indigenous Calvinism, 193, 195–96, 199, 201–15
    and transatlantic market culture, 21–26, 28–29, 32–36
    and twentieth-century American theology, 166–69, 172–73, 183, 185
    and vitality of Calvinist theology in nineteenth century, 126

biblicism, 151–52

Bismarck, 227, 233

Boise, Idaho, cross, 44

Bomberger, J. H. A., 124, 143–44n41

"Book of Sports," 230

Boston, Mass., 19–22, 25–28, 31–34

Bostwick, David, 198

Bouma, Clarence, 178–79

Bouwsma, William J., 22–23, 186n1

Bratt, James D., 131n6

Breckinridge, Robert J., 124, 129

Bres, Guido de, 77

bride of Christ, church as, 95–97, 99–100, 106, 108–9n10

Briggs, Charles, 172

Brooks, Joanna, 194–96, 206, 214

Brooks, Lisa, 194

Brooks, Van Wyck, 242, 244–45

Bross, Kristina, 194

Brotherton settlement, 192, 194, 210, 213–14

Brown, Charles Brockden, 220

Brown, William Adams, 172–73

Brunner, Emil, 179, 182–83

Bucer, Martin, 4–5, 6, 140–41n36

Buell, Lawrence, 225, 235n16

Buell, Samuel, 196–99, 201

Bullinger, Heinrich, 6, 122–23

Bunyan, John, 66

Burckhardt, Jacob, 9

Burial Hill Declaration (1865), 148, 156, 161n2

Bush, George W., 264–65

Bushnell, Horace, 131n6

Calisch, Richard, 245
Calvin, John, 3–9, 23–24, 37–38n12.
　　　See also Calvinism
　　anniversaries of, 3, 11–12, 107, 170,
　　　　172–73, 175, 186, 186n5
　　biographies of, 157–59, 163nn28–35,
　　　　186n1
　　birth of, 3, 4, 11, 107
　　on clerical celibacy, 93, 98–100, 104
　　and Congregational-Unitarian
　　　　discourse, 148–50, 152–57, 159–61,
　　　　161nn3,6, 164n40
　　conversion of, 4
　　death and burial of, 5, 9–10
　　on doctrine of Eucharist, 113–19,
　　　　121–23, 125, 134–35nn14,17,
　　　　135–36n21, 139–40n32, 140–41n36,
　　　　141–42nn37,39, 142–43n40
　　Edwards influenced by, 91–108
　　illnesses of, 8–9
　　implacable foes of, 3–11, 13n1,
　　　　14–15nn3,10
　　and indigenous Calvinism, 195–97,
　　　　200, 202, 204, 206
　　influence on American culture,
　　　　268–70
　　loyalists of, 3–4, 7–9
　　and paradox of freedom, 259–60,
　　　　264–65
　　pastoral ministry of, 92–93, 95–100,
　　　　106–8, 108–9n10
　　as "pope of Geneva," 9, 14–15n10
　　and Protestant ethic, 219, 226–27
　　Robinson's views on, 268–70
　　in Strassburg (1538–1541), 4–5, 122,
　　　　140–41n36
　　Twain's views on, 240–41, 243–48, 251,
　　　　253
　　and twentieth-century American
　　　　theology, 165–86, 186nn1,5,
　　　　187n14, 188nn34,35,38
"Calvin and Common Grace" (Bavinck),
　　175

Calvin and English Calvinism to 1694
　　(Kendell), 166
Calvin and the Calvinists (Helm), 166
Calvin College and Seminary, 174–75
Calvinism, 4, 9–11, 15nn11,12
　　and American national identity, 47,
　　　　55–60, 60–61n7, 62nn34,36,38
　　and American politics, 65–86
　　and Congregational-Unitarian discourse,
　　　　12, 147–61, 161n3, 162n18
　　indigenous, 191–215
　　influence on American culture,
　　　　268–70, 271n7
　　and paradox of freedom, 257–65
　　and Protestant ethic, 219–33
　　and transatlantic market culture,
　　　　19–36, 37–38nn5,12
　　Twain's views on, 239–53
　　and twentieth-century American
　　　　theology, 165–86, 186n1
　　vitality of in nineteenth century, 12,
　　　　111–30, 131–32nn6,7
　　　　Princeton versus
　　　　　　Congregationalist New England,
　　　　　　112–13, 125–29, 144–45n45
　　　　Princeton versus German Reformed
　　　　　　Mercersburg, 112, 113–25, 129,
　　　　　　134–35n17, 135–36n21
Calvinism and Modern Thought
　　(Beattie), 73
"Calvinism in American Theology Today"
　　(Bouma), 178
Calvin's Institutes: Abridged Edition
　　(McKim), 188n31
Calvin Theological Seminary, 178
Calvin: Theological Treatises, 181–82
Calvin Translation Society, 182
Cambridge Agreement (1629), 48–49
Cambridge Synod (1648), 155
"Can the Immortality of the Soul Be
　　Proved by the Light of Nature?"
　　(Stowe), 223, 235n15
capitalism, 20–23, 35–36, 41n41, 230, 232

Carlyle, Thomas, 119
Carrasco, Davíd, 60n4
Catholicism, 4–5
  and American national identity, 45, 55,
    62n30
  and American politics, 73, 80, 82, 85
  and doctrine of Eucharist, 118, 124,
    133–34n13
  and indigenous Calvinism, 193, 199,
    215n3
  and paradox of freedom, 259
  and practical ecclesiology, 94, 97–98
  and Protestant ethic, 219, 225, 230,
    232–33
  and transatlantic market culture, 22,
    27–29, 32–33
  and twentieth-century American
    theology, 167, 173, 175, 181
Cautantowwit, 211
celibacy, clerical, 93, 98–100, 104
Channing, William Ellery, 6, 11, 14n3,
  150–53
charismatic leaders, 261, 264
charity, 23, 26, 35
Charles I, King of England, 80–81, 230
Charles II, King of England, 53
Charleston, S.C., 21–22, 31–33
Cherokees, 193–94
Child, Lydia Maria, 6, 221
"Chinese Temple, The" (Twain), 247
Christ and Culture (Niebuhr), 181
Christianity and Barthianism (Van Til),
  182, 188n38
Christianity and Liberalism (Machen), 175,
  182
Christian nation, America as, 43–47,
  49–51, 59–60, 76, 257
Christian Reconstructionists, 170, 182–83
Christian Reformed Church, 179
"Chronicle of Young Satan, The" (Twain),
  251–52
Chronicles I, 102
Church Dogmatics (Barth), 183, 187n36

"city upon a hill," 10, 15n11, 210, 242
civic Republicans, 46
civil authority, 5–6
  and American national identity, 50–60
  and American politics, 67–86
  and twentieth-century American
    theology, 167
civil religion, American, 10, 258
Civil War, U.S., 124, 126, 147–48, 157
Clarke, John, 53
Clelland, Robert, 200
Clemens, Samuel Langhorne. *See* Twain,
  Mark
Cloppenburg, Johannes, 29
Cohen, Charles, 20, 211
Coleridge, Samuel Taylor, 119, 136n25,
  137n29
Collected Writings of Samson Occom, The
  (Brooks), 196
Colman, Benjamin, 27, 100–101
colonial America
  and Congregational-Unitarian
    discourse, 154, 159–60
  and indigenous Calvinism, 191–215,
    215n3
  and national identity, 43, 45–55
  and politics, 68–69, 74–75, 78, 86n4
  and practical ecclesiology, 12, 91–98,
    100–108
  and transatlantic market culture, 12,
    19–36
  and twentieth-century American
    theology, 172, 178
Columbia Seminary, 129
commercial trade in colonial America,
  19–35
common law rights, 49–50
Common Sense philosophy, 223
communal ethic, 19–20, 24, 34–35
communion, sacrament of, 5, 79. *See also*
  Eucharist, doctrine of
  exclusion from, 29, 32
  and practical ecclesiology, 97, 105

Compend of the Institutes of the Christian Religion (Kerr), 182
Compleat Body of Divinity (Willard), 28
Confederacy, 81, 147
Confessio Augustana Variata (1540), 122–23, 141–42n37
Congregationalists
  and American politics, 68–69, 74
  Congregational-Unitarian discourse in nineteenth century, 147–61, 161n2, 162nn17,18
  in fiction, 269
  and indigenous Calvinism, 191, 198
  National Council of (Boston, 1865), 147–48, 154–56, 161n2
  and practical ecclesiology of Edwards, 105
  versus Princeton in nineteenth century, 112–13, 125–29, 144–45n45
  and Protestant ethic, 222–23
  and transatlantic market culture, 34–35
Congregational Way, 156
conscience, freedom of, 51–52, 54–60, 62n30, 66, 69, 72, 84, 169
Consensionis Capitum Expositio (1553), 123
Consensus Tigurinus (1549), 122–23, 135–36n21, 140–41n36, 141–42n37
conservatives
  and American politics, 76
  and practical ecclesiology, 92
  and transatlantic market culture, 22, 30–31
  and twentieth-century American theology, 177, 179, 182–83
  and vitality of Calvinist theology in nineteenth century, 117, 125, 127–30
"Consistency" (Twain), 243
Constitution, U.S., 44, 46, 74, 76, 82–83
constitutionalism, American
  and national identity, 43–59, 60–61n7
  and politics, 71, 74, 76, 82–83
consumption, personal, 23, 26, 28–29, 35

conversion
  and Calvin, 4
  and indigenous Calvinism, 193–95, 197–99, 207, 211, 216–17nn15,16
  and practical ecclesiology, 101–2, 104, 106
  and Protestant ethic, 222–25, 230
  Twain's views on, 241
  and twentieth-century American theology, 180
  and vitality of Calvinist theology in nineteenth century, 126, 143–44n41
Corinthians I, 10, 98, 202, 204–5
Cotton, John, 25, 49, 51, 54, 56–57, 59–60, 61n10, 160–61
Council of the Alliance of the Reformed Churches Holding the Presbyterian System (Philadelphia, 1880), 170–71
Counter-Reformation, 166, 232
Covenanters, 81–83, 85
covenants
  and American national identity, 46, 48, 56, 62n34
  and American politics, 81–83
  and Congregational-Unitarian discourse, 160
  and indigenous Calvinism, 207, 210–15
  and practical ecclesiology, 94, 103
  and twentieth-century American theology, 166–67
creation, 37n5, 74, 96, 211, 213, 269
credit as commodity, 23–27, 30–32. *See also* usury
Creeds and Platforms of Congregationalism, The (Walker), 156–57, 159
criminal procedural rights/protections, 50, 53
Crocco, Stephen D., 12, *165–88*
Cromwell, Oliver, 66
Cronin, Brian, 44
Crossed Fingers: How the Liberals Captured the Presbyterian Church (North), 188n33

"Cry Aloud, Spare Not" (Occom), 210, 212
Cummings, Sherwood, 244

Danforth, Samuel, 207, 210
Daniel, 206–7
Daniel, Curt, 188n32
Danville Seminary, 129
Darkened Sky, The (Frederick), 248
Dartmouth, Lord, 197
Dartmouth College, 200, 223
Davenport, James, 197
Davidson, James West, 102–3
Davis, James Calvin, 62n30
Davis, Thomas J., *3–15*, 195, 206, *267–71*
"Deacon's Masterpiece, The" (Holmes),
        221
Death of Adam, The (Robinson), 268–69
Declaration of Independence, 68, 75, 258
declension thesis, 112, 131n5
democracy, 49, 53, 61n10, 70–71, 75, 81,
        83, 85, 169, 177
Deuteronomy, 23–24
Dévay, Matthias, 171
Diet of Worms, 13n1
DiPuccio, William, 125
disestablishment, 46–47
dissenting Protestant culture, 43, 46–47
divine sovereignty, 7, 21, 92, 111
    and American politics, 72–73, 75
    and Congregational-Unitarian
        discourse, 150–51, 155, 159–60
    and indigenous Calvinism, 195
    and Protestant ethic, 226–27
    Twain's views on, 243, 246, 248–49,
        252–53
    and twentieth-century American
        theology, 175, 177, 181
Dogmatics (Brunner), 183
Dogmatic Theology (Shedd), 172
dogmatism, 21, 151–52, 158–59
"Dominion of Providence over the
        Passions of Men, The"
        (Witherspoon), 68–69

Donatist debates, 96
Dorner, I. A., 134–35n17
Dort, Synod of (1618–1619),
        150–53, 171, 178
double predestination, 166–67, 169–70,
        177–78, 184
Douglas, Ann, 235n22
Douglass, Jane Dempsey, 170
Doumergue, Émile, 163n28
Dowey, Edward A., 187n14
dream images, 206–7
Dutch Calvinism. *See* Neo-Calvinism
Dutch Reformed Church, 10, 21–22,
        28–31, 33, 35–36, 45
    and twentieth-century American
        theology, 171–72, 174–75, 183
Dutch West India Company, 29–30
Dwight, Timothy, 154

East India Company, 29
Ebrard, Johannes, 122
Ecclesiastical Ordinances of Church of
        Geneva, 32, 58
ecumenical theology, 126, 144–45n45,
        166, 168–69, 179, 182, 184–85
Edict of Nantes (1685), 31, 226
Edwards, Jonathan, 12, 34–35, 91–98,
        100–108
    and Congregational-Unitarian discourse,
        149–50, 152–56, 161, 162n18
    in fiction, 220–25, 234n9
    and indigenous Calvinism, 192, 197–98
    pastoral ministry of, 92–93, 95–98,
        100–108
    and Protestant ethic, 225
    on revivals, 93, 100–106
    Twain's views on, 239–43, 245, 248–53,
        255n17
    and twentieth-century American
        theology, 167–68, 172, 177–78, 181,
        183, 186n6
    and vitality of Calvinist theology in
        nineteenth century, 125–27

election, 6–7, 46, 163n33. *See also*
     predestination
  and Congregational-Unitarian
     discourse, 150, 152, 154, 158–59
  and practical ecclesiology, 92, 96–97
  and Protestant ethic, 219–20, 229, 231
  Twain's views on, 240, 249
  and twentieth-century American
     theology, 168, 184
  Updike's views on, 258–59
  and vitality of Calvinist theology in
     nineteenth century, 138–39n31
elections, political, 49–51, 82–83
Eliot, John, 193
Ellis, George, 151–52
Elrod, Eileen, 194
Emerson, Ralph Waldo, 242
England. *See* United Kingdom
English Civil War, 25, 81
English Separatists, 10, 105, 157
English Trust for Moor's Indian Charity
     School, 212
Enlightenment, 13n1, 46, 84, 134–35n17
Ephesians, 7, 95, 138–39n31, 139–40n32,
     203
Episcopalians, 113, 223, 225
Erastianism, 79
"errand into the wilderness," 207, 210
eschatology, 28, 95–96, 99–100, 106–8
Ethics from a Theocentric Perspective
     (Gustafson), 183
Eucharist, doctrine of, 114–19, 121–25,
     133–34nn11,13,14,16, 134–35n17,
     135–36n21, 140–41nn33,36,
     141–42nn37,39, 142–43n40
evangelical system, 21, 34–35, 75–76
  and Congregational-Unitarian
     discourse, 150, 154
  and Edwards, 91, 107
  and indigenous Calvinism, 193, 199
  and Protestant ethic, 222
  and twentieth-century American
     theology, 177

Updike's views on, 258
  and vitality of Calvinist theology in
     nineteenth century, 113, 119,
     121–22, 125, 132–33n9, 138–39n31
excommunication, 25, 29–30, 32, 79
executions, 5, 8, 13n1, 196, 202, 207, 226.
     See also Paul, Moses; Servetus,
     Michael
Exodus, 210, 213

*Faithful Narrative of the Surprising Work of
     God, A* (Edwards), 100–101, 221–22
Faith Seminary, 75
Farel, Guillaume, 171
feudal system, 49–50, 85
fiction, American, 6, 11–12, 14n3, 223–25,
     235nn16,19
  anti-Calvinism in, 220–22, 225
  Calvin's influence on American
     culture, 267, 269–70
  Twain's views on Calvinism, 239–53
"Fight the Good Fight of Faith" (Occom),
     200–201
Finneyites, 113, 132–33n9
Fisher, Alexander Metcalf, 223
Fisher, George Park, 127–28
Fiske, John, 8
Flowering of New England, The (Brooks), 242
Forming of an American Tradition, The
     (Trinterud), 74–75
Foster, Charles H., 223
Foster, Stephen, 20
France, 4, 9, 23, 31–33, 171, 226–27, 231
Franklin, Benjamin, 69
Franklin and Marshall College, 132–33n9,
     138–39n31
Fraser's Magazine, 66
Frederick, John, 244, 248
Freedom of the Will (Edwards), 91, 221,
     241, 248–53
freedoms. *See also* liberties
  of conscience, 51–52, 54–60, 62n30,
     66, 69, 72, 84, 169

freedoms (*continued*)
  in Occom's preaching, 195
  paradox of in contemporary America,
    13, 257–65
  and Protestant ethic, 226–27
  of religion, 43–44, 46–47, 67–69
  of speech, 65–66
  and transatlantic market culture, 34–36
free markets, 34–35, 258, 265
free will, 151, 162n18, 231
  Twain's views on, 239, 241–43, 248–52
French and Indian War, 199
French Reformed Church, 31–33, 35–36,
    171–72
French Revolution, 66
Friedman, Benjamin, 21
Froude, James Anthony, 66–67
Fuhrmann, Paul T., 176, 180
Fulton, Joe B., 12–13, 239–55
fundamentalism, 73, 75–76, 165, 179,
    182–83

Gallican (Gallic) Confession of Faith
    (1559), 32, 51
Gast, Frederick, 121, 138–39n31
Genesis, book of, 210–11
Geneva
  Calvin's life in, 4–6, 8–10, 23–25, 97,
    103, 182
  and Congregational-Unitarian
    discourse, 154, 157, 159
  consistory in, 5–6, 8–9, 13–14nn2,3,
    99–100
  "pope of," 9, 14–15n10
  Registers of the Consistory of Geneva,
    99–100
  Servetus trial in, 5–6, 8, 13n1, 14–15n10,
    57–58, 226
  Stowe's trip to, 12, 219, 226, 233
  and transatlantic market culture, 23–25
  and twentieth-century American
    theology, 171
geomythology, 194

German Evangelical Synod of North
    America, 177
German Reformed Church, 11, 112,
    113–25, 129, 134–35n17, 142n38,
    143–44n41
  and doctrine of Eucharist, 114–19, 121–25,
    133–34nn11,13,14,16, 134–35n17,
    135–36n21, 140–41nn33,36,
    141–42nn37,39, 142–43n40
  and romanticism, German, 118–22,
    131n6, 136n25, 137–38nn28–30,
    138–39n31, 142–43n40
Germans/Germany, 9, 24, 45. *See also*
    German Reformed Church
  and Congregational-Unitarian
    discourse, 157–58, 163nn30,32
  and Protestant ethic, 227, 233
  and twentieth-century American
    theology, 171, 173, 176–77, 179
Gerrish, Brian A., 123, 142–43n40, 170,
    188n35
Gerstner, John H., 187n14
Getting to Be Mark Twain (Steinbrink),
    244
Gifford, Andrew, 200
Gilead (Robinson), 269–70
Glorious Revolution (1688), 27, 232–33
glory, theology of, 101–3, 107
Gnesio-Lutherans, 123
God, "arbitrariness" of, 6, 122, 151–52,
    154, 158–59, 161, 162nn9, 18,
    163n35, 164n40, 170
Godin, Benjamin, 32
God Who Is There, The (Schaeffer), 76
grace, 13
  and Congregational-Unitarian
    discourse, 153, 159
  and doctrine of Eucharist, 114, 118,
    120–21, 133n13, 138–39n31
  and indigenous Calvinism, 193–94,
    196, 203, 207
  and practical ecclesiology, 92–93,
    95–98

and Protestant ethic, 229, 231–32
Robinson's views on, 269–70
Updike's views on, 262
Great Awakening (1739–1740), 193,
    197–98
Great Britain. *See* United Kingdom
Gress, David, 84
Griffith, Andy, 228
Gura, Phillip, 248
Gustafson, James M., 169, 183, 188n35

Hall, David D., 4, 12, 14n3, 147–64, 161n3
Hall, Thomas Cuming, 172–73
Hamilton, Alastair, 232
Hannabal, Temperance, 216–17n16
Hanoverian monarchy in England, 27, 30
Harnack, Adolf, 159
Harold, H. Gordon, 75
Haroutunian, Joseph, 168, 177–79, 182
Hart, D. G., 12, 65–88, 86n4, 112–13,
    131n6, 144n43
Hartford Female Seminary, 223
Hartford Monday Evening Club, 243
Hartford Theological Seminary, 156
Harvard University, 149, 159, 163–64n38,
    172
Hatch, Nathan O., 131n5
Hawley, Joseph, 221–22
Hawthorne, Nathaniel, 222, 243
"Heavenly Merchandize" (Willard), 28
Hebrew language, 154, 196
Hedrick, Joan, 224
Heidelberg Confession and Catechism
    (1563), 123–24, 171, 178
He Is There and He Is Not Silent
    (Schaeffer), 76
Helm, Paul, 166
Heppe, Heinrich, 142n38
heresies, 58, 78
    and vitality of Calvinist theology in
        nineteenth century, 111, 120,
        124–27, 129, 144–45nn42,45
Hesshus, Tilemann, 123

His Dark Materials (Pullman), 14–15n10
History and Character of Calvinism, The
    (McNeill), 180–81
History and Theology of Calvinism, The
    (Daniel), 188n32
History of Dogma (Harnack), 159
Hobomok (Child), 221
Hodge, Charles, 69–70, 111–12, 117–30,
    130n2, 131n6, 134–35nn17,18,
    135–36n21, 137nn28,29, 138–39n31,
    139–40nn32,33, 144–45nn42,45, 172
Holmes, Oliver Wendell, 221
Home (Robinson), 270, 271n7
Hopkins, Samuel, 34, 91, 153, 155,
    162nn17,18, 223, 225, 235n23, 243,
    255n17
Hopper, Kenneth, 21
Hopper, William, 21
Horton, Michael, 182
Housekeeping (Robinson), 267, 269,
    271n2
How Should We Then Live? (Schaeffer), 76
Huguenots, 10–11, 21–22, 31–33, 35, 71,
    227
human depravity, 21, 83, 184. *See also*
    original sin
    and Congregational-Unitarian
        discourse, 153, 159, 163n19
    in fiction, 220–22
    and indigenous Calvinism, 194–95, 211
    and paradox of freedom, 259
humanism, 4, 22, 76, 158, 178
Humble Inquiry, An (Edwards), 105–6
Huntington, Samuel P., 43–45, 47, 59,
    60n4
Hutchinson, Anne, 162n14
hypocrisy, 5, 55, 96, 99, 104–5, 207

immigrants, 11, 24, 31–32
    and national identity, 43, 45, 60n4
    and Protestant ethic, 228
    and twentieth-century American
        theology, 166, 170–79

imperialism, 22, 28, 33–36, 206
independence, American, 68–69, 72, 74–75
Independency, 156
indigenous Calvinism, 12, 191–215, 215n3, 225
inerrancy of scripture, 74, 166, 169, 175, 181, 183, 188n38
infancy, death in, 129
Ingersoll, Robert, 240, 255n17
Innes, Stephen, 20
Institutes of Elenctic Theology (Turretin), 172
Institutes of the Christian Religion (Calvin), 4, 56, 58, 62n36
  and Congregational-Unitarian discourse, 149–50, 152, 154, 157, 163–64n38
  on doctrine of Eucharist, 123, 139–40n32
  and paradox of freedom, 259
  and practical ecclesiology, 92, 99
  Twain's views on, 241, 247
  and twentieth-century American theology, 174, 176, 182
Internet, 169–70, 184
In the Beauty of the Lilies (Updike), 258–61
"Introduction to the Literary History of the *Institutes*, An" (Warfield), 182
invisible church, 96–97, 105–7, 229
Isaiah, book of, 206, 210, 212–14, 234n9
Islam, 55, 248
Israel, 94, 210, 213

Jakob, Heinrich von, 136n23
Jakob, Therese Albertine Luise von, 136n23
James I, King of England, 81, 230
James VI, King of Scotland, 80–81
Jefferson, Thomas, 69, 75–76, 119, 136n24
jeremiad, 26, 207
Jesuits, 173, 193, 215n3, 232

John Calvin: The Organiser of Reformed Protestantism, 1509–1564 (Walker), 157–59, 163nn28–35
John the Baptist, 173
Jones, Joe R., 106
Jones, Serene, 22, 169
Joshua, book of, 214
Journal of Religion, 178
Judaism, 45, 55, 210, 212
Judd, Sylvester, 6, 221
judicial review, 43–44

Kant, 138–39n31
Keach, Benjamin, 200
Keayne, Robert, 25
Kehm, George H., 168, 184
Keillor, Garrison, 11, 15n12
Kendell, R. T., 166
Kennedy, Earl, 129
Kerr, Hugh Thompson, 74, 182
Kingdon, Robert, 13–14n2
King Philip's War, 26
Kis, István Szegedi, 171
Knowledge of God in Calvin's Theology, The (Dowey), 187n14
Knox, John, 9, 66, 77, 171
Krauth, Charles Porterfield, 129
Kriex, Johann, 31
Kuyper, Abraham, 65–66, 85, 175–76

laissez-faire economic system, 34–35
Lancaster Seminary, 132–33n9
Landis, Robert, 129
Lane Theological Seminary, 223
Lang, Andrew, 245
Latin language, 196, 200
Lectures on Calvinism (Kuyper), 175
LeFévre d'Étaples, Jacques, 171
Legare, Solomon, 32
LeMaire, Isaac, 29
"Letters from the Earth" (Twain), 241
Lex Rex (Rutherford), 76

liberals/liberalism, 21, 34, 46
    and American politics, 69–77
    and Protestant ethic, 220, 225, 227, 233
    and twentieth-century American
        theology, 167, 175, 177, 179,
        188nn33,35
    Unitarian, 148–54, 158–60, 162nn14,17
liberties. See also freedoms
    and American national identity, 46,
        49–53, 55–57, 59, 61n16
    and American politics, 65–86
    civil liberty vs. spiritual liberty, 84
    and paradox of freedom, 264
    and transatlantic market culture,
        34–35
Library of Christian Classics
    (Westminster Press), 181–82
Liebner, Karl Theodor Albert, 144n42
Lincoln, Abraham, 147
Lindbeck, George, 94
Little, David, 12, 43–63, 60n4
Liturgy; or, Order of Christian Worship, A
    (Schaff), 124, 143–44n41
Locke, John, 75–76, 151
Lockridge, Kenneth, 20
lombards, 29, 31
Long Island Presbytery, 198
Lopenzina, Drew, 193, 213
Lord's Supper. See communion,
    sacrament of; Eucharist,
    doctrine of
Louisville Presbyterian Theological
    Seminary, 73
Louis XIV, King of France, 226
Lowell, Robert, 221–22, 230, 234n9
Luther, Martin, 6–7, 13n1, 66, 113, 119,
    163n33, 226–27, 259
    and twentieth-century American
        theology, 168, 176–78, 181
Lutherans, 30, 85
    and Protestant ethic, 227, 230–31
    and twentieth-century American
        theology, 173, 177, 181

    and vitality of Calvinist theology
        in nineteenth century, 115, 118,
        122–23, 129, 135–36n21,
        140–41n36, 141–42n37
Lydius, Jacobius, 29

Machen, J. Gresham, 175, 179, 182
magistrates. See civil authority
Magna Carta (1215), 49
Margaret (Judd), 221
market economy in colonial America,
    19–35, 37–38n12, 209
marriage, 22, 96, 98–100, 105–7
"Marrow of Puritan Divinity" (Miller),
    159–60
Marrow of Theology, The (Ames), 149–50,
    172
Marsden, George, 97, 103
Marsh, James, 137n29
Marshall, John, 113
Marshall College, 113, 132–33n9
Martin, John Frederick, 20
Massachusetts Bay Colony, 10
    Body of Liberties, 49–53, 61n16
    charter of, 48–50, 53
    and national identity, 48–57,
        61nn10,16,23
    revocation of charter (1684), 20, 26
    and transatlantic market culture,
        19–21, 24–27
maternal imagery, 94–95, 97, 106
Mather, Cotton, 27–28, 160
Mather, Increase, 26–27
Matthew, gospel of, 10, 15n11, 94, 100,
    205, 209
Mayflower (ship), 10, 16n2, 192
Mayhew, Jonathan, 34, 193
McCarthy, Kelly, 204
McCormick Theological Seminary, 74,
    179
McCullogh, William, 103
McIntire, Carl, 75
McIntyre, Alasdair, 186n3

McKim, Donald K., 188n31
McNeill, John T., 180–82
Mead, Sidney, 106–7
Mead, Walter Russell, 21
Meeter Center for Calvin Studies (Calvin
    College), 174
Melanchthon, Philipp, 122–23,
    141–42nn37,38, 177
Melville, Andrew, 66
Melville, Herman, 222, 243
Memories of the Ford Administration
    (Updike), 261
Mencken, H. L., 11
mercantilism, 28–31, 33–34
Mercersburg German Reformed, 112,
    113–25, 129
Mercersburg Review, 117, 121, 124, 142n38
Methodists, 11, 74, 113, 197, 228
Mexican immigrants, 43, 60n4
Michaelius, Jonas, 29–30
millennialism, 106–7, 199
Miller, Perry, 12, 20, 148–49, 159–61,
    163–64nn38,40,43, 172
Miller, Samuel, 143–44n41
Milton, John, 66, 93–94
Minister's Wooing, The (Stowe), 153,
    162n17, 223–24, 229–30, 232,
    255n17
minorities, religious, 44–45
Moby-Dick (Melville), 222
"Model of Christian Charity, A"
    (Winthrop), 10, 15n11, 242
modernity, 19–21
    and American politics, 65–67, 73,
        84–86
    and Congregational-Unitarian
        discourse, 151–52, 159
    and twentieth-century American
        theology, 175, 180–81, 183–84
    and vitality of Calvinist theology in
        nineteenth century, 112–18,
        129–30, 134–35n17
Mohegans, 12, 191–215

Montcalm, Marquis de, 199
"Moral Argument against Calvinism,
    The" (Channing), 150–53
moral ideals
    and Congregational-Unitarian
        discourse, 150–56, 163n19
    and Protestant ethic, 226–30
    and transatlantic market culture,
        19–35, 37n5
Mother Country (Robinson), 267–68
Mount Airy, N.C., 228–29
"Mr. Edwards and the Spider" (Lowell),
    221, 234n9
Muller, Richard, 158
Münch, Paul, 232
Mystical Presence, The (Nevin), 113–19, 121,
    134–35nn17,18

Napoleonic Wars, 119
Narragansett Indians, 52–53
Nation, 147
National Council of Congregational
    Churches (Boston, 1865), 147–48,
    154–56, 161n2
    Declaration of Faith, 148, 155–56
national identity, American, 12, 43–60,
    60n4
    Calvin as background of, 47, 55–60,
        60–61n7, 62nn34,36,38
    and New England Puritans, 43, 45–60,
        60–61nn7,10,16
    and Rhode Island colony, 53–57, 59–60
Native Americans, 25–26, 52–53, 55
    and indigenous Calvinism, 191–215,
        215n3
natural man/natural law, 31, 46, 50,
    54–55, 58–60, 60–61n7, 176–77,
    179, 183, 188n34
Neander, August, 120–21, 138–39n31
Neo-Calvinism, 175–76
neo-orthodoxy, 177–79, 182–83
Netherlands, 28–31, 33, 66, 77, 174, 178.
    See also Dutch Reformed Church

Nevin, John, 113–25, 127–28, 132–33n9,
133–34nn11,13,14,16, 134–35nn17,18,
138–39n31, 139–40nn32,33,
140–41n36, 142–43nn38–40,
143–44nn41–43
"New Chinese Temple, The" (Twain),
246–47
New Divinity, 153, 220
Newdow, Michael, 44
Newell, Margaret, 20–21
New England Congregationalists. See
Congregationalists
New England Mind: The Seventeenth
Century, The (Miller), 159, 161,
163–64nn38,43
New England Puritans. See Puritans
New England Soul, The (Stout), 196–97
New England Tale (Sedgwick), 220
New England Theology (Park), 126
New Haven Colony, 222
New Haven theology, 153–54
New Jerusalem, 26
New Lights, 103–5, 191, 197–99
New Modernism: An Appraisal of the
Theology of Barth and Brunner, The
(Van Til), 182
New Stockbridge settlement, 198, 210,
214–15
"New Wildcat Religion, The" (Twain),
245–46
New York, 10, 21–22, 28–31, 33
consistory in, 30
and indigenous Calvinism, 192, 196–98
Nichols, James Hastings, 125
Niebuhr, H. Richard, 35, 41n41, 107, 148,
177–78, 181, 183, 187n18
Niebuhr, Reinhold, 35, 41n41, 177, 187n18
nineteenth century
and American literature, 220–25,
235nn16,19, 239–53
and American politics, 65–73
Congregational-Unitarian discourse in,
12, 147–61

implacable foes of Calvin in, 3, 5–11,
13n1, 14n3
and Protestant ethic, 219–33
textbooks used in, 7, 13n1
vitality of Calvinist theology in, 12,
111–30, 131–32nn6,7
Princeton versus Congregationalist
New England, 112–13, 125–29,
144–45n45
Princeton versus German Reformed
Mercersburg, 112, 113–25, 129,
134–35n17, 142–43n40
Noll, Mark A., 123–24, 131n5
non-Christians, 43–45, 59, 73
North, Gary, 170, 182, 188nn33,34
Northampton church, 97–98, 100–105,
107
Norton, Andrews, 150, 152

Obama, Barack, 265
Occom, Samson, 12, 191–215
conversion of, 197–99, 216–17nn15,16
and covenant narrative, 207, 210–15
ordination of, 198–99, 203
and Pauline paradox, 200, 204–6
prophetic voice of, 206–10, 214–15
style of, 200–210
use of irony, 197, 200, 203–6, 209
Oecolampadius, Johannes, 171
Old Calvinists, 153–54
Old Princeton Calvinism, 170, 173–76,
187n14
Oldtown Folks (Stowe), 223–25, 230–31,
235–36nn19,29
On Clemency (Seneca), 4
Oneida tribe, 192, 196, 212
On the Bondage of the Will (Luther), 6
Ordeal of Mark Twain, The (Brooks), 244
Oriel College at Oxford University, 66
original sin, 92, 126, 152–54, 156, 159,
220. See also human depravity
orthodoxy, 10–11. See also neo-orthodoxy
and American national identity, 51, 57

orthodoxy (*continued*)
    and Congregational-Unitarian
        discourse, 148–53, 157, 162n17
    Twain's views on, 244
    and twentieth-century American
        theology, 175, 177–79, 182, 185,
        188nn32,38
    and vitality of Calvinist theology in
        nineteenth century, 111–12, 114,
        121–22, 128–29, 130n2, 137n29
"outsiders," 44–45, 59
Oxford movement, 66

Paine, Thomas, 244
pantheism, 119, 124, 137n29, 138–39n31
Paradise Lost (Milton), 93–94
paradoxes
    affinity between Miller and Unitarians,
        159–60
    afflictive model of Christian existence,
        103–4, 107
    Calvinism and liberty, 68
    and doctrine of Eucharist, 125
    ecclesial images of mother
        and bride, 95
    of freedom in contemporary America,
        257–65
    Occom's use of Pauline paradox, 200,
        204–6
    and Twain's views on Edwards, 252
    in twentieth-century American
        theology, 181
Park, Edwards Amasa, 125–26, 128,
    131n6, 144–45n45
Parrington, Vernon L., 164n40, 242
Partee, Charles, 165–66, 186n1
Pasewark, Kyle A., 13, 257–66
pastoral ministry, 92–93, 95–108
patriotism, 28–30, 68, 71, 74
Pauck, Wilhelm, 168, 178–79
Paul, Moses, 196
Paul, the apostle, 6–7, 10, 34, 57, 62n38,
    98, 155

and indigenous Calvinism, 199, 201–2,
    204–5
Pauw, Amy Plantinga, 12, 91–110
Pelagian system, 111
Pemberton, Ebenezer, 27
Perry, Ralph Barton, 84
Peter, Saint, 103, 205–6
Peterson, Mark, 21
Petition of Right (1628), 49
Peyer, Bernd, 197, 206
Philadelphia, Pa., 21, 34
    Synod of, 78–79
Philosophy of Revelation, The (Bavinck),
    175
Pierre (Melville), 222
*Piety versus Moralism: The Passing
    of the New England Theology*
    (Haroutunian), 177–78
Pilgrims, 10
Pledge of Allegiance, 44–45
politics, American, 12, 65–86
    and authoritarian Calvinists, 67, 77–83
    and libertarian Calvinists, 67, 68–77,
        83
    and paradox of freedom, 258, 262–65
Pollution and Death of Man, The
    (Schaeffer), 76
poor/poverty, 23–27, 34–35
Porter, Noah, 119–20, 136n25
practical ecclesiology, 91–108
    Calvin on clerical celibacy, 93, 98–100
    Edwards on revivals, 93, 100–106
    eschatology and providence, 106–8
    and Reformed ecclesiology, 93–98, 101,
        108–9n10
pragmatism, humanistic, 22–23, 27,
    33–36
Prairie Home Companion, A, 11, 15n12
predestination, 6–7, 14n3, 21, 66, 154,
    158–59, 184. *See also* double
    predestination; election
    in fiction, 220–21, 225, 243
    and Protestant ethic, 225–26, 229

Robinson's views on, 269–70
Twain's views on, 243, 245–49
"'Preparation for Salvation' in
    Seventeenth-Century New
    England" (Miller), 159–61
Presbyterian Board of Education, 182
Presbyterian Church (U.S.A.) (PCUSA),
    67, 72, 74–75, 78
Presbyterian Historical Society, 69–70
Presbyterianism: Its Affinities (Barnes),
    70–72
Presbyterians
    and American politics, 65–86
    Confession of 1967, 187n14
    in fiction, 270
    and indigenous Calvinism, 191–215
    Princeton Theological Seminary,
        65–66, 70, 72, 111–30
        versus Congregationalist New
            England, 112–13, 125–29, 144–45n45
        versus German Reformed
            Mercersburg, 112, 113–25, 134–35n17
    and transatlantic market culture, 21,
        34–35
    Twain's views on, 241, 243–47
    and twentieth-century American
        theology, 168, 170–71, 173–74,
        178–79, 187n14, 188n33
"Present-Day Attitude toward Calvinism:
    Its Causes and Significance, The"
    (Warfield), 173–74
Prince, Thomas, 27, 34
Princeton Review, 117–18
Princeton Theological Seminary, 65–66,
    72, 111–30, 130n2, 182. *See also*
    Old Princeton Calvinism
    versus Congregationalist New England,
        112–13, 125–29, 144–45n45
    versus German Reformed
        Mercersburg, 112, 113–25, 129
    and twentieth-century American
        theology, 170, 173–76, 187n14
    Updike's views on, 258

Principle of Protestantism, The (Schaff),
    120–21, 134–35n17
Prioleau, Elias, 32
privateering, 25, 29
prophetic voice, 34, 94, 179
    and indigenous Calvinism, 199–200,
        202, 206–10, 214–15
Protestant ethic, 219–33
    Stowe's views on, 219–20, 222–27,
        232–33, 235–36nn15,16,19,22,29
    Weber's views on, 219–20, 227–33,
        235–36n29
*Protestant Ethic and the Spirit of
    Capitalism, The* (Weber), 20–21,
        158, 219, 228–29, 231–32, 263
Prussian Union (1817), 177
Psalms, book of, 68
psychology, modern, 116, 134n14
Pullman, Philip, 14–15n10
Puritans, 10–11, 24, 26, 58
    and American politics, 71
    and Congregational-Unitarian
        discourse, 148–49, 155, 159–60,
        161n3, 164nn40,43
    and doctrine of Eucharist, 114–15,
        117–18
    and indigenous Calvinism, 195, 199,
        210, 214–15
    and national identity, 43, 45–58,
        60–61nn7,10,16
    and paradox of freedom, 263–64
    and practical ecclesiology, 12, 91–98,
        100–108
    and Protestant ethic, 219–32
    and transatlantic market culture,
        19–29, 33–36
    Twain's views on, 239–45
    and twentieth-century American
        theology, 12, 166, 171–72, 183
Pym, John, 171

Quakers, 220, 228–29
Quarterly Christian Spectator, 127

Rabbit novels (Updike), 260–65
racist stereotypes, 119, 136n24
Ramsay, William, 113
rationalism, 114–15, 134–35n17,
        138–39n31, 151–53, 178, 208–9
rationality, economic, 20–21, 27–28, 31
Rauch, Frederick A., 134n14, 138–39n31
Reagan, Ronald, 10
Reasonableness of Christianity, The (Locke),
        151
Recollections of Jotham Anderson (Ware), 220
"Reflections on the Sabbath" (Twain), 243
Reformation
    and American national identity, 66
    and American politics, 76, 78
    and Congregational-Unitarian
        discourse, 148, 155–57
    and practical ecclesiology, 97
    and Protestant ethic, 232
    separation of "good"/"bad" parts in,
        5–9, 13n1
    and Servetus affair, 5–6, 8, 13n1,
        14–15n10
    and twentieth-century American
        theology, 168–69, 172, 177
    and vitality of Calvinist theology in
        nineteenth century, 113, 117–18,
        124, 134–35n17, 139–40n32
Reformation, The (Schaff), 163n30
Reformed Church Monthly, 124
Reformed Dogmatics (Bavinck), 175
"Reformed ever Reforming," 184
Reformed French Protestant Church,
        32–33
Reformed Presbyterian Church of North
        America (RPCNA), 81–83
    "Declaration and Testimony," 82–83
Reformed Presbyterians. *See* Covenanters
Reid, J. K. S., 182
religion, freedom of, 43–44, 46–47
Religious Affections (Edwards), 92, 104–5
religious right. *See* fundamentalism
Religious Situation, The (Tillich), 177

republicanism, 69–71, 73–77, 81, 83, 85
resistance theory, 84–85
Revelation, book of, 106
revivals, 93, 100–106, 174, 206, 221, 224
Rhode Island colony, 53–57, 59–60
    charter of, 53–54
Ripley, George, 162n9
Roberts, William Henry, 72
Robinson, Edward, 119, 136n23
Robinson, Marilynne, 7–8, 13, 267–70,
        271nn1,2,7
Rockwell, William Walker, 172–73
Roger's Version (Updike), 258
Romans, epistle to, 6–7, 57, 62n38, 211, 241
romanticism, German, 118–22, 131n6,
        136n25, 137–38nn28–30,
        138–39n31, 142–43n40
*Romantic Revolution in America: Main
        Currents in American Thought, The*
        (Parrington), 242
Rouchefoucauld, Marie de, 33
Roughing It (Twain), 241, 252
Round, Philip H., 194
Rutherford, Samuel, 76
Rutman, Darrett, 20

S. (Updike), 261, 263–65
Sabbath, 230–31
Saints' Everlasting Rest, The (Baxter), 240
salvation, 7
    and Congregational-Unitarian
        discourse, 154, 158, 160, 163n33
    and doctrine of Eucharist, 115–16, 133n11
    in fiction, 224–25
    and indigenous Calvinism, 193–94,
        196–97, 199, 208, 212–13,
        215–17nn15,16
    and paradox of freedom, 259–60
    and practical ecclesiology, 92–94, 96–97
    Twain's views on, 241
    and twentieth-century American
        theology, 168, 177
Samuel, Old Testament prophet, 199

Saumaise, Claude de, 31
Savoy Declaration (1658), 155–57
Scarlet Letter, The (Hawthorne), 222
Schaeffer, Francis, 75–76
Schaff, Philip, 113, 120–21, 124,
    134–35n17, 137–38n30, 144n43,
    163n30
Schleiermacher, 119–21, 138–39n31, 168,
    183, 188n35
Schneck, B. S., 143–44n41
scholasticism, 127, 134–35n17, 166, 172,
    184, 197
Schweizer, Alexander, 163n30
Scottish Confession of Faith (1560), 77, 80
Scottish King's Confession (1580), 80
Scottish National Covenant (1638), 80
Scottish Presbyterians, 67, 71, 76–77,
    80–81, 149, 171–72
Scottish Reformation, 67, 81
Sedgwick, Catharine Maria, 6, 10–11,
    14n3, 220–21
Seeberg, Reinhold, 163n30
Selina, Countess of Huntington, 197
Seneca, 4
separation of powers
    and American national identity, 43–44,
        46–47, 51–60, 60–61n7
    and American politics, 80–81
    and Congregational-Unitarian
        discourse, 158–59
    and twentieth-century American
        theology, 173
Sermon on the Mount, 10, 15n11
Servetus, Michael, 5–6, 8, 13n1, 14–15n10,
    57–58, 226
    and twentieth-century American
        theology, 170, 173, 181, 186n6
shamanism, 206
Shedd, William G. T., 129, 172
"Short Formula of a Confession of Faith"
    (Calvin), 152
Shurr, William, 243
Simmons, William, 193

"Sinners in the Hands of an Angry God"
    (Edwards), 97, 152, 186n6, 221,
    234n9, 240
slave trading/slavery, 27, 32, 34, 207–9,
    225–26
Smith, Adam, 34–35
Smith, Henry Boynton, 129, 131n6
Social Gospel, 41n41, 179
sola fides, 6, 195, 216–17n16
sola scriptura, 195, 216–17n16
Solemn League and Covenant (1643), 80–81
Some Thoughts on the Revival (Edwards),
    102–3
soteriology, 92, 102
South Carolina, 10–11, 21–22, 31–33
spiritualism, 245–46
Sproul, R. C., 170, 187n14
Staloff, Darren, 20
St. Andrews University, 66
Stapfer, Johann Friedrich, 92
Stark, Werner, 235–36n29
Stebbins, Rufus, 144–45n45
Steinbrink, Jeffrey, 244
stereotypes, 4, 7–9, 12, 13, 161, 206, 232,
    269–70
Stockbridge frontier, 107
Stokes, Anson Phelps, 136n25
Stone Lectures (Princeton Theological
    Seminary), 175
Stout, Harry, 196–97, 199, 210
Stowe, Calvin Ellis, 223
Stowe, Harriet Beecher, 12, 153, 162n17,
    219–20, 222–27, 232–33,
    235–36nn15,16,19,22,29, 243, 255n17
Stuart, Moses, 136n23
Stuart monarchy, 26–27, 81
Stuyvesant, Pieter, 30
Sweeney, Douglas A., 12, 92, 111–46
Systematic Theology (Hodge), 144–45n45,
    172

Tawney, R. H., 20
Taylor, Nathaniel W., 92, 144–45n45

Ten Commandments, 24, 57, 59, 77
That the People Might Live (Weaver), 194
theocentrism, 177–81, 183
Theology of John Calvin, The (Partee), 165
theonomy, 81, 182–83
Theopolis Americana (Mather), 28
They Seek a Country (Harold), 75
"Thirty Years of Calvin Study" (McNeill),
    180
Thoreau, Henry David, 261
Thornwell, James Henley, 124, 129
"Thou Shalt Love Thy Neighbour as
    Thyself" (Occom), 208–9, 212
Thuesen, Peter J., 12, *219–37*
Tillich, Paul, *177*
Timothy I, 99
Tocqueville, Alexis de, 43, 84
Toughest Indian in the World, The (Alexie),
    204
Toulmin, Stephen, 22
Toward the End of Time (Updike), 262
Townsend, Meredith, 247–48
transatlantic market culture, 19, 21–22,
    25–35
    and Dutch Reformed Church, 10,
        21–22, 28–31, 33, 35–36
    and French Reformed Church, 31–33,
        35–36
    and Puritans, 19–29, 33–36
"Transcendentalist, The" (Emerson), 242
*Treatise Concerning Religious Affections,
    A* (Edwards), 149
Treaty of Paris (1763), 34
Triglund, Jacobus, 29
Trinterud, Leonard, 74–75
Troeltsch, 188n35
*Tropologia: A Key to Open Scripture
    Metaphors* (Keach), 200
TULIP, 184
Turner, James, 129
Turretin, François, 92, 171–72
Twain, Mark, 12–13, 221, 239–53, 255n17
twentieth century

American politics in, 73–76
development of American theology in,
    12, 165–86, 186n1
paradox of freedom in, 13, 257–65
Twichell, Joseph Hopkins, 221, 248–49,
    252
Twisse, William, 152, 171
typology, 102
    and indigenous Calvinism, 199, 201,
        210–11, 213–15
    and twentieth-century American
        theology, 166, 184–86, 188n38

Unabomber, 261
Uncle Tom's Cabin (Stowe), 219, 223
Under God: Religion and American Politics
    (Wills), 76
Union Theological Seminary, 129–30,
    172–75, 182
"Unitarian Christianity" (Channing), 151
Unitarians, 12, 144–45n45, 147–61,
    162nn9,14,17, 220
United Kingdom, 9, 23–24, 27
    and American politics, 66–69, 71,
        74–75, 78–81
    and Congregational-Unitarian
        discourse, 154–56
    Occom's journey to, 191–92
    and transatlantic market culture,
        23–28, 30, 33–35
    and twentieth-century American
        theology, 171–72
United Presbyterian Church of North
    America, 75
University of Chicago, 179, 183
University of Freiburg, 227
University of Iowa, 267
Updike, John, 13, 258–65
Ursinus, Zacharias, 171
Ursinus College, 124, 143–44n41
usury, 23–32, 37–38n12, 207, 209

Valeri, Mark, 12, *19–41*

Van Dyke, Henry, 124–25
Van Mastricht, Peter, 92
Van Til, Cornelius, 168, 175–76, 182, 188nn34,38
"Views of Calvinism" (Norton), 152
visible church, 96–97, 101, 105–7, 153, 229
Voetius, Gisbert, 29, 31
Vos, Geerhardus, 175

Wadsworth, Benjamin, 27
Walker, Williston, 12, 156–60, 163nn28–35
Ward, Nathaniel, 49–50, 54, 56, 59–60
Ware, Henry, Jr., 150, 154, 220
Warfield, B. B., 112, 173–76, 182, 184
Warrior, Robert Allen, 194
Washington, George, 69
Weaver, Jace, 193–94
Weber, Max, 12, 20–22, 37n5, 84, 158, 219–20, 227–33, 235–36n29, 261, 263–64
Weekly Messenger, 121, 140n33
Wesley, John, 168
Westminster Assembly, 67, 79, 82, 152, 172
Westminster Confession of Faith and Catechisms
  and American politics, 78–85, 87nn23–27
  and Congregational-Unitarian discourse, 148–50, 152–57, 162n18
  Twain's views on, 241, 247
  and twentieth-century American theology, 168, 171–72, 175, 178, 181, 183
Westminster Larger Catechism, 152
Westminster Press, 181–82
Westminster Seminary, 188n34
Westminster Shorter Catechism, 178, 243
Westminster Theological Seminary, 75, 175, 182
Westphal, Joachim, 123

What Is Man? (Twain), 239–40, 248–50, 255n17
What the Presbyterian Church Stands For (Kerr), 74
Wheatley, Susannah, 198
Wheelock, Eleazar, 191, 193, 197, 200
"When He Drowned His Reason" (Occom), 209–10
Whitefield, George, 191, 197, 206
Whose Justice, Which Rationality? (McIntyre), 186n3
Wieland (Brown), 220
Wilhelm I, German Emperor, 233
Willard, Samuel, 28
Williams, Roger, 52–57, 59–60, 62n30, 162n14
Wills, Garry, 76
Winthrop, John, 10, 15n11, 25, 49, 51–52, 54, 57, 59–60, 210, 213, 242
Wisdom and Folly in Religion (Haroutunian), 177–78
Witherspoon, John, 34–35, 68–69, 72, 74–76, 78, 86n4
Witsius, Hermann, 92
Witte, John, 45–46, 61nn16,23
Women, Freedom, and Calvin (Douglass), 170
Woods, Leonard, 150, 154, 163n19
World Alliance of Reformed Churches, 186n5
World War I, 176
Wyss, Hilary, 194

Yale University, 127, 130, 144–45n45, 150, 153–54, 156, 183
Yankee disposition, 20, 220, 225–26, 231

Zakai, Avihu, 101
Zuckerman, Michael, 20
Zwingli, Huldrych, 6, 126, 140–41n36, 163n33, 171
Zwinglians, 118, 122–23, 135–36n21, 140–41n36